**Lauren Mackay** is a Tudor historian and researcher. She is the author of *Inside the Tudor Court: Henry VIII and His Six Wives Through the Writings of the Spanish Ambassador Eustace Chapuys* and a regular contributor to *BBC History* and *All About History*. She has lectured at the Tower of London, Hever Castle, Leeds Castle and the National Archives at Kew.

'A fascinating and long overdue re-evaluation of Thomas and George Boleyn based on extensive research. Lauren Mackay cuts through the stereotypes and myths which have for so long overshadowed her subjects.'

**– Elizabeth Norton, author of *The Lives of Tudor Women***

'Brilliantly researched, beautifully written and filled with wonderful detail, this is a superb biography – it will make you see the Boleyns in a completely different way. Lauren Mackay has gone deep into the documents and brought the Boleyns to vivid and important life. Essential reading.'

**Kate Williams, author of *Rival Queens***

'*Among the Wolves of Court* is an elegant, groundbreaking, persuasive reinterpretation of a powerful family. Impeccably researched and thoroughly readable, Mackay's book shatters the entrenched legends surrounding the tragic, frustrated, and fascinating lives of Anne Boleyn's father and brother.'

**Gareth Russell, author of *Young and Damned and Fair***

# AMONG THE
# WOLVES
## OF COURT

*The Untold Story of*
*Thomas and*
*George Boleyn*

## LAUREN MACKAY

BLOOMSBURY ACADEMIC
LONDON · NEW YORK · OXFORD · NEW DELHI · SYDNEY

BLOOMSBURY ACADEMIC
Bloomsbury Publishing Plc
50 Bedford Square, London, WC1B 3DP, UK
1385 Broadway, New York, NY 10018, USA

BLOOMSBURY, BLOOMSBURY ACADEMIC and the Diana logo
are trademarks of Bloomsbury Publishing Plc

First published in Great Britain by I.B. Tauris 2018
This edition published by Bloomsbury Academic 2019

A catalogue record for this book is available from the British Library.

A catalog record for this book is available from the Library of Congress.                      .

ISBN: HB: 978-1-3501-4353-1
eISBN: 978-1-7867-2552-3
ePDF: 978-1-7867-3552-2

Typeset in Stone Serif by OKS Prepress Services, Chennai, India
Printed and bound in Great Britain

To find out more about our authors and books visit
www.bloomsbury.com and sign up for our newsletters.

*For my parents*

# Contents

List of Plates                                    ix
Acknowledgements                                  xiii

Introduction                                        1

1.  Men of Mark                                     6
2.  Fortune Ruleth our Helme                       21
3.  A Courtier to his Fingertips                   35
4.  Fortune, Infortune                             46
5.  The Picklock of Princes                        64
6.  Betwixt Two Princes                            83
7.  The Balance of Power                          102
8.  Declare, I Dare Not                           113
9.  Treasonous Waters                             131
10. The Boleyn Enterprise                         146
11. Ainsi sera, groigne, qui groigne              160
12. Nowe Thus                                     174
13. Turning Tides                                 186
14. Trying a Queen                                205
15. Aftermath                                     219

Appendix I                                        227
Appendix II                                       229
Notes                                             231
Select Bibliography                               267
Index                                             279

# List of Plates

PLATE 1 Tomb and Brass of Thomas Boleyn, St Peters' Church, Hever. © Lauren Mackay.

PLATE 2 Will of Sir Thomas Butler, Earl of Ormond, Page 1 and 4, with specific reference to Butler bequeathing the white horn to his grandson. National Archives, Kew, PROB 11/18/184.

PLATE 3 Boleyn coat of arms, Hever. Courtesy of Hever Castle.

PLATE 4 The rules for the 1511 Joust to celebrate the birth of Prince Henry. From the Harley Charter. Courtesy of the British Library.

PLATE 5 Cardinal Wolsey's letter of introduction on behalf of Thomas Boleyn to Charles V, 1522. Courtesy of Haus-, Hof- und Staatsarchiv, Vienna, Austria.

PLATE 6 Example of an ambassadorial report from Young, Boleyn, and Wingfield to Henry VIII. Courtesy of the British Library.

PLATE 7 Anne Boleyn's letter to her father, from Margaret of Austria's Court. Corpus Christi College, Cambridge.

PLATE 8 Thomas Boleyn to Cardinal Wolsey; about the Imperial Election and a treaty with the Swiss. Courtesy of the British Library, Cotton MS Caligula D, VII.

PLATE 9 Thomas Boleyn's salutation to Cardinal Wolsey. Courtesy of the British Library, Cotton MS Caligula D, VII.

PLATE 10 Sample page from Thomas Boleyn's account book during his tenure as Comptroller of the Household. Courtesy of the National Archives, Kew.

PLATE 11   Anne Boleyn's music book, with the phrase 'Nowe Thus'. Courtesy of the Royal College of Music, London.

PLATE 12   Letter from Anne Boleyn to Cardinal Wolsey, 1528. Courtesy of the British Library.

PLATE 13   Portrait of Imperial Ambassador Eustace Chapuys. Seventeenth century Musee Chateau, Annecy, France.

PLATE 14 A letter from Chapuys to Charles V, reporting on George Boleyn's mission to France with his uncle, the Duke of Norfolk, 29 May 1533. Courtesy of Haus-, Hof- und Staatsarchiv, Vienna, Austria.

PLATE 15   James Butler. This half finished portrait by Hans Holbein, which is titled 'Ormond', was claimed to portray Thomas. There is, however, overwhelming evidence that this is James Butler, who also claimed the Earldom of Ormond. It is also worth noting that Holbein would not have simply referred to Thomas by his Irish Earldom, but by his English earldom – Wiltshire – which was his premier ennoblement. Royal Collection, Windsor.

PLATE 16   Imperial Pensions of 1525 to certain individuals of the English court, with Cardinal Wolsey, Duke of Norfolk, Duke of Suffolk, Sir Thomas Boleyn, among the top four. Courtesy of Haus-, Hof- und Staatsarchiv, Vienna, Austria.

PLATE 17   George Boleyn's signature in his copy of *Les Lamentations' de Matheolus et 'Le Livre de Leesce' de Jehan Le Fevre, de Resson*, Jehan le Fevre, f. 2v. Courtesy of the British Library.

PLATE 18   1535 Order of the Garter Procession from the Black Book of the Garter. Courtesy of St George's Chapel Archives & Chapter Library, Windsor. Courtesy of St George's Chapel Archives & Chapter Library, Windsor.

PLATE 19   Thomas Boleyn Garter Stall Plate. Courtesy of St George's Chapel Archives & Chapter Library, Windsor.

PLATE 20   Thomas Boleyn, Earl of Wiltshire, to Lord Cromwell, sending him his collar and his 'best George' to be returned to his chaplain. Courtesy of the British Library.

PLATE 21   First page of Indenture between Henry VIII and Mary and William Stafford following Thomas Boleyn's death. Thomas, his brother James, and Henry would all have had lawyers assisting them in drawing up the agreement, with James left to ensure everything was carried out after Thomas' death.

But there is the suggestion that Henry was not pleased about the arrangement. Henry confirms Mary's inheritance due to her hereditary right, restoring a number of estates and lands to the couple. It would seem that William had also petitioned Henry for control of Thomas' lands in Essex but Thomas had made it clear they were to go to his mother and, upon her death, his granddaughter, Elizabeth. This document suggests a far more proactive Mary, as they had already taken possession of several properties before this document had been drawn up. Kent Archives.

PLATE 22   Boleyn family crest, Hever. © Lauren Mackay.

PLATE 23   Anne Boleyn. Courtesy of the National Portrait Gallery.

PLATE 24   The white Butler Falcon, prominently displayed on a set of Virginals owned by Elizabeth I.

PLATE 25   Henry VIII. Courtesy of the National Portrait Gallery.

PLATE 26   Cardinal Wolsey. Courtesy of the National Portrait Gallery.

PLATE 27   Thomas Cromwell. Courtesy of the National Portrait Gallery.

PLATE 28   Marguerite of Navarre. Courtesy of Getty Images.

PLATE 29   Richard Fox. Courtesy of the National Portrait Gallery.

# Acknowledgements

This book owes a great deal to family, friends, and historians, all who have contributed to the Boleyn story in different ways. I am indebted to the late Professors David Loades and Eric Ives, both of whom were generous with their time and advice, but who never saw the finished work. I am also incredibly grateful to Professor George Bernard for his sharp observations and insights, as well as Dr Susan Brigden, for her enthusiasm, suggestions, and encouragement. My deep gratitude to Professor Barry Collett, for his constant inspiration and guidance, and my PhD supervisor, Dr Camilla Russell, for her support, assistance in the Papal and Vatican archives, and persuasive charm in the face of challenging Italian bureaucracy.

My thanks to Dr Ernst Petritsch from the Haus-, Hof- und Staatsarchiv in Vienna for his assistance over the last few years, Euan Roger from the National Archives, Kew, and staff from the British Library, in particular Debbie Horner from the Imaging department, and Jeff Kattenhorn from the Manuscript and Maps department, for his minor detective work on my behalf. I must also thank the staff of three venues which play a part in the Boleyn story, and who have invited me to present my Boleyn research over the last few years: Viscount and Viscountess D'Lisle and the staff of Penshurst Place, the staff of Hever Castle, especially Anna Spender, and, finally, the staff of Blickling Hall, in particular, Diana Shaw. Also my thanks to my editor, Jo Godfrey, for reading the many versions of this manuscript with unending enthusiasm. My thanks to Elizabeth Norton for our lengthy discussions over many a glass of wine about the Boleyn family, and the duplicity of the Tudor court.

Also to my partner Klemen, for the unwavering support and love, and all that you put up with – I am eternally grateful.

Finally, my heartfelt gratitude to my parents, who have been there from the beginning, when I first decided this story was worth telling, as a doctoral thesis and biography. Thank you for all that you do, and for believing in this book, and in these men, as much as I do.

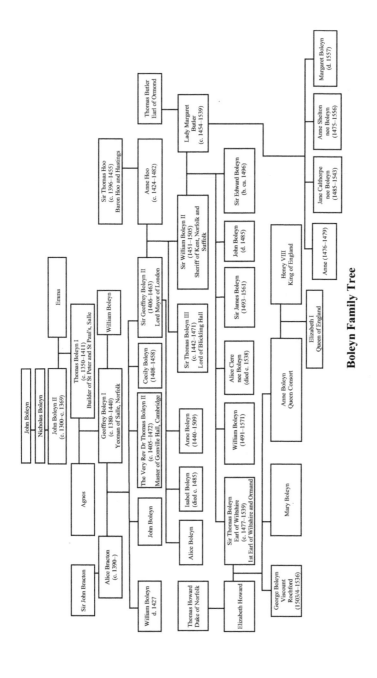

**Boleyn Family Tree**

# Introduction

15 May 1536

*Incest. Adultery. Treason.* These highly charged accusations reverberate throughout the city of London, scandalising the populace. Never has a queen of England been found guilty of such crimes. Henry VIII's 'entirely beloved' queen, Anne Boleyn has been stripped of her exalted status, and awaits her violent fate in the Queens' Apartments in the Tower. Her brother, George, one of Henry's most charming and successful young courtiers, awaits his fate nearby in Beauchamp Tower alongside four co-accused, all men of the court who served the King – Francis Weston, William Brereton, Henry Norris and Mark Smeaton. The Boleyn reputation is blackened as Anne's queenship is systematically dismantled. Through Anne and the power brokers of court, Henry discovered his unbridled power; they had, in the words of Thomas More, himself executed a year earlier, *shown the lion his own strength*. And now, not even a queen is safe.

On 17 May, George, the highest ranking of the men, is the first to be executed. In a lengthy and impassioned speech, he declares that he deserves death and warns the sombre crowds, who have come to witness the violent events, not to trust in the vanity of the world, and especially in the 'flatterings of the court', or the favour and treacheries of Fortune. He admits to reading the gospel of Christ, but not following its lessons as he should have. And if he 'offended any man that is not here now, either in thought, word or deed, and if ye hear any such, I pray you heartily in my behalf, pray them to forgive me for God's sake'.[1]

He kneels at the block, and the axe severs his head in a single stroke. His body is packed into a wooden box and taken to the vault of the chapel of Peter ad Vincula, within the Tower. His hastily stored body remains to this day hidden from view. The other condemned men follow him to the block and are beheaded, their bodies joining his below.

Two days later, Anne kneels on her own specially constructed scaffold within the Tower grounds. Henry's final parting 'gift' to his wife is to hire an expert swordsman from Calais for her execution, ordered before the trials had commenced. Anne too addresses the crowd and declares that according to the law and by the law she had been judged, and therefore she would not speak against it. Nor would she 'speak of that whereof I am accused and condemned to die, but I pray God save the King and send him long to reign over you, for a gentler nor a more merciful prince was there never, and to me he was ever a good, a gentle, and sovereign lord. And if any person will meddle of my cause, I require them to judge the best. And thus I take my leave of the world and of you all, and I heartily desire you all to pray for me.'[2]

Anne kneels, her lips moving in quiet prayer, as the blade of the highly skilled swordsman ends her life. Her body is wrapped in a white cloth and packed into a wooden box made for arrow heads, and buried under the high altar in the same chapel as her brother. Their parents – Elizabeth and Thomas Boleyn – do not witness the executions. They have left court, bearing their grief in the peaceful family home of Hever, Kent. For centuries the name, for many commentators, becomes a moral lesson in what happens when the natural order is disturbed, and the ethical free-fall in which the Tudor court was seen to operate becomes a theme of particular attention.

The lives and careers of the Tudor pantheon have been examined in detail. Studies of Henry VIII and his six queens, Cardinal Wolsey and Thomas Cromwell appear on bookshelves every year, and the average reader might be forgiven for assuming the Tudor court only comprised about ten people. The popularity of Anne Boleyn is undeniable and certainly justified, as there has been considerable research on the cultural, social and political imperatives that shaped her – particularly from the time she became the object of the King's lust and determination to have her. She is now arguably one of the Tudor period's most popular and celebrated figures. Her sister, Mary Boleyn, who did not enjoy a particularly brilliant career, and by comparison lived a very modest life, has warranted a handful of biographies, novels and a movie.

George has remained, for many, no more than a handsome but useless ornament of the court, yet he spent a great deal of time away from it, as his administrative responsibilities and ambassadorial career began to blossom. George, more so than his father, struggled to be seen as a man of skill and determination, with every mark of favour attributed to his sister.

Any exceptional qualities George possessed have been undermined by later accusations that he was arrogant, wild, violent and promiscuous at court, that he tormented his wife, and indulged in multiple homosexual relationships.[3]

There were no rumours that George was homosexual or abusive during his lifetime, or evidence to support the suppositions now. Yet these accusations stem from various sources, often with questionable motives. The scintillating narratives of the Boleyn children greatly overshadow their father, Thomas, whose successful career spanned 40 years as a courtier, ambassador, special envoy, parliamentarian, public servant, and patron. His domestic appointments included the influential and significant political positions of Comptroller of the Household, Treasurer of the Household and Lord Privy Seal from 1530 to the fatal, inglorious year of 1536. He was a dutiful son, loving husband, supportive brother and uncle and, most famously, father and grandfather of two queens of England. The narratives of Thomas and George Boleyn are only mentioned *in medias res*, as scenery to Anne's star-billing. Neither Thomas nor George have fared well in the hands of historians, usually consigned to the margins of the bloody narrative of Henry VIII's reign, poorly served by historians who view them by their contemporary standards rather than by those of the sixteenth century. When the conservative eighteenth and nineteenth-century historians appraised the morality of events during Henry's reign, there was a need to review certain events. This was an idealised time for the English monarchy and therefore an attempt was made to clean up Henry's image. In the early nineteenth century, J. S. Brewer, historian and editor of the *Letters and Papers of Henry VIII*, wrote that Mary Boleyn, the *other* Boleyn daughter, had been 'sacrificed by thoughtless and greedy parents'.[4] Several years later, a less scholarly P. W. Sergeant, who wrote biographies of numerous individuals from various centuries, wrote 'It is clearly hopeless to attempt a defence of Sir Thomas,' which Eric Ives quoted in his own biography, adding that Thomas, 'on his way on his way to an earldom, slipped, or appears to have slipped, two daughters in succession into the king's bed.'[5] In the same vein in 1884, Paul Friedmann dismissed Thomas as 'greedy and grasping'.[6] Thomas was accused of sacrificing his own daughters to the royal bedchamber for the family's personal advancement, and of accepting the violent and unwarranted deaths of his children as the indivisible price of playing the game of power.

The Boleyns are often portrayed as predators who pursued wealth and status, working in close-knit political units to destroy those who opposed their ambition, making them, in effect, wolves of court.

In the works of modern historians, the judgement is unchanged. David Loades commenced his assessment of Thomas thus: 'It was through the sexuality of his daughters that Sir Thomas Boleyn became a great man, and by the same means was brought low.'[7] In the single doctoral thesis on Thomas, besides my own, the author stated that Thomas was not equipped with courage, imagination, innovative skills, vision, charisma nor the ability to command. He added that in his dissertation he hoped to evaluate if Thomas Boleyn was *responsible for his own misfortune*, or if he was caught up in events beyond his control.[8] Eric Ives, whose biography of Anne Boleyn is still considered to be definitive, has little sympathy for her relatives and commented that most historians felt that Thomas personified all that was 'bad about the court', and noted that Anne and George Boleyn followed their father on the path to power, prestige and profit, but whether it was the road to 'honour' was, in Ives' opinion, a very different matter.

Ambition was not the sole domain of the Boleyns: they were in no way unique in their perfectly respectable ambitions to advance themselves and their family. We may ask why Thomas Boleyn, a courtier and diplomat who sought to improve his family's standing, like so many of the courtier families, has been castigated for successes he achieved well before the King noticed his daughters. We might ask why Thomas has been so harshly judged. It was the ambition, if not the duty, of every man at court to establish a firm base for the family and ensure the prosperity of their progeny, just as earlier generations of Boleyns had done. Perhaps it was because Thomas surpassed all expectations when Anne achieved a royal title, rather than the more acceptable level of enrichment and noble status. After all, what family could refuse the attentions of the King of England?

Historians to some extent are cognisant of the issues. In his biography of the Boleyns, framed as a series of essays, Loades admitted that George was not an easy man to get to know, pointing out that in his youth he was overshadowed by his father and, in later years, by his sister. Similarly, David Starkey remarked that historians have been slow to recognise Thomas Boleyn, and it is my view that a reappraisal of George and Thomas is long overdue. Historical novels are now blurring the lines between fact and fiction, with fictional portrayals as influential among readers as scholarly ones. As my PhD supervisor remarked, at the end of my doctoral journey: 'We've all really made monsters of the Boleyn men, haven't we?'

Even Hilary Mantel's artfully constructed Tudor saga, which rescues Thomas Cromwell from the centuries of vilification, does nothing to rescue the Boleyn men – they are cut from the same dated cloth as they have always been. Thomas is cold, and cunning, and Mantel's Cromwell asks 'what is the *point* of George Boleyn?' On screen, they have fared little better.

The Showtime series *The Tudors* – where an impressively toned Henry VIII cavorted through his palaces, his scheming courtiers always two paces behind – is arguably one of the most enduring depictions. While writing this book, I interviewed Nick Dunning, who played Thomas Boleyn in the series, and he personally offered a far more nuanced view than his script allowed. In response to two quotes, already noted, which called into question Thomas' ambition and treatment of his children, Dunning stated

> I think the whole idea of the King is hard for us nowadays to understand – this was God on Earth … He walked near to us – breathed near to us – the spirit made flesh. So, the possibility to have any kind of connection with this living God was desirable. In Thomas' terms it meant not only were you (and your family by association) closer socially and personally but also spiritually.

To my question as to whether he felt history had misjudged Thomas, he replied 'I think he was well intentioned and a good father doing his best. Did he fail at times to do that, tell me a parent who hasn't. I loved him, and still do.'

While acknowledging that the series chose to take the character in a somewhat negative direction, Dunning took profound issue with the negative historical judgements which have marred Thomas' reputation, and understandably so. We have constructed a character, mostly through fiction, and when an interpretation of a particular character – which suits a fictional narrative – is mistaken for the historical reality, what then is history? This book attempts to dispel the traditional stereotypes, relying on the textual traces of both Boleyn men, which are dispersed in a wide variety of sources across English and European archives and libraries.

I want to present a more complete account of these men – their political and personal trajectories, the evolution of their careers, and what mattered to them. Where judgement can be made it has been done so cautiously. In the absence of any extensive scholarly consideration, they have remained captive to a dated historiography which is a reflection of the frame within which the world continues to view them, and from which this book seeks to unburden them.

While this is a biography of two generations of Boleyns, I should note that there is far more evidence on Thomas than George, whose career had barely taken off before he was executed, therefore a great deal of the book naturally follows Thomas' lengthy career with George brought in as the evidence allows. I should also note that some Tudor studies alter their references to Thomas and George Boleyn as their careers progress, referencing ennoblements of Wiltshire and Rochford respectively. For simplicity, I refer to them as Thomas and George. Additionally, as this is a study of the Boleyn men, I avoid *la petite histoire* of the Tudor period, for the well-traversed narratives require no repetition.

CHAPTER ONE

# Men of Mark

*In no country but England could a race of merchants have risen in the feudal times to the highest rank under the Crown, have become the mark of more than one Parliamentary impeachment, and have wedded ladies of the blood.*

– T. L. Kington Oliphant

In death, the remains of the Boleyns are scattered across England. The clever, vivacious Boleyn children, Anne and George, lie close to where they met their fates in the Tower. Their mother Elizabeth, who hailed from one of the most powerful families in England – the Howards – is buried among her ancestors in the family vault in the parish church of St Mary-at-Lambeth, London, as was customary for the family.[1] Where the church once stood is now the Garden Museum, adjacent to Lambeth Palace, dedicated to the art, history and design of gardens. Many of the visitors here, sitting in the cafe near what was once the high altar, may be unaware that beneath their feet lies the mother and grandmother of two of England's arguably most famous queens. The whereabouts of the remains of Mary Boleyn, eclipsed in life and in death by her sister, is a mystery. But what has united this family for over 500 years, in all these locations, is their connection to Hever Castle in Kent.

The town of Hever is best known for its gothic turreted castle, accessible only by the small drawbridge across its moat, which carries thousands of tourists every year. Dating back to the 1270s, it was built as a defensive castle, with a gatehouse and walled bailey: later additions of Tudor-styled dwellings came in the fifteenth century. Today, it is arguably the family's most defining symbol when we think of their role in Tudor history – certainly for the followers of Anne Boleyn.

Some visitors to the castle might forego a visit to the small unassuming St Peter's Church, tucked away on the right of the main entrance to the castle grounds. It faces a rather more popular venue, a local pub, once a hunting lodge visited by Henry VIII. Vines clamber over the cracked stone tombs in the small gardens surrounding the building and, if you were to venture inside, you are likely to tread over centuries of graves beneath the stone floor. At the front of the church, in the Boleyn Chapel added to the original church in the middle of the fifteenth century, lies a large chest tomb inlaid with the brass effigy of Thomas Boleyn, dressed in his knightly robes and collar of the Order of the Garter, which Henry VIII awarded him in 1523. The arms of the Order is a cross of St George circumscribed by a garter with the motto *Honi soit qui mal y pense* (evil be to him that evil thinks). A coronet crowns his head, with a falcon to his right, entwined with icanthus leaves (or oak leaves) and braided cord; on his left knee is the garter of the Order just above his jousting armour – chausses protecting his legs and sabatons covering his feet – common features on knightly tombs. They also testify to Thomas Boleyn's jousting prowess: He stands on a prostrate gryphon, its claws fully extended. His only immediate family in this eternal grave is his infant son Henry who lies nearby: his tomb marked by a plain brass cross.

Hever is synonymous with the Boleyn family, Anne Boleyn, specifically, as it was her childhood home and where she was pursued by Henry VIII. But Anne was not a Kentish woman, nor was her father a Kentish man. The Boleyns were proud East Anglians, and to understand their trajectory is to trace their ancestry over a couple of hundred years back to the early years of the Norman conquest; they hailed from over 150 miles north-east of Hever, somewhere between the cathedral city of Norwich and the sandy coast of Cromer and Sheringham, looking out over the North Sea.

In exploring the Boleyn family history, we face an immediate challenge. Firstly, it is not until shortly before Thomas' generation that the Boleyns become visible in the extant records, when they had already become quite politically significant and financially successful: prior to this, there is limited available information that can shed light on the family. Thankfully, court records do provide some insight into the histories of non-noble lineages such as that of the Boleyns.

We also owe a great debt to the research undertaken by the eighteenth-century antiquary, Francis Blomefield, who compiled and published detailed accounts of the city of Norwich and numerous villages throughout the county of Norfolk, and W. L. E. Parsons, the Rector of Salle Church, whose 1935 work, modestly titled, 'Some Notes on the Boleyn Family', was published in the Norfolk and Norwich Archaeological Society's journal.[2] Both men drew on a variety of primary sources including the Court Rolls of the manors of Salle and

Stinton, and contemporary wills, to try to establish the roots of the Boleyns. Relying on the surviving official court and county records available, helpfully enlisted and (in some cases) reproduced by these two writers, we become acquainted with members of the earlier generations of the family, and how they rose generation by generation to accumulate wealth, position and prestige. Tracing the Boleyn family and the nature of their trajectory over time allows us to consider the *kinds* of records in which they appear, and those in which they do *not* appear, that is, documents relating to established elites with ancient noble lineage, and reveals that the Boleyns of the fifteenth century prior to Thomas' birth were not born to wealth and privilege, but were among those who achieved it.

There are two other slight difficulties: the different spellings of surnames and the repetition of Christian names across the generations can play havoc with constructing a family tree and the Boleyn lineage is no different, having suffered from historians' misinterpretation, confusion and entanglement.[3] There is considerable debate among genealogists as to how many members were named Geoffrey, Nicholas, Thomas or John, or how many men with each name there actually were.[4] Then there are countless spellings of the name: Bolleyn, Boleyne, Boulen, Bulleen, Bullyn, Bollayne and Bolen.[5] The name – in one of its forms – probably appeared in England in the wake of the conquering Normans who, under Duke William's banner, defeated the Anglo-Saxon King Harold at Hastings in 1066.[6] One Norman who fought with William was Eustace II (*c*.1015–*c*.1087), Count of Boulogne from 1049 to 1087, who was well rewarded for his service, receiving large grants of land and honours.[7] He is one of the few proven companions of William the Conqueror, and some historians believe that Eustace commissioned the Bayeux Tapestry to commemorate this extraordinary victory in which he had a starring role: in the tapestry's narrative, *Eustasius* appears above the figure, next to William, dressed in blue.[8]

Areas in northern France during the medieval period – Boulogne, Normandy, Anjou, Flanders – have interested historians for a number of years because of their kin-based model of government. Boulogne was a particularly successful region as it was based on shared territorial and common interests of its kinfolk, through blood, marriage, amity and patronage 'with a highly fluid constituency, including anyone with some social bond to its central figures, direct or indirect'.[9] This may well be the source for the view that the Boleyns hailed from Boulogne, possibly directly related – as kinfolk – to its central character, Eustace. We cannot prove it, but we do know that many of the great Norman families which settled in England used French toponymic names: Aubigny, Beaumont, Bully Montfort, Tosny, among others.

For the early part of the twelfth century English and French influences were spread across the country as the importance between localities and the central government of the king in London began to emerge, and the famous 'self-government at the king's command, provided the seed bed from which the gentry grew'.[10]

The expansion and advancement in population and agriculture saw the growth of the market economy with a large amount of trade through eastern towns including London, York, Winchester, Lincoln, Ipswich and Norwich. Norwich became the most prosperous city and port, second only to London, with the River Wensum its artery to the sea providing the vast prospect of international trade.

We can say with some certainty that the ancestors of the Boleyns were firmly rooted in the county of Norfolk during this period because our first reference to the *Boulen* family was found on a deed for the sale of a *messuage* (a small plot of land) in Woodrising, Norwich, sometime in 1188. Prior to this, information is speculative but this deed provides a crucial link to future generations.[11]

The branch of the large Boleyn family from which Thomas was descended can be traced back to one John Boleyne of Salle, from where the Boleyn story begins to take shape and is on much stronger footing. Salle, a village and civil parish in the county of Norfolk, made much of its wealth in the wool trade. Wool for export or for the domestic cloth trade was a commodity that brought a general rise in the standard of living in rural communities in the mid to late Middle Ages.

Salle was a close-knit community of four to five hundred people, dominated by four manors belonging to several 'great and less-than-great gentry families'.[12] Much like Hever today (its local pub notwithstanding), there is no town or village to speak of, only a large parish church that stands alone amongst the fields, a testament to an earlier time. This is perhaps the most curious feature of the town. In these early centuries, the church underpinned the world of villagers and townspeople: it is where every aspect of their lives took place and was recorded – baptism, confirmation, marriage, Holy Communion, confession and the last rites. The church gave meaning to this life and promised the afterlife, if one lived by its teachings. Although the local parish records tell us that either John or Simon Boleyn had two sons, John and William, we must look elsewhere for the rich and informative commentary of their lives. Our next reference to the Boleyns is in 1318, when we become acquainted with Nicholas Boleyn of Salle who was likely born just before the turn of the century.[13]

Misdemeanours and misdeeds now become the order of the day, as rough-natured Nicholas was accused of theft in 1318, and his poor reputation continued because he was later accused of robbing a man in Lincoln in 1333.[14]

He appears again in the same year and was ordered by one of the manorial courts in Salle to repair the bank between his land and that of the lord of the manor after he had damaged pastures and trees, although it is unclear what he had done to cause the damage. Records are irregular and incomplete at best, but we have to persevere and eventually we find a reference to John Boleyn in court records in 1369, but he dies soon after. Our first Thomas Boleyn appears in the records in 1370, holding much of the same land as the recently deceased John Boleyn, and this leads us to presume that he was the latter's son. This Thomas was a modest landowner and member of the community, but he was also connected to the wool trade and agriculture of the region. We may assume that he was buried in Salle Church, but the first church was destroyed, to be rebuilt during his son's lifetime. Upon his death he bequeathed his six-and-a-half acres of land to his son, Geoffrey, and it is with this individual, Thomas Boleyn's great-grandfather, that the Boleyn family starts to take shape.

Geoffrey Boleyn was not a lord of a manor, presiding over land and tenants – instead, like his father, he worked on the land, involved in farming and the wool trade. He extended the family's local prominence but not significantly. He was very much an *ends justifies the means* sort of man, and somewhat reckless, if his appearance in numerous court hearings is any indication. Our first encounter with him is in 1408 when he was among six other men accused of two incidents of trespassing and storing timber that they had been keeping to help rebuild the church in Salle. The men had destroyed a small building on the same land, probably for building material, but more seriously, they had also ransacked one of the four manor houses, which they could not explain away as being for the greater good of the town. It was left to the lord and his council to determine the punishment – it is unclear what the lord decided.[15]

Later that year, Geoffrey was once again before the court, this time with the parson of Salle Church, with both men accused of occupying a ditch or bank belonging to the lord of the manor, without permission. It seemed that they were trying to store an ash tree to preserve the wood, which they claimed was required for the church. They must have been convincing because on this occasion Geoffrey and the parson were dealt with more leniently and merely ordered to remove the tree within seven days or face its forfeiture.[16] However, there were three other charges unrelated to the church; on one occasion, Geoffrey failed to pay what was owed for property he had purchased;

on another he was charged with drawing water from a well without permission or payment.[17] Later, in 1412, he was accused of ploughing over a field division, effectively extending his own land illegally.[18]

So, at first glance, Geoffrey would appear to be lacking somewhat of a moral compass, or at least seems to have been an opportunist, although these sorts of misdemeanours were commonplace at the time. But the crimes related to the building of the church, assisting it rather than taking from it, indicates that the church was clearly an important part of his life, so much so that he was willing to break the law, and this points to some degree of piety. The Church of St Peter and St Paul, dating from the first part of the fifteenth century, was quite large for a village the size of Salle, and was the barometer by which the local community could measure its rising prosperity. The Boleyns were among several families vying to fund its construction. The townspeople of Salle loved it, as did the Boleyns, who were not just patrons of the church but benefactors and contributors to its creation. It remains a perfect example of a late medieval East Anglian parish church, containing 'one of just about every architectural feature and interior furnishing'.[19] Historian Eamon Duffy elegantly describes the interior: 'this huge building was never full and was never intended to be full; its space was intended as the setting for elaborate liturgy and processions, involving the whole parish, but also for the smaller-scale worship in screened-off side chapels, which housed the daily and occasional activities of the guilds and family chantry-chapels.'[20]

The church tells us a great deal about the Boleyn family's social distinction within the community. A memorial brass, commissioned by Geoffrey for both him and his wife, Alice, stands prominently in the middle aisle a testament to his importance to the church and its congregation. Geoffrey and Alice rest side by side, both fashionably dressed, Geoffrey wearing a cap and knee-length gown, and large sleeves. His wife is wearing a pleated floor-length gown, with draping sleeves, and a large cloth head-dress that covers her hair is draped over her shoulders. Above the couple is written: 'God be merciful to us sinners.' These brasses demonstrate that the couple saw and asserted themselves as local dignitaries, that the church was very important in their lives, just as important as they were in the life of this parish and surrounding area. Equally significant is the fact that the town honoured the Boleyns by calling a narrow street Old Boleyn's Lane and a field Boleyn's Croft.[21]

Geoffrey and Alice had numerous children, but their two sons, Geoffrey and Thomas, presumably named for their father Geoffrey and grandfather Thomas, were the first to embark on the family's foray into the world of trade and commerce. Their accomplishments would henceforth connect the Boleyn name with the higher echelons of nobility – and away from petty crime.

The two brothers appear to have been close throughout their lives, despite taking very different paths. Thomas embraced the spiritual life, taking holy orders in 1439, and then attending Trinity Hall, Cambridge University, earning a BA and MA.[22] He was as ambitious as his brother, and moved through the spiritual ranks. He was ordained a priest in 1421, becoming Canon of St Stephen's Chapel, Westminster, then Canon of St Paul's in 1447, Prebendary of Wells in 1448, and Master of Gonville Hall in Cambridge.[23] Yet Thomas also had a minor diplomatic role when he accompanied Edmund Beaufort, Count of Mortain, and great-uncle to the future Henry VII, to the Council of Basel as a representative of King Henry VI in 1434. It was an extraordinary honour, suggesting this Thomas had demonstrated impressive diplomatic skills, as they attended the council at a highly political time, when the council was starting to fragment over debates as to whether the Church was a corporate body or not.[24]

Henry VI appointed Thomas as one of six men to frame the statutes for the college of St Bernard of Cambridge, later known as Queen's College in 1446.[25] The esteemed scholar, Desiderius Erasmus would later teach and attend the college between 1506 and 1515. His connection with the Boleyns would continue. During the reign of the Yorkist Edward IV, Thomas was among a small party of men who presented the land and castle of Sudeley to the King's brother, Richard, Duke of Gloucester.[26]

Geoffrey on the other hand travelled to London to make his mark as the capital held countless opportunities for young and ambitious men. The English guilds that emerged in the twelfth century were appropriate for local markets in towns and merchants in small communities, and continued to represent specific trades, but they were less capable of dealing in trade and commerce at a national level. In the fourteenth century, Edward III chartered companies focusing on business and finance, known as livery companies. Evolving from guilds, they became corporations under the Royal Charter, responsible for everything related to their particular trade, from training, regulation and quality control, to conditions for workers and industry standards. Each company had their own livery, a specific form of dress, which each member wore to signify which company they were a part of. They were essentially trade bodies that formed the backbone of business in the city of London. To work in a particular trade, you had to first be apprenticed, and upon completion become a freeman or master of your trade and thereby secure your future. There were originally

48 companies, out of which grew the Great Twelve, one of which was the Hatters' Company.[27]

Geoffrey chose the perfect career path, being apprenticed for a short while to a hatter, then becoming a freeman of the city through the Hatters' Company in 1428.[28] The hatters were a modest guild and would later be incorporated into the larger haberdashers' guild, but it was a start. After almost eight years, Geoffrey transferred to a far grander livery company (for there was a hierarchy among the companies) in 1429, the Mercers' Company. The record of Geoffrey's career change still exists:

> Geoffrey Boleyn, *hatter*, before Henry Frowik, the Mayor, and the Aldermen in the Chamber of the Guildhall, and showed that whereas he had been admitted into the freedom of the City in the Art of Hatter ... he had long used, and was now using, the art of Mercery and not the art of Hatter. He therefore prayed that he might be admitted into the freedom of the City in the Art of Mercery. His prayer granted at the instance of the Masters.[29]

Geoffrey's petition had the support of over a dozen mercers, demonstrating that he was well liked and respected.

The Worshipful Company of Mercers was the leading guild of the top 12 London guilds, and certainly the most powerful, wealthy and influential. Whatever Geoffrey's reason for joining the Mercers, it was a clever move as it would be the making of him. Mercers were merchants who traded in a wide assortment of goods, linens, wools, furs, velvets, silks, wood, oils and many more luxurious and lucrative items. As with all guilds the Mercers had their own premises and church: they held their meetings in the hospital of St Thomas of Acon (off Cheapside), with a chapel in the south-west side of the adjoining church. Geoffrey eventually applied to be independent of the Mercers' Company, while retaining their livery, a peculiar request which was, even more unusually, granted – only Geoffrey received such a concession in the history of the Guild. But he was so successful within the company that he became master in 1454.

His diligence and advancement in the competitive London world of business had been substantial and now it was time to find a wife and start a family. His first wife was the strikingly named Dionise, of whom we have only fleeting mentions.[30] The name conjures up literary soirées and engagements of a later era, but we know only that she may have had a son, named Dionysius Boleyn, who appears alongside Geoffrey Boleyn and his uncle Thomas, in a list of early benefactors to Queen's College, Cambridge.[31] We might well speculate that Dionysius, an unusual name in itself, was named in honour of his mother, suggesting she died in childbirth. This is most likely although we have very little information on the son, who lived into adulthood but died before his father. This rather distinctive diversion in the family tree was short lived, and the family soon returned to the endless cycle of Christian names, Thomas, Geoffrey and William, leaving the resplendent Dionise and Dionysius behind.

Geoffrey's second marriage was considerably more successful, and would set the pattern for the next three generations of marrying into the nobility. Like the sons of other newly rich merchant families, he used the well-established tradition of bettering the family name by marrying into, and bringing wealth to, noble, ancient families, and in turn, acquiring gentility, land and wealth.[32] He married Anne Hoo, daughter of Lord Thomas Hoo, sometime in 1437 or 1438.

Anne's father, Lord Hoo, was the son and heir of Sir Thomas de Hoo, who won fame at the Battle of Agincourt, before easing into the role of diplomat and courtier. The Hoo family were socially superior to the Boleyns, but it was not uncommon for gentlewomen to marry into the merchant classes, and Geoffrey's wealth, and presumably his intelligence and drive, made up for any difference in social standing. Opportunities for advancement and prosperity were there for the ambitious and well connected, and for Geoffrey, his marriage now linked him to the networks of Thomas Hoo, which firmly cemented his status as a gentleman.[33] Geoffrey, unlike his father, appears in official records but not in relation to crime. He was elected Sheriff of London in 1447, in 1449 he was a Member of Parliament for London, and in 1451, he was one of five men who lent the king the combined sum of £1,246 to pay for the war in France, which suggests he was rising in esteem and was also financially secure.[34] In 1457, Geoffrey reached the pinnacle of his career when he was elected Lord Mayor of London.[35] This opened up a new tier of social network to him as we learn that in ceremonial processions and banquets, he was now situated with barons, mitred abbots and three chief justices, and was sworn of the Royal Council.[36]

In June 1453, he hosted the officers of the Mercers' Company in his own home while elections were held for wardens of the company, further evidence that he was one of the most prominent and wealthy of his fellows in the city. He was also given a commission with other wardens to legally enter houses, warehouses and cellars of any foreign merchants in London (especially Genoese and Venetians who monopolised the trade routes) in order to make inventories and could, if need be, confiscate their goods and merchandise.[37] Such a task was evidently at odds with his own mercantile loyalties, and the commission was later vacated because no action had actually been taken to carry out its commands, suggesting he had not exercised his authority.

Geoffrey maintained cordial alliances with both Lancastrians and Yorkists throughout the Wars of the Roses, displaying a nascent diplomatic ability. In 1451, he lent King Henry VI £1,246 for an expedition into France in the final phase of the Hundred Years' War.[38] A decade later, during Geoffrey's term as mayor, Richard Neville, the Earl of Warwick, known as 'the Kingmaker', attempted to lay siege to London. Geoffrey responded decisively: he put 5,000 men under arms to keep order within the city walls, and then personally patrolled the city walls, ever vigilant, as protector of the city.[39] Interestingly, when the members of the Mercers' Company agreed to lend £100 to the Earl of Warwick, Geoffrey contributed the largest portion. That same year the company granted 1,000 marks to Edward IV, 'for the speed of the earl of Warwick into the North', with Geoffrey supplying one of the highest sums of over 13 pounds.[40] Despite a highly successful London career, Geoffrey seems to have preferred life in Norfolk and sought a suitable residence for his family. In 1452, he opened negotiations with one Sir John Falstolf of Caister, a wealthy landowner and a member of the king's council, who took Geoffrey under his protective wing when they were younger. Geoffrey wished to purchase the manor of Blickling in Norfolk from Falstolf, which he remodelled into a very handsome family estate as befitted such a well-respected family. Shakespeare's disreputable, sack-drinking Falstaff was based on this Falstolf, and on Sir John Oldcastle, a close companion of Henry V. In real life, neither man fared particularly well; Oldcastle eventually rebelled against the Crown and was executed, and Falstolf was indicted for cowardice after the English defeat at Patay, a major battle between the English and French in 1429; he was temporarily stripped of his knighthood and would never recover from the scandal.[41]

The sale of Blickling to Geoffrey was far from smooth and Falstolf ended up taking Geoffrey to court before the Lord Chancellor, Cardinal Kemp, claiming an unpaid portion of the agreed purchase price.[42] Geoffrey made a counter-claim stating that Falstolf had withheld several hundred sheep which were to be included in the sale of the manor.[43] The loan was not due to be paid until 1453, suggesting Geoffrey may have been short of funds. But if he was, he hid it well, or navigated his way around it, as his ever-expanding property portfolio included land, parishes and tenements, including Chidingston, and what would later become the beloved family home – Hever. Sometime in 1457, he and his brother Thomas purchased the manors of Stivekey and Poswick in Norfolk; three years later, they added the manor of Little Carbrook, and then he began to branch out, moving south into Kent where he purchased the manors of Kemsing and Sele.

Geoffrey's success would continue, with forays into property transactions, bringing prominence and prestige to the family, and all the privileges that accompanied serious wealth. So, as nobility became restricted to the aristocracy and peerage, *Nobilitas major*, landed gentry became the next, lower strata of society, *Nobilitas minor* – landowners who became landlords in possession of estates, living entirely from rental income.[44] The criteria for entry into this next stratum required one to have a country home or estate, or many of either; and one should sever all financial ties with the business that had created one's wealth, so as to cleanse the family of the 'taint of trade'. In the fifteenth century there were some knights, like Sir John Falstolf, who were richer than many peers. From the late fifteenth century, the gentry would emerge as the class most closely involved in politics, the military and law, and would eventually supply the bulk of Members of Parliament, with many gentry families maintaining political control in certain localities.

Geoffrey's keen business sense may have been due to a rather exacting and meticulous nature which coloured his personal life, including his instructions for his own funeral, which he had planned to perfection in his will, made on 14 June 1463. If he died within the Realm of England, he wanted to be buried in the church of Blickling: if he died in London, he wished to be buried in the chapel of St John in the church of St Lawrence Jewry in Gresham Street, named for the large population of Jews who had once lived in the area.[45] It was also the official church of the Mayor of London. When he did finally die in 1463 in London, his brother, Thomas, as his executor, made the appropriate arrangements, including having erected a prominently placed gravestone on which were written the words *Nowe Thus*.[46] This rather enigmatic phrase must have had a great emotional significance for the family because his grandson, our Thomas, and his daughter, Anne Boleyn, took this as their motto.

Geoffrey wanted the ceremony to convey the right impression: he requested *black* candlesticks, not, heaven forfend, *gilt* candlesticks, and that 13 torches be carried by 13 poor men (but not beggars).[47] These men were each given a rosary, a gown lined with russet or black and a hood of black, as well as 12 pence.[48] He eschewed ostentation and extravagance, and asked that his brother Thomas should attend a dinner held in his memory, and that he should be one of the people asked to compose the guest list. It was a modest yet classy interment commensurate for a wealthy and respected man which, needless to say, Geoffrey was.

His property inventory at the time of his death included at least a dozen manors, plus land and tenements in Norfolk, Kent, Surrey, Sussex and Middlesex. Geoffrey's sons, Thomas and William, each received 300 marks, the currency still used in the Middle Ages, which was roughly two thirds of a pound. But to his daughters, Isabel, Anne and Alice, who he expected to make advantageous marriages (or forfeit their inheritance) he left each the substantial sum of 1,000 marks, leaving his brother to assent to the daughters' marriages. The three girls married prominent men of court – William Cheyne, Sir Henry Heydon and Sir John Fortescue, which would have satisfied their father. Geoffrey also bequeathed the incredibly vast sum of £1,000 to poor householders in London, and £200 to the poor in Blickling, Holkham, Stukey, Mulbarton, Kemsing and Salle; £20 was given to Blickling Church, and other monies were left to priests to pray for his parents, his first wife and the testator himself.[49]

Of Geoffrey's brother, Thomas, we know very little of his later years, only that he died in 1472, and was given a dignified, and substantial, marble tomb in Wells Cathedral, which still stands.

Geoffrey's two teenaged sons, Thomas and William, became the heads of the family. Thomas was the elder, and would have borne much of the responsibility of the family, but he died, unmarried, only eight years after his father, in 1471.[50] William was now heir, and had sufficient ambition and more importantly the ability to embark on enlarging the wealth his father had left him, and to establish himself as a leading gentleman of Norfolk. William would spend his life building on his family's foundations of commerce and trade within Norfolk, but he was equally extremely capable and confident in royal employment. He was present at the coronation of Richard III in 1483 and was one of 18 men chosen to become a knight of the Order of the Bath, and later that same year he was made a Justice of the Peace.[51] The role of Justice of the Peace figures prominently in all studies of the English gentry from the fourteenth century onwards as their numbers and duties increased under the Tudors and are considered to be the cornerstone of English local government. Their authority extended over local parishes and eventually the counties where they resided. They were not formally elected but appointed and so represented the collective social power of the gentry. With wealth amassed in industry and trade, and political influence, the gentry had what sociologists call 'social mobility' and became devoted to the acquisition of stately homes and their social appurtenances. The divisions between classes were becoming blurred, as heiresses of great families who had fallen on hard times were married into the merchant classes, securing the wealth necessary to maintain their great estates.

William lived during a time of social change, which had been characteristic of the middle to late fifteenth century and came to a head during the 30 years' war between the Houses of Lancaster and York, the two rival branches of the royal House of Plantagenet. The wheel of fortune had spun quickly, with both families holding the throne for a time. Most families of all classes throughout England had been adversely affected in some way by the wars, losing their men, land and income as the power struggle continued as York and Lancaster clamoured for the throne. William's mother, Anne, became an advisor of sorts, and was instrumental in William's choice of wife, and most particular with which family the Boleyns might align themselves. Wisely, Anne looked to the Butler family.

The Butlers were Irish, and held the prestigious title of Earl of Ormond, bestowed upon Theobald Butler by Edward III in the early fourteenth century, with the title thereafter passing from father to son through the generations.[52] Prior to the war they were a respected and powerful family; however, as Lancastrians they were on the losing side of the Wars of the Roses, with the Yorkist Edward IV having won the throne, and were eventually stripped of the earldoms and lands, although these would be partially returned. With William's marriage to Margaret, who was born in Kilkenny Castle in Ireland, the Boleyns slowly transitioned from a well-off merchant family to wealthy landowners, with close links to nobility.

We see flashes of William's character, through what is admittedly a distant mirror, but enough to make out a capable and talented man who would be as enterprising and ambitious as his father, and share his sense of duty and responsibility to his family. Even from a distance of over 500 years, it seems that William and Margaret enjoyed a successful marriage, having ten children. Not all the siblings made it to adulthood: John was born sometime around 1481, but died aged three, and Anthony, born in 1483, died aged ten. The eldest surviving son, our Thomas, was born in 1477, followed by William, born in 1491, James, in 1493, and Edward, in 1496. Their sisters were Anne, born in 1476, Alice, born in 1487, Margaret, born in 1489, and Jane, born in 1485. With the exception of Jane, the Boleyn children would enjoy longevity.

It is likely that the siblings were all born at Blickling Hall, the 'fair house of bricke' which had been in the family for generations.[53] To link Thomas to the romance of Hever, however, tradition has it that he was born there, rather than Blickling, but this was not the case – and the most compelling evidence comes from Thomas himself. In a letter to Thomas Cromwell, Thomas, commenting on a crime in the county, remarked that in his 33 years of living in Kent, he knew of no such act committed by his folk.[54] This letter was written in 1538, which would date his first year at Hever as 1505, which is when the records have Thomas and his young family at Hever. The phrasing strongly suggests that Thomas was not born in Kent.

Other evidence can be found in Henry Spelman's *Icenia*, a topographical history of Norfolk, in the seventeenth century, in which he wrote: 'To the left lies Blickling, once the seat of the Boleyns, from whence sprung Thomas Boleyn.'[55] It would make little sense, nor is there evidence to suggest, that William and Margaret moved between Blickling and Hever. Norfolk was the focal point for the whole family, and William was highly invested in Norfolk. Blickling was their ancestral home, and a symbol of their status. Hever, a small Kentish manor, was something of a 'fixer upper' and did not yet boast the grander additions that Thomas would add. Certainly Thomas' connection with Blickling, which had now been in the family for three generations, was strong, and this connection lasted throughout his life, suggesting an affection for his family home. Despite his later move to Kent and then to frequent embassies abroad, Thomas maintained his connection with Norfolk. He served as Justice of the Peace in both counties and was appointed Sherriff of Norfolk and Suffolk in 1509–10, before performing the same role in Kent in 1510–11. In 1513, he was described as 'Sir Thomas Boleyn of London, alias of Hever, Kent, alias of Blickling, Norfolk', so it is possible that he wished to be viewed as a man of Kent, without sacrificing his Norfolk roots. The Boleyn children grew up in a milieu of wealth and privilege, as William had expanded upon the political and cultural foundations set by his father and grandfather. Thomas remained close to his siblings throughout their lives – William, James and Edward would, like Thomas, become courtiers, and Thomas would be called upon to assist his sisters, through his own network, with various financial and legal matters. He would also remain close to his sisters, in particular Anne and Alice.

William and Margaret invested heavily in their eldest son Thomas. He was an educated young man which was evident, as we shall see, in his intellectual interests and associates. Although the details of his education, like so many of Henry VII's courtiers and nobles, are sparse, one may speculate and put forward a few generalisations. Thomas' father, William, was a Fellow of Lincoln's Inn, and it is possible that Thomas Boleyn followed this path. He may have been educated there or at home with private tutors, but considering his great-uncle's link with Cambridge, it is also possible that he spent some time there. Certainly his parents nurtured his flair for languages, talent for diplomacy, and keen intelligence. When the time came, they would also invest in an advantageous marriage. With a large family to provide for, William continued to become more involved in the business of the Crown, and was given the significant responsibility of repairing and guarding the beacons on the sea coast in Norfolk in the event of an invasion.[56] In August of 1483, during Richard III's reign, John Howard, Duke of Norfolk, made William his deputy for the coasts of Norfolk and Suffolk for life, a benefit which included a 'pipe of good wine yearly'.[57] This burgeoning relationship between Boleyn and Howard would be fortuitous for both families in the years to come.

William's mother Anne, the Boleyn matriarch, died in 1485, and was buried not at the chapel in Blickling but in the gothic cathedral in Norwich, her grave marked by a memorial brass. Sadly, her memorial was moved some time in the sixteenth century and all that survives is the outline of a woman on the re-positioned stone. She left her son the manor of Mulbarton and, when her uncle, Thomas Hoo, died in 1486, all the estates went to William. Anne died just before Henry Tudor's rebel forces plucked the crown from Richard III – the last king of the House of York – in a bloody battle on 22 August 1485. The defining encounter at Bosworth Field, near Stoke Golding, Leicestershire, ended the bitter 30-year Wars of the Roses, and also ended the Plantagenet reign. Whatever roses the Boleyns had once followed, they were now very much Tudor men.

# CHAPTER TWO

# Fortune Ruleth our Helme

*Let not us, that are squires of the night's body, be called thieves of the day's beauty; let us be Diana's foresters, gentlemen of the shade, minions of the moon: and let men say, we be men of good governance, being governed as the sea is, by our noble and chaste mistress the moon, under whose countenance we steal.*

– Shakespeare, *Henry IV Part I*

The accession of Henry Tudor in 1485 did not signify some extraordinary shift in the fortunes of the Boleyn family, but it had an impact on William's father-in-law, Thomas Butler. Under Henry VII, the Butler family were fully restored to their former wealth and status; the Boleyns, already connected by marriage, now found themselves joined to one of the wealthiest families in England, as William's mother, with admirable foresight, had always intended.[1] Thomas Butler was an astute, highly intelligent man who steadily gained influence at court, becoming Chamberlain to Henry VII's consort, Queen Elizabeth of York, the daughter of Edward IV and mother of the future Henry VIII. To serve as the head of her household was a prestigious position as he was obviously favoured by Henry VII, who wrote to Thomas Butler referring to him as his 'well beloved cousin'.[2] Such connections could only benefit the Boleyns, who anticipated being brought further into the court sphere. But Henry VII and England would be haunted by Yorkist spectres and violent insurrections for some years before uncertainty would give way to peace, prosperity and a country united.

Barely a year passed before Henry faced his first challenge when Richard Symonds, an Oxford priest and Yorkist supporter, noticed that a student of his, young Lambert Simnel, bore a striking similarity to one of the two sons of Edward IV, the boys who became known as the Princes in the Tower. The story became more specific: the boy was declared to be Edward Plantagenet, Earl of Warwick, and son of George, Duke of Clarence. Simnel sparked a coup, and was taken to Ireland, which had been a centre of Yorkist support, where the Lord

Lieutenant, Earl of Kildare, proclaimed Simnel as King Edward VI.[3] It is not clear whether Kildare truly believed the pretender was in fact a lost York prince, but his cause was strengthened when Edward IV's sister, Margaret of Burgundy, sent 2,000 soldiers and mercenaries to assist the Yorkists, already planning an invasion of England.[4] Henry looked to his nobles, including William Boleyn's father-in-law, to defend the realm. Unfortunately for the king, one of the premier nobles of the realm, John de la Pole, Earl of Lincoln, who had been named successor to the deposed Richard III, had also fled to Ireland in May 1487.[5] If Henry lost control of his senior nobility, his chance of remaining king was at risk, and renewed civil war was inevitable.

It was widely believed that the east coast would be Simnel's landing stage and, as Norfolk gentry, William Boleyn and his sister Anne's husband, Sir Henry Heydon, were appointed commissioners, tasked with preparing coastal defences and ensuring word was spread of an impending invasion.[6] It was implied by some at the time that William and Henry reluctantly rode as far as Thetford, but then returned home before reaching the coast, believing the King might be defeated. There is the ever-so-faint suggestion that William and Henry Heydon were secret Yorkists, but the orders came from the Earl of Oxford and were delivered via Sir Edmund Bedingfield, a fellow Knight of the Bath who was held in high favour by Henry VII. With the civil war recent history, William may have hesitated to obey a command that had not come with a royal seal.[7] They had to be sure they were responding to royal orders. The Earl of Oxford later wrote to Bedingfield reporting that the Norfolk gentry had been excused from their duty in Kent, since the rebels had clearly chosen not to land in the south of England, but hundreds of miles away, in Lancashire. This explanation is supported by the fact that Henry VII continued to favour William Boleyn, and did not treat him as a potential dissenter. Thus, the implication of cowardice, and disobedience, rings false.

Eventually the Simnel rebellion collapsed, and while Richard Symonds was arrested and sentenced to life in a bishop's prison, his young student, Simnel, was sent straight to the King's kitchen as a spit roaster as Henry recognised that he was not the cause of the invasion but a mere pawn in a very dangerous game; Simnel was later given the post of King's Falconer in recognition of how well he had worked. The Simnel affair had shown Henry that, for the moment, it was more prudent to concentrate on domestic issues. Between challenges from pretenders to the throne, Henry was eager to adopt a more aggressive foreign policy, despite the fact that the Wars of the Roses had depleted England's manpower and in the first years Henry did not have the men and financial resources for foreign adventures.

England and France had been major rivals since 1066, and it was the nearest country to present Henry VII with potential problems. The two realms had clashed over English-held land in France for many years, the most acrimonious conflict being the Hundred Years' War from 1337 to 1453. When Henry won the Battle of Bosworth in 1485, he signed a one-year truce with France that was later extended to 1489, but by 1491, France had three times the resources in terms of manpower and revenue, and Henry, fearing a now-stronger France, decided on a pre-emptive attack on the latter, in alliance with the Holy Roman Emperor, Maximilian of Austria.

William Boleyn was appointed to a commission of array for Norfolk as one of 36 commanders, this time to mobilise English forces against possible incursions by King Charles of France.[8] William and his father-in-law, Sir Thomas Butler, were a part of the contingent sent to Calais in September 1492.[9] They sailed early in the morning; we may wonder what words William and his son Thomas exchanged before William set off.

It was soon discovered that Maximilian defaulted on his promise of war preparations and would not in fact be sending any troops at all.[10] Left holding the sword, Henry pressed on. He besieged the town of Bolougne, though with no great zeal as the town was hardly a prize, but it quickly moved the French king to sue for peace before any real bloodshed could occur.[11] William returned to England just months later, but he continued to advance at court, and in 1494, he was invited to a feast and tournament at Westminster, to celebrate the three-year-old Prince Henry's (future Henry VIII) instalment as the Duke of York.[12]

With two male heirs, the Tudor king should have felt secure and hopeful for the longevity of his reign, but such hopes were thwarted when another imposter, Perkin Warbeck, older than Simnel, led a rebellion which lasted almost eight years. Warbeck's career as another 'Duke of York' began in 1491 in Cork, Ireland, where he was initially acclaimed as the Earl of Warwick. But soon he adopted the identity of Richard of York, the younger of the two 'Princes in the Tower'. He claimed to have been permitted to escape when his brother was murdered, a story plausible to those who wanted to believe it.

The Yorkist Margaret again funded the enterprise, and Warbeck landed in Kent on 3 July 1495, but his small army was routed and 150 of the pretender's troops were killed without Warbeck even stepping off the ship. He was forced to retreat almost immediately, and sailed for Scotland, where James IV, more than happy to rattle the English, gave Warbeck refuge and a pension of £1,200 a year, more than enough for Warbeck to attempt another invasion of England. An incensed Henry VII was determined to go to war with Scotland and demanded a special subsidy from Parliament, which required a new tax.[13]

This provoked a violent reaction in the south of England, especially in Cornwall; Henry now had to deal with a domestic rebellion as well as a potential invasion. In 1497, Thomas Boleyn finally emerges from the sources, aged 20, alongside his father, William, as a part of the Kentish contingent of the king's army against a force of approximately 30,000 Cornish rebels.[14] They were joined by men who would become major figures at Henry VIII's court: Sir Edward Poynings, George Neville, Lord Abergavenny and Thomas Boleyn's future brothers-in-law, Robert Clere and Philip Calthorp.[15] On 16 June, Henry VII with his forces rode out of London and attacked the rebels on the hill in St George's Field. It was violent and bloody: a rabble thoroughly routed by an organised royal force. Two thousand rebels were slain, against Henry's loss of 300 men.[16] We have no way of knowing how Thomas fared in battle, but it was the honourable entry into manhood that most young men of the period would have desired, and Thomas could be seen as a young man with certain prospects.

He was also of a good age to make a fortunate marriage alliance. The Boleyn family followed a pattern of investing, by marriage, in families who had encountered financial misfortune during the Wars of the Roses, but who were on the cusp of being restored to their former glory. Such families were not uncommon, as many had suffered a great deal through the 30 years of war which ended in 1485. In this context, Thomas made a very favourable marriage with Elizabeth Howard, eldest daughter of Thomas Howard, Earl of Surrey, sometime between 1497 and 1500. J. S. Brewer made a scathing assessment of the union: 'but what was the connection of his family with the Howards, or what could induce the premier and proudest duke of England to match his daughter with a commoner of no distinction and of little wealth, must be left to conjecture'.[17]

Thomas' lineage, already discussed, shows the inaccuracy of the statement that he was a commoner of no distinction, but it is also important to note that the Howard family had been politically influential under Yorkist rule when they held the premier title of nobility, the Dukedom of Norfolk.[18] However, they fought against Henry Tudor in the Wars of the Roses and, as a result, during Henry VII's reign, were subject to state-sponsored political restraints, which diminished their significant income and status.[19] We do not know what sort of dowry Elizabeth brought to the marriage, but Thomas and his new wife were relatively secure. Thomas' personal income was £50 per year, and remained so until his father's death.[20] Without the evidence of any personal correspondence between the couple, it is impossible to determine how compatible they were. Was there love in the marriage, or respect? What sort of woman *was* Elizabeth? Thomas' linguistic expertise and charm were traits he passed to his children, but the evidence is scarce concerning Elizabeth. Later records suggest, as we shall see, that she became an influential woman at court, the ideal companion for a man like Thomas. His parents, William and Margaret, moved down to Rochford Hall in Essex, which had been in the Butler family since the fourteenth century, leaving Thomas and his young wife in the premier Boleyn estate. The move might indicate that William intended for Thomas to be the figurehead of the family, stepping back and allowing his heir to take the reins. In any case, when Henry VII visited Norfolk in 1498, he visited Blickling Hall, and it is likely that Thomas rather than his father played host, as William Boleyn would have been referred to as 'Sir' whereas in the account of the King's progress, a 'Mr Boleyn' is listed.[21] While a visit from the monarch and their entourage usually put a dent in one's finances, it was a mark of respect that the King chose to visit the new couple and added a royal touch to their general wedding celebrations. William meanwhile also spent considerable time at Hever, as he was described as being a gentleman of Kent.[22]

The marriage was successful and we know from Thomas' own statement that they had at least four or five children by 1505.[23]

So many details regarding the Boleyn children's formative years remain out of reach – Mary, Anne and George – and a brief discussion at this juncture is unavoidable. It is likely that George was the youngest of the siblings, as his entry to court came later, around 1524. Had he been older than his sisters, there would be reference to him much sooner as son and heir, and his would have been the first marriage negotiated, rather than that of his sister, Mary. Even on his first embassy in 1529, discussed later, he was considered to be quite young for the position. George was likely privately tutored, although it was at one time claimed that Thomas sent George to be 'educated in all kinds of polite learning among the Oxonians'. This is difficult to prove, as records show that between 1500 to 1600, the age for entry to Oxford University was invariably seventeen. But as George became a page to the King in 1514, and from that time, a permanent member of court, it is unlikely that he went to university at all.[24]

Regarding Mary, her position as the eldest of the siblings would seem to be corroborated by a letter written in 1597 by her grandson, George Carey, 2nd Baron Hunsdon, to William Cecil. In the letter he makes it clear that he wished to petition his cousin, Queen Elizabeth I, for the Irish Earldom of Ormond, which had been held by our Thomas Boleyn. Carey wrote that the title 'should have passed to his father and then on to himself by virtue of their descent from Sir Thomas Boleyn's eldest daughter, Mary'.[25] This would seem to close the door on debate, were it not for the fact that Cecil advised him not to pursue the request on several grounds including the fact that Mary was not the eldest. Additionally, the Inquisition Post Mortem following Thomas Boleyn's death lists Mary as the 'only and next daughter and heir'. Her education is equally mysterious, but it is likely that Mary, like her brother, was privately educated as a woman befitting her status.

This brings us to Anne, who, according to several schools of thought, was either born sometime between 1501 and 1504, or in 1507.

Those who support the date of 1507 are persuaded by two sources, a marginal note in the 1615 edition of Camden's *History of Elizabeth*, in which he wrote 1507 in Roman numerals, but this date was removed from the second edition in 1625.[26] The other source is Henry Clifford's *Life of Jane Dormer*.[27] Neither Clifford nor his subject, Jane, were Boleyn contemporaries: Jane was born two years after Anne's death, and Clifford, who was born about 1570, only finished his book in 1643, over a hundred years after Anne's death. These two sources are not necessarily the strongest pieces of evidence, and 1507 seems unlikely, for, briefly looking ahead to her education, this would mean that in 1513, a six-year-old Anne would have been sent by her father to Margaret of Austria's court – one of the most sophisticated courts in Europe.

This was, as Retha Warnicke notes, a highly prestigious educational advantage.[28] Margaret not only seemed pleased with Anne, but was also anticipating meeting Thomas again – he had just left her court – writing:

> I have received your letter by the Esquire Bouton who has presented your daughter to me, who is very welcome, and I am confident of being able to deal with her in a way which will give you satisfaction, so that on your return the two of us will need no intermediary than she. I find her so bright and pleasant for her young age that I am more beholden to you for sending her to me than you are to me.[29]

Margaret assigned Anne a tutor named Symonnet to help her improve her French. It is likely that he assisted with the composition of Anne's well-known letter to her father which demonstrates a stated earnest desire to please him, and a declaration that she wanted him to be proud of her:

> Sir, I understand by your letter that you desire that I shall be a worthy woman when I come to the Court and you inform me that the Queen [Queen Claude of France] will take the trouble to converse with me, which rejoices me much to think of talking with a person so wise and worthy. This will make me have greater desire to continue to speak French well and also spell, especially because you have so enjoined it on me, and with my own hand I inform you that I will

observe it the best I can. Sir, I beg you to excuse me if my letter is badly written, for I assure you that the orthography is from my own understanding alone, while the others were only written by my hand, and Semmonet [Symonnet] tells me the letter but waits so that I may do it myself, for fear that it shall not be known unless I acquaint you ... you can, if you please, make me a declaration of your word, and concerning me be certain that there shall be neither ... nor ingratitude which might check or efface my affection, which is determined to ... as much unless it shall please you to order me, and I promise you that my love is based on such great strength that it will never grow less, and I will make an end to my ... After having commended myself right humbly to your good grace.[30]

The letter is not that of a six-year-old, but more to the point, why would Thomas have sought such a position for a child? Surely a young girl of 13 would benefit more from the position. Furthermore, when Thomas moved Anne from Margaret's court to the French court in 1514, he explained to Margaret that Henry was marrying his sister Mary Tudor to King Louis, and Anne, who now had a good grasp of French, would be needed to attend upon her. If Anne was indeed born in 1507, she must have been the most in demand seven-year-old in all of Europe. It therefore seems likely that Anne was born sometime between 1501 and 1504, followed by Mary, and finally George. All three were probably born at Blickling, and it was their ancestral home, but mystery surrounds two other Boleyn children – Henry and Thomas, one buried near his father at Hever, and the other in the Sidney chapel in nearby Penshurst.[31]

The memorial brasses for both young Boleyns have been dated as 1520, and a record exists in the Ashmolean Museum, Oxford of the brass, stating that the younger Thomas died in 1520. The date is peculiar, for Penshurst was owned by Edward Stafford, Duke of Buckingham in 1520, so why would a Boleyn be buried there at that stage? Thomas would not be appointed Keeper of Penshurst until 1522, so perhaps it was simply a memorial brass. It is a popular theory that these two Boleyns died as young men, and while there is no evidence to support such an argument, the size of the brass does not necessarily indicate a child. But as there is no mention of a Henry or Thomas Boleyn of this generation in any record, it is therefore more than likely that they never reached adulthood.

In these early years, it was clear that the family could hardly move back and forth between Blickling and London. Sometime in 1505, Thomas, then aged 28, moved his young wife and family down to Hever, in Kent, a far more convenient home for a family on the rise at court. Although it has been said that Thomas did 'nothing to transform their house into a worthy expression of their ambitions', the manor was a respectable estate for a man of his position.

Significantly for Thomas, with the first Tudor king came 'new men', courtiers chosen primarily on merit, rather than the hereditary lords who, during the previous reign of the Yorkist Edward IV, dominated England. The new men were not necessarily of noble blood, but they were educated, intelligent, ambitious, and they took advantage of their opportunities to advance themselves and their families through service to the first king of a new dynasty.[32]

The court of Henry VII might be imagined as sombre and oppressive, watched over by a shrewd and miserly king. True, Henry VII was fiscally conservative, and his court maintained a strict observance of religious fasting which bordered on oppressive. But Henry suffers from comparison with his over-indulgent son. Apart from the threats to Henry's kingship, the court Thomas and his family knew was experiencing a glorious age. Henry VII and Elizabeth of York had named their first son and heir Arthur, and the myth of Camelot permeated the court. Henry not only understood the power of display, he recognised the need to promote the magnificence of the monarchy. The English court cultivated relationships with some of the finest European poets, philosophers and humanists of the age. Desiderius Erasmus for instance, the great humanist scholar of the sixteenth century, whose name is linked with the Reformation and the Tudor period, was a guest at Henry VII's court and later a patron of Thomas Boleyn: perhaps they first met in England. Some of these great scholars were chosen as tutors for the King's sons, Arthur and Henry, and helped shape the future king's attitudes towards the arts. Henry Tudor was something of a scholar himself, and an avid reader, employing numerous musicians and court actors, although frugality was also observed.

Henry VII may not have been as athletic or handsome as his son, nor do we have evidence that he participated in the same physical pursuits his son would later enjoy, such as wrestling or jousting, but this is not to say that he was incapable or uninterested. The royal residences that Thomas and his father would have visited included the new palace of Richmond, opposite Westminster, which boasted dancing chambers and halls where musicians played while king and court played chess, dice and cards. Archery, tennis and lawn bowls in the expansive gardens were also popular, and Henry VII, surrounded by his courtiers and entourage, enjoyed hunting; not even his deteriorating eyesight and an unfortunate incident involving a crossbow and a farmyard rooster who happened to be in the wrong place at the wrong time dampened Henry's love of such pursuits. He also took great care in investing in the royal parks, maintaining them and ensuring they were filled with game. He was keen on hawking, owning at least 20 hawks, two gyrfalcons, a sparrowhawk and a hobby. Jousting was also popular at court, and it was Henry who introduced the Burgundian tradition of the tournament to England, conscious of this trend at the most fashionable courts of Europe. The tournaments held in these years were thematic spectacles, and it is more than likely that Thomas participated whenever he was at court.

But in such a competitive environment, how would a man like Thomas have been noticed? There was really only one corridor of power, and it was always crowded, as Henry VII insisted on being personally involved in all matters. He wrote many letters himself, trusted his mother, Margaret Beaufort, more than any other councillor, and had no qualms intervening in legal processes and local quarrels. There are very few signposts, such as letters, which locate the Boleyn family within the court, apart from the odd appearances already noted. However, Thomas would nonetheless have been present at every event that presented an opportunity to prove himself: battles, coronations, weddings and funerals.

Thomas' first grand event was the wedding of Henry VII's son and heir, Arthur. William brought his son to court, and both Thomas and his father were present in Henry VII's large entourage – led by the young and precocious Prince Henry, Duke of York, the future Henry VIII – to welcome Katherine of Aragon, Arthur's bride to be.

When the young, Spanish, auburn-haired Katherine of Aragon arrived in England, the country became besotted with her. She represented the future: an England finally looking towards Europe. William was part of Prince Henry, Duke of York's entourage, riding from London to St George's Field to meet the Spanish retinue and escort them into London. It was the same field where William and his son, along with Henry's army, had camped on the night before the battle at St George's Field four years before. Now, it was the scene of celebration. Thomas is not mentioned as part of the retinue, but he was present when, on 14 November 1501, Arthur married Katherine in old St Paul's Cathedral.[33]

The marriage of these two 15-year-olds was a diplomatic triumph for England and Spain. The House of Tudor had united with an old and powerful European dynasty which could promote peace and security for the kingdom. Thomas and his father were among the revellers following the wedding, and it is worth noting the extraordinary scenes that they would have witnessed and taken part in. The centrepiece of the celebrations was a week of tournaments and jousting. The tilt was 'arranged at the whole length from the Watergate well nighe up to the Entrance of the Gate [at Westminster] that openeth into the King's Street towards the Sanctuary'.[34] A tree had been erected and decorated with delicate leaves, flowers and fruit; underneath hung various shields bearing the crests of the lords, knights and challengers for the tournaments. On the first day rode the challengers, men of high nobility like the Duke of Buckingham, captain of the forces sent to subdue the Cornish Rebellion years earlier, who was dressed in white and green; on the second, the defenders, who broke countless staves. Various nobles had their own pavilions, which together would have resembled an army encampment: indeed, their entrances into the hall prior to the tournament was described as a 'goodly Manner of Warre'.[35] Thomas would not have previously witnessed such an extravagant display.

One chronicler noted with disappointment that it rained on the Saturday, so the celebrations continued indoors, but numerous pageants were held, including a mock castle being carried through the hall of Westminster while children, some dressed as maidens, sang sweetly from the turrets, followed by a ship built on wheels that was pushed through the hall.[36] A beautiful young woman, dressed in silver and gold like the newly wed Katherine, stood in the centre, while two young men calling themselves 'Hope' and 'Desire' clambered down the ladder and marched on the castle. They were the ambassadors from the Mount of Love, which, incidentally, was the third pageant to be carried into the hall. And so it went on, this spectacle of chivalry, majesty and glory. The Boleyns were a part of the court revels, and would have danced and feasted long into the night, and William and his son were present when Arthur, flushed from the excitement of the celebrations, arose the next morning, and, among his attendants, felt bold enough to make a few impertinent remarks about his own personal exploits with his new wife. These off-the-cuff remarks would come to light and haunt Katherine years later.

The young couple were sent to Ludlow in Wales to begin their married life. Five months later, the King and Queen were woken in the middle of the night by their confessor with the heartbreaking news that Arthur had died.[37] Katherine too had fallen ill, possibly of the Sweat. Arthur would be buried without his close family in attendance.[38] While dirges were sung in St Paul's Cathedral and every church in London, Arthur's body was carried out of Ludlow Castle and into the nearby church, where a candlelight vigil was held.[39]

Then the coffin, covered with a tight-fitting black cloth with a white cross, made its way to Worcester Cathedral, in a special wagon upholstered in black and drawn by six horses, also caparisoned in black. Thomas and his father were present for the funeral and Thomas, wearing funeral robes, carried the canopy over Arthur's coffin. Thomas' father-in-law, Thomas Howard, presided as Chief Mourner. So foul was the weather that the horses struggled in the mud and oxen were brought in to carry the coffin.

Katherine's position was now uncertain, and it was unclear whether she should be sent home to Spain – yet she was still a highly desirable match. There was a question of whether the marriage to Arthur had been consummated, but with Katherine and her attendants strenuously denying anything had occurred, it was agreed that Katherine would be betrothed to Henry VII's 11-year-old son Henry, Prince of Wales, and upon Henry's fourteenth birthday, they could wed. To cover all bases, a dispensation from the impediment of affinity (just in case Arthur's marriage had been consummated) was requested from the Pope.[40] To cement his new alliance with the Spanish monarchs, Henry VII agreed to financially support Katherine. And for his part, Ferdinand agreed to pay the last installment of his daughter's dowry, a promise somewhat complicated by the fact that Ferdinand could not actually afford to pay the rest of the dowry; thus he had no intention of sticking to his end of the deal. Caught between these two monarchs, it was Katherine who was fated to suffer.

Tragedy struck again six months after Arthur's death. On a bitter morning on 11 February 1503, the bells of St Paul's Cathedral rang out again in mourning: Queen Elizabeth had died in the Tower of London, nine days after giving birth to a daughter, who died shortly after. Henry leaned heavily on Thomas' father-in-law and the Comptroller of his household, who would both oversee the funeral. The King, as was the custom, did not attend the funeral, which lasted two days, but every detail of the event showed his love and his grief at losing her.

The procession was led by 200 poor folk carrying torches, dressed in black cloth from the great wardrobe of the King himself. Behind them came numerous household members, clerics, the Mayor of London and then, finally, the Queen's coffin, in a carriage drawn by six horses.[41] Thomas and his father were among those who rode alongside the coffin, carrying banners representing the royal arms, the Virgin Mary, other saints and the parents of the Queen. Foreign delegations from the French, Spanish, Venetian and Portuguese courts attended, carrying torches decorated with their country's arms. It was a tremendous mark of respect for the first Tudor queen.

Prior to her death, Elizabeth and Henry had brokered an alliance with James IV, with a proposed marriage between the Scottish king and their daughter Margaret as part of peace negotiations following Scotland's role in Warbeck's attempted invasion. Right up to her death, Elizabeth had spent a great deal of time with Margaret, teaching her how to comport herself, and preparing her for her role as queen. She would not live to see the result of her hard work, and Margaret was to embark on the long journey to Scotland, only a few months after her mother's death.

Among Henry's personally written instructions to those chosen to be part of the royal escort for the wedding of Princess Margaret was an invitation to Thomas, but interestingly, not his father. This may have been due to William's health, or the fact that he had, by this time, retired from court life. Thomas, now 26, was appointed to the royal escort, accompanying several relatives including his father and brothers-in-law.[42]

For all intents and purposes it was a royal progress, designed to inspire and display the magnificence of the English court. Those chosen were urged to wear their best and brightest apparel so as to remove any idea of sad solemnity for what Henry wanted looked upon as a joyous occasion. The English were bright, glittering and imposing. With military precision and a vast budget, every hour was choreographed for what would be a week-long display of one-upmanship between the Scots and the English. It made a change from all-out hostility. More importantly, Thomas Howard oversaw every move. 'Maister' Thomas Boleyn, along with several of his relatives and friends, rode behind the princess alongside Henry, who escorted his daughter to Richmond to the house of his mother, Lady Margaret Beaufort, in Collyweston, Northamptonshire.[43] At that point he gave the young princess over to the care of Thomas' mother and father-in-law, who led the procession through Grantham, Newkark, Tuxford, Doncaster, Pontefract, Tadcaster and York. The crowds turned out to watch the spectacle, and to catch a glimpse of the young Margaret Tudor, whose train of cloth of gold was carried by Thomas' mother-in-law.[44] In York, the feasting seems to have got out of hand when an altercation broke out between the Mayor of York and the sheriff, which Thomas' father-in-law had to settle, but otherwise the progress was smooth. The impressive spectacle lasted five days, as the royal party progressed through England and into Scotland where the wedding would take place at Holyrood House in Edinburgh, the official royal residence in Scotland.

James IV converted Holyrood House, once an Augustinian abbey, into a palace and while virtually nothing survives today of the former palace buildings, it appears that they were laid out around a quadrangle. Principal rooms, including the royal lodgings and the chapel, occupied the first floor, and a tower was added on the south side to provide extra accommodation for the king. Thomas would have gazed up at Arthur's Seat, the group of hills resting above the palace. He may have admired Holyrood's round towers and canonical roofs, and observed how very different it was from the royal residences of London. It was Thomas' first foray into some semblance of a diplomatic mission, and he may have even begun to appreciate that diplomacy was an avenue to which he could aspire. When the English party finally met the young, slender James IV in Edinburgh, it was Thomas' father-in-law Thomas Howard who stole the scene. Princess Margaret wrote to her father, happy with her situation, but could not help but mention 'My Lord Surrey [Thomas Howard] is in great favour with the King here and he cannot bear to be without his company at any time of the day.' James was fascinated by Surrey, who had served in numerous military campaigns; we are left to wonder what he made of Thomas Boleyn.

William died two years after Thomas' Scottish adventure, in October of 1505, when Thomas was 28. Thomas took care of the funeral arrangements for his father, who left him, among other miscellaneous items, a large piece of valuable new tapestry material and his gold collars of Esses.[45] William chose to be buried with his mother, Anne, in Norwich Cathedral, which is evidence, according to some historians, of a frosty relationship with his wife Margaret. But all it really suggests is that he was close to his mother, and still felt connected to Norfolk. William also bequeathed to his son Thomas and his heirs the four manors of Calthorp, Wykemere, Mulbarton and, of course, Blickling, where he had already been living, with the proviso that William's widow, Margaret, receive 200 marks per year and that she stay at the family home of Blickling.[46] Thomas kept his word and, when the family moved down to Hever that year, he brought his mother with them. Having lost a father and mentor, Thomas was now the head of the Boleyn family.

In February 1506, Thomas was given licence of entry, as the son and heir of his father, to his lands in England, Wales, Ireland and Calais.[47] Now a well-respected and wealthy courtier, Thomas and his wife spent a great deal of time at court, and while documentation of their next few years is scarce, we know that Thomas at least was present for major court functions: coronations, weddings and funerals.

The royal household was central to Thomas' career and consisted of two main divisions: the household proper, which was the 'below stairs', presided over, in theory, by the Lord Steward; and the chamber, or household 'above stairs', under the control of the Lord Chamberlain, and sub-divided into the 'King's household' and the lesser 'Queen's household'.[48] The innermost room on the King's side was the King's bedchamber, where the Gentlemen of the Privy Chamber slept on pallets or folding beds. As we shall see, George Boleyn would eventually become a member of this inner sanctum under Henry VIII. The men would be on call from 7am, or sooner if needed, to help the King dress in the Privy Chamber. The King's clothes were brought to the door by the Yeoman of the Robes, taken by the grooms and then handed to the gentlemen. Besides the gentlemen, two gentlemen ushers, four grooms, the barber and the page, nobody was allowed entry to the Privy Chamber unless summoned.[49] Beyond the Privy Chamber lay the Presence Chamber, and it is here that we can locate Thomas as, during the last part of Henry VII's reign, he was appointed as one of the 'Esquires of the Body', which was an advancement, and one of six coveted positions that granted personal access to the King.[50] Apart from state ceremony, their only daytime duty seems to have been to serve the King's pottage at dinner and supper. But the principal, most essential and most honourable part of an esquire's duty was at night, when he had absolute command of the house above and below stairs, after the King had retired to bed.[51]

Records show that, at the end of Henry VII's reign, Thomas was listed 'Thomas Boleyn, Yeomen of the Crown', which meant he was a servant of the royal household, and would have dealt with general domestic duties at court.[52] He was the closest to the inner circle that any Boleyn had come and, above all, this gave Thomas access to the King. He clearly made an impression, for when Henry VII died in April of 1509, Thomas played a part in his funeral. The king who had united a country and rescued it from a dark period of civil war, was laid to rest next to his queen, Elizabeth. The funeral was held at St Paul's Cathedral before the coffin was taken to Westminster, and Thomas was present, alongside a number of men, all of whom would become key figures of the next reign. John Fisher, Bishop of Rochester, preached at the funeral, William Compton, a ward of the King's, marched behind the coffin, and Thomas' brother-in-law, Edward Howard, took on a symbolic role and wore the dead king's armour.[53]

A chaplain by the name of Thomas Wolsey took part in the procession, and Thomas walked behind the effigy of the King, which was dressed in robes of state, a crown on its head, holding a ball and sceptre, as it processed through Westminster Abbey, to the magnificent Lady Chapel commissioned by Henry.

Under Henry VII, Thomas had progressed significantly up the ladder, but only within the King's household. Henry's style of kingship made courtiers less influential and it was difficult to change one's career trajectory. Henry VII would never have chosen a man like Thomas Boleyn for important diplomatic missions, for example. But under Henry's son, and his new sphere of advisors, men like Thomas were given an opportunity to prove their capabilities.

# CHAPTER THREE

# A Courtier to His Fingertips

*In court to serve decked with fresh array,*
*Of sug'red meats feeling the sweet repast:*
*The life in banquets, and sundry kinds of play,*
*Amid the press of lordly looks to waste,*
*Hath with it join'd oft times such bitter taste.*
*That who so joys such kind of life to hold,*
*In prison joys fett'red with chains of gold.*

'Of the Courtier's Life', Thomas Wyatt

Thomas Wyatt – poet, courtier and diplomat – wrote several satires on life at the Tudor court. From his privileged position as the son of a wealthy royal councillor, and himself a capable diplomat, Wyatt's biting satires portrayed Tudor courtly life as an empty facade and its participants as lacking moral integrity, intent on enriching themselves and their families, often at the expense of others.[1]

But why should Wyatt's descriptions matter? They do so because he reflected a contemporary view towards the court and courtiers that has been recycled by scholars for the past 400 years to highlight the most negative and grasping attributes of an early modern courtier, specifically those attributed to both Thomas Boleyn and his son George.

But this should not be our lingering impression of the men's careers as courtiers, for Wyatt's satires are not the only views of the courtier and courtly literature. Many writers of the day began to theorise about, and move towards creating, the archetype of the courtier, particularly in Italy where they identified more resolute attributes and skills required of the courtier. The subject was one of the most popular themes of Renaissance political writing, found in the works of Desiderius Erasmus, Baldassare Castiglione and Niccolo Machiavelli. But while Machiavelli sought to advise the prince, Erasmus and

Castiglione were focused on courtiers. Castiglione's *Il Libro de Cortegiano* (*The Book of the Courtier*) was first published in Italy in 1528, in which he detailed his expert and experienced advice to fellow courtiers like himself.[2] His courtier was a multi-faceted individual, who exhibited skills that ranged from warrior to diplomat, someone who was educated, was *au fait* with a broad range of topics, and possessed knowledge of art and literature, and further, he stated that there were 'many of humble birth who, through their virtues, won glory for their descendants'.[3]

Castiglione's model of the ideal 'professional' courtier was well known in English court circles and reflected a new level of awareness regarding the function of courtiers, with his step-by-step guide as to how to achieve excellence in the role.[4] Castiglione's *Book of the Courtier* elevated the virtues of public affairs and the concept of the 'active' life, as opposed to the 'contemplative' life of a scholar, and viewed the acquisition of wealth and service to the crown not as an impediment to knowledge and salvation, but rather a means to promote learning and morality. The ideal courtier was a man who joined the chivalric qualities of courage and prowess to the humanist ideals of culture and learning: he could demonstrate eloquence, wisdom and rhetorical skill in order to ingratiate himself with his prince, so that he might persuade him to rule wisely. The courtier, according to Castiglione, must be adept at dissimulation, and had to:

> Steer away from affectation at all costs, as if it were a rough and dangerous reef, and (to use perhaps a novel word for it) to practice in all things a certain nonchalance [sprezzatura] which conceals all artistry and makes whatever one says or does seem uncontrived and effortless. ... So we can truthfully say that true art is what does not seem to be art; and the most important thing is to conceal it.[5]

Castiglione also believed that the successful courtier was projected, through self-awareness as an actor, with a careful sense of timing.[6] This concept of self-awareness and comportment complements the concept of 'self-fashioning', the way in which courtiers presented themselves to the world.[7] In fact, Castiglione's work could easily be seen as a manual for ambassadors, as much as courtiers – as it has been noted, great courtiers were often successful ambassadors, Castiglione himself a prime example.[8] Thomas and his son George, with their skill in languages, demonstrated attributes of the European intellectual and fashionable context set by Castiglione, and were exemplars of this style. Thomas, whose career at court began to take shape at the beginning of Henry VII's reign, was able to cultivate his own persona, and move from the role of courtier to the father to become one of the son's most trusted ambassadors. Although we do not know which positions he may have held at this time, we do know that he was active at court and in the social sphere. He could be described as a freelance courtier, and his steady rise began with Henry's coronation in 1509, three months after his accession to the throne.

The uncontested transition from Henry VII to Henry VIII held great promise as it launched a new and stable time for England, at least initially, and offered career opportunities for the 'new men' like Thomas. With the new accession, the Boleyn name, as we will see, begins to appear more frequently in official documents as almost immediately his world began to change. Henry VII's death also changed the fortune of Katherine of Aragon, who had been the unwanted princess for seven years. Her stock had declined following the death of her mother Isabella in 1504, who had ruled the kingdoms of Aragon and Castile with her husband, Ferdinand, their union uniting Spain. Katherine was no longer the Princess of the Iberian Peninsula, but none of this mattered to the new king, Henry. Katherine was still beautiful, probably the most intelligent and educated woman he had ever met. Above all, Henry had fallen in love with her; the matter of her six-month and reputedly unconsummated marriage to his elder brother would take many years to haunt him. They were married in a quiet ceremony at Greenwich on 11 June, but their coronation just ten days later would be a lavish affair.

English coronations were held on a Sunday, at the end of a week of feasts and processions.[9] Unusually Henry and Katherine had a joint coronation with celebrations that began on 21 June 1509. The first preferment for both Thomas and his wife came when Elizabeth was appointed 'Baroness' of the Queen's Chambers, where her duties included the privilege of arranging Katherine's Great Wardrobe for the joint coronation. Henry and Katherine rode from the palace at Greenwich to the Tower of London, where they hosted a lavish dinner and spent the night before their coronation.[10]

Both Thomas and his wife were in attendance at this dinner where 26 honourable persons (Thomas being one of them) were chosen to serve the dishes and wait on the King. Assuming the role of humble servants to their king was a purely symbolic but significant gesture and, for their reward, all those who served 'in token that they shall never bear none after that day' were made Knights of the Bath at the coronation, a late medieval order of chivalry.[11] The elaborate ritual required that after the feast, 26 baths were laid out in a hall of the White Tower where they were draped with fresh white linen, covered in a canopy. Thomas and the other knights would have bathed ceremoniously before Henry VIII entered the hall, skimming the water of each bath before making the sign of the cross on each knight's bare back, vowing:

You shall honor God above all things; you shall be steadfast in the faith of Christ; you shall love the King your Sovereign Lord, and him and his right defend to your power; you shall defend maidens, widows, and orphans in their rights, and shall suffer no extortion, as far as you may prevent it; and of as great honor be this Order unto you, as ever it was to any of your progenitors or others.[12]

With the others, Thomas spent the evening in a candlelight vigil in the stone hall of the chapel, guarding their knightly armour – helmets, swords and spurs – which had been arranged around the high altar.[13]

On Saturday 23 June, the eve of the coronation, Henry and his new queen processed through London, from the Tower to Westminster. The procession started at 4pm and Boleyn, as a Knight of the Bath, dressed in: 'Blue long Gowns with hoods upon theyr shoulders spread after the manner of the persons or priests, and tassles of white and blew silk fastened upon one of they shoulders'.[14]

The streets of Cheapside and Cornhill, through which Henry and Katherine progressed, were hung with tapestries and cloth of gold. The new royal couple were magnificence incarnate: Henry, resplendent in a robe of crimson velvet trimmed with ermine, his jacket of cloth of gold luminous with diamonds, rubies, emeralds, pearls and other precious stones, Katherine, her long, auburn hair, falling from a coronet 'set with many riche orient stones', draped about her shoulders, her white satin dress embroidered in gold, silver and tinsel.[15] Henry was described as being of 'amiable visage, princely countenance, with the noble qualities of his royall estate, to every man knowen nedeth no rehersall'.[16] Thomas' father-in-law, Thomas Howard, was Earl Marshal for the day followed by his companions 'Armed at all poyntes, their Basses and Bardes, or trappers were of grene velvet, beaten with roses and pomegranates of gold, bordered with fringes of Damask Gold.'[17]

A banquet of 'high and long solemnitie' followed the coronation in the Great Hall of Westminster and, for the next few days, tournaments and jousts were scheduled, in which Thomas and his kin played a part. Tensions seemed to run high among the competitive courtiers – no man wanted to lose in front of the king, and when, on the last day, a mock war, complete with a general on horseback took a violent turn, the king's guard was called in and the contest was stopped only with 'grate payn'.

Despite the slightly awkward conclusion to the coronation festivities, the new reign was to be a new, golden era. The poet, John Skelton, welcomed the changing of the guard, writing: 'Astrea, justice hight, that from the starry sky. Shall now come and do right.'[18] George Cavendish, who later became servant and biographer of Cardinal Wolsey, also wrote that England was 'A golden world where grace of plenty Raygned.'[19] And, ensuring that he would not be eclipsed, Thomas More wrote his own tribute, moving from the deferential to the simply obsequious, declaring that the people of England were so enraptured by Henry that all they could utter was 'The King, The King'.[20] For this new, glorious reign, the young king had chosen the wisest of men, namely those who he knew had been dear and loyal friends of his father's, including the Boleyn family and their Howard and Butler kin. They would all continue their rise in this new, glittering realm. Thomas' first opportunity arrived within months of the coronation: he was made Keeper of the Exchange of Calais, and Keeper of the Foreign Exchange in England, the duties of which included taking care of all the money which travellers or merchants required to send abroad, and being responsible for Bills of Exchange.[21] It was a start, but despite his knighthood and these new responsibilities, Thomas was still only a member of the Presence Chamber, not the Privy Chamber, Council or Star Chamber. That was where fortunes were made.

Two spheres orbited the young king – his friends and councillors – and there was often competition and hostility between them, requiring a delicate balance between the two. Henry's personal sphere consisted of court favourites and boyhood friends, men who loved the more informal pursuits in life, and to whom the 18-year-old Henry gravitated, spending much time in their company.

On the other side of this personal power base stood the King's advisors: the clerics such as Bishop Richard Fox and Archbishop Warham, and the secular advisors, Thomas Howard, Earl of Surrey, George Talbot, Charles Somerset, Thomas Lovell, Henry Wyatt, Thomas Ruthal and Edward Poynings.[22] In between the two groups stood a young man called Thomas Wolsey, a force in his own right, of whom we will hear more later. These men were Henry's core group of advisors who instructed him daily on political matters at home and abroad, forming an 'attendant council' when he went on progress throughout his realm. Thomas' father-in-law, Thomas Howard, alongside Wolsey, Fox and others, tutored the King in the art of diplomacy, briefing him on the royal courts of Europe, current alliances and hostilities, where England's opportunities and challenges lay.[23] They were all men of strong opinions, all jostling to influence the King.

Fox particularly was a colossal influence on the Tudors, a supporter of Henry VII during his early years in Paris, then fighting alongside him when he claimed victory at Bosworth Field. Although Fox was a commoner, Henry trusted him implicitly, making him his Secretary, then Lord Privy Seal in 1487, a position he held for almost 30 years and one which would later be bestowed on Thomas Boleyn. Fox was a consummate politician; his cleverness and judgement exceeded that of courtier and noble alike. Artful in the direction he guided his king, he devised and promoted the Scottish-Anglo union, which resulted in Princess Margaret's marriage to King James IV.[24] Fox had also seen the potential of a Spanish alliance and sought the union of Henry's son Arthur to Katharine. His fiscal policies of taxing the poor and wealthy alike filled Henry's coffers, which pleased his king. Fox looked to the common men, the clever *new men*, who were capable and, if so honoured with advancement, would be most loyal and trustworthy. Fox was a founder of careers, as evidenced by his most famous protégés – Thomas Wolsey and John Fisher.

The court was a place where, as scholars have noted, 'a name dropped could mean much, and a career could be built through second, third, or fourth-hand access to those in power', and where family connections could make all the difference.[25] Family interests were also integral to Thomas, and he was fortunate enough to have such connections at court. Apart from his father-in-law, his grandfather, Thomas Butler, who as mentioned was a great friend of Henry VII, also served as Lord Chamberlain to Henry's queen, Elizabeth of York, and Katherine of Aragon from her first year as queen.[26] Butler was close to his grandson, and would have assisted in providing opportunities, but he was very much in the domestic realm. Thomas' father-in-law, on the other hand, while also involved in the affairs of the realm, was from an older generation in the political sphere of court, but he had one foot in the door of Henry's personal sphere. Howard ensured that his two sons-in-law, Thomas, and Anthony Knyvett, as well as his own sons, Edward, the elder, and more charming brother of the younger Thomas, later Duke of Norfolk, extended their reach into social *and* commercial spheres. A good courtier was not just a shape-shifter, servant or advisor, but needed to be able to entertain, advise and engage in manly activities, all while displaying virtue. It was vital that the young men like Thomas acquired the skill to deftly alternate between the formal sphere of court, and the informal one, as well as demonstrating a physical prowess which in the young king's case was highly desirable.

Celebration and revelry were promoted throughout the new king's court, and performing well at all events ensured one was noticed. It was vital that Thomas and his wife engaged in everything that went on at court, and regularly found themselves taking part in the expensive and often ostentatious entertainment given by and for the youthful king. Among the favourite revels of the carefree monarch and his devoted court were masques, mummeries and plays.[27] The court masque or revel was the most favoured royal entertainment which involved music, singing, dancing and acting; elaborate productions usually featured several courtiers enthusiastically portraying historical or classical characters. In 1510, Thomas took part in a revel at Westminster to honour Queen Katherine. Masques were a favourite of Henry's and he took delight in surprising his young wife. Thomas was one of 11 men who joined the King elaborately dressed as Robin Hood's men in their 'Lincoln' green coats and hose made of Coventry Blue and Kentish Kendal in order to fawn over Queen Katherine, who was rather suddenly transformed into Robin's beloved Maid Marian.[28] Thomas had his share of acting in Henry's masques and was often required to wear bizarre attire, to portray a moor or Muscovite, in Henry's endless merrymaking.

Thomas also showed a considerable passion and skill for the tiltyard and other physical pursuits and, that same year, he took part in one of four days of scheduled knightly combat. The King, Charles Brandon, Edward Howard and Sir Thomas Knight, challenged all to tilts and jousts, and Thomas appears to have accepted a challenge from the King's team.[29]

As well as jousting, Thomas also participated in hand-to-hand combat and wrestling, and was at one point paired against the King in a Feat of Arms.[30] What does this activity tell us about him? We know that in his youth, Henry was tall, athletic and incredibly fit, which required that his young companions must have been similarly strapping to keep up with their king. Without a portrait to use as a reference, we can only imagine that, at 34 years old, Thomas Boleyn must have exuded strength, agility and prowess to engage in such a physically demanding sport as wrestling. Jousting too was not for the faint-hearted of the court; it was not for show, and required a high level of fitness to be able to withstand the heavy armour, then to hold and aim the lance and charge, bracing for the inevitable contact which might result in the opponent's lance splintering into the body or the face, or worse. All these considerations had to be made while one attempted to remain upright in the saddle, and required years of fitness and experience.

Thomas had further opportunities to prove his physicality when the court celebrated the birth of a prince on 1 January 1511, causing the court to whip themselves into an absolute frenzy of celebration. Henry was so moved and overjoyed with this heavenly blessing that he made a pilgrimage to the Priory of Our Lady of Walsingham, Norfolk, to give thanks for the birth. He returned to Richmond Palace to see his son, and then set off for Westminster with the Queen, where the celebrations could begin. On the first day, Henry himself, Edward Howard, Charles Brandon and Edward Neville all jousted, handsome in their coats of green satin and crimson velvet. They jousted against Thomas Howard, the Earls of Essex and Devon. A few weeks later, yet another tournament was held, and Henry jousted for his queen under the banner of *Coeur Loyal* – Sir Loyal Heart, in his wife's colours.[31] Thomas rode in with Charles Brandon, Henry Guildford and the Marquess of Dorset, dressed like pilgrims, wearing black velvet tabards and hats over their helmets, all decorated with the gold shells of Santiago de Compostela.[32] Their servants, with matching attire, followed them. When he jousted, Thomas performed admirably, his young wife watching from the stalls, and as the day of festivities carried on into the night, with a great feast held at Whitehall, Thomas danced with his wife, who was a part of the court pageant. Even the people of London, who had been invited to witness the spectacle, became so crazed by the excitement of the celebration that they mobbed the lords and ladies of court, stripping even the King himself down to his hose. But Henry and his men were good-natured about the intrusion; the guards were called to calmly restore order, and the court continued their merrymaking, with whatever finery had not been pilfered.[33]

The future for Henry and Katherine and their newborn prince was full of promise – promise which was dashed only two months later, when the royal couple were told the devastating news; their young prince had died on 22 February. It was heartbreaking for the couple, and it was a major blow politically. Thomas was one of the chief mourners for the deceased infant, bearing the coffin through Westminster Abbey.[34] While Katherine locked herself away in prayer and contemplation, Henry turned to his young sphere of men, hoping to be diverted with court entertainment; in particular he looked to his 'primus minister in regis cubiculo'– his premier member of the Privy Chamber, Groom of the Stool, William Compton.[35]

William Compton had been a ward of Henry VII and became a part of his household, growing up alongside the young Prince Henry. Understandably they forged an enduring relationship, as he became Henry's most trusted companion. Where Fox was a founder of careers, Compton was a founder of fortunes – if a courtier sought favour or position, it was worthwhile cultivating William Compton's favour first.[36] This may have influenced Thomas' decision to form a rapport with the notoriously influential young courtier, for even close advisors often had to seek Compton's approval before getting near Henry. We might regard Compton as a sort of 'gatekeeper' and he would even act as intermediary when the royal signature was required.[37] Compton served at court, received grants, deputised offices, and became the conduit through which one could access the King and his favours, so it could surprise no one that along the way he acquired great personal wealth. Yet, in all of this, he remained a highly independent figure as he was void of any political persuasion or alignment: as one historian remarked, 'Compton merely served Compton.'[38]

Compton did enormously well out of royal service, receiving a mass of grants and using his influence to create a landed patrimony. Among the most significant grants made to him by the Crown were those of custody of several castles. He and Thomas both seemed to do well in terms of land and property, and the latter's own grants and acquisitions from 1509 to 1512 suggest considerable success.[39] As young men who spent a great deal of time with the King, the two knew each other well, and nothing speaks of trust more than money, in this case a loan. At some point between 1513 and 1520, Thomas took a large loan of over £1,000 (over £500,000 in today's currency) from Compton.[40] If nothing else, business dealings with such a court favourite gave Thomas excellent credit rating and could even lead to further business dealings.[41] In short, Henry's personal sphere of companions provided an important social connection for Thomas, who was still without any discernible political affinity. Crucially, he would build on faint connections with those orbiting Henry's political sphere: Thomas was already moving towards the next phase of his career.

Within the first years of Henry's reign, 60-year-old Fox, who had overseen foreign diplomacy for decades, felt he was at the tail end of a long career, overburdened by work with no prospect of it diminishing, and saddled with an unreliable young monarch. During 1510 he began to groom Thomas Wolsey, the Royal Almoner, to work with him and the Royal Council. He hoped that Wolsey would lessen their workload, perhaps displace the belligerent Earl of Surrey, Thomas' father-in-law, and eventually become heir-protagonist of Fox's peace policies.[42] Tradition has it that Wolsey, who was only four to six years older than Thomas, was the son of Robert Wolsey, a lowly Ipswich butcher, but he was actually a grazier and wool merchant with financially successful relatives. When we think of Wolsey, we think of the imperious Cardinal of later years – a mountain of scarlet robes, stretched across a jowly barrel of a man. But in 1510, Wolsey was only 38 and in a time of political restlessness he would emerge as a most versatile statesman. Wolsey himself was particularly brilliant – enrolling at Oxford at the early age of 11, and completing his Bachelor of Arts when he was 15.[43] He served as Fox's secretary through Henry VII's reign, and was therefore trained in traditional policy, which was not interested in making England glorious, but simply safe and secure.

With dark hair, his face slimmer than in his later portraits, he was charming, highly articulate and learned and, like Thomas Boleyn and William Compton, moved between the spheres of court. He was a good friend of King Henry's companion, Charles Brandon, and, according to historian Polydore Vergil (who meant it disdainfully), made friends through 'singing, laughing, dancing and clowning about with the young courtiers'.[44] Knowing that Henry disliked routine administrative work, Wolsey willingly took on additional tasks. George Cavendish, Wolsey's senior aide, noted that he was 'puttyng the kyng in Comfort that he shall not nede to spare any tyme of his pleasure for any busynes that shold necessary happen in the Councell as long as [Wolsey] beyng there'.[45] Wolsey was the perfect diplomatic protégé for Fox, cultivating these new men.

The court was the site for several competing agendas, and one such example coincides with the beginning of Thomas' diplomatic career. From 1511 onwards, Thomas' reputation as a skilled courtier who enjoyed good relations with numerous individuals across the court circles contributed to his promotion from domestic duties to foreign affairs. As Fox began to gradually step back from duties from 1511, Thomas' father-in-law used his sons' (Edward and Thomas Howard) popularity, and his own influence, to persuade Henry to go to war with Scotland.[46] The evidence suggests that Howard appealed to Henry's youth, his virility and enthusiasm to this end.[47] Wolsey, perhaps on Fox's suggestion, made a counter-move, encouraging Henry to concentrate on France, where he knew that engaging in a battle with the French would be noticed by the rest of world, and place Henry on the European stage. Wolsey won as Henry turned his aggression from Scotland back to France, with its greater opportunities for military glory (and Wolsey's career). Perhaps feeling that he had been ill-advised, and that Howard's urgings had not been in Henry's interest, Henry became quite hostile towards the latter who prudently and promptly left court.[48]

But there was a considerable degree of consternation at how easily swayed the King could be by particular individuals, and the older generation of Henry's advisors, and Fox in particular, referred to these issues not as sin or wickedness, but as damage caused by human weaknesses and error, defining 'evil courtiers' as those 'who never learn upright behavior', a defect of character and lack of education.[49] Navigating potentially fractious spheres suggests that Thomas now had to tread carefully as he was also close to several men of whom Fox disapproved, but Fox seems to have worked well with Thomas himself. Like Castiglione's ideal, Thomas must have been a charismatic, charming, intelligent and trustworthy courtier, likeable enough for men from various social circles to engage with him, to trust and solicit his opinion, and to facilitate his career. These connections to individuals such as William

Compton, Fox and Thomas Wolsey, all of whom were part of Thomas' social and professional circle, formed a network of influence upon which his own influence gradually expanded.

In 1511, Fox and Wolsey were tasked with forming a team of diplomats with the right experience, education and sensitivity for a foreign embassy, and Thomas was chosen alongside the most experienced of Henry VII's and Henry VIII's diplomats, men with whom Fox had worked: Sir Edward Poynings, Richard Wingfield and John Young. Thomas, listed as Knight for the Body, stands out as a new face in the line-up set by Fox and Wolsey.[50] Fox had begun to cultivate personality politics – he had in mind a new breed of courtier and ambassador, highly educated men but with guarded minds who could be personal, flexible and adaptable.[51]

Fox recognised that England was at the very end of Europe's negotiating table, and sought to remedy this, strategically placing England – militarily, politically and diplomatically – on the political chessboard of Europe and beyond. Henry would need Fox's administrative skills to co-ordinate preparations for war; he would need the talents, energy and enthusiasm of Wolsey; and they would both require the most reliable and persuasive ambassadors.

CHAPTER FOUR

# Fortune, Infortune

*There is a tide in the affairs of men,*
*Which taken at the flood, leads on to fortune;*
*Omitted, all the voyage of their life*
*Is bound in shallows and in miseries.*
*On such a full sea are we now afloat;*
*And we must take the current when it serves,*
*Or lose our ventures.*

– Brutus in Shakespeare's *Julius Caesar*

From the moment of his coronation, Henry VIII made clear where he wanted to stand on the political chessboard of Europe and which monarchs he would choose to call 'brother'. His marriage to Katherine had allied him with Spain and the other countries who had married into the Hapsburg Empire. England's traditional enemy was France and, despite the warnings from his advisor, Richard Fox, Henry was vocal about his antipathy towards an Anglo-French relationship. Henry spent a great deal of his reign preoccupied with foreign policy as he sought to be regarded as a major and respected power within the European community of monarchs; he began to leave matters of war, diplomacy and domestic administration largely under Wolsey's control. In Wolsey's hands, the quality of England's diplomatic service improved and evolved as he sought to secure a role for England in European politics. As was customary for a new monarch, Henry sent messages to his European counterparts formally requesting their friendship and a desire for peace. The older French king, Louis XII, courteously sent an ambassador with a formal reply. But during the ambassador's presentation to Henry at Westminster, the man was rudely interrupted by Henry himself, who turned to his courtiers and loudly and rhetorically asked who had bothered to request peace from Louis of France 'who daren't look at me, let alone make war?' and ended the audience.[1]

Fox was embarrassed, Wolsey uneasy at such a bold and unprovoked slur, and Thomas, like many courtiers, no doubt taken aback, but a further indignity awaited the ambassador. When he was invited to a display at the tiltyard scheduled that afternoon, he found no seat had been reserved for him. Only when he stormed off did Henry, more than likely under stern advisement, call him back and order a cushion for him. This was just a small example of the increasingly complicated and volatile state of English – French relations that would allow men like Wolsey and Thomas to display and develop their diplomatic skills.

Thomas was only seventeen in 1494, when Italy, divided into numerous states, kingdoms, and republics, became the battle ground between the Valois and the Hapsburgs. Decades of struggle would ensue for control over the powerful Italian states of Florence, Venice, Genoa, the Papal States, the Duchy of Milan, and the Kingdoms of Sicily and Naples, and from 1509, all eyes in Europe, when not focused suspiciously on each other, looked towards the increasingly powerful state of Venice. Pope Julius II, seeking to curb Venetian influence in northern Italy, established an anti-Venetian alliance consisting of himself, Louis XII of France, Spain's Ferdinand of Aragon and the Holy Roman Emperor, Maximilian.[2] Known as the Venetian Alliance (also the League of Cambrai), its initial success (the very fact that they had formed the alliance) emboldened the allies, until friction between Pope Julius and Louis caused it to collapse in 1510. In April 1511, Julius called a General Council to meet at St John Lateran Basilica in Rome, where they formed a Holy League to oppose the French, rather than Venice. The League was formed in October 1511 and comprised the Papacy, Venice, Henry's father-in-law King Ferdinand of Aragon, Maximilian and England. The fact that the Pope now chose to ally *with* Venice *against* France, in contrast to the earlier Venetian Alliance, demonstrates the volatility of European politics at the time.[3] At great expense, Venice and King Ferdinand hired another 10,000 Swiss mercenaries to fight the French and asked Henry to join them.

Henry needed little persuading to join the League: he envisioned an isolated France, ripe for invasion, allowing him to reclaim the French throne for England. In 1340, England's Plantagenet king, Edward III, had claimed inheritance of the French throne through his French mother, Isabella, on the death of her Plantagenet brother and Edward's uncle, King Charles IV of France. England's continued assertion of this claim fueled the bloody Hundred Years' War (1337–1453) between England and France. Regaining France was not only Henry's ambition, but Wolsey's too.

Joining an alliance was the easy part; investing in it by committing money and troops was another matter entirely. In May 1512 Henry wrote to Margaret of Austria, daughter of Maximilian, who had appointed her as Governess of the Low Countries, and she had been instrumental in all negotiations. He informed her that he was sending two men to her court – John Young and Thomas Boleyn – as special envoys to negotiate an alliance, and they were to be paid 20 schillings (approximately 50 pounds in today's currency) a day. Henry, Fox and Wolsey would have given this appointment considerable thought, as so much was at stake. Coaxing the Holy Roman Emperor Maximilian, of the powerful Hapsburg Empire, to commit to any political alliance would be a delicate and frustrating task requiring considerable skill, patience and self-confidence.

It is necessary to make a distinction between the roles of special envoy and ambassador for, in the course of his career, Thomas Boleyn would be both. A resident ambassador was described by the seventeenth-century ambassador, Henry Wotton, as an honest man 'sent abroad to lie for the good of his country'. They had full diplomatic status, and their task was not to discharge a significant piece of business and then return, but to remain at their post until recalled. Special envoys, on the other hand, were given specific commissions, usually to negotiate particular treaties in authority: a special envoy represented the sovereign and had the power to negotiate and sign treaties. Alternatively, an ambassador was authorised to promote the sovereign's policies, which could only be modified in consultation with the monarch.

It was common for special envoys to be selected from the nobility, often members of the royal family, or from those of very high rank such as ambassadors and even courtiers might aspire to. Ambassadors on the other hand could be of the nobility or outside it. However, the difference between the roles extended far beyond the duration of one's embassy. This is particularly evident in the first decade of Henry VIII's reign when the men chosen by the King, Fox, and Wolsey – the architects of the young king's foreign policy – to serve as resident ambassadors lacked social and political importance and were treated differently from those appointed to special embassies. As Henry's reign progressed, the benefits of employing resident ambassadors became more apparent; both the calibre of the men chosen and the degree to which they were involved in their sovereign's diplomatic affairs altered considerably.

Thomas was 35 years old when he was sent on his first mission. His kin at court, the equally dashing and charismatic Edward Howard and Anthony Knyvett, were embarking on their own impressive military careers, and Thomas was no doubt eager to make *his* mark in European politics and diplomacy. At first glance, the inclusion of Thomas in such an important embassy might seem unusual. He joined a trio of experienced ambassadors. Richard Wingfield had been the uncle by marriage to Henry VII, which continued to place him among the elite. He was an experienced ambassador who had twice attended Maximilian's court, and had been assigned to a council convened by Pope Julius at the Lateran. Thomas Spinelly, appointed as the resident English ambassador to Margaret's court, was originally from Florence, and had commercial and banking connections with many Florentines; he was believed to be a member of the same Spinelly family who, at that time, transacted the papacy's financial business in central Europe.[4] He was also a nephew of Philip Gualterotti, who was in charge of one of the largest banking houses in the Low Countries, with establishments in Bruges and Antwerp, and thus an important connection for the English. Meanwhile, John Young had already served as ambassador in the Low Countries in 1504 and 1506, at one point even attempting to negotiate a marriage between the widowed Henry VII and Maximilian's daughter, Archduchess Margaret; by chance she was the person with whom the men were to negotiate.

The mission was to conclude a military alliance between Henry and the Holy Roman Emperor Maximilian, allied with other anti-French states against France. It should have been quite straightforward. Thomas' presence as special envoy has not gone unnoticed by some scholars. This was a European arena and men of nerve and intellect were needed. He was fluent in French, and, as noted in the previous chapter, had been Keeper of the Exchange at Calais and of the Foreign Exchange in England since 1509, two important and highly profitable appointments.[5] As an attendant and then friend of Henry VIII, he was also well versed in the customs and ceremonies of state. He had a track record in important areas of government, and must have already exhibited qualities that Henry, Fox and Wolsey needed for this mission. And in any case, every ambassador must have a first mission. Thomas would have eagerly looked forward to Brussels, at that time the elegant artistic and cultural hub of the duchy of Burgundy. The Archduchess Margaret's life had been marred by misfortune. Considered beautiful in her youth, with striking and imperial presence, she had been given in marriage no fewer than three times. Her first intended, the French crown prince, had sent her back to her family at the age of 11 because he had found a better match. Several years later, Margaret married the Spanish heir to the throne, Juan, son of Isabella of Castile and Ferdinand of Aragon, and younger brother of Katherine of Aragon. In a tragic parallel to Katherine's ill-fated marriage to Prince Arthur in England, Juan died only a few months after the marriage. Finally, Margaret married Philibert of Savoy, said to be the love of her life. He too died after only three years of marriage, and Margaret lost a child who was stillborn. Thus, Margaret was a widow from the age of 24, preferring black garments and always wearing a small white coif as a widow's cap. She refused to marry again and be used as a bargaining tool, preferring to become a woman of power. Her motto seems apt: *Fortune, Infortune, Fort Une* – fortune and misfortune make one strong.

It was a strength she had also learned from some of the most powerful and influential women of Europe, who had helped raise and educate her. Among them was the woman she thought would be her sister-in-law, Anne of France, daughter of King Louise and regent of France. Known as 'Madame la Grande', Anne was also responsible for the education of another powerful woman who would play a part in Thomas' life: Louise of Savoy, future mother of King Francis I. During her marriage to Juan, Margaret spent time at the court of the formidable and remarkable Isabella of Castile, a fiercely intelligent and pious queen in her own right. These women deeply influenced Margaret; she took on her own position of power and, following in the footsteps of Anne of France, she took responsibility for raising her nieces, Eleanor, Isabella and Maria, and nephew, the future emperor Charles V.

Disembarking on the Continent, Thomas, Young and Wingfield rode not to Margaret's court in Mechelin, or Malines as it was then known, but to Brussels, the major centre for trade.[6] At the very heart of the walled city lay the Palace of Brussels, which sprawled on the hill above the city, called Coudenberg, or 'cold hill' after the cold northern wind which buffeted the region. It was considered one of the most splendid palaces in Europe and had for centuries been the seat of government of the counts, dukes, archdukes, kings and emperors of Leuven and Brussels, as well as Burgundy and the Hapsburgs. Engulfed by fire in the eighteenth century, all that remains of the palace Thomas knew are its foundations, preserved beneath the new buildings. Today, one must venture underground to explore what is left of its corridors, with its high, curved arches and bare brick walls, on which once hung ornate tapestries, textiles and countless works of art. It is difficult to imagine the expansive splendour and sophistication of a place that was once described by Albrecht Durer – one of the most influential artists of the sixteenth century – as a paradise.

The resident English ambassador to Margaret's court, Thomas Spinelly, awaited the three on horseback in the grand park, known as Warande.[7] As he escorted them to their lodgings, he informed them that a rather covert meeting had been planned with the Emperor for the next day, away from the palace and prying eyes.[8] He explained the situation at court to the trio and no doubt offered an insight into the characters of Margaret and Maximilian. With

Spinelly a part of negotiations, they anticipated that the next few days would consist of routine negotiations in Brussels. The reality was far from straightforward.

In the early hours of 28 May the three ambassadors and Spinelly rode to a secret meeting with Emperor Maximilian, who had chosen the countryside rather than his palace to open discussions. The ambassadors' first report to Henry suggested the meeting was brief and full of the usual platitudes, but added that Maximilian, whilst cordial, spoke of an alliance between himself and Henry against France in only the most general terms, without making any commitments. He would not hear the men's commission, but he did promise, out of respect for Henry, to dismiss the French ambassadors, whom he had also planned to see. Maximilian then departed, promising to hear their presentations the following day; instead, he left very early the next morning to rendezvous with the French, who were determined to prevent the proposed alliance, and its intended war against them. The ambassadors complained in their report to Henry about being unable to disclose their mission to the Emperor, and were now left to wait for his return; the intended two-day visit had already been prolonged to six. The Emperor's strategy was either a reversal of policy or simply stalling tactics – they were left to deal with Margaret almost exclusively for the rest of the embassy.

The men were invited to a formal audience with the Archduchess during which they explained at length why Emperor Maximilian and England should continue a union against France.[9] This was Thomas' opportunity to charm Margaret, only three years younger than him; but she was neither malleable nor easily persuaded. She cut short his no-doubt rehearsed address and pointedly asked whether Henry had despatched the fleet of ships and 10,000 men that he had promised to the service of the Holy Roman Empire.[10]

This suggested that she knew more than she let on: despite Thomas' assurances that the ships had been ready before they left England, only tarrying for wind, the envoys' report makes clear that the ships had not left, and no one seemed to know when they would.[11] Margaret proved to be as shrewd as her father, keeping the embassy on the back foot, making further financial demands and insisting that no further negotiations would be considered until money was received.

The diplomatic trio had not made the roaring start they had hoped and seemed unsure of their next move. Thomas, new to the game, quickly learned to adjust his strategy accordingly. The demands were too numerous and complex to be agreed to without further consultation, nor could they wait for Henry to reply to their letters, so Thomas made a bold decision: he left the court at 3am without taking formal leave and rode at a gruelling pace to cover the 125 miles to Calais in only six hours, likely changing horses at least once. He crossed the channel, reaching Dover in the afternoon, and rode the 70-odd miles to Greenwich, arriving in the early evening to meet with Henry personally. His discussions with the King behind closed doors were not recorded but, based on the handling of other English diplomatic embassies, we can reasonably assume Thomas was also debriefed by Wolsey.

Meanwhile, Maximilian, who had not yet returned from his French negotiations, decided that in Thomas' absence he would put all negotiations on hold until his return. He arrived in Brussels for the Feast of St John, held on 23 June, inviting Young and Wingfield to enjoy the great bonfire in the evening, but they arrived just as he was leaving; it seemed Maximilian had a propensity for arranging meetings with the English just as he was dashing off elsewhere.

It was a tense ten days for the embassy, but Thomas returned on 26 June. Having ridden from Calais, he wasted no time giving Margaret letters written in Henry's hand.[12] Very few experienced ambassadors would break with protocol by failing to take formal leave of a court to which they had been posted, but this was proving to be an unconventional mission and Thomas demonstrated that results trumped protocol: Henry was promising full financial aid and confirmed that a treaty was to be drawn up joining England, the Emperor, the Pope, Margaret, the Prince of Castile, the King of Aragon and the Venetians against France. Margaret seemed to approve of these developments and proposed to Thomas that she assist the embassy in further negotiations. Soon after, Maximilian wrote to her to tell Thomas he was 'glad of his coming and waits for him here, so that he should make haste'.[13] 'Here' was the castle of Turnhout, a few hours ride from Brussels. It seems that Thomas met Maximilian there, but it is not clear what the meeting entailed.

The mood at Maximilian's court in Brussels seemed to improve greatly, as the next morning Boleyn, Wingfield and Young were invited and attended Evensong in the royal chapel before being taken on a tour of the royal gardens.[14] There, the men were introduced to Maximilian's grandson and Margaret's nephew, Charles, who lived and was educated at Margaret's court at Mechelin, one of the most sophisticated courts of Europe. The young boy would feature heavily in Thomas' life: he would become Charles V, Holy Roman Emperor, ruling over the most powerful empire in Europe. The English courtiers were invited to watch the 12-year-old prince practise archery, later commenting that he 'handled his bow right well favourdly'.[15] Charles was tall, with cropped dark hair and the distinctive protruding Hapsburg jaw, and was by all accounts shy and awkward, with an aversion for learning, at least in his teens. Margaret doted on her nephew, and on this afternoon she praised his aim as the court and ambassadors clapped politely.

As mentioned, from the very first weeks of their embassy Margaret had singled Thomas out as chief negotiator, and now we see a definite elevation of his authority: he began to write most of the reports to Henry, and no negotiations took place without him being present.[16] Maximilian had told Margaret he would meet Thomas upon his return from England, but he continued to stay away from court. This put Margaret in a difficult position. She wrote to him, 'I shall do my best to entertain the ambassadors, but they are impatient and I cannot think that they will be pleased with so long a delay.'[17]

Although Margaret still promised that her father would sign the treaty, as the weeks passed with no sign of Maximilian, she advised the ambassadors to send Wingfield to the Emperor; Young and Thomas stayed at court, reporting that they were not as well entertained as previously. What the embassy did not know was that Maximilian and Margaret had also been in secret negotiations with the French.

Up to this point, Thomas is quoted in many of the reports as having been the main ambassador involved in discussions with Margaret, suggesting that she singled him out as chief negotiator, passing over Ambassador Wingfield. In the end, Boleyn had to reassure Maximilian that he was writing the reports, in effect replacing resident ambassador Wingfield as the main diplomatic representative at Margaret's court, although his appointment was as special envoy, not ambassador. It was now a matter of who had Maximilian's ear, and although Spinelly was ambassador, Thomas' trip to England with news direct from the King himself promoted him to the most important player. It was also Thomas who persuaded Maximilian to agree to a formal meeting on 3 July 1512, it was Thomas who dealt with him, and it was also Thomas who advised Ambassador Spinelly to arrange a meeting between him and Margaret.

These weeks reveal much about Thomas' developing ambassadorial style: to attempt to cultivate a more sincere relationship, beyond diplomatic statecraft. While Maximilian stalled, Thomas encouraged an air of friendly informality with Margaret. He also took the initiative of insisting that Margaret forbid any exports of artillery and food provisions to France. This might have caused indignation with other individuals, but Margaret reacted well. As evidence of their good personal relationship, Thomas succeeded in both endeavours and Margaret wrote to her father to appoint commissioners to draw up the treaty against France.[18] But Maximilian again stalled, forcing the English embassy to wait several more weeks. It is not clear what the ambassadors did to pass the time while matters were delayed, week after week, but as their despatches are written at times from Brussels, then Mechelen, and Antwerp, it would seem that they travelled with Margaret, and at least would have been glad of a change of scene. For her part, Margaret continued to express her regret at the long delay, excusing it, as the ambassadors wrote to Henry, first, because Maximilian was not ready, then because he wished to consult the princes of the Empire; and, finally, he blamed the backwardness of his defence of his country. It also seemed that absence made the emperor 'forgetful' – in late July, the ambassadors noted that Maximilian remained in Cologne, and 'required to have his memory refreshed'. July crawled into August, and the ambassadors' reports paint a picture of increasingly desperate men, who wrote to their king simply 'to avoid being thought remiss'.[19]

But finally, on 12 August, Margaret received word that Maximilian would appoint her as commissioner with the power to draw up the treaty, and the necessary documents would follow.[20]

But the waiting game continued. Perhaps sensing that the ambassadors were becoming weary of the delay, Margaret, as a diversion, wagered with Thomas that the commission would arrive within ten days. The stakes were decidedly equine: if she lost, she would give Thomas a horse, a Spanish courser; if he lost, he was to give her a small horse commonly known as a hobby.[21] As only Thomas was invited to join the wager, it is possible that the Spanish courser was Margaret's light-hearted reference to the impressive speed with which he had ridden from Brussels to Calais, then Dover to London weeks before.

In the end, Margaret lost the bet. Whether or not she fulfilled her end of the bargain is unclear, but we may well wonder if, in lieu of a horse, Thomas requested a more advantageous reward: a future position for his daughter Anne at this most prestigious of courts.

What Margaret did next, while highly unusual, shows her trust in Thomas and her firm commitment to deliver a treaty against France. Fully aware that her father was stalling by promising to give her power to draw up the treaty, Margaret sent her secretary one evening to the ambassadors, to suggest that either Spinelly ride to the Emperor, or else the ambassadors should write, in her words, a 'pricking letter in Latin' to her, accusing her of causing this delay.[22] The men acquiesced, though what they thought of the slightly bizarre tactic it is not known, but they reported to Henry that they wrote the letter, and that Margaret seemed pleased. Their ploy appeared to work, as the long-awaited commission arrived, with strings attached.[23] Any thoughts Thomas had of returning to England during August were now dashed, for Maximilian fed Margaret just enough positive information to keep the ambassadors at court.

In England, Henry was livid and pressed the ambassadors to threaten to return home. This put Thomas in an awkward position for, as the embassy noted to the King, Margaret had been 'been such a good friend that they did not like to displease her'.[24]

Finally, in early September the Imperial Council under the newly empowered Archduchess met to deliberate on the treaty. It proposed forming an alliance of powers dedicated to the destruction, dismemberment and partition of France.[25] However, instead of a treaty amongst various nations, the council suggested a treaty between the King and the Emperor only. This was not the grand alliance Henry had envisioned. The ambassadors had also assumed Margaret would play a prominent role, which would have made sense after being empowered by her father. Instead, she only wanted to be listed as a participant, not as negotiator or commissioner. Thomas, dismayed at having come so close, declared that he could hardly agree to such requests without further consultation.[26] The ambassadors withdrew to discuss their position. They were aware of the games being played at their expense, and in his report to Henry, Thomas admitted that Margaret, in whom they had trusted, now shied away from the full authority her father had given her. She could act on Maximilian's behalf but chose not to. The embassy had expected not only Margaret to be included in the treaty, but also her nephew, the future Charles V. As the embassy noted, this had in fact been some of the conditions included when the Emperor demanded 100,000 ducats.[27] Margaret seemed aware that she had caused supreme disappointment and, unsure of how to proceed, wrote to her father that negotiations had now stalled. He praised her for keeping the course and, although he would not come to Brussels, he sent her what he probably supposed was a gift to soften Henry: a beautiful crossbow in a case, which was mounted with silver gilt.[28] Margaret presented it to the embassy to give to Henry; but they would rather have sent him an alliance.

September dragged on, and on 13 October the men were brought in for a meeting with Margaret and the council, who, either stalling or playing for more money, made excuses, assuring Thomas that the real issue was Henry – he had misunderstood the terms. This was too much for Thomas, who must have had visions of never being appointed to another mission again. He snapped at the surprised council, retorting that his king had made the same interpretation of the articles as anyone with common sense. Thomas would not allow Henry to be played for a fool.[29]

Margaret attempted to defuse the situation, warning the embassy that if England did not pay 50,000 crowns now to get the war against France moving, it would surely cost four times that amount later. Furthermore, mercenaries, who were expensive, would have to be hired to take the place of the English, who lacked fighting skill after so many years of peace.[30] Thomas' response was firm: he would not tolerate any more demands for money from an absent emperor. Further, having served in the English army with his father and knowing first-hand the skill of the English troops, he replied that a war might last three years, and the English were neither weary nor lacked experience.

The embassy took their leave, stalking out of the chambers. They might just have to turn to veiled threats, and it was Margaret, caught in between, who was most susceptible to pressure. Thomas and Young met with the Archduchess soon after, and put on a show. Sighing in resignation, Thomas told Margaret that Henry had said the season for war was past and that they should return to England – he made every sign that the embassy was at an end, having achieved nothing. Margaret became visibly upset – she had already heard that their colleague Wingfield, who was not at the meeting, had intended to leave court, for a pilgrimage to Canterbury and had not taken her leave, an incredible snub to the Archduchess if the rumour was true.[31] She begged them to stay a little longer at court, promising to do what she could. Thomas, who may have felt slightly guilty at causing such drama, sought to placate her, assuring her they would wait for further instructions.[32]

The ambassadors dined privately that evening, and 'made good cheer' as they went over letters from England. One mentioned the possibility of Thomas' and Young's return, which seemed to please them: a mission that should have taken days had now lasted seven wearying months. But it was the far more experienced Wingfield who rather dramatically took a ring from his finger, slammed it on the table, swearing that he would go home, regardless of the cost.[33] The men probably ignored the outburst, but the next morning, according to the remaining ambassadors, Wingfield *did* depart without taking leave to go on pilgrimage, leaving his colleagues in an awkward position, making them even more restless, which Margaret sensed. She wrote to her father explaining Henry's final terms and urged him to modify his demands, stressing that Thomas was making plans to return home. Maximilian had again promised and failed to come to Brussels, and Thomas and Young advised Henry to send a proper, official ambassador (Spinelly was clearly inefficient) to the Imperial court who could do more than Margaret's letters:

Therfore yt semeth to us very necessary as we have hertofore written to your highness that your grace have oon contynually resseant in his [Maximilian]

comite whose presence with such enformacion as he shall [gather] unto hym wuld
do more in your matters than either my lady's letters or any other writings, for a
letter is soon seen and lightly cast in some corner and forgotten, where the
presence of your ambassadors ... shal force hym to declar hys mynde one wey or
the other.[34]

As October faded into November, Thomas and Young reported frankly to
Henry that they regretted not having anything more substantial to send him
but 'fair promises and sweet words when spending the king's money, but
doing him no good'.[35] The ambassadors remained at Margaret's court for the
winter – no reports were sent to England. We have only fleeting glimpses of
the men in correspondence between Margaret and her father, referring to the
ambassadors, but it was not until 5 April 1513 that the treaty was finally
ratified. The treaty specified that, within 30 days, they would declare war on
France and, within two months, the Pope and the Emperor would invade
Provence or Dauphiny.[36] It was hastily signed by Sir Edward Poynings,
Young, Thomas, and Wingfeld, who had managed to find his way back to
court just in time for the conclusion of the embassy.[37] It was almost one year
since their arrival.

Thomas had been at the forefront of negotiations for a war on France and,
back in England, his Howard brother-in-law was now given the opportunity to
shine in the realm of warfare – Henry appointed the dashing and much loved
Edward Howard Lord Admiral of the English Fleet. Edward was desperate to
meet with the French at sea, and decimate their fleet, but the latter were far
superior in numbers. Despite the odds being stacked against him, Edward
managed to board French galleys lying in shallow waters, but before his men
could follow him their cable was cut away, and he was left stranded, facing the
French pikes. Before they could strike, he tore the whistle from his neck – the
silver whistle of the Admiralty – and cast it into the sea. Then, he was taken.
Thomas lost a dearly loved brother-in-law – we have no evidence of how he or
his wife took the news.

Not until 11 April would the ambassadors personally witness the tendrils of
war their treaty had outlined. As they prepared to cross the channel from
Calais, which England controlled, Thomas wrote that they had seen four
French ships chasing the fishing boats into the harbour. One of the Frenchmen
came on shore to capture a boat laden with wine but withdrew when he was
fired on by English artillery. They also reported that the French were lying in
wait for them but, after a brief interval, they sailed safely home.[38]

For Thomas it was both a positive conclusion to his first embassy, and a
personal triumph in that he secured a position for his daughter, Anne – who

would have been approximately 13 at the time – at Margaret's court. To have secured such a position speaks volumes about Margaret's relationship with him, and about Thomas' relationship with his daughter, his trust in her to conduct herself well and represent the family. But Thomas also saw in Margaret a role model for his daughter: powerful, intelligent and respected. Anne would be exposed not only to the European stage but also to a progressive way of thinking not necessarily seen in England. Margaret possessed a vast library that reflected the intellectual, religious and cultural interests of the day. These included works by authors such as Christine de Pizan, who was known for challenging misogyny and the stereotypical views of women, and the works of Boccaccio, Aesop, Ovid, Boethius and Aristotle. Margaret was a patron of the arts and her court was renowned for welcoming a diverse range of poets, painters and some of the most progressive thinkers of Europe, including the humanist priest and theologian, Erasmus of Rotterdam.[39] Margaret's collection of paintings included works by masters such as Jan van Eyck, and her illuminated manuscripts and music books were highly regarded. She also favoured the tradition of courtly love, which was an integral element in chivalry, the complex of attitudes and institutions, which were central to the life of the Tudor court and the elite.

Thomas did not accompany his daughter to Margaret's court when she arrived sometime in the summer, only a few months after her father had left. Instead, Flemish Esquire Claude Bouton, who had been in the service of Phillip the Fair and now served Margaret, escorted Anne from England to Margaret's palace of Mechelen.[40]

What is perhaps most touching, however, is that her first letter – discussed in the first chapter – from a young daughter to her father, has passed down through the centuries, perfectly preserved. He must have kept it safe throughout his life and, considering how few personal letters have withstood the centuries, Thomas cherished the letters from his daughter. He was proud of her accomplishments and proud of her.

Ultimately, Thomas did not return to Brussels, and his absence seems to have been keenly felt. Within weeks, both Henry and Wolsey were berating Wingfield, who remained at court, for not reporting frequently enough. Clearly Boleyn had been frustrated by Maximilian, and at times manipulated by Margaret, but he was new to the game, finding his own identity and diplomatic style. This worked to his advantage as he was willing to take risks: rushing back to England for further instructions to avoid the embassy stalling and seizing the opportunity to take charge of the embassy, not because he was ambitious but because the embassy required it. He was successful as a special envoy, knowing how far he could ingratiate himself with Margaret, but he also no doubt learned valuable lessons. This embassy might have been concluded sooner, but it was an important stepping stone for his career.

In 1513, just months after returning home, Thomas' focus shifted from diplomacy to battle. Aged 36, he was drawn into military service in the inevitable war against France, heading a contingent of 100 men, which made up the advance guard of Henry's army.[41] There are no official records of Thomas' exact movements, but the progress of Henry's army has been recorded in detail, and from this we are able to interpret Thomas' involvement. As Knight of the Body, Thomas' would have been with the King and may have acted as interpreter during the Anglo-Burgundian negotiations.[42] We know that Richard Fox, who was passing beyond active duty, also accompanied Henry to Calais. Fox was part of the diplomatic corps, and it is more than likely that Thomas, fresh from a successful diplomatic mission, was part of this corps.[43] We find him also listed in The Vanguard, or the King's harbingers, alongside men of note: Sir Richard Carew, Lord Lisle, who was also Lord Marshal; Sir Nicholas Vaux, Sir Thomas Parr, Sir John Seymour and Sir Edward Hungerford. Thomas accompanied the King and his army to France on 30 June, where 14,000 troops awaited him. From Calais, they marched towards the city of Therouanne, which together with the neighbouring city of Tournai, were fortified towns that Maximilian had recommended be conquered as a first step to conquering France. Henry concurred and, on 16 August 1513, the English and Imperial troops won the battle in Therouanne, known somewhat sardonically as the 'Battle of the Spurs', where the English forces chased the French army (which had orders not to fight) from the field.

The war that Henry had so desired against France did not truly come to fruition; the conquest of a handful of French towns was not the glorious campaign he had envisioned. He had been outclassed by his own allies – Emperor Maximilian and Henry's father-in-law, King Ferdinand – who from the beginning had a game plan in which England and Henry were pawns. They had encouraged Henry to go to war, then abandoned him, letting both the French and English exhaust their resources fighting each other, and then used the threat of further invasion with their support to make demands of the desperate French. At the same time, they offered France an alliance from which England would be excluded, unless Henry agreed to all terms. Henry was humiliated, and would not forget their duplicitous behaviour.

On Wolsey's advice, Henry changed diplomatic course, and England now favoured France. The process of *rapprochement* in fact took some years but, by

1514, Henry and the French king Louis XII were both disillusioned with the Imperial approach to war and peace, and reopened negotiations.[44] The first step towards peace was to betroth Louis, whose wife had recently died, to Henry's younger and beautiful sister, Mary, originally destined to marry Charles of Castile.[45] Wolsey was the architect of this peace treaty, and there is the suggestion that Thomas played no part in the negotiations, omitted deliberately as he was one of the councillors most committed to war. But Thomas was associated with the strategy that had not worked, a strategy advanced by Henry and Wolsey to align with Maximilian against France, and ultimately for Henry to invade France. It was a flawed scheme because England was never significant for Spain, France, the Pope, Venice or the Holy Roman Empire. Wolsey, possibly urged by Henry, or Henry urged by Wolsey, had overestimated their relevance and standing, forcing a reversal of English policy. Thomas' lack of success in his first mission was due to Maximilian's playing the better hand. And, as he had just spent over ten months promoting Henry's war-mongering, it stands to reason that he would not immediately be involved in the peace negotiations with France. But there is nothing to suggest that he personally was committed to war with France: he was a special envoy acting for his king.

Thomas who, as we have seen, had escorted Henry's other sister, Margaret, to marriage in Scotland, was chosen in 1514 to escort the other English princess to her future home, France. He then wrote to Margaret, asking that Anne be released, explaining that Henry was marrying his sister Mary Tudor to King Louis, and Anne would be needed to attend upon her. He almost apologetically added: 'To this request [To have Anne serve Mary Tudor] I could not, nor did I know how to refuse.'[46]

The marriage proposal had only come about because Henry and Maximilian could not maintain an alliance, and Margaret was highly displeased that Henry was now leaning towards their joint enemy, France. Here we see Thomas being ever-responsive to his masters, but knowing how to take opportunities as they arose, and adapting to circumstances. It is unclear who suggested appointing Anne to serve Mary, but logic suggests it might have been Wolsey: the Cardinal had begun to rely on Thomas and knew his character well. It is at this point that some scholars have identified George Boleyn's entry to the political and courtly scene. In the translated *Letters and Papers*, Brewer included a question mark after the name of one 'Le Poulayn', questioning whether this referred to the young George Boleyn, as it might seem because it follows the heading 'enfans donneur'.[47] However, in the original manuscript, Le Poulayn is listed under 'Pannetiers, eschancons, et valets trenchans'.[48] A William Poullain is also described as a native of Normandy who was at court during this time, and granted 'denization' meaning he was granted certain rights normally reserved for a citizen; it is more than likely that he is the Poulayn listed.

The wedding procession was just as grand as the one Thomas had been a part of years before. The bridal train, 3,000 strong, progressed to Dover, accompanied by Henry, Katherine and the court. Thomas' daughter Anne was not a part of it, for she would have made the journey straight from Brussels to Paris.

Fierce winds and storms detained them for several days and, when calm weather finally allowed them to sail – at four in the morning on 2 October – the winds returned and scattered the little fleet. Some of the ships reached Calais while others ended up in Flanders. Only the royal vessel reached its destination, narrowly escaping destruction. When the princess and her attendants approached the shore in a small boat sent to fetch them, the churning waves were so violent that Sir Christopher Garnish, a man of court reputedly just over 7ft tall, waded into the water and carried the princess in his arms to safety, before assisting with the other ladies, with Thomas' other daughter, Mary, possibly among them.

The wedding of Mary to the king of France was reportedly a boisterous and glittering affair, but the following day Louis discharged most of the English entourage. He made an exception for a few of Mary's attendants, including a 'Mademoiselle Boleyn' but it is likely that this was Anne rather than Mary.

Thomas spent the next few months back at the English court with his wife. It is from 1514 that we catch glimpses of the young George Boleyn, Thomas' male heir. He became a page to the King in 1514, roughly at the age of ten, and from that time, a permanent member of court. It would have been a triumphant Christmastide for the family, with his daughters in secure positions in a foreign court and Thomas' own career well on track. Thomas is listed as a participant in a mummery during the 1514 Christmas revels. The invited participants were dressed 'After the fashion of Savoy' and were invited into the Queen's chamber to 'dance for Katherine's pleasure'. Curiously, a *Master Bollen* is also listed as taking part in the mummery.[49] In subsequent interpretations of the list, historians have identified this person as George Boleyn and the occasion as that of his first entrance to court. J. S. Brewer, Ives and Starkey, for instance, note that George was listed alongside his father, participating in a mummery with other children, but a reading of the revel list shows this is unlikely. We must look at Chronicler Edward Hall's account:

This Christemas on Newyeres night, y king, y duke of Suflblke [Suffolk] and. ii. other in mantels of cloth, of sihier, & lyned with blew veluet, the syluer was pounsed in letters, so that y veluet might he sene through, the mantels had great capes like to the Portingal slopys … iiii. ladycs in gounes, after the fashion of Sauoy, of blew veluet, lyned with clothe of golde, the veluet all to cuttc, and mantels like typpettcs Knytte together al of siluer … the. iiii. torche bearers were in satten white and blewe. This straunge apparell pleased muche euery person, and in especially the Queue, & thus these, iiii. lordes and. iiii. ladyes came into the Queues chamber with great light of torches, and daunced a greate season, and then put of their visers, & then they were well knou en, and the Quene hariely thanked the kynges grace for her goodly pastyme, and kyssed hym.[50]

Hall makes clear that the participants were seven men, four of whom carried large torches, and four ladies. We know their names: Thomas Boleyn, the Duke of Suffolk; Nicholas Carew, who was a cousin of the Boleyns, and his wife, Elizabeth; Henry Guildford and his wife, Margaret; Thomas' sister-in-law, Anne St Leger; Elizabeth Blount who became Henry's mistress; Robert Coke, William Coffin, and the mysteriously named Master Bollen. There is compelling evidence that this 'Master Bollen' was Thomas' younger brother, Edward, who would have been 18 at the time and who did frequent the court.[51] This age matches that of the rest of the group, most of whom were in their late teens or early twenties. The specific references to 'ladies in gowns', 'torch bearers' and 'Lords and Ladies' make it highly unlikely that a young boy like George, at this time between the age of eight and ten, would have been a part of such a group. The only Christmas pageant that year which included children lists those of a Mr Cornishe, Mr Kran, and Mr Cranys, 'men of the Chapel'.[52] This mummery thus probably does not mark George Boleyn's entrance to court. It is a minor detail but one worth making, since this is among many episodes that have become entrenched in the Boleyn historiography and have shaped the dominant interpretations of the family.

On 1 January 1515, King Louis of France died, and Thomas quickly secured Anne a position in the household Louis' daughter, of the new French queen, Claude, wife of the newly anointed King Francis. Up to this point, Thomas had spent little time in France, a mere few days during the wedding of Mary and Louis, so it is plausible that Wolsey assisted Anne's move. The appointment had to be approved by the French court, so it seems that Thomas was held in high regard as his young daughter was considered a desirable maid of honour. Eventually it would prove most advantageous to England as well. It has been argued that Mary Boleyn was also moved to the new household, but there is no concrete evidence, and she may well have returned home with the newly widowed Mary Tudor.

If she did, this calls into question much of what we know of Mary Boleyn, and in turn alters to a degree how we view her relationship with her father, for it is commonly accepted, without much evidence, that Mary not only stayed on at the court but also developed a highly promiscuous reputation, becoming mistress to Francis himself and later being labelled a 'great and infamous whore'. What sort of father – cried those Victorian historians – would allow such a thing? Mary's reputation, much like her siblings, has been seen as a reflection of Thomas. The main source is a letter between two Italians, written in early March of 1536 by Ridolf Pio, Bishop of Faenza, to a Signor Prothonotario Ambrogio, Da Monte Plaisant. It slanders Mary:

> Francis said also that they are committing more follies than ever in England, and are saying and printing all the ill they can against the Pope and the Church; that 'that woman' pretended to have miscarried of a son, not being really with child, and, to keep up the deceit, would allow no one to attend on her but her sister, whom the French king knew here in France 'per una grandissima ribalda et infame sopre tutte'.[53]

We have no way of knowing what Francis said, and if he did make the remark; by March of 1536, Francis was, as we shall see, following his own political agenda. Mary's life choices would cause friction between herself and her father, for various reasons which come into this narrative as we progress, but it had nothing to do with her promiscuity at the French court.

# CHAPTER FIVE

# The Picklock of Princes

*Arrange your facial expression beforehand at home, so that it may be ready for every part of the play and so that not even a glimmer of your true feelings may be revealed in your looks. You must plan your delivery at home, so that your speech suits your looks and your looks and the bearing of your whole body suit your feigned speech.*

– Desiderius Erasmus

Thomas had been an instrument of war and peace for his monarch, but the years of 1515 to 1518 were decidedly domestic: there were no special or sensitive commissions abroad, and all resident ambassadors remained at their posts, but there is no evidence that he had lost the favour or confidence of the King. He had been part of a special mission that pursued policies concerning France that were now being reversed, so it may have been politic for all concerned that he was absent from further diplomatic work while these political shifts took effect. Instead he was dedicated to improving the Boleyn balance sheets. Since the beginning of Henry's reign, Thomas had been rewarded for his service and dedication, and with each year, the rewards and responsibilities attached to them grew greater. In 1511, Thomas had been granted Keepership of the Park of Beskwode, Nottinghamshire; Borham and Powers, Essex; Busshy, Hertfordshire; Henden, Kent; and Purbright, Surrey. The next year, rather than parks, Henry awarded him the manors of Walkerfare and Wykmere in Norfolk, and made him joint Keeper and Constable of the Norwich Castle and Gaol alongside Sir Henry Wyatt. More manors would follow in 1514, with Thomas being awarded life grant of the Norfolk manors of Saham Tony, Nekton, Panworth Hall, Cressingham Parva, and the hundreds of Waylond and Grymmeshowe.

Another avenue of wealth could be found in the wardship of minor heirs of a royal tenant – a child from a well-to-do family who had lost their father. The king was entitled to all the revenues of the deceased's estate, with one third remaining with the widow. Wardships were lucrative commodities, with revenue coming in until the heir reached his majority of 21, or 14 for a girl. Henry, like his predecessors, had either sold such wardships, or bestowed them on those he favoured. In 1512, he did just that for Thomas, awarding him joint custody of the lands and wardship of John, son and heir of Sir George Hastings, and a year later, partial wardship and custody of the lands of Elizabeth Grey, daughter and heir of Viscount Lisle.[1] Thomas now looked to his own district – he had already been appointed on numerous occasions as Commissioner of the Peace since the beginning of Henry's reign – nominated by the King to perform specific tasks within an assigned county, usually relating to minor crimes. This continued throughout the rest of his career at court, and Thomas would be assigned to numerous counties alongside men like Bishop Warham, the Dukes of Norfolk, Suffolk and Buckingham, and Lord Cobham, among others.[2]

On 3 August that year, Thomas' maternal grandfather, Thomas Butler, who had retired as Lord Chamberlain in 1512, died and was buried in the Mercers' Chapel of the Hospital of St Thomas of Acre in London. His death set affairs in motion which would occupy Thomas for over a decade.

Thomas had always remained close to his grandfather, and we see firm evidence of this in the latter's will. Despite the fact that Thomas' mother Margaret was the younger sibling, Butler senior bypassed the son of his eldest daughter and bequeathed to Thomas a precious family heirloom: a white ivory horn, garnished at both ends with gold and covered with gold-barred white silk; its gold terret ring meant it could be used as a pendant on a chain.[3] All family heirlooms require a degree of mystery and mythology, and this horn was no different. Butler claimed that the horn had been in the family since the reign of Henry II, and originally had been given to Theobald Walter, a cousin and heir of Agnes Beckett, sister of St Thomas Becket.[4] Butler's instructions were that

> my executors deliver unto Sir Thomas Boleyn knight, son and heir apparent of my said daughter Margaret the little white horn and corse [possibly meaning relic], he to keep it for the use of his male heirs of his body lawfully begotten. And for lack of male issue said horn to be delivered to George St Leger Knight, son of my said daughter Anne and to continue in the issue male of the bodies of Dame Margaret and Dame Anne as long as fortune shall send males.[5]

There is far more to the horn than its value: it would be adopted by the Butler family as a symbol of their titled inheritance and became synonymous with the Earldom of Ormond. There is some evidence that Butler had desired his grandson Thomas to succeed him to the Irish earldom, and even more evidence that his mother, Margaret, desired the title for him.

Thomas' mother immediately wrote to her son informing him of her father's death, letters which show the affection between them:

> And whereas I understand to my great heaviness, that my lord my father is departed this world to Almighty God, on whose soul I beseech Jesu to have mercy, wherefore I pray and heartily desire you that you will do for me in everything as you shall think most best and expedient. And in everything that you shall do for me after as you think best, I will, on my part, affirm and rate it in as like manner as though it were mine own deed.[6]

Margaret relied heavily on her son at this point, adding that 'if hereafter you shall think it necessary for me to come up to London to you, I pray you send hereof to me your mind, and I shall pain myself to come; howbeit if you may do well enough without my coming in my behalf, then I were loath to labour so far'.[7]

Butler's will had created a major conflict as the Earl's two daughters, Margaret and Anne, were his heirs-general and co-heiresses to any property that was not entailed upon his male heir. The Crown issued a directive that granted the women livery of the lands, and they divided his 72 manors, 36 to each.[8] The Earl also had Irish lands, but Butler and his brother, Sir John, 6th Earl of Ormond before him, had been absent from their Irish estates for a long period due to the Wars of the Roses. Their cousin, Sir James Butler, a member of the Polestown branch of the Butler family, managed their Ormond estates but regarded them as his own.[9] When Thomas Butler died in 1515, Sir James' son, Piers Butler, considered himself the rightful heir, believing the title should be entailed upon male heirs. However, the Ormond title was entailed to heirs-general, not just male heirs: thus Anne and Margaret were the rightful heirs. By 25 August, when his grandfather's will was proved, Thomas must have felt the earldom was within greater reach than ever before. Another earldom, that of Wiltshire, had also been held by the Butler family by his great-uncle but had been bestowed upon Henry Stafford, the younger brother of Edward Stafford, the Duke of Buckingham. It was certainly Thomas' ambition to regain the titles, not just for him but for his mother's family, which surviving letters from Margaret to her son make clear. Apart from the affection between them, and Thomas' sense of duty towards his mother and her sister, Anne, the sisters were clearly reliant on him to assist the family, which he went to great lengths to achieve.

The matter of the Ormond earldom was to be heard in Dublin, with a counsel representing Thomas' mother and aunts who asserted that their claim to the title as heirs-general was valid.[10] On the other hand, counsel for Piers showed no evidence at all but asked that the matter be remitted to the common law.[11] But there were far greater forces at work. Henry, who was brought into the matter, was wary of upsetting the fragile balance in Ireland and, despite Thomas' determination, the earldom was not awarded to either party. Thomas was bitterly disappointed; he had been something of a pawn in a larger political game. Until now he had been favoured by fortune, and this defeat only strengthened his determination to succeed for his family. Even without the earldom at this point, Thomas did benefit further from his grandfather (not in the least, the famous drinking horn) in terms of estates, and one in particular – Newhall in Essex – described as a *costly mancion*, caught Henry's eye.[12]

Henry approached Thomas at some stage to 'make an offer' of £1000, over £500,000 in today's currency, which Thomas accepted. And Newhall became one of Henry's passions, his largest building project on which he spent the extraordinary sum of £17,000, completely revamping and refurbishing the estate which would eventually rival Richmond Palace. In fact, Henry seemed so taken with his new estate, that he renamed it *Beaulieu*, 'beautiful place', and, for a time, he visited it more frequently than either Richmond or Windsor. Despite leaving the family's portfolio, the property continued to be linked with the Boleyns when, years later, it would become a safe haven for the trysts of Henry and Anne; and later Thomas' son-in-law, William Carey, would be named as Keeper in 1522, followed by George Boleyn in 1528.

The entrepreneurial streak that his grandfather, Geoffrey, had shown decades before was strong in Thomas too. On 26 October 1517, he received a licence 'during pleasure, to export from his mill of Rochefort (Rochford) Essex, all "wode" billet (cut pieces of firewood) made within the said lordship in a "playte" (pleyt) of his own called "the Rosendell"'.[13] A pleyt was another term for a river boat, and although it is unclear to whom Thomas sold the wood, it was a most lucrative business that secured considerable financial advantage for him, and was financed no doubt by the generous inheritance from his enterprising Butler grandfather. Thomas was obviously an astute businessman, but he was not, nor did he consider himself, above his merchant background which provided considerable financial security for his family.

It had been five years since the bells of London had rung out in celebration of a royal birth. Henry and Katherine's hopes had been dashed several times since, with pregnancies resulting in miscarriages and still births, but finally, at the bleak hour of 4am on 18 February 1516, the couple joyously welcomed the birth of a daughter, Mary, at Greenwich. It was not the son for whom Henry and Katherine had prayed, for hours each day, but they were certain that this would lead to many more healthy children – preferably sons, of course. A week later, the princess was proudly carried out of Katherine's apartments, through the court gate to the door of the Church of the Observant Friars, which was railed and hung with arras, the way being well gravelled and strewed with rushes. Thomas' sister-in-law, Elizabeth Howard, Countess of Surrey, carried the princess under a gold canopy, borne by Sir David Owen, Sir Nicholas Vaux, Sir Thomas Aparre and Thomas Boleyn.[14] To be a part of another royal christening showed that Thomas and his family were now at the heart of the court elite, part of the innermost circle of the King and his family.

In early 1517, Henry's older sister Margaret, who Thomas had accompanied to Scotland years before, visited the English court.[15] It had been 13 years since Margaret had seen her brother and, in the preceding years, she had endured a tumultuous marriage with James IV, and had been widowed since his death on the battlefield at the hands of the English army in 1513.[16] While she had been named as regent in her husband's will, it was also expressly stated that she could not remarry, as any future husband could then lay claim to the Scottish throne. It seemed that the propensity to ignore formal stipulations was a Tudor family trait – she ignored the stipulation, and married Archibald Douglas, the Earl of Angus, resulting in her first husband's cousin, John Stuart, Duke of Albany, seizing power from her. To protect Scotland, he imprisoned Margaret, taking control of the throne through her son, the young James V, and Margaret appealed to her brother for help.

She briefly escaped this political nightmare and, whether Henry liked it or not, his sister was headed his way. Margaret was an English princess and missed England, and while Henry was adamant that she belonged in Scotland, in England she was for the time being, and in royal state she would be kept. Thomas was awarded the lucrative post as her 'official carver' for 40 days, being paid £10 for the post. This required him to personally attend to her when she dined and accompany her throughout the visit, a position only a highly respected individual would be given. But it was a short-lived assignment. Margaret was sent back to Scotland, on the proviso that she would not interfere with Scottish politics.

By 1518, it had been almost five years since Thomas' very first mission. In that time, he had furthered his family's interests, cultivated his position and reputation, and secured an enviable position for his daughter, Anne. At court, he also continued business arrangements with William Compton, to whom he sold the manor of Long Compton (perhaps William liked the name) for £400.[17] He must have been desirous of another embassy, however, and it was therefore imperative that when a position did come his way, Thomas proved his worth as a skilled diplomat thereby ensuring that he would not have to wait so long between ambassadorial postings again.

The peace negotiations between England and France, which began with Mary's betrothal to Louis, for which he had sent Anne to the French court, had continued into 1518.[18] Once again, an embassy was required to negotiate the conditions of this clause, but the unsettled issue was the city of Tournai, in the Walloon area of what is today Belgium, lost to the English in the war of 1513, and which the French sought to reclaim.[19] Francis I was a great patron of the arts, commissioning a good deal of the painting, decorative sculpture, and architecture for the French court, and he had a particular passion for tapestries. The royal factory in Paris, the Gobelins Tapestry, produced the finest European tapestries, along with other major centres of Arras, Aubusson, Tournai and Brussels, each one a major supplier of exquisite works of art that began to flourish in the fifteenth and sixteenth centuries, when they became wealthy centres as the prosperous classes and courts of Europe fuelled the trade in textiles.[20]

But the English were equally resistant to relinquishing Tournai to France. It was such an impediment to the two countries moving forward that an embassy of French diplomats was sent to England to meet with an equal number of English diplomats to negotiate the fate of Tournai. Thomas was among those chosen to entertain the French embassy when it landed at Dover and then to escort them to London to meet his father-in-law, Lord High Admiral Surrey, who was attended by 160 richly apparelled men including Boleyn. The arrival of this embassy gave the gentlemen of the Privy Chamber an official position in the court procession: they were paired with their French counterparts, in a gesture of brotherhood, as they walked arm in arm, two at a time, through the city of London to the Merchant Tailors Hall where a banquet was held.[21]

It was an event of great ostentation and extravagance; Henry had spent a considerable fortune on beds, hangings for chambers, carpets and cushions. Wine was brought in, wood for the fires, coals, table cloths, towels, napkins and sheets. The palace at Greenwich was the perfect venue for the French and English delegations' festivities and entertainments which competed with sessions of hard negotiations that stretched into October. Eventually, however, there was a major breakthrough and terms were reached, one of the most important that the city of Tournai would be returned to the French for the modest sum of one million crowns, plus an annual payment.

But Wolsey had masterminded something quite unprecedented, which sealed his reputation as one of the great diplomatic minds of the period: the Treaty of London in 1518. More than just a truce between France and England,

Wolsey's vision encompassed almost a dozen other states, all of whom signed the treaty, which bound the signatories to unite against any power that undertook an act of aggression against any one of the participants.[22] It has been noted that the treaty evolved into a sophisticated attempt to address European international relations, and was dependent on skilled public servants and diplomats to bring it to fruition, of which Thomas was one.[23] On 3 October, the English hosts and their French counterparts rode from Greenwich to St Paul's Cathedral where the 'Universal' peace was proclaimed. Henry and the ambassadors took their oaths to the treaty, and Wolsey sang High Mass.[24] A treaty of marriage (which was what high-born children were for, partly) was signed on 4 October, pledging Henry's two-year-old Princess Mary to the one-year-old dauphin of France, an agreement to which Thomas and several others witnessed their king's signature.[25] Against this historic backdrop, Thomas had acquitted himself well in the eyes of his king: it is from this date that we can mark the point of his accession to the Privy Council, gained entirely through his well-demonstrated skill, loyalty and dedication.

After the conference, Wolsey finally tapped Thomas on the shoulder for a new embassy to France, deliberately choosing a man whose diplomatic skills had already been proven, but also someone who would see negotiations to the very end, regardless of potential difficulties. There were several crucial differences between Thomas' first two embassies. Now, Thomas was no longer reporting to Henry but was working in collaboration with the king's closest advisor, the most influential and powerful man at court and the architect of Henry's diplomacy, Cardinal Wolsey. This second embassy is significant as it marked the consolidation and intensification of their relationship, which would evolve into Thomas becoming one of Wolsey's right-hand men.

Although he departed for France alongside fellow ambassador Richard Weston and others, Thomas' appointment was as an individual ambassador. This meant that he alone was ultimately responsible for conducting the numerous sensitive diplomatic exchanges between monarchs. More importantly, this embassy coincided with two events that would have an impact throughout all concurrent English embassies, namely, the Imperial election of 1519, which was crucial in dictating the balance of power in Europe, and the Papal election the following year.

Thomas' first French reports began in January of 1519 but he had actually arrived in France much earlier. He was listed amongst the French embassy who left England, reaching Calais on 14 November and we also see in a report to Wolsey as early as 2 February that Thomas noted in 15 days' time, the first 100 days of his diets would have been spent.[26] Since diets were dated from the day an envoy left court, Thomas' mission to France can be placed exactly as starting on 19 November 1518, and Thomas was present for the Christmas festivities in Paris, which the ambassadors finally reached a week later, for a sumptuous banquet held in the Bastille on 22 December. A three-tiered gallery was built, over which was stretched a blue awning, waterproofed with wax and painted to represent the night sky.[27] Torches lit the room, throwing 'a marvelous blaze of light on the starry ceiling to rival the sun'.[28] A raised platform draped in a white carpet formed the embassy's table, with each member placed among their French counterparts and their ladies of the court. Thomas and his colleagues were regaled with a sumptuous nine-course banquet as they delighted in the entertainment, including a masque, after which the young king Francis, who had been dancing, finally revealed himself. He joined his wife Queen Claude, and his mother, Louise, on the royal dais, as the party enjoyed the confections, served by ladies dressed in the Italian fashion. It was to be a period of revelry and merrymaking to rival any display of Francis' English brother.

The next day, a grand tournament took place at the Bastille with Francis himself taking pride of place in the competitions. No business was conducted, and it looked as though the men would have to wait for the New Year. But there was a silver lining – Thomas had not seen his daughter, Anne, who had now been in France for several years and, despite their differing duties, it must have been a warm reunion for father and daughter. To see Anne at home in France, a young woman in her element among the sophisticated splendour of the court, must have instilled a sense of pride. When the court moved to Poissy, Thomas relocated to larger quarters a few kilometres away from the court. These were grand rooms which would have cost a considerable amount, and he would surely not have needed such lodgings for himself. We may speculate that Anne spent time there with her father, or he may well have been briefly joined by his son George as part of his entourage. Being slightly removed from court no doubt offered a brief respite from the unending drama. But we might consider the possibility that Anne's position within the French court was very useful to her father in terms of feeding him inside information and keeping him well informed, which he often seemed to be. Ambassadors often paid courtiers or inserted spies into royal households for this kind of information – his daughter, already installed was a considerable asset.

France and England were fortunate enough to be ruled by fit, young monarchs – Henry was just 27 in 1518 and Francis was 24. These were men in their prime, unlike the Holy Roman Emperor Maximilian, who had long seen the zenith of his power during the Italian wars which sought to secure and defend the dynastic interests of the Hapsburgs, and, at 59 years old, was somewhat frail and in poor health. He had long seen the zenith of his power during the Italian wars which sought to secure and defend the dynastic interests of the Hapsburgs. Always a patron of the arts, particularly of music – he was himself a composer – he was also a man of deep melancholy.[29] Morbidly, he had his own coffin carried with him on campaign as early as 1514. It was not until January 1519 that he died, leaving the position of Holy Roman Emperor vacant. This was not an hereditary title but an elected one, conferred by an electoral college comprising the nobles and important echelons of clergy, although any sovereign with enough financial backing was eligible.[30]

The Holy Roman Empire consisted of 1,800 semi-independent states spread across Central Europe and Northern Italy. While every state should have had a say, such a process would have been too lengthy, and the number of voters in the Imperial electoral college was just seven: the Archbishops of Mainz, Trier and Cologne, the king of Bohemia-Hungary, the Margrave of Brandenburg, the Count of the Palatinate, and the Duke of Saxony.

Charles was the strongest candidate, but Pope Leo feared that this would provoke a violent confrontation between Charles and Francis and thought a third candidate might ease the tension in the electoral college.[31] He did not particularly have Henry in mind as the third candidate but, with Wolsey's encouragement, Henry put himself forward. Henry had no idea of the ring into which he had just thrown his cap, but he seemed to genuinely believe that this was a democratic election. Thomas was already at the French court when the Imperial vote was about to begin, but he was unaware that Henry had put himself forward as a candidate and, in a report to Wolsey, Thomas wrote of Francis' relief that Henry showed no enthusiasm to enter the contest for the Imperial ring, and added that Francis would be one of Wolsey's strongest allies should he aspire to the Papacy. These electors were keen see the rise of another Hapsburg, but they also expected to be bribed for their loyalty, so it was more a case of who could afford what, and who could afford to pay up front. Substantial loans would need to be secured from either banks or private lenders, with the competition to finance the election almost as fierce as the election itself. One of those most likely to be able to afford it was a German merchant and one of the wealthiest men in Europe – Jakob Fugger, *the Rich*. The Fuggers were from the German city of Augsburg and had made their money in textiles trading with the Venetians. They had already funded Maximilian, and now Charles' aunt, Margaret of Austria, urged him to borrow from Fugger: even an electoral commissioner told him frankly that the electors 'have neither faith, letters nor seals from any merchants other than the Fuggers'.[32] It was more of an auction than a contest.

With Europe in the throes of the election, part of Thomas' mission was to assess the likelihood of Francis becoming emperor. But Wolsey had another protégé, Richard Pace, who he despatched to Germany with instructions to advance Henry's candidature and do all he could to harm the chances of the French king.

In addition to the Imperial election was the potential Papal election – Wolsey's own Papal ambitions are well documented, although they have been the subject of debate.[33] The Pope was ageing, and while he showed no imminent signs of vacating the Papal throne, it was essential to have allies on side in the event of his death. Thomas' intimation to the Cardinal was that if he kept Henry out of the contest, Francis would support his bid to become the next Pope. This information, if correct, was highly useful to Wolsey, who was aware that Francis would soon see opposition from England.

Before entering into the details of the embassy, it is worthwhile noting Thomas' writing style, specifically his correspondence to Wolsey and the manner of his address, for this was the first opportunity he had to craft his own reports. While Thomas' counterparts – Richard Pace, Thomas Spinelly and even men like Archbishop Warham – address the Cardinal simply: 'To my lord Cardinal's grace', 'To the cardinal of York and legate de latere' or 'To my lord Legate's grace', Thomas, in these first months, preferred: 'To myn most especial and singular good lord, my lord Legate, Cardinal and Chancellor of England.'[34] Interestingly, he concluded his letters to Wolsey with the following: 'Beseching the holy Trynyte long to preserve your Grace' and used 'Beseching the holy Trynyte long to preserve your Highnesse' when writing to Henry.

There is no particular sign of false flattery here, although we may assume that Thomas was anxious to do well, eager to please, and his capacious address to Wolsey may indicate that he desired the Cardinal's continued trust and favour. It also suggests a formality that had yet to ease into a collegial relationship, and this may also account for the meticulously detailed, lengthy and frequent reports of which the Cardinal must have been appreciative.

Maximilian died in February, and within days of hearing the news, Thomas had been invited to an audience after Mass in the King's chambers, along with Francis' mother, Louise of Savoy, who wielded enormous influence over her son. Thomas visited the court and delivered letters to the King and his mother telling them that Henry hoped that they would act in unity in their response to Maximilian's death. When he apologised to Francis for the delay in presenting the King's correspondence, Francis responded enigmatically: 'contrary winds hindereth [many] matters'.[35] Thomas reported to Wolsey that he spent over an hour with the French king discussing the upcoming Imperial election and that Francis was 'very much set upon being made Emperor', and his mother even more so.[36] From the first weeks of the embassy, the ambassador made numerous references to a growing rapport between himself and the French royal family. In one of his first reports from France, Thomas wrote that Francis asked him to lean out of the window with him so they could speak on the subject of the Imperial election so as not to be overheard by gossips.

In his February report, written only four months into the embassy, Thomas wrote that he:

> Was so familiar with him [Francis] that I asked him in earnest, if he were Emperor, whether he would make a voyage against the Infidels in his proper person, as the voice went. He took me hard by the wrist with the one hand, and laid his other hand upon his breast, and sware to me on his faith, if he attain to be Emperor, that within three years after he [would] be in Constantinople, or he would die by the way.[37]

Francis preferred a style of informality – adept at creating a sense of trust, and making the ambassador feel as though he and Francis had a deep understanding. He may have with Thomas, but unbeknownst to the latter, this air of formality was one Francis cultivated with various ambassadors. Thomas also spent time with the royal family at their palace in Blois and reported to Wolsey that the King received him in his dining chamber, embraced him, and led him by the hand, 'To a beddys syde in the same chamber, and so stonding there talked with hym half a quarter of an howre' when he delivered the King a letter from England, which he read; and calling the other Legate, 'talked with hym, lenyng on the bedde more than half an howre'.[38]

Louise also demonstrated her respect for Thomas and a papal legate with whom he would become very well acquainted in the years to come: Lorenzo Campeggio. On one occasion, the Queen mother:

> Took him [Campeggio] [by the] right hand, and me [Boleyn] on the other hand, and brought us [to the] Queen, [Claude] where she was accompanied with 14 or 15 [lords and] gentlewomen, in a nightgown, and nothing [upon her] head but only a kerchief, looking always her ho[ur when she shall] be brought in bed.[39]

For Thomas to be brought to Claude, alongside a representative of the Pope, speaks volumes of the high esteem in which Thomas was held.

Thomas began to spend a great deal of time with the royal family. His letters to Wolsey indicate that like all skilled ambassadors, Thomas cultivated good relations with individuals closest to the king, especially Rene of Savoy, the Grand Master, (commonly referred to as the Great Bastard of Savoy) with the pair dining together frequently. He also enjoyed lengthy conferences with Francis until the arrival of John Stuart, Duke of Albany, considered to be the Scottish thistle in England's side at the French court. On one occasion Francis warmly invited the Duke into his rooms towards the end of a meeting with Thomas, which irritated him, and he wrote that the *auld alliance* remained as strong as ever. Thomas had to contend with the duke at court into March when they were both present for a wonderfully Italian styled masque on 7 March, and an elaborate jousting tournament the next day. Thomas would certainly have partaken in this lavish event where the court participants presented themselves to their king dressed in fabrics of gold, lush velvets and shining taffeta, their gilded masks ornately designed with jewels and ostrich feathers.

Despite the court distractions, and the unwelcome Duke of Albany, Thomas remained focused on Francis' position in the Imperial election, looking for any indication of what support there was for him. Francis on the other hand wished to appear to Henry non-committal about the election, somewhat detached, above the fray, stating only that he hoped for Henry's and Wolsey's good offices on 'this interesting occasion', but that he would be interested to hear if there was anything worthy of note. In another letter to Henry, Francis wrote he 'preferred to know all of his [Henry's] thoughts by way of [ambassador] Boleyn'.[40] Clearly Thomas had risen further in the esteem of the French king and now even had his ear: as chief negotiator, he became the conduit between England and France.

Wolsey and Henry were supporting Francis' rival, Charles, for the mantle of Holy Roman Emperor while maintaining the appearance of supporting Francis.[84] They may well have realised that he would eventually control much of Europe, including Spain, and therefore seemed the better ally for England. The continuing expansion of the Ottomans threatened all of Europe and their success in the Ottoman Egyptian/Mamluk wars now meant that they were closer to controlling many trade routes in the Mediterranean. They had already taken Damascus, Beirut, Gaza and Jerusalem, and now they were on the doorstep of Cairo, posing the greatest threat to all of Christendom.

Thomas spent much of his time and energy putting out the political fires the King and Cardinal had started. Within a few weeks of his embassy, he was struggling to convince Francis that he had Henry's support when he then had to discredit a further report that Henry and Wolsey were attempting to influence German states to support Charles' candidacy. In a letter to Wolsey, Thomas reported that he had to convince Francis to pay it no mind, 'as it was contrary to Henry's letter written to the King here. He replied that he believed it not, but prayed Boleyn to show Wolsey by this what manner of man the Cardinal was.'[41]

His loyalty to the Cardinal was commendable, although it is not clear whether Thomas knew at this stage that Wolsey was undermining Francis, although he soon would be aware. From Calais, Pace wrote to Thomas, warning him, 'if he hears of any sinister report of his journey, he shall say that Pace is only sent to be present at the coming imperial election, and if he does not hear anything, Boleyn is to keep quiet. Do this for the safety of his own person, for if the French king should by evil information suspect his journey, he might intercept him, and perhaps destroy him.'[42]

Despite the subterfuge swirling around him, Thomas continued to be warmly received within the court and was well enough informed to be able to report on intimate matters involving the King's family. His daughter Anne, positioned in Claude's inner circle, may well have kept him abreast of developments in the Queen's chamber, for he reported to Henry that Queen Claude had gone into confinement and was 'very sickly, worse than she has been in any former confinement'.[43]

He also devoted a great deal of time to discussion with the King's Great Master (the French equivalent of Lord Steward), Artus Gouffier de Boissy, in relation to the complaints of numerous English merchants whose vessels had been damaged by notorious French pirates.[44] Thomas was very aware that his intercession on behalf of English merchants was paramount as their only recourse to compensation was to have their grievances before the King of France. The ambassador drew up articles to be presented to Francis with figures and details for damages from the plundered merchants, claims that had already been agreed to. However, now the claims were considered insufficient.[45] As he had done with Margaret five years earlier, Thomas remained firm in the face of powerful, persuasive individuals who wanted a better deal for themselves.

The spotlight was now on Anglo-French relations and Thomas was sensitive as to how the English were perceived at the French court. By this time there were several English gentlemen who were causing havoc at court. The men were reported to be seen brawling in public, drinking and frequenting brothels; one was now very ill with, in Thomas' words, 'the haunting of harlots'.[46]

He was fastidious in his adherence to protocol, a concern which is evident following the birth of Francis' son, Henri, whom Thomas was invited to sponsor in the name of his king. Francis enjoyed sumptuous celebrations and lavish feasts, and for the christening of his second son, the pomp and ceremony of a Catholic christening.[47] Thomas was most attentive to what protocol required on this occasion and fussed greatly until he had found the suitable gifts – a salt-spoon, a cup and (layer) sheet of gold – to be presented to Queen Claude; a customary present warmly received. Wolsey also sent Boleyn £100 to be distributed at his discretion as baptismal gifts which Thomas dutifully accounted for.[48]

Despite the fact that Francis personally wrote to Henry that Boleyn 'performed the ceremony with all possible honor', Thomas reported to Wolsey that: 'Officers of Armys which with importune manner asked reward saying that the Duke of Urbyn [Ubino] at the crystenyng of the Dolphyn [Dauphin] rewarded them.'[49] The startled English ambassador gave them the best answers he could as to why he did not have money for them which did not appease them, and they went away discontented.[50]

Another, far more personal, incident gave cause for alarm months into the French embassy. As early as 1515, years before Henry's affair with Anne, Henry took steps to reward Thomas for his service by promising to appoint him Treasurer of the King's Household when the incumbent Thomas Lovell resigned from the position.[51] On St George's Feast Day, May 1519, Lovell did step down, and Wolsey wrote to his ambassador in France to inform him that Edward Poynings, who was then Comptroller of the Household, would replace Lovell, and that Thomas was also not in the running for the lower position of Comptroller. All Thomas could do was reply to Wolsey:

> Notwithstanding his promises to Boleyn the King thinks 'that without greatly discouraging Sir Edw. Ponynges, he can do no less for the laudable service which the said Sir Edw. hath done than to advance him for a season.' Wolsey however, informs him [Boleyn], on the King's behalf, that before long, he will create Sir Edward a baron, and will then undoubtedly make Boleyn treasurer. He intends to appoint to the controllership someone with whom Boleyn will agree when treasurer, and has desired him to let Wolsey know his mind by letter.[52]

Sections of the letter to Wolsey are candid and impetuous and, in an unguarded outburst, he claimed he would have been better off to stay home, if absence from the court was a hindrance to promotion.[53] With a great sense of dejection, Thomas wrote that he supposed Wolsey had found some fault in him, and clearly intended to promote a worthier person. If Wolsey objected to the promotion, we might ask whether he could have persuaded the King to renege on his promise. But, contrary to the usual interpretation of the incident, this exchange is not indicative of any manipulation on Wolsey's part, but suggests that he had the task of conveying a decision that may have been made without his involvement.

Thomas' tone is not one that he would have presumed to adopt with the King; however, in sending this letter, he probably wanted the King to know that he was upset and felt betrayed, sentiments he could convey to Wolsey with whom he had sufficient familiarity and trust to be completely candid. Many historians argue that Wolsey's letter bearing the news added insult to injury, because Wolsey also asked Thomas to approve of a candidate for the Comptrollership.

Yet Wolsey's letter made it clear that Poynings' appointment would be brief because he was about to be made a baron, and that Thomas would be the next Treasurer; he did not think it sensible to appoint him as Comptroller for such a short period. It would seem that Wolsey was arranging his personnel, which is why he wrote to Thomas in the first place, assuring him the job was his, next time around. Wolsey seems to have genuinely wanted Thomas' input, as he would have to deal with whoever became Comptroller in his future role as Treasurer. Furthermore, Thomas was far from court and beseeched the Cardinal to act on his behalf to ensure the King fulfilled his promise: this suggests he felt Henry had been mercurial, not Wolsey.

In any case, Wolsey must have wanted to reassure his ambassador, as news filtered through the English court that Thomas would soon be made Treasurer, news of which reached the latter who then wrote to Wolsey that he surrendered any claim that he might have had to the Comptrollership, as per Henry's previous promise. He said that he understood: 'Thay favourable mind that your grace beareth to me intending my advancement to the treasurership. Wherein I think myself more bounden to your grace than ever I can deserve.'[54] Wolsey, ever keen to keep his staff happy (especially his favourites), also engineered things so that not only was Thomas briefly awarded the position of Comptroller of the Household sometime in 1520, after Poynings, but he also successfully granted Thomas the higher position of Treasurer later on.

In the first weeks of summer, the French court learned that the Electors in Frankfurt had voted on 17 June and the duplicitous role of the English in the Imperial election was now clear. Francis' prospects had started to decline: he could not raise the necessary funds to buy his votes, and had even asked Henry for a loan of 100,000 crowns, which had been refused. The French ambassador lamented that even if it rained gold in England, Francis would not get so much as a piece, so it is little wonder that Charles, who had banked with the right merchant, was elected Holy Roman Emperor. On hearing the news, Francis' mother, Louise, Thomas wrote, 'is right glad that the King Catholique is chosen. Sayeng that though the Kyn her sonn is nat Emperor.'[55] Thomas doubted her sincerity and wrote to Wolsey that Louise would have preferred any other monarch in Europe. Francis was naturally disappointed that his rival had taken what he had so coveted, and Wolsey's letters of commiseration no doubt rang rather hollow.

Charles' election delivered him the prize, but the result drew Henry and Francis closer to each other, and sometime in August of 1519, Thomas relayed Henry's intention that the two monarchs should meet. In the final months of Thomas' French embassy and his first weeks back in England, the ambassador was appointed as a key operator in Wolsey's plans for this event, one of the most famous of Henry's reign. The Cardinal made him responsible for fixing with King Francis the ceremonial and logistical aspects of the intended meeting (referred to at the time as an 'interview') between the English and French monarchs. Thus began preparations for what would be become known as the Field of Cloth of Gold. In a spirit of camaraderie, Henry ordered Thomas to announce to Francis his intention to grow his beard until the meeting, and Francis also agreed to the gesture of mutual trust and admiration. We can detect, beneath the bravado of both monarchs, their sense of dejection at losing the prize to Charles, and how reliant they now were on each other, which explains Louise's alarm in November when she heard that Henry had failed to keep his promise and shaved his beard. His reasons are unclear; he may not have taken his oath as literally as Francis, but this morning ablution almost caused a diplomatic incident. Thomas promptly shifted the blame to someone who made a perfect scapegoat. Thomas assured Louise that it was none other than Henry's wife, Katherine, who had forced him to shave it. Louise of course knew that Katherine was Charles' aunt, and political pressure coming from these quarters through his wife may well have informed Henry's action, but Thomas ably reassured Louise of Henry's loyalty, and Louise finally conceded that 'their love us nat in the beards but in the harts'.[56]

Thomas had thus averted a potential crisis and showed an adeptness at dealing with Louise, whose confidence was perhaps even more important than that of Francis; he recognised the role that she played in Francis' decision making and knew how to exploit it. The newly found friendship between Henry and Francis was still delicate, and Thomas' intervention ensured it remained cordial. That Louise accepted his explanation for what she saw as a serious breach of their agreement may be interpreted as Thomas merely being good at his job, but her esteem for the ambassador could be traced back over several months, from the time of his arrival, and was indicative of his personal style. Numerous reports to Wolsey and the king demonstrate the increasing responsibilities imposed on Thomas, particularly in the organisation of the delegations on both sides, something that he remarked was easily done whilst he was still in France.

In late March, Thomas reported that he had an audience with Louise of Savoy and, as instructed, begged her to use her influence to have the meeting in Calais, 'where they might be honourably received, well and easily lodged, it should be convenient for their estates', rather than closer to Paris.[57] Such was Louise's respect for Thomas that she successfully lobbied Francis, and Calais was chosen: 'She saying always that it shall be more and triumphant to be lodged in summer in the fields in tents and pavilions than it should be in any Towne.'

Writing to Wolsey, Thomas asked how many people the King and Wolsey would bring over, as Francis would appoint an equal number to meet them. The Great Master, Boissy, the French counterpart of the Duke of Norfolk's position as Treasurer of the Kingdom, wanted Henry and Francis lodged at different locations to prevent a fracas between their men. Thomas agreed with King Francis that people tended to drink the most during July, the hottest month of the year, and the more inebriated the men, the more likelihood of a brawl.[58] Instructions were sent to Thomas with his formal recall in early 1520 and instructions were issued to his former colleague, Richard Wingfield, to replace him. In March Wingfield arrived at the French court as part of the ambassadorial handover, and he had only to tie up the few, but important, loose ends that remained to be worked out within the framework that Thomas had constructed. Both ambassadors had a lengthy audience with Francis at which Wingfield delivered letters from Wolsey and Henry to Francis, who expressed his 'great and sincere pleasure at their amicable terms'.[59] Francis also expressed his joy at the Cardinal's good convalescence, and said he was putting his life and safety into Wolsey's hands. Francis added that 'he should always be anxious to recompense Wolsey for the cares he had taken', Boleyn reported, 'and if there were anything in his realm elsewhere which might do the Cardinal pleasure, he might be assured thereof.'

It seemed to be a very simple exchange, but the orders for recall have been seized upon as evidence that Thomas somehow failed in this embassy. The accusation was that Thomas was 'uncourtly, plodding, and overly business-like, in short, like a middle-class merchant'.[60] Another ambiguous allegation, made by Venetian ambassadors in England, was that Thomas imparted too much information to Margaret of Austria, with whom he continued to correspond, and for that reason he was universally hated by the French court.[61] This is a bizarre accusation – there is no evidence that Boleyn wrote to Margaret, save for the discussion of his daughter's placement at her court years earlier, nor is Thomas mentioned as a source in any correspondence between Margaret and the Imperial court.

Thomas' recall after a year was not necessarily indicative of any dissatisfaction on Henry's part: he may have accepted the posting for only one year, given his commitments and family in England.

Henry's letter to Francis, to be conveyed by Wingfield, stated:

> Henry, remembering the peace and amity between them, is desirous to hear continually of the prosperity of Francis; and although he is informed of his affairs by the French ambassador in England, and by Sir Thomas Bolain, his own ambassador in France, he could not be satisfied without sending one of his 'trusty and near familiars' to him for this purpose, and to declare his love and affection for him ... He has accordingly licensed Bolain to return, and sends Wingfield in his place.[62]

A logical explanation would be that Henry and Wolsey were moving Thomas to where he was needed most, to deal with sensitive diplomatic issues that were closer to the heart of England's foreign policy. We must consider that within a few months of his return, the lavish and grand-scale meeting between Francis and Henry would take place, a meeting in which Thomas would play an important part. It seems more likely that Wolsey was positioning his key players where they would be most useful.

From the French perspective too, there is no evidence to suggest that Thomas had lost favour, or that confidence in his ability had waned. Francis wrote to Henry that Thomas was grateful to be returning home, and although this may have been the language of diplomacy, after so many months away from court and his family, it is likely that this was also the case. Louise of Savoy and Queen Claude both made specific and warm references to Boleyn upon his departure, and Louise, in her own hand rather than that of a secretary, wrote to Henry praising his ambassador, informing him that he had executed his charge in a very virtuous manner.

Thomas was still in France in the first weeks of 1520, and he was not present for the first family wedding – that of his daughter, Mary, to one young William Carey on 4 February. The greatest mark of respect to the family shows in the venue – the Chapel Royal of Greenwich Palace, where Henry and Katherine had quietly exchanged vows years before. Henry himself was present, bestowing an offering of six schillings and eight pence. Despite his absence, Thomas had clearly brokered the match with the Carey family. William was the younger son of Sir Thomas Carey, who had died in 1500. They were not astronomically high on the social ladder, but they had connections enough. His grandmother, Eleanor Beaufort, was the daughter of the Duke of Somerset, and a first cousin of Margaret Beaufort, Henry VIII's grandmother. He was much like Thomas had been in his younger years – athletic and a fine jouster. Henry had taken a liking to him, making him Esquire of the Body and Gentleman of the Privy Chamber. Thomas, as we shall see, also seemed to have a good relationship with his son-in-law, becoming a quasi father figure and advisor to the young man. The match showed great promise.

Thomas returned to England in late March 1520, and became immediately immersed in preparations for what was about to become part of one of the most highly anticipated and now famous events of Henry's reign – the Anglo-French summit, the Field of Cloth of Gold, between King Henry VIII of England and King Francis I of France. He laid the significant diplomatic groundwork for the upcoming meeting, and his replacement, Wingfield, had only to tie up the few remaining loose ends for the upcoming event. Three centuries after his death, Thomas was given the epithet of 'Picklock of Princes' – there is considerable evidence that the title was well earned.[63]

CHAPTER SIX

# Betwixt Two Princes

*Those Sons of Glory, those two lights of men,*
*Met in the Vale of Arden*

– Shakespeare, *Henry VIII*

It was a scene of enchantment, staged in a narrow field in northern France in the balmy first weeks of June 1520. This legendary Anglo-French meeting, known as the Field of Cloth of Gold, was a conscious form of political self-advertising, designed to usher in a new era of 'Universal Peace' between France and England, and Christendom, we are told, had never witnessed such a scene.[1]

Meanwhile, Charles V was showing signs of alarm at the thought of the Anglo-French meeting and pushed for his own conference with Henry and Katherine (his aunt) beforehand. Wolsey arranged to have Charles meet with Henry prior to his crossing to France and Charles was asked to wait in Calais, a French town under English jurisdiction, until after the Cloth of Gold, so the two monarchs could continue their negotiation. Unable to prevent the Anglo-French meeting, and uncertain of its consequences, Charles acquiesced in the hope of neutralising any alliance between the other monarchs. Above all, the Emperor was wary of Wolsey.[2]

Imperial ambassador Jean De la Sauch recommended that Charles be as charming and politically seductive as the French: 'We must turn their own arts against the French, and not be sparing of our promises, or Francis will make them drink his *aurum potabile* [liquid gold], and they will tipple *à la bouteille*, while our ambassadors sit looking on with folded arms ... though some may have already tasted the bottle.'[3] De la Sauch added pointedly: 'Had this been provided for three or four months ago, the French interview would never have taken place, and our own would have been arranged more consistently with our honour.'[4]

Charles went overboard in his haste to see Henry before the French interview, throwing protocol out the window.[5] Letters flew between Charles' ambassador in England and Lord Chievres, a nobleman and politician, concerned with logistics of the meeting, namely the time when Charles would arrive, how long he could stay in England before Henry left for France, and whether the time allotted was long enough to discuss all matters. But they were also anxious: would it be better to conclude everything Charles and Henry had to discuss at their meeting *before* the French interview, or should they defer everything until after it? What was clear was the exclusivity of the affair. The Archduchess Margaret, with whom Thomas was well acquainted, would be present, and Henry would be accompanied by his queen and Wolsey. Apart from bodyguards, the retinues would all be unarmed, and both groups were to be equal in number.[6] In his new position as Comptroller of the Household, Thomas worked closely with Sir Edward Poynings, the Treasurer, to arrange all accommodation for the Imperial side.

Unfavourable winds delayed the journey, but on 26 May Charles landed at Dover where he was met by Henry, Wolsey and a small group of men, Thomas and Poynings included, all of them passing the night at Dover Castle. The next day, Whitsunday, they rode to Canterbury where Katherine awaited them. What transpired at this first meeting is not known, nor is it entirely clear what Thomas' role was in the preparations for it, or in the meeting itself, but he was present at almost every public and private negotiation between Henry and Charles. Both sides are decidedly vague as to what had been achieved during Charles' visit, and Charles was forced to wait until Henry and his court returned from the main event: the Field of Cloth of Gold, which was proving to be so anticipated that commissioners found it difficult to restrict the English and French retinues to a manageable size. Henry's was eventually set at 3,997 people and 2,087 horses, while the Queen was permitted 1,175 people and 778 horses.[7] The English court arrived in Calais on 31 May, remaining there until 4 June, when they moved to Guisnes. The whole Boleyn family took part in events. Elizabeth Boleyn was appointed to attend Queen Katherine, as was their daughter, Mary Carey.[8] Her husband, William, was also in attendance, and Thomas was probably accompanied by his son George in his retinue of attendants. Thomas' younger brother, Edward, and his wife, Anne, were also a part of both royal households.[9] Across the field on the French side, Anne, who had been in France for several years, was more than likely part of the retinue as a maid of Queen Claude's.

Tentative tendrils of communication stretched out over a series of days, beginning with the Cardinal riding out to meet King Francis, accompanied by a small army of 100 archers of the guard and 50 gentlemen of his household, clothed in crimson velvet with chains of gold. Crimson velvet was *de rigueur*, for in the middle of it all rode Cardinal Wolsey, resplendent in a 'velvet upon crimson velvet figured', his red hat hanging with tassels, and Wolsey himself mounted on a barded mule with buckles and stirrups of fine gold, and the trappings of – what else – crimson velvet.[10]

Following the Cardinal were other clergymen and a further 50 archers, dressed in red velvet with golden roses, their bows bent. Wolsey rode in this state to Ardres, where he was met by King Francis with a fanfare of trumpets. The next day Francis sent his own group, including the Archbishop of Sens, and the Admiral, La Trimouille, all dressed in cloth of gold. Henry welcomed them warmly into his tent, and it was reported that 'the lords of England feasted the French lords in their tents marvellously, from the greatest to the least'. Trust had been earned on both sides, it did not seem as though either party would betray the other, and a day was fixed for the two young kings to meet. On the Thursday, artillery sounded on each side, to let the kings know of each other's departure. Thomas was one of the 40 specially appointed men from government, the nobility and the Church, who rode out with Henry to personally greet Francis, on the evening of 7 June. They each marched with splendid retinues, blazing with the nobility, captains, constables and admirals, accompanied by musicians.

Henry was dressed in silver damask, decorated with cloth of gold, and riding on a horse also trapped in gold. Francis was equally handsome, wearing a mantle of cloth of gold, covered with jewels. The two kings pulled ahead of their respective parties, urging their horses forward and gaining speed as they rode towards each other. Both raised their right arms and doffed their feathered caps as they passed each other. Their retinues cheered loudly as Henry and Francis dismounted and embraced.[11] Now, festivities could truly begin.

Three hundred tents were pitched, their tapestried walls and ceilings stitched with roses. Henry and Katherine slept in a temporary palace of timber, pierced on every side with oriel windows glazed with gold and joined to Guisnes Castle.[12] The hallways and galleries flowed with fluted white silk, and the walls were panelled with antique carvings and dozens of priceless tapestries, Turkish carpets and cushions.[13] A chapel was attached, extravagantly adorned in cloth of gold tissue, pearls and priceless materials. To render the chapel especially fine, the vestments from Henry VII's chapel at Westminster were brought in for the occasion and real stained-glass windows inserted. Outside the palace gate there stood a beautifully wrought gilt fountain, with a statue of Bacchus whose cups literally ran red with claret, cleverly pumped in by secret conduits so the wine seemingly sprang from the earth. Even the palace gate was imposing, boasting the figures of Hercules, Alexander the Great and other ancient heroes all richly decorated and painted. Wolsey seems to have been taken with the extravagant display: shortly after his return from France he went on a spending spree, ordering 22 sets of tapestries (comprising more than 200) from the Netherlands, through London merchant Richard Gresham, to adorn his palaces. The next day Thomas, George and William Carey would have stood under a summer sun so scorching that a Venetian ambassador accompanying Francis wrote 'that it could not have been hotter in St. Peter's at Home'.[14] The young kings seemed not to mind the heat, walking slowly towards the tents, where they remained for a short time, before dismissing a red-faced and sweating Wolsey who wished to escape the sun. According to the Venetian, the Cardinal gratefully returned to a tent 'where the wine was'.[15]

With the summer heat came storms and gales, which blew relentlessly through the camps. Thomas may well have taken satisfaction that his side were more prepared – the English timber structures, masterminded by Wolsey, were built, for the most part, to withstand such a force, but the pretty French tents were constantly being blown away. Following this first meeting between the two monarchs, the main attraction was the jousting tournament. Specially built galleries which seated the Kings and Queens of England and France were hung with rich tapestries. Fourteen teams, comprising of ten to 12 men were the 'Answerers' to the French challengers.[16] Altogether, over 100 men participated, however the Venetian and Florentine records have up to 300. Somewhere among them, it is highly likely that Thomas participated, as did his brother-in-law, Thomas Howard, and his son-in-law, William Carey. George, approximately 16, would have been among the spectators. It was without a doubt one of the most extravagant displays of medieval tourney in Henry's entire reign.

The events of the Field of Cloth of Gold wound down after 17 days and the two kings parted. Henry now returned to Charles, awaiting a conclusion to the meetings begun in England. Thomas was amongst the knights who accompanied Henry and Wolsey to these Imperial negotiations as he had already proved to be adept in negotiations, but more significantly, also present was his friend and sparring partner at Mechelin, Charles' aunt, the Archduchess Margaret. This second meeting between Henry and Charles achieved several key aims: the renewal of older treaties between the two, and an agreement that neither party was to enter into treaty with any prince without the consent of the other. Both meetings had taken months of preparation and cost an obscene amount of money, and yet, despite the sheer scale of these two meetings, all three kings – Henry, Francis and Charles – viewed the treaties they signed, hand on heart, more as guidelines. It had been a politically significant year and, after months abroad, the Boleyn family patriarch was able to spend time at the English court with his family, attending to domestic duties and concerns, but the peaceful pattern of court life was short lived.

Within the space of a few months, the Boleyns had to contend with two unrelated but significant issues, one which caused friction between Thomas and his brother-in-law, Thomas Howard, now Earl of Surrey upon his father's elevation to the Dukedom of Norfolk. Surrey was unquestionably one of the wolves of Henry's court. He was a ruthless soldier, with a disdain for diplomacy and ineptitude for tact, which partially informed his appointment as Lord Lieutenant of Ireland in the spring of 1520. Among other matters of governance, he turned his attention to the unresolved matter of the Earldom of Ormond, which Thomas had pursued for several years. But Surrey's solution was for young Anne Boleyn to marry James Butler, son of Piers Butler, their rival to the Earldom of Ormond. Norfolk had not even consulted his brother-in-law, taking the matter to the King and the Cardinal.

While such a marriage would see the title go to Anne and her husband, thus benefitting the family on the whole, it would skip Thomas entirely. The title was a personal issue: it was his grandfather's title, and it was obviously deeply symbolic for him, and his mother was probably against the idea of her father's title being lost within the family. This may have been why Henry cautiously responded to Surrey's proposal, suggesting that he ascertain whether the current Earl of Ormond was open to the idea, while he would advance the matter with other parties. Conversations may well have occurred behind closed doors between Thomas and the King, but there is no written record of Henry discussing the proposal with his courtier.

Surrey, on the other hand, did discuss the matter with Wolsey, who, at first, seemed inclined towards the proposal, but made no effort to bring anything about. Then, in a rather pushy move, Surrey wrote to Wolsey on 6 October 1520, declaring that he thought 'it would be advantageous if a marriage were solemnised between the Earl of Ormond's son, now in England, and Sir Thomas Boleyn's daughter'.[17]

At the time, James Butler, the potential groom, was being raised in Wolsey's household, and his presence there was, to some degree, used as an incentive to keep Butler Senior in line.[18] So did Wolsey have any intention of marrying Anne off, especially considering he must have known that her father was less than pleased about the match? It is unlikely, but he could at least feign enthusiasm. The most interesting part of this correspondence is what it tells us of Thomas and his brother-in-law, and it would not be the last time tension ignited between the two. The matter of Ormond was put on hold for the time being which suited Thomas – he would wait it out. And within a few weeks, both King and Cardinal had another, more pressing, concern – Edward Stafford, Duke of Buckingham.

Stafford was powerful in his own right, a little too regal for his own good, and wealthier than any other man save for the King, but it was the ancient Plantagenet blood running through his veins that had always marked him as a potential threat. But Stafford, reputedly articulate and witty, had always played a major role in court events, much like the Boleyns, present for the myriad of royal weddings, births, christenings and funerals. Although he danced on the periphery of Henry's inner circle, he was never a close confidant of the King but he was well respected among the elite and was something of a representative for the nobility. But it was Wolsey, who had clashed with Stafford on occasion, and whose eyes followed the proud Duke whenever he attended court, who quietly planted the seed in the King's mind – how loyal *was* Stafford? Throughout the latter half of 1520, evidence was secretly compiled and, in April of 1521, Stafford was accused of having listened to prophecies of the King's death and of his own succession to the crown, and of having expressed an intention to kill the King. The charges seemed to come without warning or logic.

On 16 April Stafford was sent to the Tower, and Thomas, among other nobles, was appointed to special commissions of Oyer and Terminer – meaning to 'hear and determine' in both East Greenwich in Kent and at Southwark in Surrey. These two commissions found indictments against the Duke on 6 and 7 May respectively, and Buckingham was tried before 17 of his peers, presided over by Thomas' father-in-law, the 80-year-old Duke of Norfolk, on 10 May in the Court of the Lord High Steward at Westminster. The evidence was no more than hearsay, but he was found guilty and executed on Tower Hill on 17 May 1521.[19]

The Duke's lands were all returned to the Crown, and Henry wasted little time distributing them. The Boleyns did well, receiving the manors of Penshurst, Tunbridge, Northleigh, Fobbing and Northlands. It is not clear how Thomas felt about the trial, but his father-in-law was said to have wept as he read out the guilty verdict. If the King could execute a duke of such prestigious lineage, what else might he be capable of?

Beyond England's shores, the accession of Charles V to the throne of the Holy Roman Empire intensified Hapsburg–Valois struggles for supremacy, among the Italian states. After allying himself with the papacy against Francis in 1521, Charles moved to replace French rule in the powerful Italian state of Milan.[20]

Wolsey's desire for the papal tiara had not abated, and it may have, to some degree, dictated his diplomatic policy, tying England to Charles, whose alliance with the Pope placed Wolsey closer to his papal goal.[21] But as we have seen, England did not align itself only with Imperial interests, but sought to get closer to French ones as well. Acting as an intermediary between the two empires placed England in a strong position, and it was a great honour for Henry to defuse the situation 'betwixt these two princes'.[22]

It was decided that Cardinal Wolsey would set sail for France, and Thomas was chosen as part of the retinue alongside Sir Thomas More, the Bishops of Ely and Durham, and Lord Docwra.[23] Wolsey may well have chosen Thomas as both Francis and his mother considered him to be a reliable diplomat, and his presence would perhaps assuage any concerns and suspicions they may have had.

On 2 August, the English embassy landed at Calais in style, and Thomas was among a number of nobles, knights, courtiers and servants, with the Great Seal of England carried proudly as part of the display. The French had become quite apprehensive due to the recent provocative actions by Robert de La Marck, Duke of Bouillon, who marched on Charles' city of Luxemburg.[24] The Duke's dominions straddled France and the Holy Roman Empire, but his act of aggression was interpreted as being on Francis' behalf, and they anticipated retaliation.

As this development required a swift response, Wolsey immediately divided his embassy into two, and assigned a special envoy to reassure Francis, while the Cardinal personally accompanied a delegation, which included Thomas, to Charles in Bruges. The two groups carried the same message, that England would undertake to negotiate a peace settlement between them, but should either party refuse to negotiate, England would be forced to intervene.

Perhaps the seriousness of these terms was part of the reason why Wolsey chose to take Thomas; Charles was now the potential aggressor, but Thomas had excellent credibility with Margaret of Austria, Charles' aunt, and Wolsey had to make use of any advantage they might have and perhaps thought it prudent to bring along a man who had an intimate and affectionate first-hand knowledge of her methods and character. Despite the lack of evidence, it is reasonable to assume that Margaret and Thomas were glad to be reacquainted, almost a decade after their last meeting.

The negotiations in Bruges lasted 13 days and, on 25 August 1521, the two sides reached an agreement, which was a considerable departure from the

English embassy's original mission statement. Charles, Margaret and Wolsey had agreed to form an anti-French alliance, and that they were 'henceforth friends of friends, and enemies of enemies', and were to declare themselves open enemies to King Francis in March 1523 and 'make war upon him by land and sea'.[25] The Treaty of Bruges, as it was known, would include an English invasion of France before 15 May of that year, in which 'the Emperor shall furnish [Henry] with ships or hoys [haenes] for transporting his army'.[26] It would be a conquest of monumental proportions – if it became a reality.

Unfortunately for Wolsey his duplicitous scheme had been discovered when letters from Charles to the Cardinal were intercepted. This forced the latter to despatch Thomas back to the French, this time accompanied by Lord Docwra, to dispel reports that England was preparing its forces with Charles against France – which they were. Thomas embellished the truth, assuring the French Chancellor, Du Praet, that such manoeuvres were merely customary for that time of year, but his assurances were not accepted.[27] Wolsey did not leave him with the French long enough for the ambassador to redeem himself or the Cardinal; he was replaced at the French court by other less talented ambassadors, who would continue to attempt to soothe Francis' disquiet. Instead, Wolsey sent Boleyn and Docwra to Charles once more to persuade the Emperor to postpone any altercation he might be planning; Francis' and Charles' troops were now close enough to engage in battle. The ambassadors picked up Richard Wingfield, who had replaced Thomas at the French court over a year previously, and travelled to meet the Emperor at Oudenarde, modern day Belgium.[28] Wolsey's anxious instructions to them were indicative of an older man surrounded by young and battle-hungry monarchs. Thomas and Docwra were instructed to assure the Emperor of the 'faithful mind and will he [Wolsey] bears to the Emperor, and the desire he has for the safety and advancement of his affairs, to which end he stays on this side of the sea, leaving all his business, and that of the realm'.[29] The Cardinal was also concerned that, much like his own king, Charles was surrounded by 'young folks' who, Wolsey fretted, would goad him into a battle. If this were the case, the ambassadors would have to exert pressure on the Emperor to dissuade him, by focusing on Charles' weak points: he would lose a great deal of money, his troops had suffered illness and disease recently, and, as it was not the right time of year for a campaign, a victory was far from assured.

But Thomas modified this approach somewhat. Rather than tell Charles what he should *not* do, he confided that Henry was not ready for war, financially or otherwise, to which Charles grudgingly admitted that he too had neither the numbers nor military strength.[30] But persuading him to keep to his territories and not provoke France was another matter. As Wolsey complained to his ambassadors in Oudenarde: 'I have been laboring for such a pacification between the Emperor and the French king as you advise, and have gained the confidence of the chancellor of France here ... but the more the French give way, the more obstinate I find the Emperor's chancellor.'[31]

It had been a rather circuitous and pointless exercise, and there is little point in delving deeper into what were extraordinarily convoluted and seemingly endless negotiations. In the end, Wolsey wrote to both sets of ambassadors, stating that if no one could come to an agreement, both embassies were to accompany him back to England. The details of negotiations provide no further insight into Boleyn's involvement, and therefore it is only necessary to note that with matters concluded, the men prepared to take their leave. However, the ever-suspicious Charles requested that the English contingency not leave all at once. Wingfield was ill, and so Thomas and Docwra left for Bruges.

By 10 November, Wolsey had officially ordered the two groups to make ready to return to him at Calais. Arriving the next day, the men all attended Mass, after which Docwra too became so ill that the return home of all three was delayed for several days. Only Thomas remained in good health, though whether this was due to a rugged constitution or luck is unclear. Shortly before departing, Thomas learned that Edward Poynings, Treasurer of the Household, had died. Wingfield hastily wrote to Wolsey that Thomas hoped to succeed Poynings as Treasurer (which Wolsey already knew) and pleaded with the Cardinal to be awarded Comptroller, who would work with the Treasurer, for 'I cannot use any other way to come to further promotion but by the advancement and setting forth of your grace.' Thomas would formally be made Treasurer in a few months; Wingfield was unsuccessful. The Treaty of Bruges was ratified in Calais, with England, The Holy Roman Empire, and the Pope joined in an alliance against France.

As the embassy prepared to leave, Francis suspected that Henry was in the process of selling him out in favour of Charles. He had found out about the Treaty of Bruges against him, and that shipments of gunpowder and cannon balls were going to Antwerp and that England was building ships, and he noted that 'the daughter of Mr. Boullan' (Anne Boleyn) and several English scholars who had been studying in Paris were returning home.

Francis was right to be suspicious – several members of the English embassy, led by Thomas, were also engaging in espionage. A merchant trading in England, Perpoynte Devauntter, had been captured by the French at Boulogne and interrogated about England's war plans, although why a merchant would have knowledge of the government's war plans in this case is unclear. He was eventually released on the proviso that he should henceforth report to the French from England any information about the English movements which he might think useful to the French.[32]

Thomas, assisted by Sir Henry Marney, interviewed the merchant for two days and allowed him to return to France. Recognising that a merchant could travel freely without arousing suspicion, Thomas and his fellow inquisitor turned the merchant into a double agent. They instructed him not to conceal what ships and men were being prepared in England because the French had their own spies and would know England was preparing for war.[33]

In these early months of 1522, English policy displayed every colour of the spectrum – from missions of peace to grand campaigns.[34] Thomas had to keep up with these changes, and sometimes he was wrong-footed, although he displayed a remarkable flexibility and resilience in the face of English changeability in this period. Following the English departure from the continent in late 1521, another meeting between Charles and Henry had been arranged, and would take place in England in May of 1522. Charles felt that England needed further coaxing to go to war. Charles was escorted by the King, the Cardinal, and a retinue which included Thomas and other ambassadors, to Canterbury for a conference, at which Thomas was one of the courtiers appointed to attend upon the King. Now Treasurer of the Household, as Wolsey had promised, Thomas along with other household officials, was in charge of making numerous arrangements, and with the Comptroller of the Household arranged lodgings for Charles at Dover – where he would first land – and Canterbury, as well as the other various stops along the route to Windsor where a peace treaty would be signed. The treaty of Bruges had amounted to nothing, and Wolsey, like his predecessor and mentor Bishop Fox, always found wars too expensive, and attempted to pause the Treaty of Bruges which had stipulated war on France, advised Henry to agree to another alliance with Charles, including a marriage agreement between the Emperor and Princess Mary, to be deferred until England could prepare for an active role in Charles' war with France. The Treaty of Windsor, as it was known, was negotiated on 19 June 1522 and concluded the next day. Thomas was one of the witnesses.[35]

Jousts and celebrations were planned, and while the English thought they were showcasing the very best the Tudor court had to offer, the Imperial ambassadors' reports suggested that they were far from impressed. Martin De Salinas, Ambassador of the Archduke Ferdinand at the Imperial court, cousin of Maria De Salinas, a dear friend of Queen Katherine, had no good news to report. The weather was abysmal, the food served in Dover was almost inedible, although Henry had promised to send 600 horses, the necessary number could not be obtained, and the journey to London was extremely fatiguing. Charles' lodgings were subpar, the jousts feeble, and no foreigners were allowed to take part. De Salinas also doubted (rightfully) that Charles would marry Princess Mary, as per the treaty, writing: 'I will not believe it until I see it.'

Despite the complaints, if nothing else, the negotiations resulted in Thomas and Dr Richard Sampson being appointed in August as special ambassadors to Charles V in Spain, alongside Thomas' former colleague, Spinelly, already appointed as resident ambassador.

It is of particular interest that Wolsey assigned the men to Charles' court, as it is reasonable to presume that, as Charles was well acquainted with Thomas, he may have even requested his attendance. Wolsey must have realised that appointing Thomas as special envoy would undermine Spinelly's credibility.

However, Wolsey and Henry not only continued to use the special envoys to Charles, but sometimes directed the envoys to circumvent their resident ambassador. We know this because for this mission there were two sets of instructions – Spinelly was only aware of one set. The formal instructions were primarily concerned with negotiations against the French.[36] A second, secret set of instructions ordered Sampson and Boleyn to report on the progress of the preparations:

> First, they are to dwell much on the King's great affection for the Emperor, with as pleasant words as they can devise, marking his gesture and countenance, and how he receives it; and to discover in what sort of esteem he is held by his subjects, and whether they are likely to provide him with money. 2ndly, what is really the state of the enterprise against France. 3rdly, how he is stored. 4thly, on what terms the Burgundians stand with the Spaniards. 5thly, what means were used with the Pope for an abstinence of war between France and the Emperor, what is the Emperor's inclination, and what secret messages pass. 6thly, what drifts are practised between the Emperor and the king of Portugal. 7thly, to urge him to invade Guienne.[37]

Two sets of instructions would mean two sets of negotiations, and the Imperial court would be aware that one member of the embassy was not privy to all negotiations, an embarrassing position for Spinelly.

The two special envoys journeyed to Plymouth from where they would sail to Spain, but violent weather delayed the voyage. With no end in sight to the bad weather, the fleet had no choice but to risk setting sail, and was almost immediately caught in a storm which decimated a number of ships. The *Mary James*, carrying Thomas, ran aground, and the ambassadors later reported that Thomas' priest lay near death, and two of Sampson's servants, plus one of the

Windsor Herald – an officer of arms from the College of Arms – had drowned.[38] The men transferred to one of the undamaged ships and they sailed again, but within two days they were besieged by six Breton ships which attacked them on their windward side. With only one defence ship left, the crew 'hadde cowchyd such beddes stuffyd with straw' and other things for barricades while Thomas' ship was 'rent open in all the one side of the stern that scarcely two hides might stop it'.[39] The ship Thomas and Sampson were aboard managed to capture and board one of the Breton ships as the others fled. The storm which eventually took the life of Thomas' priest and threatened to engulf the entire fleet had a deep impact on him. Between the storms buffeting the body of the ship as it lurched between the waves, and the roar of cannons from enemy ships, Thomas vowed to himself that if he survived the crossing, after his embassy, he would go on pilgrimage to Santiago de Compostela.[40]

The embassy did survive and, finally, the small fleet arrived at Laredo on 11 October 1522.

The bad luck continued. Thomas and Sampson, nerves frayed and longing for home before they had even begun, were despondent that lodgings were scarce, and Charles was out hunting when they arrived. Instead, Cesar, Charles' master of the horse, amused them with running the swift 'genets'.

Their arrival was also met with the news that Spinelly had recently died, which precluded a debriefing, so without their first point of contact, they wrote to Wolsey to ask what ciphers they should use to encode any sensitive information, sending him a few to choose from.[41] The ambassadorial reports over the next months are as numerous as they are detailed, and both men were constantly trying to ascertain how seriously Charles was regarding a joint war against France.

A competent ambassador surveys the court to glean intelligence. An exceptional ambassador surveys the fields and the land beyond the court, to assess the true health of the nation, economic or otherwise. And Spain, as far as Thomas was concerned, was a far cry from France or England. Dry, not very fertile, and much depleted from the civil wars of the previous year, it was clear to Thomas that Charles would not be able to raise much capital in Spain to help with the conquest of France. Of Charles, the ambassadors initially reported that they thought 'there is no man more faithful to the King than the Emperor', but soon they conceded that: 'We have less comfort of the Emperor now than at any other time. He [Charles] complains of poverty, and declines to raise more than the ordinary number of men; – makes many excuses.'[42]

Regardless of their complaints, Wolsey wrote to his ambassadors on 10 January 1523 and addressing them as 'My loving Friends' he urged the men to continue their mission, and instructed them to deliver the letters he had sent with the correspondence, which congratulated Charles on 'his good health, of his daily successes, his prudence in pardoning his disobedient subjects, of the good speed of those sent by his majesty for the discovery of new lands and finding of the spicery'.[43]

The Cardinal also acknowledged their warning regarding Charles' finances, but instructed them to ask for naval assistance, 'for fleets to guard the seas'. It might seem as though the Cardinal was ignoring his ambassadors, with their reports to England which hinted at Charles' weakness, but they spurred Henry and his Cardinal on to be more uncompromising in negotiations. Charles, like his grandfather Maximilian, was adept at stalling, and kept negotiations in the same circuitous route from mid-December to mid-January of 1523. It was clear that Charles had no serious intention of invading France with Henry – he would rather Henry pay all the costs of a war, and keep France occupied, while Charles himself secured key Italian states such as Navarre and Naples.[44]

In addition to the stress Charles' stalling caused, Sampson was also in the midst of his own personal issues. In March of 1523, Sampson asked Wolsey for an increase in his allowance, writing that: 'things are so dear he will not be able to continue here. If he had a more agreeable and liberal colleague, he could get on better.'[45]

Sampson seems to be suggesting that he asked Thomas for financial assistance, but was rejected: yet Thomas borrowed money himself from several merchants, so he may have been a little short of cash himself.[46]

There is no evidence that Thomas had to chase payment or extra funds, or his ambassadorial diets from the Cardinal, not because it was unnecessary, but perhaps because he wished to maintain favour: to become a burden to the Cardinal, however warranted, was undesirable.

Thomas seems to have been recalled, or asked to be recalled, and was replaced by Sir Richard Jerningham. This replacement suggests that the embassy had not concluded. Thomas departed court on 18 March, but not for England. He had made a vow at the beginning of his embassy, and it was no empty promise. It was the same pilgrimage Katherine of Aragon had made years before, when she was a young princess on her way to England, to see the relics of St James. It was not an easy road to travel, and the details of Thomas' journey – who, if anyone, accompanied him, if he walked all or part of the way or used a mule – are lost to history. By this time, pilgrimage was not as popular as it had been in previous decades, and the fact that Thomas chose to embark on such a physical and spiritual journey marked him as a man of deep medieval tradition. After quietly giving thanks for his survival, he returned to the bustling Imperial court in late April and met once more with the Emperor. Upon his departure for England, Charles wrote to Wolsey saying that he had given the English diplomat oral instructions concerning the two sovereigns and was sending letters to the King and Cardinal. But Charles then wrote a personal letter to Thomas, suggesting his deep respect for the ambassador and that he was aware of how much sway Thomas held:

> When you first spoke to me about a truce it seemed to me a holy object, and for our common good. I have since heard from my maréchal de logis, who has just returned from Rome with letters from the pope, that the French show little disposition toward a truce, making unjust and unreasonable demands which it would be neither honourable nor profitable for Henry and me to grant. There seems little likelihood of a truce, therefore, until we can force the French to accept one. They are often fickle, and may change their minds, but the surest course is to be ready to compel them to see reason ... I am writing as above to M. de Praet, my ambassador, but I have found you so good and loyal a servant of the king of England, and so zealous for the common cause, that I wish you to be fully informed of all these things, which your prudence will know how to bring to a good conclusion.[47]

Thomas arrived back in London saddled with unexpected baggage – Charles had sent an unofficial ambassador named Bewreyn to accompany him. When the men arrived in London, Brewreyn was shocked that Thomas abandoned him to find his own accommodation, as the latter made his way to court. He must have complained to someone, as it got back to Jerningham, who reported the incident to the Duke of Suffolk, albeit months after the fact: 'Boleyn suddenly shook him off in the midst of London, and would not help him to a lodging.'[48]

But as Brewreyn was not an official ambassador, what was his role, exactly, and why should Thomas have been responsible for assisting him with lodging? Thomas must have been anxious to get to court, and no one else seems to have offered any assistance, either. Perhaps the men had a disagreement en route, or Thomas assumed the man could make his own arrangements. In any case, it was a minor incident that in no way affected the latter's reputation, or overshadowed what he had achieved while in Spain.

After his departure the letters coming out of Spain decreased in frequency to the point that Henry complained to Wolsey, who in turn chastised Sampson and Jerningham:

> The King is much surprised that he has received no letters since their last mentioning the arrival of Jernegan. This is a great disadvantage to his affairs, as the negotiations of Beaureyn with the Duke have been concluded, as they will see by the copy of his letter enclosed.[49]

Wolsey's reprimand resulted in more frequent correspondence, but it is clear that both Wolsey and Henry had become accustomed to Thomas' detailed and frequent despatches, suggesting his performance was preferred.

Once back at court, Thomas resumed his domestic duties. His role as Treasurer of the Household was an enormous responsibility. So often this title is referred to almost glibly, without much attention to what this job entailed. Close to the centre of the King's household, second only to the Lord Steward – George Talbot, Earl of Shrewsbury – Thomas was required to spend time in the counting house, monitoring the supply of provisions, keeping supply books current, and appointing and instructing purveyors. He would get down to business at 8am, and, alongside his second-in-command, Henry Guildford, Comptroller of the Household, they were to examine daily, between eight and nine, the books of all the officers of the household to determine the expenses of the previous day.[50] While Thomas was in office, job descriptions and rules of procedure were devised for the conduct of the principal household officers, and he was one of the few officials who could grant licences for other members of the household to leave the court. He would only remain in the position between 1521 and 1525; nevertheless, he may well have played a part in the formulation of 'practices and procedures' in his department. It was a role he took seriously, but further rewards and responsibilities were on the cards.

As demonstrated by the countless pageants, tournaments and elaborate processions, Henry loved chivalric tradition but also wanted to be as *au courant* as the courts of Europe. Henry's father had, as mentioned, introduced the Burgundian tradition of tournaments, and he had also continued to revamp the chivalric orders, namely the Most Noble Order of the Garter, founded by Edward III in 1348, and regarded as the oldest and most prestigious order of chivalry. Henry VIII's grandfather, the Yorkist king Edward IV, had been spurred into competition by the – not quite as ancient, but certainly more glorious – Order of the Golden Fleece, founded by Philip the Good, Duke of Burgundy, in 1430. Under Edward, St George's Chapel at Windsor was redeveloped – being the spiritual home of the Order of the Garter, and the Tudors continued what Edward had begun. Henry VII introduced the great collar of the Order to rival that of the Golden Fleece and, while the Order consisted of only 25 members, for the first time, foreign princes and dignitaries could also be inducted. Under both Tudor monarchs, the Garter Feasts and ceremonies became an important representation of royal prestige and glory, and, for those chosen, it was one of the highest ceremonial honours one could receive. According to tradition, each knight was assigned to a stall in the chapel, and to commemorate the induction, a small brass plate was created, emblazoned with the knight's family crest. Thomas' plate displayed the Butler falcon, and his grandfather's motto: 'Nowe Thus.' It would have to be updated to correspond with Thomas' continued rise.

Thomas became part of an order to which his Howard father and brothers-in-law and his great-grandfather, Thomas Hoo, had belonged. Besides the premier nobility, Henry had bestowed the honour on men he liked, such as Charles Brandon, and those who had performed exemplary service to king and country, as Thomas had. And yet, in the eyes of many historians, this honour was for services rendered. Mary, his lively, pretty daughter, had captured Henry's attention, though when, and for how long, is unclear. All references to this are to be found years after the fact, brought to light during Anne's own relationship with the King. The generally accepted date is sometime in 1522, and it is of course understandable that many would suspect, or even expect, that a monarch would reward not only his mistress (then wife, in Anne's case), but her family as well. This great honour has been attributed to this liaison.[51] There is no way to determine which honours Thomas *might* have received as the father of the royal mistresses and which honours he earned for his loyal and extremely valuable services to the King, which continued throughout Mary's and Anne's association with Henry.

Another piece of evidence that can appear to suggest that Thomas profited from Mary's liaison concerns the materialising of a ship in the Tudor fleet in September 1523, with the name of *Mary Boleyn*, and an assumed possible link to Thomas' daughter. Rather than being named in her honour, however, the records of the ship provide a different insight into the matter. The several documents that survive name a captured French warship called the *Mary of Boloyne*, Boloyne being another variation of the French town of Boulogne. The circumstances for the ship's appearance in the fleet, and its naming, would seem to derive from the war between France and England (the latter assisted by the Holy Roman Empire), which commenced with the Duke of Suffolk's invasion of France in 1523.[52] Crucially, the English naval fleet had intended to attack Boulogne harbour, but were unable to do so due to adverse weather conditions and, on 20 August 1523, Wolsey recalled the fleet, instructing them to return to Portsmouth.[53] But the ships were involved in numerous skirmishes, and the English managed to capture several French ships. The ships were listed in January of 1524 as: the *Mary of Homflete* (Hornfleur), the *Galley of Dieppe*, the *Michael of Dieppe*, the *Griffin of Dieppe*, the *Yennett Purwyn* (Jenette Purwyn), and the *Mary of Boloyn* (Boulogne).[54] With the exception of the *Jenette Purwyn*, a Danish ship captured in 1511, the remaining ships were all captured in 1522, and Dieppe, Boulogne and Hornfleur were all coastal towns south-west of Calais, but only appear in the list in 1524 as they were to change hands. It is also worth noting that in 1528 Francis I travelled 'from St. Germain's to the abbey of St. Genevra, and thence to St. Mary of Boleyne, not far from Paris, thanking God and St. Mary'.[55]

This is not necessarily irrefutable evidence that the ship was not in any way linked to Mary Boleyn – but there is enough evidence to suggest other, equally plausible theories as to the provenance and naming of the ship, and it is certainly difficult to argue absolutely that the ship was named specifically to honour or reward Thomas himself, or his daughter. Henry sold the moieties of the *Mary of Boloyne* in 1524, along with the other naval prizes captured late in 1523, to Captain Christopher Coo.[56] As we are unable to determine when Henry's interest in Mary waned, it is difficult to link the ship's acquisition and later sale to the affair. But it is clear that Thomas' star was on the rise long before his daughters became mistresses to the King. It even managed to remain stable to some extent after their fall, as we shall see, most likely because Thomas' sources of power, wealth and influence were numerous, with several foundations, and evidently not solely tied to his children.

Thomas' service to the King continued unabated during his daughter's association with Henry and, in 1523, he was again part of a commission, alongside William Warham, Cobham, and others to 'practice' with all persons in Kent having £40 or more in goods or land whose names were on the King's subsidy list. For purposes of the subsidy, Thomas' wealth was assessed at £1,100 in lands, wages and fees – a number of his colleagues were only assessed at £300.[57] Thomas continued to serve as a loyal courtier and, on 5 September 1523, when Henry's army, led by Suffolk, invaded France with a force of some 20,000 men, it became necessary to fortify England's coasts from French raiders. Thomas had played a part in the diplomatic process which had set the war between the Holy Roman Empire, England and the Papal States against France in motion. Now, if war came to England, he would be among several men chosen as part of a commission to repel the landing of enemy forces. By the end of October, coastal watches were stationed along the Cinque Ports – the five port towns of Sandwich, Dover, Hythe, New Romney and Hastings – while ships patrolled the coast. Commissioners were required to organise and superintend the men in this service who resided in their own areas of jurisdiction; Thomas would be in command of troops in the event of invasion.

After some delay Suffolk finally invaded France on 5 September with a force of some 20,000 men and would eventually advance to within 50 miles of Paris. Unfortunately he made it no further, the rhythm of war grinding to a halt.

Events conspired against him – lack of provisions, unending rain and a lack of reinforcements meant that the army had to retreat to Calais. Henry had emptied his treasury in an illusory quest for the crown of France. He had badgered Wolsey to request £800,000 from Parliament over four years – he had initially been awarded only £600,000 over two years, of which only about £150,000 was finally collected. It was not enough to help Suffolk. Charles and Francis continued their war, but England was out for the time being. Insolvency for Charles, however, was quite common – his dominions were littered with promises of repayments – but Francis arrived in the south of France at the head of around 40,000 men and the Imperial army was forced to retreat back into Italy, and his troops, months in arrears, had only two options before them: victory or a truce.

In mid-October 1524, Francis crossed the Alps and advanced on Milan at the head of his army, taking the city from Imperial forces without much difficulty, though the fact that the Imperial troops were weakened by plague may have helped. The French council of war, held after Francis captured Milan, was faced with two options – either besiege the town of Pavia, which would remove the threat to their flank, or pursue the Imperial army and destroy them at Lodi, to where they had retreated, before they had a chance to reform. Francis chose not to listen to his highly experienced advisors, especially Anne de Montmorency, Admiral of France, who favoured the latter option, and followed the brash suggestions of one Guillaume Gouffier, Lord of Bonnivet. It was a foolish choice – the Imperial army had not had a chance to fortify their position at Lodi, whereas the Pavia garrison *was* heavily fortified and led by de Leyva, a supremely skilled and experienced commander. The decision perplexed the English too, as Henry's ambassador, Richard Pace, wrote that Francis had recklessly attacked, and in half an hour the French lost 2,000 men, adding 'I know not what hope he can have, except that the Imperials may lack money'. Francis then adopted another tactic – fortify his camp and starve the garrison into surrender. Time, he must have reasoned, was a far more dangerous enemy, and indeed it was, but for both sides. Francis continued the siege throughout the bitter Northern Italian winter, plagued with sickness throughout his army and lack of provisions.

In England, Wolsey had been informed that Francis had boasted of invading the powerful city state of Naples, but would have to journey through the Papal States, currently aligned with Charles. By mid-December, Francis and Pope Clement were formally allied, and Francis despatched a force of 11,000 men to conquer Naples, led by John Stuart, Duke of Albany, who Thomas had taken a disliking to when he was last in France. These troops would be badly missed at Pavia.

On the evening of 23 February, the Imperial armies, commanded by Charles de Lannoy, the Viceroy of Naples, began their march north along the walls from their camp located outside the east wall of the city. Imperial artillery began a bombardment of the French siege lines, successfully decimating the French. In an extraordinarily daring move, Francis himself was captured by Habsburg troops and pulled off his horse by the helmet, but de Lannoy rescued him from the soldiers. Francis was taken to Madrid, where he was imprisoned. Humiliated, he wrote to his mother, Louise: 'Nothing is left but the honor and the life that is saved.' It was an unprecedented defeat for Francis and in England, Henry could scarcely believe what Charles had achieved. With a temporarily vacant French throne, Henry, eager to launch an invasion and claim the throne for himself, had to first contend with almost empty coffers – which the Cardinal believed he could remedy. But England could not know that the ripple effects from the war between the princes would spread throughout Europe, and even Eastern empires would take notice.

# CHAPTER SEVEN

# The Balance of Power

*But that all-disposing fate*
*Which presides o'er mortal state,*
*Where it listeth, casts its shroud*
*Of impenetrable cloud*

— Bacchylides

The constellation of older, experienced advisors, some of whom at one stage had mentored the young Thomas, and who had surrounded Henry since his accession, had begun to fade. Men like Fox, Thomas' father-in-law the Duke of Norfolk, and others reached the age at which they were no longer desirous of life at court or able to perform their duties. On 21 May 1524, the Boleyns lost their Howard patriarch – the Duke of Norfolk, who had left the court in 1522, aged 80, to spend his remaining days in peace, died at his castle of Framlingham in Suffolk, and would be buried at Thetford Priory. Thomas had the utmost respect for his wife's father, for his generous assistance had been vital for Thomas in those first unsteady years at court following his own father's death. The funeral by all accounts was extraordinarily elaborate, lasting several days, as the Duke's corpse was slowly carried from Framlingham to the priory, and Thomas, alongside his brothers-in-law, was present for the entire event as one of the chief mourners.[1] On the first day, he knelt by the coffin as solemn masses were sung throughout the day and, that night, he was one of the men who watched over the body.

His son, George may have been present, for numerous men had brought their sons and the next day, both men were part of the large procession of 400 hooded men carrying torches as they followed the coffin from Framlingham to Hoxne. That night, the Boleyn men may have been two of the 28 men chosen again to watch over the body. Finally, the coffin arrived at Thetford, and the mourners took their places around the coffin once more as they sang a solemn dirge. For a final night, they kept watch, and early the next morning, the funeral commenced. One of the most honourable parts of the procession involved carrying 'offerings' – some of the Duke's effects. Thomas, partnered with Lord Willoughby, carried the Duke's sword up the aisle and presented it to the Bishop, the sword pointing upwards.[2] The whole event had cost a small fortune, and involved over 1,500 people, but it was a fitting tribute to the man who had once been one of the most powerful and influential nobles in the country. Thomas had lost his father figure and mentor, and he would henceforth have to contend with his tactless and charmless brother-in-law, who now assumed the mantle of Duke. Thomas Howard senior had been one of the last tendrils of the old world in which Thomas had begun his career.

It was the end of an era, but now Howard's grandson, George Boleyn, probably about 20 years of age, begins to emerge from the historical records, with the first grant of the manor of Grymston in Norfolk. George was the ideal age for a young man to consider marriage and, in 1524, the Boleyns entered into negotiations with one Henry Parker, for the hand of his daughter Jane. Thomas may have discussed the matter with his mother, the Boleyn matriarch, as Boleyn marriages had been family affairs for the last few generations. But unlike the previous generations, they chose a family whose trajectory was similar to their own, rather than a noble family in a temporary eclipse.

Where the Boleyns had favoured neutrality in the Wars of the Roses, Henry Parker's family had been loyal Yorkists, and he had served as standard bearer to Richard III. Parker was on the wrong side of the field that day, which may have led to his imprisonment by the victorious Henry VII.[3] Henry Parker's mother, Alice Lovel, could trace her lineage to Henry II, and his uncle, Henry Lovel, Lord Morley, was the husband of Elizabeth de la Pole, a niece of the Yorkist Edward IV, Richard III, and George, Duke of Clarence, through their sister, Elizabeth. They were therefore a family on the make, with certain noble ties, much like the Boleyns themselves, and they were connected by marital links which preceded George and Jane's union. Henry Parker's father had died in 1510, and his widowed mother, Alice, married the handsome, ambitious, Admiral Edward Howard, Thomas Boleyn's brother-in-law, who was over a decade younger than his new wife – unfortunately the marriage was short lived, as we may remember that Edward died in 1513. As to Henry Parker himself, his career as an ambassador and an admired translator placed him in the same circles as Thomas, and the family were closely connected to the Queen – therefore the match was a desirable one.[4] From the very beginning of their union, popular history tells us, George and Jane disliked each other intensely. A lack of records about Jane in particular makes this difficult to disprove, considering where history has placed her in the tragic events to come, but perhaps we are reading their lives backwards – we know the eventual outcome. Why would the young couple be anything but optimistic for the future? Arranged marriages were the norm, and every Boleyn match thus far had been successful, and seemingly emotionally fulfilling. More importantly, George and Jane would have appreciated the benefits of such an alliance. Jane's older sister, Margaret, married one of Thomas' nephews, John Shelton, so it was a successful alliance between the two families. This was not a forced marriage between two unwilling partners, but a new partnership. The marriage signified the beginning of what they both no doubt hoped would be a transition into adulthood and a successful life at court.

In early 1525, as Henry dreamed of expanding his realm and claiming France, Charles wrote to his ambassadors in England of Louise of Savoy's desire for peace. In his words this was: 'not without reason, for otherwise she will never see the King her son again'.[5] Charles added that he had always desired peace and had no desire to make war upon a prisoner who could not defend himself – peace was higher on his list of priorities. If peace negotiations fell through, England was prepared, but if the English wished for war, *they* would have to bear the responsibility. Charles had little faith in Henry, especially considering how quickly the English army had disbanded.[6]

Henry remained captivated by his own desire for the French throne, but such a campaign required significant funding. Wolsey's solution was surprisingly old-fashioned – he conjured up an Amicable Grant, based on the old feudal obligation of contributing aid to the King when he led an invasion in person.[7] On 21 March, commissions were sent forth to demand one sixth of lay and one third of clerical incomes, hoping to gain an estimated £800,000 for the proposed war. It was a thankless task, and Wolsey chose his commissioners carefully – 'the greatest men of every shire' – one of which was Thomas Boleyn. Cleverly, Wolsey ensured it was not a formal tax because it was only a means for people to give monetary 'gifts' to fund the King's war. After receiving his commission, Wolsey, who was not at court, relied on Thomas to communicate between himself and the King.[8]

In the cities and counties, however, Wolsey's scheme stirred deep resentment, hardly surprising, as famine had begun to bite. In London the demands were ignored; in Suffolk a revolt broke out among the weavers; Cambridge men united in resistance; and Norwich threatened insurrection.[9] Thomas, assigned to Kent, faced strong opposition, with jeering crowds greeting him everywhere and the clergy leading the opposition.[10] According to one account, Lord Cobham, assigned alongside Thomas, handled men roughly, even sending one man to the Tower. This move made them both, but particularly Thomas, unpopular with the people of Kent, resenting him: 'And in this grudge they evil entreated sir Thomas Bullein at Maidstone.'[11] By 3 May conditions in Kent became so volatile that Warham, Boleyn, Cobham and Guildford wrote separately to Henry and Wolsey to adopt measures which would prevent violent riots.[12] They also complained that it did not help that the King had remitted the sums due from Londoners, which infuriated the rest of the country.

According to Warham's communications with Wolsey, they were afraid of the multitude who had persecuted those who had complied, and Thomas and Guildford were begrudged by the people for allowing a favourable vote on the grant as councillors to the King. That Thomas voted for Wolsey's grant in council may say no more than that he agreed with the concept, and but it also suggests a degree of loyalty to the Cardinal. Whatever Thomas may have felt about the proposed invasion, he did as much as he could to support his Cardinal and his King, even if it meant being deeply unpopular in his own county.

Before the end of May, Henry and Wolsey realised that the grant could not be collected in an amicable manner. They abandoned their dream of invading France.

By 1525 the Boleyns had an impressive property portfolio of over 30 manors. A sample of Thomas' household accounts still exist, which lists barrels of Gascon wine, money being sent to his brother, William, fur for his mother's gown, a hogshead for his mother-in-law, and black satin for a new doublet.[13] Thomas had influence and prestige in Kent and elsewhere, both by his increasing stature at court and by the acquisition of property. He seemed to spend a great deal of time down in Kent, and undertook to co-ordinate the renovation of the 104-foot-long bridge at Tunbridge, and oversaw the extensive restoration to the castles of Tunbridge and Penshurst, which included the re-roofing of both structures.[14] He was meticulous, keeping detailed records which reveal that he did the job in stages, requesting additional funding from the when necessary.[15] Up to this point, Thomas' advancement had been steady, following the path set by his father and grandfather. In June 1525, in a great ceremony, Henry VIII elevated his six-year-old illegitimate son, Henry Fitzroy, to the earldom of Nottingham and the dukedoms of both Richmond and Somerset.[16] Thomas was one of the official witnesses at these investitures, which occurred in the sumptuously decorated Presence Chamber at the Palace of Bridewell. Then, in the same ceremony, Thomas was elevated to the peerage as Viscount Rochford, a title created for him personally, taken from his estate in Essex.[17] History has long dismissed the elevation as another reward for allowing Mary's dalliance with Henry and, if this were the case, it would seem extraordinary indeed to be granted both the Garter and this elevation to the peerage for simply looking the other way. It is an out-dated myth, repeated ad nauseum with no regard for the circumstances. Thomas was ennobled alongside other men who had performed commendable service, or who the King particularly liked: his favourite, Charles Brandon's infant son was made Earl of Lincoln, Henry Courtenay, Henry's cousin, was made Marquis of Exeter, Henry Manners was created Earl of Rutland, Robert Ratcliffe was made Lord Viscount Fitzwalter, and Sir Henry Clifford was created Earl of Cumberland. What they all had in common were years of exemplar service, in the Privy Council, in Henry's army, or in diplomacy.[18]

The ceremony also celebrated Henry Fitzroy, born of Henry's liaison with Bessy Blount. It would have been in poor taste to hold a ceremony celebrating two extra-marital affairs and the illegitimate product of one of them. Surely, if rewarding the fathers of mistresses was Henry's style, Sir John Blount, Bessie's father, should have been a recipient. Instead, we must allow that Thomas' elevation was the result of his years of dedicated service and skilled performances in his many roles. His advancement was gradual, and now he was a peer, roughly on an equal footing with the other nobles at court.

Thomas relinquished his role as Treasurer of the Household to William Fitzwilliam, though whether this was due to the elevation or not is unclear. Perhaps he had not enjoyed the domestic duties of the royal household, preferring politics. Fortunately for him, opportunity beckoned, as England was still negotiating with Charles, but both sides had cooled towards each other. Louise of Savoy had sent a barrage of ambassadors to England in order to secure support from her imprisoned son-overtures to which Wolsey was very receptive. Charles appointed special commissioners to travel to England for further negotiations following Pavia. The meeting was held in private between the ambassadors and Henry in the Council Chamber at Windsor on 7 June.[19] The Imperial group was led by Commander Peñalosa, who began by stating that although Charles was aware that an embassy was being prepared to offer him congratulations upon his last victory (just in case Henry had forgotten Pavia) he felt it more expedient to send his own men to England. It is more likely that Charles felt the bond between the two nations had a certain brittleness to it. What Charles wanted was a firm gesture of good faith, as well as funds, which came, neatly bundled together in the marriage contract which continued to be negotiated between the Emperor and Henry's daughter,

Mary.[20] Additionally, Charles requested that Henry send 200,000 ducats for the 'keeping of their common army in Italy, thereby to attack and weaken the said kingdom of France on every one of its frontiers'.[21] Mary would be sent to Spain alongside the far more precious dowry.

It was a rather audacious request, and Henry's immediate answer was that Mary was too young to travel to Spain by herself and, besides, he was not bound by treaty to give her up before she was 12. Peñalosa shrugged, replying that the application was not made in virtue of any particular treaty, but merely as a simple request. The timing of Mary's arrival in Spain was irrelevant, simply that she should arrive in the near future so that she could learn the manners and language of the people before she and Charles were wed. Perhaps Henry felt out of his depth, for he quickly called for his own cavalry – Wolsey, Thomas, Norfolk, Suffolk, Thomas Grey, Marquis of Dorset, and George Talbot, Earl of Shrewsbury were all summoned to the Council Chamber. As a viscount, Boleyn was of the lowest rank, but his presence here precedes the relationship between Anne and Henry, and therefore his presence can be taken as evidence of his capabilities. With his advisors present, Henry again made it clear that Mary's marriage to Charles was a long way off, and that sending her to Spain now was not an option. He was not bound to pay any sum of money as dower to his daughter until she had attained the age appointed for her marriage; and, as to the additional 200,000 ducats, he was under no obligation whatever to furnish them.

The ambassadors changed tack by asking, on Charles' behalf, for a loan of 600,000 ducats – 200,000 now and 400,000 over the next four months. Suffice to say it was not the wisest course of action. Going on the defensive, Henry puffed up, bellowing his amazement that they would 'dare put forward such pretensions'.[22] Surely they knew that Charles owed Henry money already, which he showed no sign of paying. But, Peñalosa pointed out, dangling France in front of him, had not Henry gained from Charles' recent exploits, which he had helped finance? Had not Charles 'delivered him [Henry] of the greatest enemy he ever had, and put him in a situation to recover all the land which the said King of France had taken from him?'[23] Henry could only mutter that the sum was still excessive. It would be interesting to know what Thomas made of the meetings, knowing his preference for the French, but it is likely that he was pleased when no further negotiations occurred between Henry and Charles, who had no intention of marrying Mary. The Emperor instead quietly revisited the marital alliance with Portugal, which he had considered in 1521. Isabella of Portugal was a more suitable bride – only three years younger, fluent in Spanish, and she came with a dowry of 900,000 Portuguese cruzados, which solved Charles' financial issues. Henry on the other hand, had turned entirely towards the French, and agreed to a new treaty with Louise. Charles and Henry had gone their separate ways, much to Katherine's sorrow – she had longed to see her daughter and nephew allied in marriage.

In early September of 1525, Henry wrote to his ambassadors – Wingfield, Tunstall and Sampson – in Spain, ensuring they had notified the Emperor of England's peace with France (while complaining that he had not heard from them in some time). Henry tried to justify his actions, noting that he had already heard that Charles had made peace with France, which would make sense, 'perceiving the inroads of the Turks, the dangers of Lutheranism, the peasant war in Germany, the general distress, the desire of the Emperor to marry with Portugal, and the urgency of the Pope'.[24] The treaty was signed on 30 August between the two belligerents and was known as the Treaty of the More, so named because it was signed at More Park, a country estate in Hertfordshire that belonged to Wolsey. In all probability, Thomas was one of the witnesses to the document, although this is not possible to confirm because some signatures were lost: Wolsey, Nicholas West (Bishop of Ely), and Comptroller Guildford signed the document, while Thomas' may have been one of the lost names.

On Saturday 9 September 1525, the treaty was to be formally ratified at Greenwich with two days of festivities arranged by the household staff. The Imperial ambassadors as well as the Papal ambassadors were also invited. Thomas was a key member of the proceedings, meeting two sets of ambassadors – Imperial and French. To be chosen to escort two sets of ambassadors suggests Wolsey's reliance on Thomas to help facilitate matters, and as the latter had served at both courts, he was well placed to encourage good relations and perhaps soothe any ruffled Imperial feathers.[25] At 2pm, the ambassadors entered court, where Henry received them, under his cloth of state in his dining chamber. Another meeting occurred at seven in the evening in the King's dining chamber, with Thomas personally escorting the Imperial ambassador. After this session was adjourned, Rochford, Docwra and others conveyed the ambassadors to residences provided to host the visiting dignitaries, with Boleyn taking the Imperial ambassador to a residence owned by his son-in-law, William Carey.[26] It is possible that Thomas was attempting to bring his son-in-law further into the politics of court. All of the parties met Henry in his dining chamber at nine the next morning where Wolsey and other high prelates did the obsequies and sang Mass.[27] Then came the oaths to the treaty by Henry and the French embassy, and the solemn affair was witnessed by the representatives of France and the Pope, who were seated on the right side, while the emissaries of the Emperor, Venice and Milan, looked on from the left. After the ceremonies, Thomas escorted the Imperial ambassador to dinner and then to a final audience with the King. There was great prestige attached to the role of escort for the Imperial ambassador but, more importantly, Henry's diplomatic realignment with Charles meant that the pensions that Charles had owed to English ambassadors since Thomas' embassy stopped being paid. Wolsey is listed first, with £9,000, followed by Norfolk, Suffolk and Boleyn, each with £1,000. Boleyn's old colleague, Wingfield, was only given £500.[28]

These were considerable sums that would have been missed, but for Wolsey at least, this financial situation was the least of his problems. Since 1519, Wolsey had attempted to reorganise and reform the royal households, and with good reason. During the reign of Edward IV, the annual running costs of the court were about £13,000.[29] In the beginning of Henry VIII's reign they had risen to about £19,000, and by the end of Henry's reign, they had risen to £45,000.[30] Wolsey's attempt at reform in 1519, when Thomas was in France, had achieved little, and in 1526 Wolsey targeted every echelon of court, from restrictions of Yeoman of the Guard from sending their servants to attend the King in their place, limiting the number of servants each noble could have with them at court, and who could join the King on hunts, to how many men were actually needed to attend upon the King in his Privy Chamber.[31]

Despite the sheer scope, the popular theory remains that Wolsey's attempt at reform, known as the Eltham Ordinances, was really an attempt to oust those he saw as political rivals and those who he viewed as persistent trouble-makers at court, and names Nicholas Carew, Francis Bryan and George Boleyn as prime examples.[32] But the evidence does not support this theory. Wolsey had drafted the reforms the year before as he sought funds for Henry's French campaign, relying heavily on Thomas and there is no mention of George as a powerful presence at court at that stage. Bryan was a well-respected ambassador who had accompanied Wolsey on numerous embassies, and would continue to do so after 1526, and there is no detectable friction in their correspondence.[33] Why would Wolsey, at this point working well with Thomas, want to eliminate his son from the household – a young man with very little political power or sway? The men listed were still given lodgings in the royal household alongside their wives, and George is listed in Wolsey's reorganisation of the households, alongside men like William Compton, William Kingston and Richard Weston, all of whom were given positions, with Wolsey writing 'A provysyon for suche as shu[ld] ... of the Kynges p ... ' at the top of the heavily mutilated page.[34] From what we can discern, the positions listed – yeoman of the wardrobe, esquires – suggest it would be the Privy Chamber. George's position was changed rather than negated, from page to cupbearer, with Wolsey writing that 'Yong Bolleyn to [have] 20 pounds yeerly above the ... the hath gottyn to hym and hys wyfe to lyve therapon.'[35] This was a generous payment – 20 pounds was over a year's wage for a skilled tradesman. Thus, despite the arguments of many Tudor historians, the evidence makes clear that Wolsey had not tried to expel the younger Boleyn, and there is no evidence that the family did not continue to work amicably with the Cardinal. Wolsey was concerned with expenditure, not eliminating young political rivals, at this stage. Within a year, however, Wolsey would have far more important things to contend with than cutting royal costs.

The year 1526 had been one of new alliances, the reverberations of which continued into 1527. Henry had turned from Charles to Francis, seeking to marry Mary to the French king, whose wife Claude had died in 1524. Not only had Henry tired of Imperial games, he had also begun to turn from Katherine of Aragon, his wife of 17 years. As for Thomas, he was about to embark on the last embassy wholly unconnected with what would be called Henry's Great Matter. The months prior to the embassy were spent in obtaining agreements with France. Thomas had a growing role in negotiations, not only as a signatory, but acting as an intermediary, meeting socially with the embassy and inviting them to visit the King when requested. Gabriel de Grammont, the Bishop of Tarbes, Claude Dodieu, and other ambassadors from France arrived in England to join Jean Joachim, an envoy already there, in order that all might negotiate terms of a permanent peace treaty with Henry.[36] The ambassadors, with Dodieu as secretary, had an audience with Wolsey at Westminster, and curiously chose to address the Cardinal in Latin, thanking him on behalf of Francis: 'for being the occasion of peace with the king of England, which peace had been the means of his deliverance; and for proposing the marriage with the English princess'.[37] Throughout the negotiations, Dodieu notes that the Cardinal was flanked by Norfolk, Suffolk, Thomas, and Fitzwilliam, the new Treasurer of the King's Household.[38] The meeting hit a snag when Wolsey brought up the issue of Madame Eleanor, Charles V's younger sister. As part of the humiliating peace treaty Charles had strong-armed Francis into, his mother, Louise of Savoy, had surrendered to Charles' main sticking point, the return of Burgundy, and agreed to the Treaty of Madrid, in which France renounced its claims in Italy. However, this treaty required that when Francis was released from captivity, his two eldest sons would be exchanged and taken hostage. In addition, Francis was required to marry Charles' sister Eleanor, and the two were betrothed by proxy on 20 January 1526. Wolsey of course was aware of this, and grilled the ambassadors, asking whether Francis was free to marry, to which the French hurriedly assured the Cardinal that Francis had protested the marriage and in no way felt bound by the treaty.

Negotiations continued for over a week, and Thomas was again one of the men present for all negotiations, escorting the men to and from court and to meet with the King when requested.

In the first week of May 1527, Henry held a feast for the French delegation. The gathering was a serious affair of state with the Knights of the Garter seated behind the King, who solemnly professed friendship for France and the desire for peace. Shortly after, on 17 May, Thomas was selected to travel to France, to work alongside the current resident ambassador in France, John Clerk, Bishop of Bath and Wells, and Sir Anthony Browne. As special emissaries, they were 'To take the oath of Francis I to the treaty of closer alliance between the two crowns.'[39]

Once more, detailed correspondence flowed out of France upon Thomas' arrival, but it is interesting to note that historians generally assume the lengthy and detailed descriptions of this mission were written by Arthur Plantagenet, Viscount Lisle, peculiar considering the fact that the commission expressly nominates Thomas and not Lord Lisle as part of the delegation. Lisle was not even a part of the embassy, so why would he write such a lengthy communication?

With respect to the tone and description of the report, it is very much Thomas' style, his typical phrasing, with a slightly familiar tone when describing the court. Additionally, both Francis and Louise of Savoy would later write to Henry that, 'he [Henry] will understand by viscount Rochford [Thomas] all that has been done relative to the oath for the ratification of the treaty between himself and England'. Therefore Thomas was the nominal leader of the group, the narrative most logically but erroneously attributed to Lisle.[40]

Wolsey was supposed to have accompanied the embassy, but had fallen ill, and could not make the crossing until he had recovered. In his absence, Thomas took charge. His reports show a marked difference between this embassy and those of his previous visits to the French court, as he now had a firmly established French network on which he could rely. He reported that he was warmly greeted by Francis in his chamber and was immediately escorted to Louise of Savoy and her daughter, Marguerite of Navarre, and Thomas noted with pleasure that he was reacquainted with 'old Mons. Montmorency', Guilliame, Anne de Montmorency's father.[41]

Thomas described in detail the splendour and glitter of the French court. Francis was in formal attire of estate, his throne perched on a dais, and at each corner knelt a gentleman usher. The French nobles sat on the right of their king, while all envoys were on the left. Thomas reported that he and his colleagues sat in the middle of the hall, directly opposite Francis, and Thomas noted the air of informality, which Wolsey would never have allowed of Henry's attendants. Francis, on the other hand, seemed not to mind the fact that some of his men were 'leaning on the pommels of his chair'.[42]

It seems as though Thomas never left Francis' side throughout the embassy. He hunted and hawked, attended Mass, feasted and sported with the young monarch, a clear sign of favour, and Francis treated the entourage well, constantly entertaining them, and they never had to dine at their own expense. Wolsey, missing out, had to contend with Thomas' detailed narrative of the nights of dancing and feasting into the early hours.[43] On Whitsunday eve, Thomas and his colleagues had had a public audience with Francis, to celebrate the peace treaty between England and France.

On Whitsunday, 9 June, Thomas and the English embassy accompanied Francis, all riding on mules through Paris to Notre Dame for the solemn Latin Mass held to commemorate the treaty. Francis, Thomas wrote, then approached the high altar, swore an oath to peace, and kissed the book of Mass. The men left the cathedral, accompanied by the sound of trumpets, as the choir sang a 'Te Deum'.[44]

The special emissary saw his host for the last time on 23 June, when Francis told Thomas and the Bishop of Bath that he still wanted to meet Wolsey in Picardy but said that it would have to be postponed for several weeks because of the Cardinal's sickness, and affairs of state required his presence in Paris.[45] It had not been the most constructive of missions, but both sides seemed satisfied, and Thomas left France with the Bishop in late June, leaving Anthony Browne to serve Francis. It was the last mission in which Thomas was not personally invested.

# CHAPTER EIGHT

# Declare, I Dare Not

*I have seen them gentle, tame, and meek, that now are wild and do not remember*
*That sometime they put themself in danger to take bread at my hand; and now they range,*
*busily seeking with continual change.*

– Thomas Wyatt

Since the earliest times throughout the Christian world people have observed the season of Lent – a time to take one's spiritual temperature, a time for fasting, self-denial, simplicity and spiritual growth in preparation for the celebration of Easter. Shrovetide, the pre-Lenten season, blended ancient pagan carnivals and Christian festivals, with Shrove Tuesday, the final day before the austerity of the Lenten fast, a day of celebrations – and at Henry VIII's court, jousting and feasting, and always a day of opulence and excess. The jousts on Shrove Tuesday 4 March 1522 had been magnificent as usual, its theme 'Unrequited Love', an added felicity that invited amorous court intrigues directed at the ladies of the court, including Anne and Mary Boleyn. Henry was as usual surrounded by his favourites, including Anthony Knyvett, Nicholas Carew, Thomas Manners, Nicholas Darrel, Anthony Kingston, Henry Courtenay and Charles Brandon, and all had participated in the jousts sporting their mottos decrying of varying degrees of self-pity: 'my heart is broken', 'my heart is bound', and 'in prison I am at liberty, and at liberty I am in prison'. Henry led the joust and blazoned across the trappings of his courser, the phrase: 'Elle mon coeur a navre' – 'She has wounded [or broken] my heart.'[1] It is unlikely that Henry had any particular woman in mind, for this was more a theme, not a message. For this special Shrove Tuesday evening, Cardinal Wolsey, 'the Golden Centre' of court, had organised a pageant in his great chamber of York Place, where a magnificently constructed and decorated Chateau Vert stood in the centre of the hall, lit by

32 large flame torches. Eight young ladies performed the virtues, including Anne Boleyn, approximately 20 years old, who had recently returned from France in time for the Christmas revels. Anne played Perseverance and her sister, Mary, Kindness; Mary Tudor played Beauty. Jane Parker, George's future wife, was Constance, and Gertrude Blount played Honour – followed by others including Bounty, Mercy and Pity. All were resplendent in white satin gowns, guarded by another eight young women playing the parts of Scorn, Danger, Disdain, Jealousy, Unkindness, Malebouche and Strangeness – the name of the eighth virtue has been lost.[2] William Cornish, master of the choristers of Chapel Royal, played Ardent Desire, leading the charge to 'free' the maidens, accompanied by the roar of gunfire from outside the hall. Thomas Boleyn had been tasked with accompanying the Imperial ambassadors who were Wolsey's guests, and must have been proud of his two young daughters who were being favoured. Whether he saw anything predatory in Henry's eyes settling on Mary Boleyn that night we can only wonder. For Henry, who liked to think that the women he pursued had a choice in the matter, saw himself as a romantic, and it is likely that his liaison with Mary began shortly after this pageant.

As fate would have it, exactly four years later, at an equally extravagant Shrovetide celebration and joust, there was another motto aimed at another Boleyn daughter – this time, Henry chose to make his feelings less ambiguous. In the crisp March air of 1526, the jousts were held at Greenwich, and Henry, iridescent in cloth of gold and silver, had chosen the motto: *Déclare je n'ose*, in English, 'Declare, I dare not.'[3] The court was thick with rumour that he was referring to his illegitimate son, Henry Fitzroy, whom he had ennobled in the same ceremony as Thomas the year before. Some even believed Henry was about to declare him legitimate but this was unlikely. This was a romantic message, designed to woo a new interest.

Anne had been at court since 1521, following seven years abroad, which had instilled in her an air of refinement and independence. Although she loved her father and respected his advice, she was becoming a woman of strong opinion. Anne, if we adhere to the likely birth date of approximately 1501, and not 1507, as discussed in Chapter 1, was not a young maiden of 20 in 1526 but an educated, cultured woman of about 26 – this is still debated. Hers was a tall stature, with dark auburn hair and eyes, described as 'black and beautiful', which may have come from her father.[4] Perhaps her 'slender neck' was a Howard feature on her mother's side. Her intelligence, quick charm and wit were very much Thomas' traits, as was her talent for French. She was utterly unlike any other woman at court.

Henry had noticed Anne and began to write his now famous (and laboured) love letters to her, 17 of which survive. These letters provide a broad, if unreliable, arc of their courtship as they are all undated, leaving us with an inexact timeline of their affair. Disagreements continue as to when the affair began, with a starting date of anywhere between late 1525 to the beginning of 1527 plausible, but Henry's dramatic statement, in February 1527, that he had been in the 'toils of love' for over a year would seem to confirm the timeline of events as beginning sometime in 1526.

Some historians are certain that Thomas, who may or may not have been present at the joust, was receptive, indeed promoted Henry's advances towards his daughter, sacrificing Anne to the royal bedchamber for the greater Boleyn good. Therefore the contemporary description of the Boleyns as 'unique in that they owed their influence to the sexual prowess of their women rather than the military or political talents of their men' remains largely unchallenged.[5] That Thomas' talents and the career he built have taken up seven chapters of this book suggests another reason entirely. As we have seen, Thomas was a rational, conservative and cautious businessman, ambassador, and courtier who had spent over a decade in steady advancement on his own merit, rather than a risky scheme that exposed not only himself, but his family, wealth, credibility and position. Anne was equally cautious and understandably guarded, and there is no evidence that capturing the King's interest was ever Anne's ambition or would have crossed her mind as she waited for the Butler betrothal to be concluded – when that collapsed, she must have wondered what her fate held.

Henry and Katherine's 18-year marriage had begun with such promise in 1509, and Thomas and his family, like so many courtiers, had borne witness to the decades of triumphs and tragedies of the royal couple, who had enjoyed a fiercely loyal partnership of over 18 years. It must have seemed unimaginable that England could have any other queen *but* Katherine, who was adored throughout the realm. Yet in the countless retellings of the story of Henry and Anne Boleyn, Henry is portrayed as a young and virile man, trapped in an unhappy marriage to a much older wife, who falls in love with a much younger woman. But the evidence presents a considerably different picture. By 1525–26, about the time Henry had privately begun to contemplate setting his wife aside, he was 36, but Katherine was only six years older. She was not a much older woman, but she had been, to some extent, emotionally and physically ravaged by years of failed pregnancies and miscarriages – as many as ten, which had produced only one living heir, Princess Mary. Not only was Henry's passion for Anne intense, it also provided him with an opportunity for a reversal of fortune.

For Henry was a desperate man, painfully aware of the limits to his marriage and the need to produce a male heir.

At some point in early 1527, before his French embassy, Thomas took Anne to Hever. Perhaps it was in the hope that Henry's obsession with Anne would abate, or at least that as a family they could gain some sort of perspective and control of the situation, away from the prying eyes of court. Henry's flagrant pursuit of Anne left the family open to criticism and judgement from other envious courtiers. But Henry was not at all pleased with this turn of events.

While two Boleyns departed court, George remained, a minor part of the royal inner circle, to whom Henry paid little attention, and granted no special favours. George was only another handsome, witty and amiable young courtier, with as yet little opportunity to prove himself, but he had his father's confidence and sense of ambition, that envisioned a career trajectory born of dedication and skill. His father had benefitted from the influence and connections afforded by his kin and, at the start of 1527, Thomas was one of the wealthiest subjects in the realm, with a fortune of £800, not to mention numerous properties, and was therefore ideally placed to facilitate his son's rise. But Henry saw George initially merely as the link to Anne, and his first chance to prove himself was not a grand or delicate mission abroad, it was as a glorified messenger, carrying love notes between Henry and Anne. Making numerous journeys between court and Hever, he was likely bombarded with questions at both ends – Henry no doubt eager to know how Anne seemed, and vice versa. We have no way of knowing how George felt at being used as a go-between between the King and his sister, but there may have been a degree of unease. His father's success had never been questioned, but this new romantic development could overshadow George's career.

We cannot say with any certainty just how involved Thomas was in the relationship, still in its early stages, but he may have encouraged Anne to refuse all pleas to be Henry's mistress, or even his generous invitation to be his *Maîtresse-en-titre* – his *official* mistress. For Thomas, Anne's welfare and future prospects were paramount, and the tenure of a mistress, finite; the chances of an ex royal mistress to make a good marriage were slim. Like all parents, Thomas and Elizabeth sought to secure Anne's future by arranging a marriage with a respectable family, which would be advantageous to both. But at some point throughout the courtship, whether in person, through George, or in a letter now lost, the offer changed. It became a question of whether Anne would be his wife. We can only imagine the commotion this must have caused, and all this proposal entailed.

George Wyatt, grandson of the poet and courtier, Thomas Wyatt, described Anne's turmoil as she remained at Hever. Wyatt wrote of Thomas' joy when Henry finally proposed marriage once he was free of Katherine, but how would Wyatt know of Thomas' reaction, writing decades later? Like many accounts written at later dates, this was an attempt to flesh out a significant event by adding dramatic detail, but it is not evidence of what took place.

We do know however that it was extremely risky to even consider repudiating a queen as powerful, well loved, and connected as Katherine. Such a course of action could be disastrous for England and would leave the Boleyns, at this stage well liked and respected at court, open to attack from those loyal to Katherine, and to the idea of peace.

In these early months of 1527, Henry confided to Wolsey his doubts regarding his marriage, without naming who he had in mind for his new queen. In a muddle of lust, necessity and conscience, Henry now believed Katherine's miscarriages and stillborn or short-lived babies were divine punishment. As Katherine was the widow of his deceased brother, Arthur, Henry (conveniently) contended that their marriage had violated an Old Testament prohibition of such a union in the Book of Leviticus: 'If a man takes his brother's wife, it is impurity ... they shall be childless.' This issue had been resolved decades earlier when Pope Julius II had issued a papal bull of dispensation, which allowed for the possibility that Katherine and Arthur had consummated their marriage. What then were the grounds for an annulment? Henry left such details to Wolsey.

His mentor, Richard Fox, had not paid much thought to a French marriage all those years ago, gaze fixed firmly on the daughter of Isabella and Ferdinand, but Wolsey, pro-French, had already begun to consider Renee, Princess of France, sister to Queen Claude. This may well have influenced Wolsey's policy throughout 1527 as, in early May, he hosted the magnificent reception for the French ambassadors, in which Thomas was heavily involved, and it was reported that the French ambassador, De Turenne, danced with Princess Mary. Curiously, it was also reported that Henry had danced with Mistress Anne Boleyn. Thomas' departure for France coincided with the beginning of several secret court sessions, which Wolsey held alongside Archbishop Warham on 17 May at York Place, for the first of the highly secret court sessions convened to investigate the validity of the royal marriage. Wolsey promoted the case in a rather ingenious way, by stating that the French had raised doubts about the legitimacy of Princess Mary during the marriage negotiations, conveniently distancing the matter from Henry, denying his instigation. Within days of Thomas' return from Paris, Wolsey left for his own mission. He was to feel, in

J.S Brewer's words, the 'pulse of the nation', and to ask Francis for advice on the best means of communicating with Pope Clement regarding an annulment. They knew that Charles would support Katherine, so Francis also needed to be won over to Henry's cause.[6] It must have been while he was in France that Wolsey was first made aware of Henry's intention to marry Anne Boleyn. This revelation elevated Boleyn to a position of considerable power, in the sense that he was a member of the Privy Council, and now the father of the woman the king wished to marry.

Unbeknownst to Wolsey, Henry sent his secretary, William Knight, on an independent mission to Rome, with an extraordinary draft bull for the Pope's signature. In it Henry begged Pope Clement to release him from 'sin' by ending his marriage, and allow him to marry a woman within the first degree of affinity, provided that his existing marriage was annulled.[7] Henry had already had sexual relations with Anne's sister, Mary.

Henry seemed confident that this discreet investigation led by Wolsey and his council would come to the right conclusion to annul the marriage. Any momentum however was lost with the news that Imperial troops, still bearing grudges from the Pope's duplicitous actions in 1525, had gone on a rampage and sacked Rome on 6 May.[8] For eight days these troops ravaged the city, butchering priests, monks and nuns, and taking Charles' desire to have an audience with the Pope into their own hands. They stormed the Vatican, looting it when they discovered Pope Clement had fled. He was quickly captured and imprisoned in the Castel Saint Angelo, while troops killed more than 12,000 men, women and children. This effectively ended any of Henry's or Wolsey's plans to secure a verdict. With the Papacy incapacitated, Wolsey promoted his desire to be named vicegerent in his absence, which would have allowed him to grant Henry's divorce; however, despite being appointed, he chose not to take the matter further.

Despite the violent and unexpected turn of events in Rome, Wolsey negotiated with the French ambassadors, with both sides assuming a French marriage was on the table. At some point during the meetings, the ambassadors mentioned that Thomas had in his possession a portrait of a prospective bride, the 17-year-old Renee of France, who knew Thomas well, and who had spent a great deal of time with Anne when she had served Queen Claude. Perhaps Wolsey hoped Thomas would assist in brokering a match, but it is more likely that Thomas was simply going along with the official programme – he remained quiet about Henry and his daughter, lest it all fall apart before their eyes.

Henry probably assumed that the last person to know of his actions would be his wife, but he underestimated Katherine. In late June, Henry privately confronted her, informing her that he felt their marriage had never been valid in the eyes of God, that she had married his brother, and she was still *his* wife. For Katherine, it was an incredible betrayal, not only of their marriage, but of their beloved daughter, Mary. Katherine raged, understandably inconsolable. Her Spanish ambassador, the quick-tempered Don Inigo de Mendoza, reported the separation, recounting Henry's tale of living in mortal sin, and his assurances that the opinion of many canonists and theologians whom he had consulted on the subject had forced him to come to such a conclusion. When Henry assured he wife that she could choose the place to which she would retire, Katherine burst into tears. All Henry could do was beg her to keep the matter quiet. Not that it would do much good, Mendoza scoffed. The 'affair is as notorious as if it had been proclaimed by the public crier'.[9]

Katherine's movements were being closely watched, to prevent her from contacting her nephew but she was too quick, smuggling word out via a Spanish servant, Felipez, who crossed the sea before English agents could intercept him. On receiving word, Charles immediately wrote in support of Katherine to Henry, and demanded that Clement refuse to hear petitions for an annulment. After being imprisoned for months, Clement had been freed by Charles in June following the payment of a ransom and the concession of certain Italian territories, allowing for a new alliance – on Charles' terms. Nevertheless, Clement could hardly offend his former captor. This was all greatly troubling to Wolsey, who saw how unfavourably events could unfold for England.

Henry and Wolsey returned to Julius II's bull of dispensation, which had been granted to Henry and Katherine decades prior, but Katherine received some powerful ammunition. In Spain, a transcript of the dispensation by Julius II dated 1503 had been discovered, which allowed Henry and Katherine's marriage, but it was worded differently from the bull. It assumed Arthur and Katherine had consummated their marriage, and stated that the brief permitting the marriage was issued on the grounds of confirming the friendship between Spain and England, and to prevent possible war. It posed a greater threat to Henry's case than the bull of dispensation, as it unequivocally stated that even if the marriage had been consummated, this was no impediment to her marriage to Henry. Understandably, Wolsey wanted a good look at this document, and Charles sent a properly notarised copy of the brief – he was hardly going to trust Wolsey with the original. Wolsey had lost the element of surprise. A quick investigation and annulment was out of the question, they now had the unwanted attention of all of Europe.

It is a popular notion that Wolsey met his ruin in the rise of the Boleyns, a family who had reached impressive heights by 1527 but, as we have seen,

Thomas and Wolsey had worked well together for years, with Wolsey helping facilitate George's modest rise at court. Neither Thomas nor his family had any reason to be at odds with the Cardinal at this stage, for who else was capable of achieving an annulment? While Wolsey believed a foreign princess would have been preferable – a royal marriage was always about benefit in terms of treaties and alliances – Wolsey gave the matter his full attention and energy. He wrote to Henry to dispel any suspicion: 'Assuring your highness that I shall never be found but as your most humble loyal and faithful obedient servant, enduring the travails and pains which I daily and hourly sustain.'[10]

But the genesis of the antagonism between the Cardinal and the Boleyns is repeatedly quoted to have begun years earlier, firstly when Wolsey allegedly thwarted Thomas' ambitions to become Comptroller of the Household in 1519, which in the face of the evidence seems highly improbable. The other popular argument that the Boleyns resented Wolsey comes from George Cavendish, Wolsey's devoted servant and later biographer, who wrote at length that Anne had once had a dalliance with and secret betrothal to Lord Henry Percy, the eldest son and heir of the Earl of Northumberland. Henry Percy was Wolsey's page and, sometime between 1523 and 1525, the pair were discovered, and Wolsey, either acting on his own, or following Henry's orders, forced them to separate. In Cavendish' account Anne was sent to Hever in disgrace, and Percy was sent north to Northumberland.[11] Anne 'was furious and she has promised that "if it lay ever in her power, she would work the cardinal as much [similar] displeasure"'.[12] Such an account may have served a loyal servant's resentment regarding his master's demise, but it was highly embellished. In these years, Anne was the daughter of Wolsey's colleague, a respected ambassador and courtier, with Howard and Butler connections. She was not reckless or foolish enough to make threats.[13]

Less histrionic references to this dalliance can be found in numerous sources, so there is little doubt that it occurred, but it does not prove that Anne was disgraced, or that she plotted Wolsey's demise. We have no way of knowing what Thomas made of his daughter's amorous adventure, but there is a curious payment found in Thomas' 1525 account book: 'For my costs to Wendesor, whan your Lordeshipe sende me to Maister Perssey [Percy].' Master Percy could not be the Lord of Northumberland but must have been his son. Could Thomas have sent his servant with a warning for Henry Percy or to encourage the match? The latter seems unlikely. In any case, it is improbable that this event caused Thomas to resent Wolsey. We do know that the Percy family had been negotiating a match between Henry Percy and Mary Talbot, the daughter of the Earl of Shrewsbury, as early as 1516, and during the event in question, Wolsey was still negotiating the Butler–Ormond marriage with the Boleyns. There is no reason to suggest that Thomas would have approved or encouraged Anne to risk scandal in a dalliance with someone whose formal betrothal was part of a serious political alliance.

Some historians speculate that Wolsey was already falling from favour as early as 1527 when his enemies (always assumed to be the Boleyns) sought to distance him from the King.[14] This theory is based on a single report by Inigo de Mendoza, Imperial ambassador to England, who referred to an anti-Wolsey group/faction led by Norfolk, which he describes in the context of the annulment as the 'finishing stroke' of all of Wolsey's iniquities.[15] But what Mendoza actually reported was that he: 'Hears on reliable authority that the Legate, as the finishing stroke to all his iniquities, has been scheming to bring about the Queen's divorce. She is so full of apprehension on this account that she has not ventured to speak with him [Mendoza].'[16]

While Norfolk, Suffolk and Thomas gained Henry's confidence, evidenced by their frequent meals with him in his privy chamber, this is not evidence of any change or shift against the Cardinal – they were already favoured courtiers who regularly dined with the King.[17] Furthermore, the letter from William Knight to Wolsey, while on his secret mission, has been interpreted as a warning to the Cardinal that Thomas and the dukes were aligning against him. But the letter merely states: 'Norfolk, Suffolk, Rochefort, [Thomas] and the treasurer [Fitzwilliam] are privy to the other letters sent to Wolsey. After which the King delivered Knight Wolsey's letter "concerning the secrets," and gives him hearty thanks for it, and for his devices about the Pope.'[18]

No more can be inferred from the letter other than the fact that the individuals listed had also read the letters, reasonably so, as they were highly invested parties.

Mendoza reported that Anne was conspicuously at Henry's side, her family close behind her, and he perceived that she held no affection for Wolsey, recounting the latter's return to court, in which he had been expecting a private audience, as was usually the case. But Anne's defences were up on his return when he had departed, he was not aware that he was moving heaven and earth on her account, and she interrupted Wolsey's messenger, who had come to inform the King of Wolsey's arrival and that he awaited Henry in his rooms, sharply retorting, 'Where else is the Cardinal to come? Tell him that he may come here, where the King is.'

What are we to make of this response? Anne was just as invested in this matter as Henry, but for her the stakes were far higher. Whatever news Wolsey carried, she should be equally privy to it. Nevertheless, Mendoza assumed that

Anne, her uncle Norfolk and father had made a league against the Cardinal, thinking that his absence (from England) might be a favourable opportunity for working his ruin.[19]

But this is at odds with the reality – they needed the Cardinal and they knew it. Knight's mission had been a disaster, he had foolishly confided in Pope Clement that Anne was Henry's intended, rather than keeping the matter vague, and the bulls Clement had issued to Knight did not grant an annulment, but merely reserved the right to deliver a final verdict. The preferred avenues had been exhausted, and Henry now required everyone's full co-operation.

Despite the drama of 1527, not every aspect of Thomas' life, or Wolsey's for that matter, was overshadowed by Anne and Henry's romance, and both men continued to work together. Thomas obtained a 21-year lease to Tunbridge manor, in addition to a series of demesne – lands attached to a manor – from Cardinal College, Oxford, and one of the conditions of the lease was that Thomas would provide the Dean and any other individuals of the college lodgings whenever they were in Tunbridge.[20] This is an interesting arrangement as Wolsey founded the college, and its welfare was close to his heart. Perhaps in acknowledgement of the business arrangement which would profit his college, Wolsey again turned his attention to a matter which had been close to *Thomas'* heart for over a decade – the Boleyn–Butler dispute over titles to the Irish earldom of Ormond. The matter seemed insoluble, with both sides laying claim to the earldom. Wolsey found the compromise.

He proposed that both sides – Thomas, his aunt and mother, and Sir Piers and his son James – renounced all their rights to the earldom, agreeing to put the case to the King.[21] Henry decided to divide the estates under the title, awarding Piers particular manors, while several others were leased to him by the Boleyn party for 30 years, for which Piers had to pay them £40 per year in two equal instalments.[22] The Boleyns were satisfied as the title remained vacant, but even though Piers was further mollified by being created Earl of Ossory in a ceremony at Windsor, he felt cheated out of the Ormond earldom he too had coveted.[23]

In 1527 another name enters the Boleyn historiography – that of Thomas Cromwell, a protégé of Wolsey's who was steadily earning a reputation as a skilled lawyer, though history has given him mixed reviews. The late Victorian historian James Froude described Cromwell as 'the most despotic minister who had ever governed England' with a 'long list of solemn tragedies'.[24] Cromwell became the 'notorious chief minister' who many historians regard as another wolf of court who deserted Wolsey to join the Boleyn ranks, until 1536 when he found their influence too dangerous.

Both Thomas and Cromwell worked for the Cardinal roughly at the same time or, at the very least, overlapped at some point, but in different capacities.[25] Cromwell belonged to Wolsey's domestic retinue, and Thomas was engaged in foreign affairs. But the very first threads of interaction between Thomas and Henry's future chief minister began in 1527. Thomas' sister, Alice, approached her brother for legal advice. It would appear that he immediately put her in touch with Cromwell, and she wrote to him on her brother's recommendation, asking for assistance.[26] Cromwell accepted, and wrote to Thomas in December, informing him that he had agreed to counsel and advise her. Unfortunately the case was complex, and Cromwell could see no other course of action but to go directly to Wolsey, which he advised Thomas to do, using his influence with the Cardinal to settle the matter. Upon reading the salutation of the letter, addressed to Thomas, it is clear that the men shared a mutual respect, but it also suggests again that Thomas was still on good terms with the Cardinal. In early April of 1528, Wolsey appointed Thomas to deal with potential riots in Kent – there was considerable agitation amongst those individuals who had loaned money to the King under duress for his war preparations prior to and including the 'amicable grant' and were demanding repayment. This was not a small matter – by mid-April, about 100 yeomen came to Knoll, begging for the money to be returned. Thomas' colleague, Warham, anxiously wrote to him that he had briefly placated the men, but they would return.[27] At the same time, Wolsey wrote to Thomas, urging him and his colleagues to use their 'unusual and accustomed wisdom' when dealing with the situation, meaning he assumed they would tell a few smooth lies and defuse the situation, which Thomas probably did.[28]

Thomas remained in Kent for the rest of the month as Warham had asked him to hear and decide a case of assault alongside Henry Guildford. It seems that Warham's bailiff, William Cheke, was waylaid by some of the servants of the Duchess of Norfolk, Thomas' sister-in-law. The outcome of this case is not known but it was an awkward choice – Thomas had worked well with Warham over the years, and the servants seemed to be at fault, but the duchess was family. This was not the last time Thomas would have to choose between a colleague and family. Soon after, Thomas returned to court, where Wolsey had been developing a new initiative in Henry's quest for an annulment.

The Cardinal had sent Edward Fox and Stephen Gardiner, Henry's almoner and the Cardinal's secretary respectively, to Orvieto where Clement had fled, to request a Papal Legate to preside over an English trial alongside Wolsey. At the same time, Thomas' priest, probably a man named William Barlow, was sent to Bologna on a secret mission, though it is not clear what his instructions were. This has been construed as Thomas going behind Wolsey's back – sending his own delegation – but Wolsey must have been privy to this second despatch as Gardiner and Fox mention the priest returning to England in April.[29] Gardiner and Fox returned several weeks later with letters of commission for the Cardinal, which they brought to his London residence of Durham House to peruse late at night, though Wolsey had gone to bed. Thomas visited the next day, and he and the Cardinal spent the morning perusing the commission, and Fox was sent to the king to give Wolsey's opinion on the matter.[30] All parties were working in harmony, and there is further evidence of Thomas advising his daughter to remain civil to the one man who could procure an annulment.

In early March of 1528, as the court dined at Windsor, Anne and her mother caught the attention of Thomas Henneage, a close friend of Wolsey's, and immediately struck up a conversation. Anne fretted that she felt Wolsey had forgotten her, for he had not sent any tokens of his esteem. Elizabeth Boleyn also asked Henneage for a morsel of 'tunny' or tuna, from the Cardinal.[31] Later that evening, when the court dined again, Henry, who was probably aware of Anne's plans, sent Henneage to deliver a special dish from the great hall to her apartments where she was dining privately. Her dainty hands fell upon his sleeve, and he was charmed into dining with the Boleyns. Anne told Henneage that she wished she had some good meat from Wolsey, as well as carps, shrimps or something else. Was this a not so subtle request for tribute? Whatever the case, it was more prudent to work *with* Wolsey towards a common goal, while making clear her position. Wolsey immediately began to correspond with Anne, sending gifts and words of encouragement, which she may have genuinely appreciated. He may have stymied her first attempt at marriage, but now that he respected her position, and was working for her benefit, they were a united front. Of course, even the most united of individuals, in such a small group surrounding the King, could still accidentally trip over each other.

Several weeks later, there was a misunderstanding between Henry and Wolsey over the complications arising from the death of the Abbess of Wilton; this is generally understood to be the first official indication of tension between Wolsey and the Boleyns.[32] Wilton Abbey in Wiltshire was one of the wealthiest religious communities for women of high birth in medieval England, but the appointment itself would not have been particularly noteworthy, were it not for the conflict it was about to create.

When the Abbess died on 24 April 1528 Wolsey, as Papal Legate, had elective rights to her successor. The Boleyns slowly becoming even more involved in court politics, had their own candidate – Eleanor, the sister of

Mary Boleyn's husband, William Carey. Carey was equally involved and ambitious for his sister – Thomas Henneage wrote to Wolsey that 'Mr. Carre begs you to be gracious to his sister, a nun in Wilton Abbey, to be prioress there, according to your promise.'[33] But Wolsey had his own candidate, Dame Isabella Jordan, who he installed once he received word that Henry had to drop Eleanor Carey as a candidate after her salacious lifestyle had been exposed.[34] Wolsey may have been under the impression that Henry had relinquished the choice to him, but in fact Henry had adopted a compromise, and chosen *his* own candidate. Was it miscommunication, or had Wolsey deliberately ignored his king and Anne? Nineteenth-century opinions pointed to Wolsey arrogantly ignoring Henry, assuming he would be able to override his king.[35] However, in the reappraisals of Wolsey by most modern historians, this drama is seen as a mistake on Wolsey's part rather than calculation or assumption.[36] The incident did not cause a major rupture between king and cardinal, but it came at a time when an element of distrust had begun to tinge the royal relationship, slowly undermining the Cardinal's position.[37]

With the summer heat of 1528 came the dreaded Sweat, and it cut a deadly swathe through Henry's court. It was said that one could be fine at breakfast, and dead by supper. Despite his conviction that as divinely anointed monarchs they would be untouched by the illness around them, Henry fled the city with Katherine at his side. We do not know how Anne reacted to being abandoned, but Thomas took his daughter to Hever. Curiously, George and his wife did not join them, but travelled with the King and Queen. We do not know where Elizabeth stayed. Within days, Anne had become gravely ill, followed shortly by her father. George was at Waltham Abbey accompanying the King, and had also caught the Sweat. He would probably have preferred to join his family, but he remained where he was. Henry sent letters to Anne along with his second-best doctor, but the fear of contamination prevented him from visiting, even when it was clear that both Thomas and Anne were slowly on the mend – Anne was young and of a strong disposition, and Thomas, despite being 51, was robust enough to survive the illness.

While at Hever, Anne received a letter from a surprising correspondent – the Cardinal. Wolsey initiated contact, sending Anne gifts and, from the peace of Hever, a weakened Anne responded in a warm and conciliatory way, thanking him 'in the humblest wise that my poor heart can think' and declaring that she was undeserving of his assistance. But once the annulment was concluded, she assured him, anything she could do for the Cardinal – if it were in her power, she would. For all the days of her life, she wrote, she was most bound to love and serve the Cardinal, and she beseeched him to never doubt it.[38] Historians, however, have. These letters are perhaps unusual for Anne, but they contain echoes of Thomas' style; he often favoured a flattering conciliatory approach. It was Wolsey who would procure an annulment, and who had finally made the breakthrough – Pope Clement had agreed at last that Henry's case should be heard in England in a Legatine Court. Cardinal Campeggio, who Thomas met at the French Court in 1519, would arrive in October to assist Wolsey with proceedings.[39] They were all still on the same page.

The threat of illness passed, and Henry was anxious to be reunited with Anne, who, though weak, continued to recover. Thomas had arranged to return her to court, but Henry begged Anne to ask her father to bring her to court a few days earlier than arranged, 'otherwise I shall think he will not do the lover's turn as he said he would, nor answer my expectation'.[40] In other words, Henry was placing enormous pressure on Thomas to facilitate the relationship, as he must have promised.

Remarkably, all three Boleyns survived the Sweat, but there was a family casualty – William Carey, Thomas' ambitious son-in-law, had caught the illness, and died on 22 June. It was a great loss to the family – to Thomas, who had assisted Carey in crafting his career at court, and Mary, as it left her a widow, and Carey had not left her financially secure. Henry and Anne discussed her predicament and, in a letter to Anne, Henry wrote: 'as touching your sister's matter, I have caused Water Welze to write to my Lord [Thomas] my mind therein, whereby I trust that Eve shall not have power to dyslave Adam; for surely, whatsoever is said, it cannot so stand with his honor but that he must needs take her his natural daughter now in her extreme necessity.'[41]

Historians have assumed that there had been a rift between Mary and her father and Thomas refused to assist her. Thomas was not as close to Mary as he was to Anne, and he could have been disappointed by her earlier behaviour with the King, which humiliated her husband, or perhaps tension had arisen from another issue. Thomas may have rashly declared that he would not assist Mary but whatever Thomas had said in anger to his daughter does not necessarily indicate that he had abandoned her, and Henry seems to be intimating that he assumed Thomas would assist Mary, further noting that Thomas was a man of honour. Shortly after, Anne took Mary's son, Henry Carey, as her ward, providing him with an education. Mary too would receive a stipend and while we cannot discern Thomas' direct involvement, the Boleyns rallied around Mary.

The Sweat had taken many influential individuals from the Privy Chamber, including William Compton, who had once been one of the most powerful men at court. George now had an opportunity for advancement and, by the end of September, he was made Esquire of the Body, about the same age as his father had been when he was first appointed to the position. The marks of favour continued: he was then made Master of the King's Buckhounds, a position within the same department as Master of the Horse. His responsibilities included overseeing Henry's hunting pack of buckhounds, which were used to bring down smaller game, in particular fallow deer. In November that year, he was made Keeper of the palace, garden and wardrobe of Beaulieu, which had been his brother-in-law, William Carey's position. The manor once belonged to George's great-grandfather, and it must have been satisfying to be in command of an estate which was such a part of the family history.[42]

George had now become a respected member of the King's Privy Chamber, but he was still ambitious, and looked to his future when his sister would be queen. He had always been on hand, when he was required as a go-between with Anne, or when illness had threatened the royal couple. With the household sustaining such loss of life, survivors like George were promoted. The latter half of 1528 saw the Boleyns, King and Cardinal working together to convince Pope Clement to agree that Henry's case should be heard in England in a Legatine Court. In September, Henry wrote to Anne to inform her that Clement had agreed to send a delegate, Cardinal Campeggio, to assist Wolsey with proceedings. The court waited for the man who, in their minds, held all the cards.

Lorenzo Campeggio had enjoyed a varied career. A diplomat, lawyer, and married father of five children, it hardly seemed that he was destined for religious life. Yet when his wife died in 1509, Campeggio was ordained as a priest earning the patronage of Pope Julius II. He was appointed cardinal-protector of England in January 1523, and he received the bishopric of Salisbury a year later which he had been promised. Beyond these appointments he had never really shown any interest in England, and he was probably less than pleased to be named legate on 8 June 1528, after a joint commission with Wolsey had been agreed. Campeggio arrived in London on 8 October, knowing the impossible position he was in, and Wolsey, who badgered the Cardinal from the moment of his arrival, did nothing to soothe his disquiet. What Wolsey did not know were Campeggio's true instructions – to delay the trial, and make no judgement. Initially he attempted to reconcile Katherine and Henry, but when this early form of marriage counselling proved unsuccessful, he suggested that Katherine, divinely appointed and royally anointed, should depart for a nunnery and take a vow of chastity. This suited Henry as he could remarry, and it was the only avenue Pope Clement, with Charles in his ear, was willing to consider. Katherine quickly made it clear that she might be pious, but she was not destined for a life of contemplation.

By early 1529 frustration crept in as Campeggio continued his preliminary investigations. Mendoza believed that Anne suspected Wolsey was responsible for the court delays, as he was afraid he would lose power once she became queen. This had forced her, Mendoza wrote, to form 'an alliance with her father, and with the Dukes of Norfolk and Suffolk, to try and see whether they can conjointly ruin the Cardinal'.[43] But Mendoza goes on to say that, blinded with passion, Henry himself was placing enormous pressure on Wolsey and Campeggio, and 'there was nothing that he [Henry] would not do or promise in order to obtain his object'.[44]

The French ambassador, Jean du Bellay, also reported that Norfolk and *his* group 'le duc de Nortfoch et sa bande' were working to rid the court of the Cardinal.[45] Whether or not these reports accurately described the situation, it was clear that uncertainty had created chaos.

Campeggio finally convened the court at Blackfriars on 18 June 1529. It was an event no one wanted to miss – the King and Queen on trial. The streets were filled with spectators but, to Henry's annoyance, they called Katherine's name. Despite her objection to the English trial, Katherine sat in her chair on the opposite side of the hall to Henry. But instead of waiting to be called to give evidence, she quickly crossed the floor and knelt before her husband, her lengthy and heartfelt speech famous enough that it need not be repeated here.[46] Katherine then left the court and, despite being re-summoned, would not appear again.

Both Thomas and George were present for the hearings, and while much of the detail, who said what about who and when, would have meant nothing to George, these were details Thomas had lived. The ghost of Arthur was conjured up for the court, as they tried to ascertain the crucial question – had he slept with his young wife or not? Had the marriage been consummated? Every living person who had witnessed the cheerful young prince that morning was called to testify, and a month into proceedings, it was Thomas' turn. He and his father William had served the young prince the morning after his wedding, and he was one of 18 people who gave a deposition concerning their recollection of events following Katherine's wedding to Arthur decades earlier. Thomas recounted the same story as the others: Katherine and Arthur lived as man and wife, the marriage was considered valid at the time, and it was assumed the marriage had been consummated. Arthur's lewd comment that, on his wedding night, he had 'been in the midst of Spain' was repeated by several individuals.[47]

Plate 1    Tomb and Brass of Thomas Boleyn, St Peters' Church, Hever.

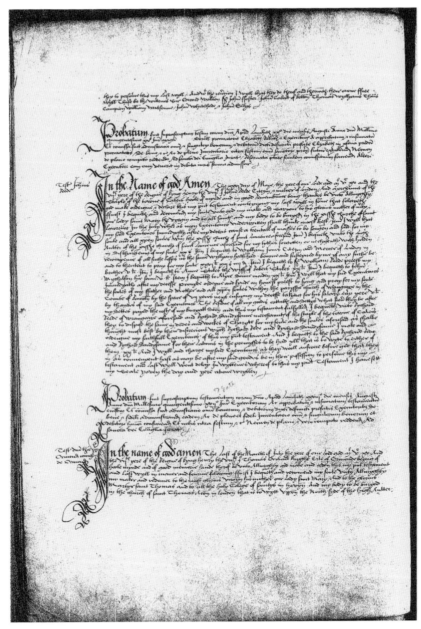

Plate 2 Will of Sir Thomas Butler, Earl of Ormond, Page 1, with specific reference to Butler bequeathing the white horn to his grandson.

Plate 3   Boleyn coat of arms, Hever.

Plate 4   The rules for the 1511 Joust to celebrate the birth of Prince Henry. From the Harley Charter.

Plate 5  Cardinal Wolsey's letter of introduction on behalf of Thomas Boleyn to Charles V, 1522.

Plate 6  Example of an ambassadorial report from Young, Boleyn, and Wingfield to Henry VIII.

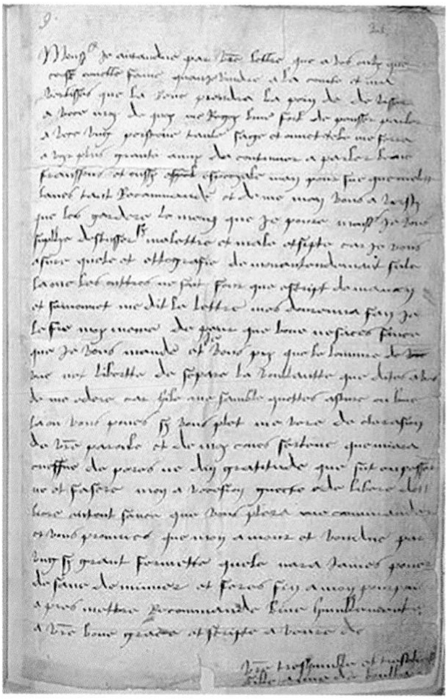

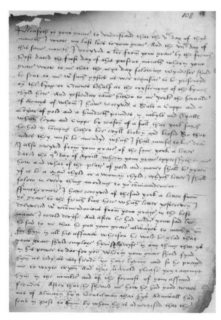

Plate 7    Anne Boleyn's letter to her father, from Margaret of Austria's Court.

Plate 8    Thomas Boleyn to Cardinal Wolsey; about the Imperial Election and a treaty with the Swiss.

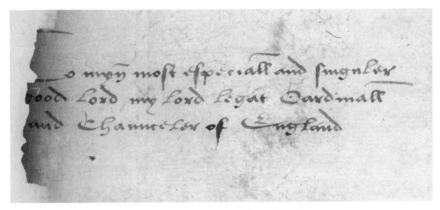

Plate 9    Thomas Boleyn's salutation to Cardinal Wolsey.

Plate 10    Sample page from Thomas Boleyn's account book during his tenure as Comptroller of the Household.

Plate 11  Anne Boleyn's music book, with the phrase 'Nowe Thus'.

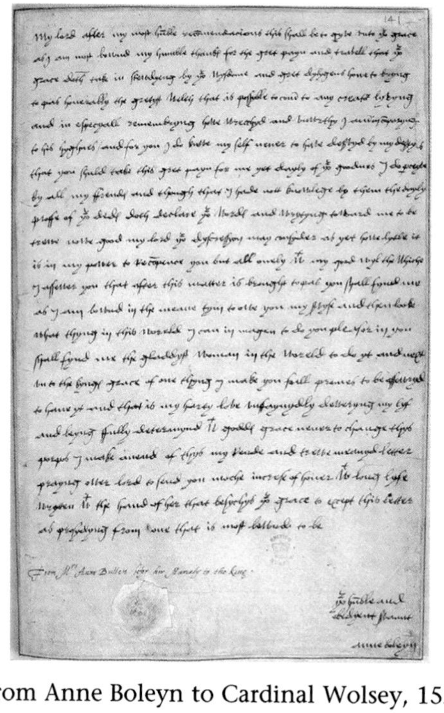

Plate 12  Letter from Anne Boleyn to Cardinal Wolsey, 1528.

Plate 13   Portrait of Imperial Ambassador Eustace Chapuys.

Plate 14   A letter from Chapuys to Charles V, reporting on George Boleyn's mission to France with his uncle, the Duke of Norfolk, 29 May 1533.

Plate 15    James Butler. This half finished portrait by Hans Holbein, which is titled 'Ormond' was claimed to portray Thomas. There is however, overwhelming evidence that this is James Butler, who also claimed the Earldom of Ormond.

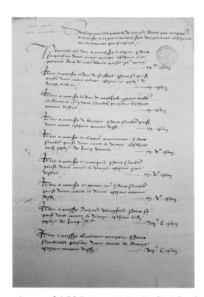

Plate 16    Imperial Pensions of 1525 to certain individuals of the English court, with Cardinal Wolsey, Duke of Norfolk, Duke of Suffolk, Sir Thomas Boleyn, among the top four.

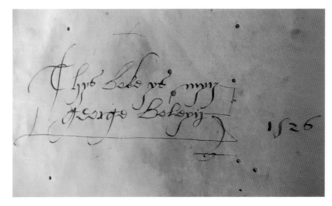

Plate 17   George Boleyn's signature in his copy of *Les Lamentations' de Matheolus et 'Le Livre de Leesce' de Jehan Le Fevre, de Resson*, Jehan le Fevre, f. 2v.

Plate 18   1535 Order of the Garter Procession from the Black Book of the Garter.

Plate 19    Thomas Boleyn Garter Stall Plate.

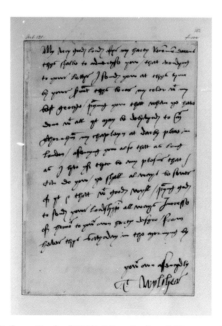

Plate 20    Thomas Boleyn Earl of Wiltshire, to Lord Cromwell, sending him his collar and his 'best George' to be returned to his chaplain.

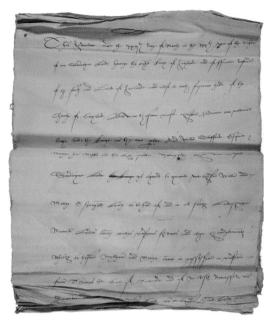

Plate 21 First page of Indenture between the king and Mary and William Stafford following Thomas Boleyn's death.

Plate 22 Boleyn family crest, Hever.

PLATE 23   Anne Boleyn.

PLATE 24   The white Butler Falcon, prominently displayed on a set of Virginals owned by Elizabeth I.

PLATE 25    Henry VIII.

PLATE 26   Cardinal Wolsey.

PLATE 27   Thomas Cromwell.

PLATE 28   Marguerite of Navarre.

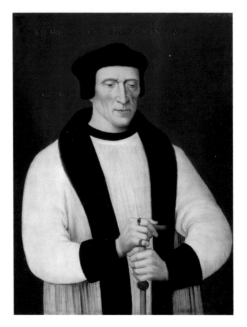

PLATE 29   Richard Fox.

Apart from his role as witness, Thomas also assisted Wolsey and Campeggio, both escorting the Legate to and from court each day. If there was discernible tension between the Cardinal and Thomas, there is no record of it. In the account of Wolsey's biographer, George Cavendish, however, Thomas and Wolsey became involved in a dramatic altercation and, admittedly, Cavendish does paint an intriguing scene. It was at the end of another trying day of court in July, when Wolsey received word that Katherine was planning to appeal directly to the Pope to have the matter heard in Rome and, if Katherine forced the trial to stall, Wolsey would bear the brunt of Henry and Anne's wrath. Wolsey considered his position as he sailed up the Thames from Blackfriars to Westminster, the heat of the day lingering in the London air without a respite in sight. He was already in a rather fragile state, despising the heat, and he needed rest, and to rethink matters. He had only just had a chance to lie down, Cavendish tells us, when Thomas knocked on his door – he had been sent by the King with a message, that they were to leave immediately to fetch Cardinal Campeggio, and beg an audience with Katherine. As Thomas explained, their job was to persuade her to place the whole matter in the King's hands, without waiting for the decision of the Legate, which might end in her slander and defamation.[48] No doubt Thomas was no more enthusiastic about the prospect of an afternoon convincing Katherine, but Cavendish was far less concerned with Thomas' feelings on the matter, describing Wolsey's reaction instead. Wolsey rose from his bed, face still flushed from the heat, and no more rested. Thomas stood quietly while the Cardinal dressed, stalking from one end of his chamber to the other and, while he did so, he proceeded to give Thomas a dressing down. It was because of Thomas and other lords of the council who had put such fantasies into Henry's mind, 'whereby ye are the causers of great trouble to all this realm, and at length get you but small thanks, either of God, or the world'.[49]

Cavendish wrote that Thomas' eyes watered during the chastisement, as he knelt before the Cardinal's bed as he was berated.[50] There is no other source to corroborate this story, or that Wolsey lambasted Thomas – he may have – but as Cavendish was writing decades after Anne's death, it is possible that he put such prophetic words in Wolsey's mouth for a reason.

After weeks of trial, Campeggio declared he would make a public announcement and, on 23 July, the court assembled. Wincing as he stood, his gout causing discomfort, he declared that he would give no judgement in this trial, and would recall the case to Rome, but as the Legatine court was not in session over the summer, the case would be adjourned until October. It was what Wolsey had been trying to avoid, his ambassadors in Rome arguing that if

Campeggio did such a thing, this would cause manifest scandal and irreparable ruin. Katherine, upon hearing the news, agreed. It would indeed cause ruin – for Wolsey.

Something had shifted too, in the perceptions of the Boleyns. The family had attracted resentment for their rise, and Katherine's popularity fuelled general dislike towards them. The whole matter divided opinion – some families remained loyal to Henry, but others sympathised with Katherine; they remembered what her marriage had signified, what it had done for England, what *Katherine* had done for England. Historians have presented Thomas as father of a queen in waiting, scheming while enjoying a position of influence but, if anything, it had so far been a thankless task. Far from enjoying the rewards that we would assume came with such a position, Thomas would still have to endure countless stressful diplomatic situations, abroad and at court. He had allowed events to play out, but it was clear already to the sharp-minded ambassador that, with the postponement of the trial, Wolsey's approach was never going to work.

In late 1529, George, emerging from his father's shadow, was proving to be a determined, ambitious young man, eager to follow in his father's footsteps. Perhaps Wolsey felt that the relationships were too fragile at this point, and approached the family. When Richard Fox, the man who made Wolsey, and who had witnessed Thomas' first foray into foreign politics decades earlier, died in 1529, Wolsey exchanged the bishopric of Durham for that of Fox's bishopric of Winchester, and Henry used the revenues of Durham as a gift for Thomas. Wolsey then offered the King a further four months income in order to expedite the payments.[51] For better or worse, the politics of the court now revolved around *his* family politics.

# CHAPTER NINE

# Treasonous Waters

In these days a minister who is no longer acceptable to his sovereign, be that sovereign one man or many, consults his ease and his dignity by resigning. He sharpens his weapons, he bides his time – sparsa ad pugnam proludit arena. He raises a mighty dust, and prepares for the future combat.

– J.S. Brewer

In the well-traversed – but not always substantiated – narratives of Wolsey's fall, the Boleyns and their Howard kin are usually portrayed as a morally corrupt faction, out to destroy the Cardinal politically, repelling his attempts to return to royal favour. For the foreign ambassadors at the English court who had seen a marked coolness towards the Cardinal following the Legatine trial, Wolsey's fate seemed obvious. He would soon fall, they predicted and, when he did, the Boleyns and their allies who would be to blame. They were right about the shift in power – Wolsey's assurances to Henry of a quick trial and favourable result, annulment, and a new marriage had not come to fruition. In Rome, the case would result in Katherine's favour. Wolsey had never been popular with Henry's councillors, and his position had been a constant source of envy. Henry relied heavily on Wolsey, and the Cardinal, for his part, had never disappointed him. But Wolsey had become a prisoner of his own promises and was now vulnerable.

As a new political landscape emerged in the final months of 1529, Henry was less reliant on his Chancellor, preferring to surround himself with other individuals. The Dukes of Norfolk and Suffolk, alongside Thomas, are often viewed as a triumvirate who took over from Wolsey, but Norfolk and Suffolk had always been, and remained, in Henry's inner circle and, alongside Anne as queen to be, they often dined, hunted and hawked together. Thomas rarely took part during these uncertain weeks following the trial at Blackfriars.

He remained at court, dealing with the business of diplomacy as well as Henry's marital issues. The pressure must have been immense for the 52-year-old – the King wanted to marry his daughter but, if they adhered to Papal law, such an outcome seemed remote at this stage. More importantly, Thomas would have felt the impact of the marital crisis which had weakened England's position, affecting Wolsey's diplomatic strategy and the missions of English ambassadors abroad. Katherine's stance increased political tension between Henry and Charles, which left only France, but they were in an equally weak position. As part of his release in 1526, Francis was forced to abandon his feudal claims to Artois and Flanders. In addition, he agreed to marry the Emperor's sister Eleanor, resign his rights to Milan, Genoa and Naples, provide a French naval fleet to accompany Charles to his Imperial coronation in Rome, and would have to join the Emperor on a crusade against the Ottoman Turks and the German Lutherans. It was a great deal for Charles. For insurance, Charles had taken Francis' two sons, the nine-year-old Dauphin, François, and seven-year-old Henri, duc d'Orléans.[1] Rescuing his children from their squalid conditions in Spain was paramount, thus Francis was focused on peace with the Emperor throughout early 1529, and French and Imperial ambassadors met at Cambrai to negotiate a treaty, in which England was eager to play a part. Wolsey had asked du Bellay to ensure negotiations would not take place until after the Legatine trial, when he could give this his full attention, to which both sides agreed. But negotiations seemed to gain ground in July when Wolsey and the English court were preoccupied at Blackfriars.

Wolsey sent Thomas More and Cuthbert Tunstall on an embassy to Cambrai. Tunstall was a stalwart of Wolsey's diplomatic stable, and he and More had worked together as ambassadors in the past. But from their arrival, and much to Wolsey's frustration, they were kept on the sidelines, and could not insert themselves properly into negotiations. The Treaty of Cambrai, or Ladies' Peace, was engineered between Francis and Charles by the women Thomas knew well – Charles' aunt, Margaret of Austria, and Francis' mother, Louise of Savoy. It was a less punitive version of the 1526 Treaty of Madrid, which restored some French territories, but Francis would only be reunited with his children after the ransom was paid. This new treaty was signed on 3 August 1529, with the English ambassadors having done no more than witness a treaty that ended hostilities between France and Spain. Wolsey feared that Francis would no longer support Henry's annulment.[2] Imperial eyes did indeed turn to Henry, and Charles' Imperial ambassador in Rome, Louis de Praet, wrote that he and Pope Clement had agreed to wait and see if England would back down from the annulment, smugly noting that the English were in shock, as they had 'not only had no hope of peace, but believed and wrote that it would never be concluded'.[3]

With an alliance between Charles and Francis consolidated, where did that leave England?[4] Wolsey still had one option – he could insist that England also be a signatory to the treaty, having loaned both nations considerable money for various campaigns. Wolsey knew that Francis would struggle to raise the ransom for his sons without England's assistance, but it was hardly the level of involvement he or Henry would have liked. Nevertheless, Wolsey quickly drew up a course of action which he submitted to the King, and waited. Henry was spending a great deal of time at his Palace of Woodstock in the summer air with the Dukes of Norfolk and Suffolk. Henry read Wolsey's suggestions after returning from the hunt late in the evening of 30 August, but he was dissatisfied with Wolsey's approach, and immediately called for Thomas, instructing him to seek out Stephen Gardiner despite the late hour. Gardiner was only slightly younger than Thomas, and also pursued an ambassadorial career, though he did not have his colleague's easy charm and tact. But he was intelligent and educated, and had spent time in Paris alongside Thomas Wriothesly – a courtier and member of Wolsey's household in those early years.[5] He had served Wolsey but, more importantly, his embassy to Orvieto with Fox in 1528 had proved his reliability and loyalty.

Thomas and Gardiner set about checking Wolsey's detailed proposal to ratify the treaty, checking for any potential loopholes or flaws before the proposal was taken to France. Gardiner's letter to Wolsey the next day indicates the pressure both men were under.[6] Gardiner was sincere in assuring his former mentor that Henry appreciated the 'great pains taken in answering with such diligence the articles proposed by the French ambassadors'.[7] He added that he and Thomas were given the highly unwelcome task of spending a sleepless night at Woodstock, examining the treaty alongside Wolsey's suggestions. By morning, the bleary-eyed men had determined that Wolsey's suggestions were harsher than necessary, possibly due to the Cardinal's distrust of the French, and he and Thomas made their own suggestions to Henry. Gardiner wrote that both he and Thomas 'urge you to consider *quod præterita dolere magis quam corrigere possumus* [the past can suffer more than we can correct]'. He further begged Wolsey not to be offended, but to 'take it in good part'.[8]

Some historians claim that Thomas staged this incident to undermine Wolsey, making him look foolish or superfluous, 'while Gardiner looked the other way', in other words, did nothing to assist the Cardinal.[9] But it was Henry who ordered the men to make the appraisal, and Henry who decided to soften the approach to the treaty.

An increasingly insecure Wolsey lashed out at Gardiner, suggesting that he assumed Gardiner had been more instrumental in persuading the King.[10] An offended Gardiner wrote again to the Cardinal, saying that whatever his opinion might be of the interpretation of the Treaty he should not judge either himself or Thomas, who were doing no more than they had been bid.[11] It would be foolish to assume that Thomas wanted Wolsey's proposals to fail, or that he and Gardiner made the suggestions to antagonise Wolsey. A peace between Charles and Francis, which Henry left isolated, did not bode well for his annulment. Most likely, Thomas was hopeful of success, and he and Gardiner had devoted a great deal of time and care to perfecting the ratification. Shortly after, a chastened Wolsey wrote to Gardiner to smooth things over, but a breach had opened.

Wolsey's failure to secure an annulment via the Legatine trial opened the door to others to try more innovative approaches. When the court moved to Waltham in late August, Gardiner was lodged with Edward Fox, who he had known for several years. Serendipitously, the two men made the acquaintance of a studious theologian, Thomas Cranmer, who, like everyone else throughout the country, had followed the Legatine trial at Blackfriars. It is believed that the three men spoke of the King's predicament over supper one evening, and Cranmer said that the problem with the annulment was its approach. Cranmer suggested that it was not an issue of canon law, but a theological issue. He believed that the theologians of universities both in England and abroad should be consulted on the legitimacy of Henry's marriage, which Fox relayed to the King. It was August 1529 when Henry instructed Cranmer to stay at Durham House, – previously Wolsey's residence until he exchanged the bishopric of Durham for Winchester, and now Thomas' residence in the Strand. Henry had instructed Thomas to 'let Doctor Cranmer have entertainment in your house at Durham Place for a time, to the intent he may be there quiet to accomplish my request and let him lack neither books, nay anything requisite for his studies'.[12] It may have re-energised Henry but it was not a radical suggestion. Campeggio reported that Henry and Wolsey had sent men to consult the theologians of the University of Paris on 21 October 1528, and in June 1529.[13] After the collapse of the Legatine trial, du Bellay reported that Henry wanted Wolsey to go to France personally to get the opinions of learned men there on the divorce, which Wolsey supported.[14] This is not to negate Cranmer's role, but that it was his idea is a misconception. Cranmer's move to Thomas' house is significant, as it reflects how Thomas was viewed. This was an intellectual undertaking and Cranmer would have required significant reading material, so this suggests that Henry saw Thomas as a man of learning and education who might be able to assist Cranmer to construct their position so as to appeal to the courts of Europe – in other words, Thomas was seen as an effective diplomat or a scholarly advisor, or perhaps both. This sentiment is echoed in the memorial of Thomas Cranmer, published in 1840 by the clergyman and historian, John Strype, who described Thomas as 'one of the learnedest noblemen in the land, and endued with a mind inclined to philosophy'.[15]

Wolsey had not seen Henry for some time, and could only come to court when expressly invited. His requests to see the King thus far had been denied, with Gardiner the messenger. When Henry did visit him for three days in late August at Tittenhanger, he made the error of complaining about the Duke of Suffolk's treatment of him.[16] It was a different landscape now for Wolsey.

Cavendish tells us that the King and Cardinal met once more; Cardinal Campeggio, gout-ridden and tired, was ready to depart England, having done little good, and Wolsey accompanied him to court to take his leave of the King. Henry, Anne and their entourage arrived at Grafton, and Henry invited Campeggio and Wolsey to visit. They arrived at Grafton but Suffolk, whose delight in making life difficult for Wolsey was evident, ensured that there were no rooms available for him.[17] It gave Suffolk perverse pleasure to cause as much discomfort as he could, forcing Wolsey to lodge three miles away at Easton Neston, in a house owned by Sir Thomas Empson. Wolsey was not aware of this until the pair arrived and, astonished, he rushed to quickly change out of his damp riding clothes in the chamber of Sir Henry Norris, Groom of the Stool, before his meeting with the King.

When Wolsey arrived, Henry was amiable and cheerful, surrounded by his court, with Thomas and his children present. Cavendish tells us that Henry drew the Cardinal to a window bay to talk as they once had. Cavendish described Wolsey as somewhat confounded by Henry's warm gestures, contrasting this with Henry and Anne's private dinner later, during which Anne spent more time pouring poison against the Cardinal into her lover's ear than eating. Cavendish was not invited to the private dinner but assures us that Anne was not in favour of Wolsey regaining his position. She was Henry's confidante and trusted advisor, and she distrusted Wolsey.

When Wolsey trudged to court from his lodgings this next day, he discovered that Henry had chosen to go hunting with Anne, who, Cavendish tells us, had convinced him to depart early. Wolsey sat with the King's council well into the night, and it was reported that Suffolk, Thomas, Brian Tuke and Stephen Gardiner were just as courteous and respectful as protocol dictated. Wolsey waited for Henry to return, but instead received instructions to depart court with Campeggio, and the two men took their leave. Wolsey would never see Henry again, nor would he see Thomas – whose career he had cultivated, and with whom he had worked so well and for so many years.

Thomas must have known that the King would soon move against his Chancellor, but of all the individuals waiting to bring the Cardinal down, it is difficult to locate either of the Boleyn men among them. George had no reason to resent the Cardinal, and Thomas obviously followed the pattern set by the King, but he was not a leader, or a particularly active participant. Henry's divorce was paramount – if Wolsey could assist, then they could work together, but Wolsey had exhausted his options, and the tide had well and truly turned.

As Wolsey's star set, George's rise at court continued. Days before the Legatine trial was postponed, George had been appointed governor of Bethlehem Hospital in London, a lucrative position, but his true opportunity came in October, when he was appointed as the new ambassador to France. George was only 25 years old, he was inexperienced – his father had been a decade older when he was sent on his first mission abroad – but Thomas had no experience either when he had first journeyed to Margaret's court, dealing with a far more experienced negotiator than himself. This embassy was George's opportunity to launch his diplomatic career. The Boleyns expected him to be taken seriously – du Bellay wrote ahead to Francis that George's family anticipated that the young man would be received with more than ordinary honour, and that his reception would be 'well weighed'.[18] The appointment had raised a few French eyebrows, with du Bellay referring to George derisively as the *Petite Prince*. He was judged before his feet had even left English soil. George's career came at a time when contemporaries immediately dismissed any perceived favour or position as owing to Anne's status, but the Boleyns were not just relatives of the future queen, they would soon be kin to the son and heir to the English throne. Who better to represent royal interests?

As in the case of Thomas' first embassy, George would not go alone nor was he the figurehead; he would be joining John Stokesley, a senior and well-respected ambassador and Church figure. Their instructions were twofold – they were to confer with Francis about the possibility of convening a General Council of the Church, most likely in regards to Henry's annulment. Stokesley was not there to support such an idea, but, as Henry instructed, to prevent the event, 'considering the influence the Emperor has over the Pope'.[19] They were also instructed to gain the votes of the Parisian theologians at the University, to persuade them to declare for the King, and write in favour of the divorce.

Although Henry asked Francis for credence for both ambassadors in October 1529 it is not clear when they arrived, or if they were even received by Francis as no reports were sent back to England.[20] Some historians assume that George returned to England briefly and then left for France again in January, but there are two intriguing pieces of evidence which shed light on the mystery. We know that Stokesley was in France from October until sometime after Christmas, only then making it to Paris. From there, he wrote a letter to Thomas back in England in mid-January, informing him that a bill was currently in circulation in Paris, protesting Henry's divorce. But he began his letter by writing: 'On the 15th your son took his journey to the French king, now being ten leagues beyond Troyes.'[21] Stokesley would not be informing Thomas about his own son leaving England. Clearly George was still in France and it is likely he had been there since October of 1529, but he may not yet have had an audience with the King of France.[22]

George's mission to France meant that he missed the arrival of the new Imperial ambassador to court, Eustace Chapuys, who, it is said, had a nose like a terrier, and smelt mischief whenever Anne Boleyn passed by.[23] Dignified, slender, with dark, beady eyes, short cropped hair, and the elegant turn of phrase of a talented ambassador, Chapuys would be a force to be reckoned with. He arrived in London in late September, having been briefed by Mendoza on the current state of play at court. The cause of Wolsey's problems, as far as Chapuys could tell, was his failure to procure a divorce, 'on which failure those parties, who for a long time have been watching their opportunity to revenge old injuries, and take the power out of the Cardinal's hands, have founded their attacks to undermine his influence … and get the administration of affairs into their own hands'.[24]

Henry chose Thomas to entertain the ambassador at dinner, and Chapuys described his counterpart as conciliatory and amiable. Thomas usually preferred a frank approach to matters, never over-articulating how his master felt, and avoiding sweeping statements of affection. Wisely, Thomas made no attempt to downplay the current marital crisis. After dinner Thomas took the ambassador aside, concerned that tensions between Charles and Henry had escalated recently with Henry recalling his ambassador, Dr Edward Lee, from the Imperial Court. Thomas hoped that Chapuys would not feel it necessary to likewise depart.[25] Chapuys assured him that Henry had mentioned a new embassy to the Imperial court, and Chapuys had no reason to leave. Thomas, according to Chapuys, effusively assured him that, despite their differences, Henry thought of Charles with 'more affection than anyone can think, imagine, or describe'.[26] Thomas stressed Henry's overwhelming love for

Charles, declaring that he would have given anything, including the whole of his fortune, for Charles to be convinced of Henry's goodwill and affectionate regard. But was Chapuys reporting Boleyn's words verbatim? We must take into account the constructed nature of Chapuys' accounts as potential acts of self-fashioning. Chapuys wrote with an eye to posterity, and his reports were dynamic and full of colour, but he was keen to show he was never bested by those he sparred with, and that he saw through any attempts to manipulate or flatter him. We cannot therefore say that this conversation took place exactly as Chapuys reported, but Thomas may well have been anxious that Charles be kept on side, especially considering he had made peace with Francis. Regardless, Chapuys' first reports are useful in placing both Boleyn men at court. He often found Thomas in conference with Henry, who called on his expertise at all times day and night, but was still by this point not a frequent member of his social circle, the other young men Henry surrounded himself with.

For several weeks there had been silence between Henry and the Cardinal, but the French and Imperial reports from England in the first week of October were full of the extraordinary news that Henry had suddenly moved against Wolsey, which must have been his intention even as he met with Wolsey at Grafton. Events continued to move at a rapid pace as the wolves descended, let loose by Henry himself. On 9 October, Wolsey was indicted in the Court of King's Bench for offences under the statute of praemunire.[27] Eighteen days later, the Dukes of Norfolk and Suffolk barged into his residence of York Place, demanding he surrender the Great Seal, thus formally resigning as Lord Chancellor, the position he had held since 1515. In their excitement, they had forgotten to bring the royal authority, which Wolsey pointed out, and the pair had to return the next day to complete the task, having lost some of their thunder.

It is hard not to feel sympathy for Wolsey, especially through the eyes of du Bellay, who visited the Cardinal shortly after his disgrace, and painted a miserable picture. He reported that when Wolsey spoke, his heart and tongue failed him completely. He wept, and prayed that Francis and Louise would have pity upon him.

Wolsey was instructed to make a detailed inventory of all his goods, which would be surrendered to the King. The inventories still exist, and make for extraordinary reading, painting a portrait of a man of exceptional taste for religious and secular art, with an obsession with tapestries and textiles from the East, which he imported through Venice. Some of these iconic tapestries still exist, including the story of Absolom; King Assuere and Queen Hester; the history of Sampson; and the history of Solomon. Each of the Cardinal's residences teemed with gold plate, silks cloth of silver and gold, and in every residence, a gold strainer for oranges, which Wolsey was famous for eating each day, believing it staved off illness. He also had countless finely carved images of saints and crucifixes, chalices, organs, silks for altars and cushions for kneeling, among other items. Decades had gone into this collection and, within a few weeks, it had all come to the King.

On a quiet October evening, Henry took Anne, her mother, and Henry Norris, Groom of the Stool, by barge, to view Wolsey's collection. Whatever she may have felt about the Cardinal, Anne must have been impressed by the exquisiteness of all that lay before her. When she next saw her father, who was evidently busy with other matters, she may well have described in detail what she saw that evening.

Meanwhile, the whole of London turned out to watch the once great Cardinal amble to Putney where he would be housed until Henry chose to proceed against him. Cavendish, who we rely on for these events despite his obvious bias, wrote that, before he reached Putney, he was overtaken by Norris, who brought him, 'from the King, a ring with a rich stone in it, as a token of the King's favor'. Norris had a message from Henry, who commanded him to be of 'good cheer'.

What was Henry's motive for demeaning his servant, only to offer a sliver of hope? The traditional explanation has it that this was a tug of war between Henry and Anne, who encouraged him to remain hardened against the Cardinal, while Henry had moments of weakness, and out of guilt gave every indication of forgiving Wolsey. But this is doubtful as Henry intended to discredit him politically.

Following the news, Thomas remained quiet on the issue, whereas Norfolk was everywhere at court in the best of spirits, and cheerfully asked Chapuys what Charles would make of the Cardinal's disgrace, to which Chapuys replied that he hoped that 'the management of affairs would now fall into the hands of men better fitted by their birth and nobility to promote the happiness and honour of the king and kingdom'.[28]

The Cardinal's despair is palpable through his letters, written in desperation to anyone who he thought might offer him assistance. One of his most frequent correspondents was his protégé, Thomas Cromwell. Wolsey spoke of Norfolk and Suffolk as the prime movers against him, and Cromwell lamented that no one dare speak to the King, lest they upset 'Madame Anne'.[29]

Wolsey had fallen from a high pedestal, and now found himself in the unfamiliar position of a suitor, relying on Cromwell and any other allies.

Cromwell, in London, prepared to defend the Cardinal's interests, first turned to the Boleyns. The Cardinal had written in his own hand that 'If the pleasure of my lady Anne be somewhat assuaged, as I pray God the same may be, then it should be devised by some convenient mean she be further laboured, for it is the only hope and remedy.'[30]

Wolsey had always preferred to personally manage the King, and as such Parliament had not sat for six years, for Wolsey despised parliamentary interference. But on 9 August 1529, Henry commanded an issue of writs summoning peers to Parliament and ordering the elections of the Commons. It is not immediately clear why Henry chose to convene Parliament so soon after the failure of the Legatine Court, but he may have hoped that one of its members might suggest a solution to his marital crisis.[31] This Parliament, which held sessions from 1529 to 1536, would be known as the Reformation Parliament, and the first session convened on 3 November 1529, accompanied by a blaze of pomp and medieval pageantry. The King set out for Blackfriars, where Parliament would convene; first came the knights, esquires and sergeants-at-law, then the bishops. Archbishop of Canterbury, William Warham, and Lord Chancellor, Thomas More, then followed. The Duke of Suffolk flanked the King, as Earl Marshal, and bore the staff of office. Norfolk, Lord Treasurer, came next, followed by Temporal Peers, Thomas among them. Thomas Audley, now part of the Boleyns' circle, was elected as Speaker.[32]

The first session of Parliament dealt with the recently deposed Cardinal Wolsey. If the Cardinal had hoped that Henry would take no action against him, he was mistaken. On 22 October, Wolsey was ordered to acknowledge his guilt in an indenture made with the King. Chronicler Edward Hall wrote that, 'when the nobles and prelates perceived that the king's favour was from the Cardinal sore minished, every man of the king's council began to lay to him such offences as they knew by him, and all their accusations were written in a book, and all their hands set to it.'[33] The charges against Wolsey varied from accusations of bungling foreign policy, taking proceeds from religious houses that should have gone into the King's coffers, to knowingly breathing on the King when he was infectious. The English clergy played a major part in the allegations, as did Thomas More, alongside numerous nobles.[34]

Thomas, who was a member of the House of Lords, signed the 44 articles, drawn up weeks earlier in Parliament, accusing Wolsey of 'enormities, excesses, and transgressions'.[35] The bill was signed by the Dukes of Norfolk and Suffolk; the Earls of Shrewsbury, Northumberland and Oxford; the Marquesses of Exeter and Dorset; and Lords Darcy, Boleyn, Mountjoy, Sandys and Fitzwalter, not all of whom were anti-Wolsey. Instead, this was a list of all those influential in the King's counsels at that time.[36]

The same day, du Bellay wrote that 'Wolsey has just been put out of his house, and all his goods taken into the king's hands ... he is quite undone ... the duke of Norfolk is made chief of the Council, Suffolk acting in his absence, and, at the head of all, Mademoiselle Anne.'[37]

These parliamentary complaints did not recommend any new charges against Wolsey, and no further parliamentary action was taken. Despite being exiled, the door was left open for the Cardinal – he continued to correspond with Norfolk and, when he fell ill in December, Henry immediately sent his own physician, and persuaded a reluctant Anne to send a small gift – a tablet of gold from her girdle.[38] A few days later, Chapuys reported that Wolsey was leading a very devout life, saying Mass daily, praising God for having afforded him this opportunity of acknowledging his errors, and saying to everyone he met that he never enjoyed greater peace of mind than at the present moment, and that even if the King would restore him to his former position, as well as give him the entire administration of the kingdom, he would not willingly resume the charge of it.[39] Wolsey thought nothing of the sort.

England's negotiations with France continued following the Treaty of Cambrai, with Norfolk and Suffolk first attempting to take control with Wolsey out of the way. The Dukes felt they were entitled to take over, and at first the French ambassadors felt they were making progress. Understandably this caused friction with Thomas; he was not only the future father of a queen but he had extensive experience with the French diplomatic technique, and especially with this particular treaty, which he and Gardiner had spent a sleepless night untangling. His colleagues had not dedicated the same time or effort – Norfolk was not a natural ambassador, with very little tact and skill for dissimulation. Suffolk preferred the more adventurous of life's pursuits; diplomacy bored him. We see an ambition in Thomas to be the new chief of foreign diplomacy, eager to step out of the shadow of the Cardinal and the dukes, and to guide through a treaty in which he had been so invested. Chapuys reported that all matters of diplomacy now crossed Thomas' desk, confirmed by the French ambassador, du Bellay, who assumed that due to tension with Charles, they would have more agreeable negotiations, and that Thomas would be more open to pleasing them. But of all Henry's councillors, Thomas caused problems. He knew this treaty inside and out, and was prepared to stand his ground, debating the finer points of negotiations.

Du Bellay incorrectly assumed that Thomas was deliberately frustrating his attempted agreements with Henry, against the wishes of his English colleagues.[40] He anxiously wrote to Anne de Montmorency, Admiral of France, regarding his difficulties, suggesting that if Louise of Savoy could send a letter which recognised Thomas' position and status as a lead negotiator, matters would be smoother. As du Bellay complained, it was Thomas who 'leads the dance expressly against the Dukes and Wolsey, whom I had so well persuaded that I thought I had gained my cause'.[41] Thomas may have expected preferential treatment to reflect his standing at court. But he only made his demands after du Bellay had mentioned to him that he had conducted business earlier that day with Norfolk and Suffolk, inadvertently excluding him. Thomas was positioning himself to be as influential as Norfolk and Suffolk, but was also keen to remind the ambassador of the connection to Anne. He made it clear to du Bellay that 'None of the other [councillors] have any credit at all [with Henry] unless it pleases the Young Lady [Anne] to lend them some.'[42] In other words, Thomas made use of his daughter's position, while maintaining an air of independence, and wanted to quickly establish that he had an integral role in the new order being established.

It was the same hall where, years earlier, Mary Boleyn had once captured Henry's attention, but the Chateau Vert in the Great Hall of York Place was but a memory, as was its former owner. Now, York Place had a new, royal owner and, on 8 December, in a small ceremony following Parliament, Henry raised three men to earldoms: Robert Radcliffe to the Earldom of Sussex, George Hastings to the Earldom of Hungerford, and Thomas Boleyn to the Earldom of Wiltshire and the Irish Earldom of Ormond. The only witnesses were the Archbishop of Canterbury, the Dukes of Norfolk and Suffolk, the Marquis of Dorset and Exeter, the Earls of Oxford and Shrewsbury, the Viscount Lisle, Lord Sands and Bergavenny, Henry Guildford, and William Fitzwilliam. These were some of the most important men of the realm and the royal household – the Earl of Oxford was Chamberlain of England, Earl of Shrewsbury was Steward of the Household; Lord Sands, the King's chamberlain, and William Fitzwilliam had succeeded Boleyn as Treasurer of the Household, working with Sir Henry Guildford, Comptroller of the Household.[43] It was the greatest achievement for the Boleyn family thus far, and of course was linked to Anne's position. Chapuys wrote that Henry probably gave the earldoms in order to raise his intended father-in-law and his family to heights exalted enough for a royal association. Chapuys suspected that the King, 'wishing no doubt to make it appear that the honours conferred upon the new earl were entirely owing to his daughter's favour, gave a grand fête in this city, to which several ladies of the Court were invited'.[44]

Chapuys was new to court and would not have been aware of Thomas' career up to this point, and while the latter's relationship to Anne may have played a part, Thomas had also been in pursuit of both earldoms for some years. Ormond was his grandfather's title, and Wiltshire was his great-uncle's title, which, without heirs, had passed out of the family.[45] Reclaiming both titles had been his greatest ambition for decades – and it had also been his mother's ambition for him. Although George was absent for the ennoblement, as son and heir, he was automatically granted the title of Lord Rochford, a tremendous honour for the young man. That night, Anne sat beside the King at the celebration feast, and would have been proud to see her father sitting at a separate table reserved for peers. It had taken generations, but the Boleyn family had risen from membership in the minor Norfolk gentry to that of national nobility.

Henry did not just raise Thomas to an earldom, he also appointed him as Lord Privy Seal, an exalted position that dated back to the Middle Ages when all legal documents that the king authorised carried the mark of the 'Great Seal'.[46] Each monarch had his own Great Seal, which was ceremonially broken after his death. Rather than the king physically carrying the seal on campaigns or while touring the country, a position was created for someone in whom the king had the greatest trust, a Keeper of the Privy Seal.[47]

This was not an empty honour. Thomas had been appointed to many government positions over the years: Comptroller, Treasurer, Royal Counsellor, Commissioner of Peace; and was an integral part of the Star Chamber.[48] The position of Lord Privy Seal was a responsibility that could even be considered a burden, requiring considerable work and effort, not thought to be a reward for a member of court. If he was being rewarded as the father of Anne, surely a less taxing position could have been found. Henry may have placed Thomas there to safeguard the political agenda, that is the King's will, for which Thomas would work for its promotion and stability.[49] Thomas would be fully committed to his role and even well respected, an essential component of a well-oiled government machine, working for the good of the realm.[50] He would not step into the role until early 1530, which would prove to be one of the busiest years yet.

It is difficult to imagine that, throughout all these events, Henry, his wife and his mistress were living under the same roof, even if it was a palace. Henry especially made sure that he and his wife were together for the Christmas festivities, and in order to gloss over a situation that might prove improper to visiting foreign dignitaries, Katherine was formally recognised as queen and presided over the events. Katherine had so far remained tight lipped, but Chapuys reported that the day after Thomas was made Earl during the feast of St Andrew's, Katherine took advantage of her public position, reproaching

Henry before all the court for his unkindness and neglect. The whole court heard her, as they did Henry's furious response, which was to boast that the opinions being collected on the case were so weighty that the decision must go in his favour. He petulantly added that, if it did not, he would denounce the Pope as a heretic and marry whom he pleased. Henry then stormed away from his first wife to seek solace from his wife to be, who was holding her own rival Christmas, only to receive another verbal dressing down. Chapuys reported: Lady Anne ... said to him reproachfully:

> Did I not tell you that whenever you dispute with the Queen she is sure to have the upper hand? I see that some fine morning you will succumb to her reasoning, and that you will cast me off. I have been waiting long, and might in the meanwhile have contracted some advantageous marriage, out of which I might have had issue, which is the greatest consolation in this world; but alas! Farewell to my time and youth spent to no purpose at all.[51]

Thomas may well have tried to calm his daughter, urging her to keep her peace and not rail at the King. It was a stressful arrangement for the family, and only Anne's uncle, Norfolk, seemed unaffected by the bizarre arrangements, and was everywhere, cheerfully gambling with du Bellay until 4am (du Bellay thought of nothing else, reported Chapuys disdainfully) and up early in the morning with the Privy Council, though how he fared may only be guessed at.[52]

Henry's attention was still fixed firmly on obtaining his divorce, but his tone in early 1530 had softened towards his old advisor. In mid-February, Chapuys reported that Wolsey had again been ill, or, as some believed, feigned illness, in the hope that the King would see him. Henry resisted the temptation, but he did send his former Chancellor, in Chapuys' words, the best remedy for his illness, namely a promise of pardon and grace, as well as absolution from all the charges brought against him. Wolsey made a miraculous recovery, especially upon hearing the news that Henry had decided to allow him to remain as Archbishop of York and give him a yearly pension of 3,000 angels on the revenues of the bishopric of Winchester.[53] Anne by all accounts was furious, but Henry ignored her, sending Wolsey a hefty gift of money, two services of plate, and enough tapestries and hangings for five rooms. Without her father's guidance – he was on a mission, as we shall see – she took her anger out on those around her, including individuals who her father would have urged her to cultivate favour with, not alienate. John Russell, for instance, a highly influential Gentleman of the Privy Chamber and ambassador, had earned Anne's wrath for quietly saying a few words in Wolsey's favour, and she had not spoken to him for nearly a month. She was also feuding with her uncle, Norfolk, who followed Henry's suit and was working with the Cardinal when necessary, even though Norfolk had made it clear that that he would 'sooner than allow the Cardinal's return to favour under such circumstances he would eat him up alive'.[54]

Eventually, Anne decided to send a messenger to the Cardinal. Either she thought that the Cardinal was upon his deathbed, Chapuys mused, or else she was trying to show her capabilities for dissimulation and intrigue, 'in which arts she is generally reputed to be an accomplished mistress'.[55]

What was not immediately apparent was Wolsey's reaction to this fortunate turn of events. He had begun to consider the possibility of a return to Henry's side and, while he had never enjoyed a close rapport with Katherine, they both had a common interest. Wolsey quietly turned to the Imperial cause and supported Charles, bolstered by the court gossip that Henry missed him, as nothing in the government had gone well since he had been sidelined. Chapuys was certain that if Wolsey were restored, the Howards and the Duke of Suffolk would pay with their heads, which was highly unlikely. Chapuys believed that only Wolsey was clever enough to find the means to end the divorce proceedings and restore the Queen; Wolsey on the other hand was hopeful that Anne could be discarded. The Cardinal had again found his nerve, but he was dipping his toes into treasonous waters indeed.

CHAPTER TEN

# The Boleyn Enterprise

*All Friends shall taste*
*The wages of their virtue, and all foes*
*The cup of their deservings.*

– Shakespeare, *King Lear*

A triumphant Charles V entered the city of Bologna on 5 November 1529, to meet with Pope Clement to arrange his coronation.[1] He had been elected Emperor almost a decade earlier in 1519, and had enjoyed an Imperial coronation, but by 1529 he had not yet been crowned by the Pope. Bologna was chosen because it was convenient for Charles, constantly in transit between his territories of Spain, Austria and Germany, but it was still within the Pope's dominion because it was the major and northernmost city of the Papal States.[2] Henry, alarmed by the thought of Charles and Clement together, had discussed the idea of sending Thomas, John Stokesley, Edward Lee, William Benet and several doctors of law and divinity to Bologna to meet with Charles and Clement regarding the divorce.[3] Not only would it be an arduous journey in the bitter winter, trailing through the mountainous north of Italy, but Thomas must have wondered why Henry thought him an obvious choice for the delegation, and may also have felt reluctance to go on a bootless errand – not that he could refuse such an appointment. His education, experience and skill made him one of the most successful of Henry's diplomats, but as the father of the woman Henry was intending to place on the throne – replacing the Emperor's own aunt as queen consort to do so – the move seemed uncharacteristically indelicate on Henry's part.[4] Stokesley's letter to Thomas, in January that year also advised Thomas to urge Henry to write to the faculties in Paris, which he would do while on his journey to Bologna.[5]

Despite being chosen to lead the embassy, Thomas would exert very little control. Henry gave him elaborate instructions – how to handle Charles and

Clement, what he should say, and how many times he should visit, assuming that Thomas would somehow be able to dominate proceedings. Thomas was to assure Charles that Henry would not have gone against the Emperor's wishes without the advice of the most learned and virtuous men that could be found in England, Italy and France, meaning the scholars of the universities currently grappling with the divorce question.

Chapuys was finally informed of Henry's plans for Bologna on 12 January, when Henry casually remarked that the Council had resolved to send to the Imperial Court one of its members, someone of weight and authority. If Chapuys was surprised by the choice, he kept his expression bland, as Henry hastily added that he had thought of sending Norfolk, but he was not in good health, his knowledge of French and Latin was inferior to Thomas' and, although not expressly stated, Norfolk lacked the delicate skills required for such challenging diplomacy. Thomas was ideal, as 'He knew more of the king's intentions than anyone else. Not being able to go himself, Boleyn was the fittest man to represent him.'[6] Chapuys admitted that many people at court half expected him to succeed, and the ambassador also feared that Thomas might omit details of the meetings in his reports, lest Henry lose his nerve and abandon hope.[7]

Therefore, Chapuys mused, the appointment made sense, for he would certainly make more strenuous efforts than anyone else to bring about the marriage: 'so, in the event of his being unsuccessful, would the King feel justified that he has done his utmost, and discharged his responsibility towards the father, daughter, and the whole family, whom, at the present moment, he does not wish to alienate'.[8]

The ambassador's reports to his master give some indication of how seriously he took Thomas' appointment, and he urged Charles to assemble as many learned men as possible in Bologna, in particular theologians who could combat Thomas' arguments. Thomas was as anxious as Chapuys, aware of the difficult position, and was eager to maintain a good relationship with the ambassador. Meeting at court, the two men spoke at length, and Thomas seemed concerned about his reception in Bologna, as well he might, and declared that he hoped Chapuys would not try to disturb the friendly relations between their two countries by sending Charles evil reports. Thomas then lightly criticised the ambassador saying 'although there being still a few points of dispute between the Emperor and the King, my master, your letters perhaps are not without their rough edges'.[9] Thomas still grappled with the notion that his daughter's marital choices had affected the family in the eyes of Europe, and seemed sensitive to the criticism. In a surprising move, he also asked

Chapuys if he wrote often to Charles, and enquired how his despatches were carried, to which Chapuys gave evasive answers. It was a clumsy and slightly obvious move on Thomas' part to find out as much about the Imperial envoy as he could but he was *too* obvious about it, and one wonders why he bothered. It could have been the case that Chapuys was embellishing his report, for such a ploy was not Thomas' style.

The two men parted and Thomas made an appointment to call on the ambassador at his London residence close to the Tower but, at the last minute, sent word that he would be unable to visit, as he still had considerable preparations to make for his embassy which was only days away. It was also, Chapuys noted, terrible weather, which may have impeded the new Earl. But should Chapuys happen to pass by, or be in the neighbourhood of Thomas' lodgings 'he begged me to let him know'. Chapuys was understanding, but slightly sceptical: 'The excuse, no doubt, was to a certain point genuine and legitimate, but I fancy that Mr. de Vulchier [Boleyn] would have liked to have it said that Your Majesty's ambassador had called upon him.'[10] It may have been a ruse to manipulate the situation so that Chapuys was seen 'paying court' to Thomas, but Chapuys may have been overly suspicious – Thomas continued to seek the ambassador out prior to his departure, and made his feelings clear, confiding that 'I cannot persuade myself that the Emperor wishes to hinder a plan which would be so beneficial to this kingdom. I would willingly have given all I possess for the King, my master, to have been able to converse with the Emperor a little while on this subject.' If Charles did fall into line (this is how Chapuys read the declaration), Henry would offer any amount of money and agree to any alliance, and Henry would be his slave forever.[11]

The French embassy observed proceedings, and scathingly reported that Thomas had been entrusted with the task of bribing the Pope: 'He [Thomas] had a commission to make great expence, and promise assistance to his Holiness with a good sum of money.'[12] If that was not the case, it was speculated, then perhaps Thomas was to negotiate with Charles as well, making a 'promise for the restitution of the Queen's dower to the Emperor, with security for the Queen's good treatment'.[13]

Chapuys appeared to change his mind regarding visiting the Earl, and attempted a quick visit on the morning of Thomas' departure, but the timing was off – Thomas had departed earlier than expected. A few days later, Norfolk had an odd conversation with the Imperial ambassador, confiding that he feared for his brother-in-law's safety, as he was travelling through places that were hostile to the mission.[14] Thomas, Norfolk confided, was not of a warlike disposition, but a timid man, and if, on his arrival in Italy, he should find any danger abroad, or even suspicion of it, he would turn back.[15] Chapuys found the whole conversation peculiar, considering Thomas had seen battle, and was highly skilled in other physical pursuits. Chapuys reported that it was quite superfluous to write to Charles about it, especially considering Charles' good reputation when it came to the treatment of ambassadors. He believed 'all this to have been simply done to give themselves importance, and gain reputation, and that the fear which they seem to entertain is only an excuse'.[16] It is not clear what Norfolk's intentions were, but it is more than likely that Thomas was unaware of his brother-in-law's dramatic approach.

In the quest for his annulment, Henry had employed some of the brightest men of court, including George Boleyn, Reginald Pole, Edward Fox, John Stokesley, Richard Croke and Cranmer. Through the cities of Europe they had spread, visiting faculties of law and theology to secure support for Anne's marriage. George, who had been in Paris since October, was one of the men searching through libraries and bookshops for various scriptures and manuscripts which might aid their arguments. Theologians were consulted, religious leaders were invited to debate, and lectures given in the universities outlining the case. As J. J. Scarisbrick elegantly stated, rarely has learning been more hungrily interrogated.[17]

Father and son were reunited when the latter arrived in Paris on his way to Bologna, where he found that George and Stokesley were in the midst of arguing and lobbying for a favourable opinion at the Sorbonne.[18]

George had struggled in his first mission, not due to his age or inexperience, but because Francis was unwilling to openly support their cause. He was anxious not to appear unfriendly to the English, as he had found Henry's friendship and support useful in the recent past, first when he was a prisoner in Madrid and then when his sons were hostages in Spain, but he could ill afford to insult Charles.

The Boleyn men then set off in opposite directions – George departed for England, and Thomas for Bologna.

George arrived in London around 20 February and was reunited with his wife, mother, and sister. Within a week, he also made the acquaintance of the Imperial ambassador, who took an immediate liking to the young man. Chapuys reported that he found George charming, exceedingly courteous, and in possession of a frankness of mind which Chapuys found refreshing. George had found France frustrating, and did not hesitate to talk about the lack of French favour towards the annulment or England in general.[19]

Apart from his conversation with Chapuys, we have evidence of George's difficulties, in a letter found in the State Papers. This letter has been dated

July of 1530, when George was back in England, but it has mistakenly been placed there. Firstly, George made clear that he was not in England, writing 'They of this country say nothing; whether it be because they cannot, or else they will not, I cannot tell.'[20] He was probably referring to the French opinions of the divorce. He then wrote that he could send no news from England 'for there is no good fellow will take the pain to write, they be so merry. As a good fellow said to me the other day, our country folks have so many pastimes they have no leisure to write.'[21] George wistfully added that he too hoped to be back home soon, passing the time with his friends. Another clue comes from the man he is corresponding with, William Benet, a distinguished ambassador and doctor of civil law. George made clear that he had chosen to write to Benet and not the latter's colleagues, Girolamo Ghinucci or Gregory Casale, as he could not write in Latin or Italian very well – Benet, Ghinucci and Casale were in Rome together in 1529/30, while George was in Paris. George asked that he be recommended to Ghinucci, adding that he had been the latter's guide in England earlier, from Notley to Oxford. Ghinucci had been appointed Bishop of Worcester in 1522, and had visited England several years later, at which point George had obviously accompanied him. George and his wife Jane lived at Rochford Hall, which was not far from Notley, so it is entirely plausible. The letter itself provides an insight into George's style and self-fashioning, but we must remember that this was his first foray into politics. He did not desire to establish himself as an integral player in negotiations, as his father had on his first mission, and where his father was proud of his linguistic accomplishments, George drew attention to his linguistic weaknesses, which Thomas would never have done. With youthful indifference, George also admitted that he might forget to respond to Benet's next letter – the phrase of an inexperienced young man not yet at ease in his position as ambassador, or appreciative of professional courtesy. Apart from this letter, we hear nothing of George for the next few months, but his embassy had obviously been difficult for him; however, a more experienced ambassador would never have admitted such shortcomings.

As for Thomas, his first port of call was the Italian Duchy of Milan, where he managed to bolster his own position (possibly because his daughter's rise was imminent) with Francesco Sforza, Duke of Milan, who hosted the embassy and entertained them lavishly.[22] No expense was to be spared, nor were they to spend their own money, and the Duke also gave orders that the embassy be provided escorts or anything they desired.[23] Over dinner, Sforza delicately hinted that he would like to do business, and Thomas assured him that, on his return through Milan, they would continue the conversation.

It had been a long journey, taking two months, but finally the group arrived in Bologna at the beginning of Lent, and could not present their credentials for they were not received. Instead Thomas, Stokesley and the others remained in their lodgings not far from the Palazza d'Accursio, where Clement and Charles resided, and Thomas moved to cultivate good relations with Gabriel Grammont, Bishop of Tarbes, who had been ordered to entertain the embassy. They met on several occasions, dining together as the Earl waited to be invited to a meeting, and Thomas assured Grammont that if Anne became queen, she would be his servant for the rest of her life, knowing that the affection and support of Francis would enable them to achieve their goal, echoing, to some extent, Chapuys report.[24] For his part, Grammont tried his utmost to assist Thomas, warning the Earl of the Emperor's (obvious) intentions to oppose the marriage, but he also advised Clement to speak with Thomas privately.[25] Finally, the embassy was invited to a meeting with Charles.

It had been over eight years since the two men had met face to face, when Charles had praised Thomas' diligence and loyalty as an ambassador. Thomas was no longer just an ambassador working for Wolsey – he was older and had the assurance of a man who had risen significantly in rank and prestige since those times. But he embodied all the problems surrounding Charles' aunt, Katherine of Aragon, and a hostile Charles made his displeasure clear. Charles interrupted the Earl in the middle of his speech, snapping that he was not to be believed in this case, as he was a party to the suit. Thomas was astonished at first by the attitude, and, collecting himself, he calmly replied that what he did was not as a father but as a subject and servant of his master. He emphasised to the Emperor that Henry was motivated by a scruple of conscience he had that he had lived in sin and, while it was unfortunate that Charles had not taken the news well, 'his displeasure would not hinder the execution of his intention'.[26]

Charles signalled the short meeting had come to an end, and Thomas left the palace and hastily with Grammont, begging him to intercede with Clement and relay a message that 'his coming hither will create a stronger affection towards you, in himself and his master. He told me yesterday, he was sure, if his daughter came to be Queen, she would be all her life your very humble servant, well knowing that all their weal depends upon you only.'[27] So far nothing had gone to plan, but Clement reluctantly agreed to meet with the embassy. We may wonder if Thomas felt apprehension before meeting the most powerful man in Christendom.

The meeting would later be immortalised in reformist propaganda, projecting a much more triumphant and defiant Thomas Boleyn. John Foxe, a protestant martyrologist, would later write a vivid account of the meeting, in which Thomas refused to submit the cause of the divorce to Clement and Charles, declaring that the case was very clear and would be submitted to an assembly of prelates and doctors, not Roman canonists.[28] This would have made the entire journey pointless, and it is difficult to imagine Thomas would travel all that way to negotiate only to declare that he did *not* want to negotiate. Foxe also wrote that Pope Clement offered his foot to be kissed by the embassy, but Thomas refused to do so by remaining standing.[29]

And a final, seemingly trivial, story circulated that a spaniel belonging to Thomas bit Clement's big toe, which was met with mild amusement by the embassy.[30] It is a fanciful story; surely Grammont or the Papal and Imperial ambassador would have relayed such an incident had there been a significant threat to Papal toes.

The reality of Thomas' audience with Pope Clement was far from triumphant. Clement refused to even hear the Earl's suit, and reiterated the demand that the King and Queen, or their representatives, were to come to Rome in order that the case might be heard there. He also presented Thomas with a citation reaffirming an earlier one that required reasonably prompt action on the part of Henry. Throughout the audience Clement was doing all he could to please Charles, which correspondence confirms: Clement had already asked Charles what answer he wished to be given to Thomas and the embassy.[31] Charles was adamant his aunt's case be 'determined by justice'.[32]

Thomas gave the order to his embassy to depart the next day, and would not take formal leave – there was little point. A frustrated and weary Earl confided in Grammont that there was more need now than ever that Francis and Henry should continue good friends and brothers, adding the English would 'act for three or four months like those who look at dancers, and take courage according as they see them dancing ill or well'.[33] In other words, the English would follow France's lead.

Following Thomas' conversation, Grammont met Ghinucci, who George had escorted from Oxford to Notley years prior. Whatever fondness he may have had for the Boleyns in 1522, it had faded. Ghinucci gossiped that, the day before Thomas' departure, he had mentioned in conversation with Ghinucci that Francis had promised him some benefices, which he believed should be given to him on his return to France. Ghinucci also told Grammont that Thomas had great influence in the government, and would act sooner out of interest than for any other motive.[34] We should pause to consider why a Papal ambassador was feeding such information to the French ambassador. Such reports may be indicative of the ill will towards the family who dared usurp the legitimate queen of England, to place their daughter on the throne.

Such criticism that Thomas had an 'acquisitive tendency' reflects a political agenda yet is taken as fact by most historians. Although inaccurate, these impressions remain in currency. But personal interests were at the very heart of ambition, so whose interest should Thomas have had in mind, if not the interests of his daughter, edging closer to the throne? Nevertheless, these reports do give us a glimpse into the reputation that Thomas, now potential father-in-law to the king of England, began to develop among some of his contemporaries.

Thomas returned to France via the same path he had taken from Paris, staying once more with the Duke of Milan, who again went to considerable lengths to entertain the embassy. Hoping to catch Thomas while at ease, Sforza made the request to borrow 50,000 ducats from the King.[35] Despite knowing the sum would never be granted, Thomas sleekly gave just enough hope for the Milanese to continue their suit for several months. The directives given to the Milanese ambassador in London, to work specifically with Thomas when he returned to England, suggests that Sforza considered Thomas the principal English ambassador and advisor to the King.[36]

While in Milan, Thomas received orders from Henry to go to Francis, who was in Bordeaux, still trying to ransom his children from Charles. The Earl was also instructed to take charge of the group of men, including Henry's cousin, Reginald Pole, and Wolsey's son, Thomas Winter, who remained in Paris trying to influence the university to vote in Henry's favour.

Thomas arrived in Lyon days later, and from there he wrote a lengthy report to Henry, that he should know how stiffly the Emperor was set against his cause. The Pope was governed by the Emperor, but if the Emperor should fall out with the French king, which was highly possible, they needed to redouble their efforts in France.[37] Henry's response to Thomas indicates that he took his advice seriously: if Thomas' report was as disappointing as his letters, Henry wrote, he would settle the matter in England, and if he refused to recognise the Pope, other kingdoms would follow suit.[38] For Thomas, Bologna had not necessarily been a defeat. It had confirmed what he and his daughter surely had suspected – the matter would not be settled by the Pope.[39]

Arriving at the French court at Angouleme in late April, Thomas was lodged in spacious apartments, and 'feasted daily'.[40] Louise, Francis and Marguerite of Navarre were there to receive him, and he reported to Henry that Francis and Louise would 'help what they can in your great matter, and speak of you with great affection'.[41] It must have been something of a relief to be at the French court with Francis, with whom he had always worked well, and Louise, for whom he had the utmost respect, and vice versa. But his spirits were somewhat dampened when part of the reason for his warm welcome was made clear by Jean du Bellay, who informed Boleyn that Francis still required Henry's assistance to ransom back his two sons from Charles. This was the second request for a loan in the space of a few days. And Thomas noted to Henry that Francis had enough wealth to ransom his children back twice over. To du Bellay, he kept up the flow of warm, conciliatory words, promising to do what he could, but he privately advised Henry that 'if the same request is moved to you by the French ambassador in England do not consent to it'.[42]

By this time, Thomas was slowly establishing a private network, and glimpses appear in a letter sent to him while he was in France from his godson, Thomas Tebald. Tebald was the son of Thomas' steward at Hever, who was executor of his estate. Thomas seemed to have doted on the young man, an affection born of his close friendship with the father.

Tebald's letters, some of which are partially damaged, are warm, detailed, and deferential, demonstrating the very close nature of their relationship. Tebald also made a great spy – he reported to his godfather that he heard that Charles would procure 7,000 horsemen from German princes, and the city of Cologne would muster 3,000 horses and 5,000 foot soldiers for the Emperor. Thomas would hear more, Tebald assured him, from his courier, Reginald Wolfe, a London bookseller who would later serve his grand-daughter, the future Elizabeth I. Wolfe was travelling to Frankfurt to the Book Fair (*Frankfurter Buchmesse*) at Thomas' behest, and we may wonder what books Thomas had asked him to collect.[43]

When news came of Thomas' arrival at the French court, his colleagues in Paris, who had been floundering for some time, anxiously wrote to him, urging him to convince Francis to put pressure on the Sorbonne University.[44] The ambassador dutifully did so, and kept steady pressure on Francis to ensure that the French universities decided in Henry's favour. Finally, Thomas arrived in Paris, and there was a marked difference in proceedings. After months of stagnation, the Earl whipped the English contingent into a frenzy, persuading and cajoling those around him, missing nothing. His son George had warned him about one of the faculty members, Noel Beda, who was disruptive, collecting propaganda against the divorce. George had demanded his dismissal but had been ignored. But Francis' response to Thomas was far more respectful – at Thomas' urging, he established an enquiry into Beda's conduct.[45]

The Sorbonne handed down their decision on 2 July in favour of Henry's divorce, but stated that they would not attach an official seal until a later date.

A lesser ambassador might have returned home with the university's promise, but shrewdly Thomas again applied pressure to Francis, and ensured the seals were delivered before he departed. He took no chances.

Desperate to have his ambassador home, Henry sent Alexander Gray, Thomas' usual courier, from London to Paris to overtake the Earl on his way home with rather redundant instructions for him to hasten his return. Obeying these orders as quickly as he could, the travel-weary diplomat arrived back in England on 3 August, and headed straight to court at Windsor. It had been an exhausting and draining eight months.

Henry immediately sent a messenger to Rome with Sorbonne's favourable determination, but for Thomas the mission had shifted his attitude towards the divorce. He had always supported his daughter, but now he saw with great clarity what they were truly up against. Thomas resented the Pope and Charles and developed a marked antipathy towards the clergy in general. And he knew just the man to take it out on. Within days of returning to court, Thomas crossed paths with Chapuys, and Thomas erupted in a tirade, criticising the Pope and all the cardinals, mortifying Chapuys who hastily withdrew, perhaps partly because Thomas intimated that he thought Chapuys himself was partially to blame for their treatment in Bologna.[46] However, as Chapuys had pointed out, Charles hardly needed encouragement to distrust the father of Henry's mistress.[47] Chapuys duly reported the incident to Charles, concerned that, should Thomas and his daughter remain influential at court, they would alienate the kingdom from the Pope.[48] In Chapuys' mind, these remarks were also evidence of Thomas' anti-Papal stance, which he assumed was related to Henry's pursuit of a divorce.

Thomas, known for his equanimity and restraint, left angry outbursts to the Dukes of Norfolk and Suffolk, so it must have been a bizarre spectacle when, on 12 November 1530, Chapuys and Thomas clashed once again, this time over two separate proposals by Charles and Henry. Charles was to convene a series of Imperial Diet in the German city of Augsburg, in an attempt to calm rising religious tensions exacerbated by the increasing threat from the Ottoman Emperor, Suleiman the Magnificent, who laid siege to Vienna, the Hapsburg capital, in 1529.

The Emperor strongly and strategically desired this Diet as it would allow him an avenue to more easily reassert control over the Lutheran cities and princedoms of his empire. But in England, the Privy Council had also put forward a proposal to discuss religious reform. Thomas made it known to Chapuys that, in his opinion, the convocation of councils was the province of secular rulers, not the Pope, except on matters of faith: but in either case the Pope should not head such gatherings.[49]

Furthermore, Thomas was reported as saying he would risk his life and property to ensure that no pope or prelate should exercise jurisdiction, promulgate laws, or enforce ordinances in England.[50]

A scandalised Chapuys declared that Thomas and his daughter were also allowing heretical literature to flow into England, and were therefore more Lutheran than Luther himself. He blamed Thomas as the principal advocate of a measure in Parliament to abolish the authority of ecclesiastical courts.[51]

But what of Chapuys' accusations? Apart from his anti-clericalism, was there evidence at this point that Thomas was anything other than a devoted Catholic, bound by his duties as an ambassador, acting for a monarch in conflict with the Pope? We could conjecture that this was Thomas' deliberate ploy to anger Chapuys and, through him, make a point to Charles and the Pope. But it was clear that Thomas was no longer interested in working with or through the Catholic Church to effect the King's purpose.

Bologna marked the end of Thomas' career as an ambassador in the field, although he continued to be involved in Henry's foreign diplomacy. But his role as Lord Privy Seal required him to remain in England. For George, France marked the beginning of his career, and he had begun to cultivate his own reputation at court, distinctive from his father and sister. Thomas had always preferred the more physical pursuits as a young man; George enjoyed such pursuits too, but he also developed an artistic streak, spending time with other like-minded courtiers such as Thomas Wyatt, whose prose was well loved at court.[52] Later Cavendish wrote extensively about George, praising his physical attributes and natural qualities, describing the eloquence of his 'pleasant *ditties*' while decrying his 'sensuall apetyte' and accusing him of 'forcing widows' and deflowering maidens.[53] There is no other evidence of George's appetites, sexual or otherwise, and therefore such a judgement must be cautiously considered. But it was evident that both he and his sister began to form a young sphere at court, exuding European sophistication. Anne and George were of a new generation, eager to shift the court away from the old ways.

Despite their efforts, life at court had barely changed since Henry had first pursued his divorce. Katherine was still queen, and Henry was still in a domestic relationship with her. This lingering affection resulted in an explosive argument over something seemingly unimportant to Henry, yet significant to everyone else. For longer than he could remember, Henry and Katherine had an arrangement whereby he sent her cloth to make his shirts.

Anne was unaware of this, but when she discovered the arrangement, she was furious. She had been a queen in waiting for three years, and here was Henry still paying deference to his first queen. Chapuys reported that 'the Lady, hearing of this, sent for the person who had taken the cloth, one of the principal gentlemen of the bedchamber, yelling at the shocked servant, threatening that she would have him punished severely'. Henry managed to soothe a hysterical Anne, putting an end to the arrangement, but it was clear that, for all her confidence in her father and brother, the weakest link was Henry.

Meanwhile Wolsey had been languishing for months, to everyone's satisfaction but his own, but it was clear to those he continued to correspond with that he did not dare leave the proximity of the court again as 'he would then have less facility for watching for his opportunity to return to it, the hope of which he has not yet relinquished'.[54] The Cardinal was thrilled to hear what had happened in Bologna, and Chapuys reported that Wolsey was not at all sorry for Thomas' failure but very much so that he was returning home so soon.

In reality, he had reason to be grateful to the Earl. For several months, the Cardinal had been anxious about the fate of his beloved Cardinal's College, Oxford, which was beginning to struggle since Henry had seized all revenues, leaving it vulnerable without the financial support of its original benefactor. This was no vanity project – Wolsey cared deeply for the college, and the education of those within its walls, and he dedicated months to begging anyone at court who would listen to restore funding. The Cardinal sent countless messengers to the King, who at one point consulted Norfolk and Thomas about the matter. Norfolk guffawed at the messenger's request, and advised Henry to ignore the Cardinal. In any case, who cared about his college? Thomas on the other hand, whatever he felt about Wolsey at this stage, was inclined to fully support it, for Thomas was a pious man, like the Cardinal, and he respected what Wolsey had created in Cardinal's College. He had a quick private meeting with his brother-in-law, where he obviously made a convincing case, after which Norfolk came back, somewhat chastened, and awkwardly apologised: 'Sirs, albeit I have spoken hardly to you at the beginning, yet will I be an helper in your matter.'[55] Wolsey may not have been aware of how vital Thomas' intercession had been.

Several weeks later, a Papal Nuncio arrived at court with a papal brief prohibiting Henry's remarriage, and ordering him to dismiss Anne Boleyn from court. Wolsey immediately bore the brunt of Henry's wrath, as his discreet correspondence with the Emperor and the Pope had been uncovered. His chaplain had been arrested with letters to Charles and shortly afterwards his physician, Agostini, was intercepted carrying dangerous letters written in cipher. Wolsey had attempted to clamber back into Henry's inner circle, but he had masterminded nothing more than his own demise. In November 1530, William Walsh, a gentleman of the Privy Chamber, and Henry Percy, Earl of Northumberland, were sent to arrest the Cardinal at Cawood on a charge of high treason, the men delivering the news as the Cardinal dined. He was to be escorted to the Tower of London to face charges of treason, but his progress from the north of England was a saga, and he fell ill on the journey south, dying in Leicester Abbey. He denied his enemies the pleasure of seeing him imprisoned or executed, but on his deathbed he said, 'If I had served God as diligently as I have done the King, he would not have given me over in my grey hairs.'[56] Such was the end of the great Thomas Wolsey.

Wolsey had fallen from grace and perhaps even in death was considered fair game by those who had watched his fall and even favoured it, while, more broadly, anti-clericism was rife in England at this time, and Wolsey was a strong symbol of the clergy. Chapuys wrote to Charles on 23 January of that year: 'The earl of Vulchier [Chapuys' way of writing Wiltshire] invited to supper Monsieur de la Guiche – Francis I's *Maître des suppliques* – for whose amusement he caused a farce to be acted of the Cardinal going down to Hell.'[57] According to Chapuys, who had not forgiven Thomas for their angry confrontation, the reaction to the farce was not what Thomas had anticipated. Chapuys reported that La Guysch 'much blamed the Earl, and still more the Duke for his ordering the said farce to be (later) printed'.[58] Had Thomas, in an uncharacteristic moment, misread the French attitude towards Wolsey – and, more generally, the mood of the moment, since mocking a dead man who could no longer defend himself might indeed be seen quite reasonably as having been in poor taste? The details of the farce are lost, and it is unclear just what it entailed: was it a dance, a monologue, or performed by a group? Farces were common and often dealt with contemporary issues, and were 'explicitly in-house affairs for the benefit of guests whose political views were sympathetic to their hosts'.[59] Drama was seen as a natural means of political expression for those with 'either the rhetorical talents to create it or the wealth to patronize it'.[60] Thomas' farce was probably a means of expressing such sentiments, a satirical, if somewhat harsh assessment of Wolsey, the clergy, and all that they represented. But Thomas intended it to be a private display – Norfolk escalated the matter by having the farce printed. However, the Boleyns were hardly the only critics of Wolsey. Thomas More's address to Parliament, not long after Wolsey's dismissal as chancellor, was far more scathing and personal (although the difference was that Wolsey was still alive at the time). In his address, More described Henry as a good shepherd and the Cardinal was a castrated male sheep:

> You se that emongest a great flocke of shepe some be rotte[n] and fauty which the good sheperd sendeth from the good shepe, so the great wether which is of late fallen as you all knowe, so craftily, so scabedly, ye & so untruly iuggled wyth the kynge, that all men must nedes gesse and thinke that he thought him self, that the[e] had no wit to perceiue his craftie doing, or els that he presumed that the kyng woulde not se nor know his fraudulent Juggeling and attemptes: but he was deceiued, for his graces sight was so quicke and penetrable, that he saw him, ye and saw through hym, both with in and without, so that all thing to him was open, and according to his defect he hath had a gentle correction.[61]

Members of court scrambled to establish their own positions as leading ministers after Wolsey's fall, with most courtiers quick to show that Wolsey and his methods were now discredited and irredeemably a thing of the past.

Despite what the French or Imperial ambassadors may have thought of the Earl following the farce, the Milanese and Venetians had the utmost respect for his reputation and influence. They had been observing the unfolding events for some time, initially focusing on Norfolk as a source of power. One may presume either the Duke's mannerisms and character were so outlandish as to necessitate a special report, or, more plausibly, he was considered as the most vocal and involved of the group. The Venetian ambassador, Falier, noted that 'His Majesty makes use of him [Norfolk] in all negotiations more than any other person', adding that, since Wolsey's death, Norfolk's 'authority and supremacy have increased, and every employment devolves to him'.[62]

His Milanese counterpart agreed, but also noted that Thomas was considered to be so highly placed and influential (and regarded by many as more reasonable), that ambassadors preferred to deal with him, and even put off negotiations with Norfolk and the King until Thomas was also available.[63] Although Thomas had promised to assist the Duke of Sforza earlier that year, it became clear that he could do no more for Sforza's cause, but Scarpinello respected his attempts, writing to Sforza that no better avenue could have been attempted.[64] The Boleyns now represented the future.[65]

# CHAPTER ELEVEN

# Ainsi sera, groigne qui groigne

*The purest treasure mortal times afford*
*Is spotless reputation: that away,*
*Men are but gilded loam or painted clay.*
*A jewel in a ten-times-barr'd-up chest*
*Is a bold spirit in a loyal breast.*

– Shakespeare, *Richard II*

The formidable Margaret of Austria had commanded the respect and admiration of the most powerful monarchs of Europe, and had a profound impact on the young Anne Boleyn. Thomas had learned his first difficult lessons in diplomacy at her court and, when she died on 1 December 1530, his reaction is not recorded, but his high regard and affection for the woman who had been instrumental in the education of his daughter would not have faded. Cromwell had been informed by his Flemish contacts of Margaret's death, and news trickled through the court, reaching Anne in the first week of December. We have no record of Anne's reaction, but within a few weeks, Anne adopted as her motto 'Ainsi sera, groigne qui groigne' – 'That's how it will be, let those who grumble, grumble.' This was Margaret's motto, and while Anne omitted the ending, a pro-Imperialist cheer: 'Vivant Burgundy', could it have been a bold tribute to the woman who had so influenced her in her formative years? In Margaret, Anne had benefitted from an extraordinary role model – a woman of confidence and wit, who stood unflinching even in the most difficult of circumstances, and with the most difficult of men. Anne channelled the strength of her former mentor as she and her family continued to live in Henry's court of two queens, and Chapuys wrote, with a degree of admiration, 'Lady [Anne] considering herself already sure of her affair, is fiercer than a lioness.'

In these early years, Anne remained relatively quiet about Katherine, but it was her fifth year of waiting. The marital landscape of 1531 looked no different from 1527, despite the endless political machinations which had taken place. Henry still had a queen and a queen in waiting, with neither woman showing signs of conceding ground.

Anne was bolder about her feelings, at one point declaring to one of the Queen's ladies-in-waiting that she wished all the Spaniards were at the bottom of the sea. When chided for using such sentiments, she replied that she cared not for the Queen or any of her family, and that she would rather see her hanged than have to confess that she was her Queen and mistress. Brash and impudent, neither George nor Anne had the patience of their father – they were anxious for matters to be settled.

On 5 January, an extraordinary Papal brief reached court, stating that, at Katherine's request, Clement forbade Henry to remarry 'until the decision of the case, and declares that if he does all issue will be illegitimate. Forbids any one in England, of ecclesiastical or secular dignity, universities, parliaments, courts of law, &c., to make any decision in an affair the judgement of which is reserved for the Holy See. The whole under pain of excommunication.'[1] This foreign interference only strengthened Anne and Henry's determination.

By 1531, Henry had secured the scholarly opinions of the various universities of Europe, which Thomas More presented to the House of Commons in March. These opinions were soon compiled into a book called *Censurae academiarum*. Cranmer later translated the work into English, and renamed it the *Determination of the Universities*. It provided a snapshot of scholarly opinion, and was a useful piece of propaganda, but with only a selection of universities it was by no means comprehensive, and it certainly was not enough to bring about an annulment. Henry continued to seek a solution.[2]

On 16 January 1531, Parliament met at Westminster. Thomas diligently attended all parliamentary sessions, with only his son George having the second highest attendance rate, clearly demonstrating their dedication to the governance of the realm, and not just the divorce. This came after Norfolk assembled a group of influential individuals including himself, Thomas, the Earl of Oxford, Lord Darcy, and several nobles to establish whether the matrimonial case should be considered as a temporal, or spiritual matter, and surely Henry could settle the matter as emperor in his own realm. By now, anti-clericism was rife in England, and Parliament's main order of business was to secure a mandate to consider the 'Manifold abuses of the clergy'.[3] Henry charged the members of the English Church with Praemunire, a lesser form of treason, committed when an attempt was made to exercise an illegal jurisdiction that rivalled that of the

Crown. As Henry demanded, the clergy paid £100,000 to buy a pardon for their 'crime', but he demanded more. He insisted that the clergy recognise that they held no jurisdiction independently of the Crown. They could not, in other words, impede his annulment.

In February of 1531, Henry raised the stakes and challenged the clergy. He issued five articles, one of which demanded that the clergy recognise Henry as sole protector and supreme head of the Church and clergy in return for a pardon for the offence of Praemunire.[4] For almost two years, a team of scholars and royal agents gathered and studied manuscripts that would provide evidence to buttress Henry's claims that his annulment of his marriage to Katherine was justified and that his matrimonial case ought to be determined in England rather than Rome. It was known as the *Collectanea satis copiosa* (*The Sufficiently Abundant Collections*), which Cranmer presented to Henry in the summer of 1530. The *Collectanea* argued that the Church of England was an autonomous province of the Catholic Church and that Henry had both secular *imperium* and spiritual supremacy in England. In other words, it was the King, not the Pope, who exercised supreme jurisdiction within his realm.

Henry was delighted with the work and wrote approving comments all over the manuscript. Now confident that he had right on his side, he began the campaign to persuade or force his clerics to accept and recognise his imperial pretensions. George was prominent in persuading Convocation of the scriptural case for the King's supremacy. For several weeks, he examined the *Collectanea satis copiosa*, and wrote several tracts regarding Henry's authority, probably with the assistance of scholars like Fox and Cranmer. Armed with these tracts, written in his own hand, George was sent to Convocation on the afternoon of Friday 10 February and, before Parliament, delivered an impassioned speech. One still survives today, and emphasises the King's power to repress heresy and error, and that Henry's 'Supreme authorite grounded on God's word ought in no case to be restrayned by any frustrate decrees of popish lawes or voyed prescriptes of human traditions, but that he maye both order and minister, yea and also execute the office of spiritual administration in the church whereof he ys head.'[5]

Henry's advisors hoped that Convocation would be convinced by George's words, but George, while a junior member of Privy Council, was not even a member of Parliament, why then would they want to deal with the 26-year-old envoy? In order to circumnavigate George, they attempted to send a delegation to the King but were told that they could communicate with Henry through the young Lord Rochford. There is no official explanation of why the inexperienced young man was appointed to act as a buffer, but it may have been a desire to promote George, or ensure that the younger Boleyn generation was seen to be as influential as the senior generation.[6]

George's tracts had immediate impact, for the next day Convocation granted Henry the title of 'singular protector, supreme lord, and supreme head of the English church and clergy'.[7] But while the bishops acknowledged Henry as Supreme Head of the Church and Clergy in England, a limiting clause 'as far as the law of Christ allows' was added to Henry's new title that rendered it almost ineffective, possibly by John Fisher, Bishop of Rochester, Katherine's champion since the Legatine trial.[8]

Thomas had clashed with Fisher just days prior, as the Clergy agonised over their decision, barking that he was willing to prove with scriptural testimony that when God left the world he left behind no successor or vicar on earth.[9] Thomas stormed off, his frustration evident, and Fisher's ally and friend, Lord Chancellor Thomas More, heard of the altercation, and was so incensed that he considered resigning from office. They probably discussed the issue when they sat down to dinner, among other guests, several days later at Fisher's residence in London, in what would incidentally become one of the most infamous meals of the year. The first course was a soup or a type of pottage, which every guest ate except More, who sat in shock, but was physically unaffected as Fisher and his guests doubled over in pain, their bodies already trying to purge whatever poison they had ingested. The remains of the dish had also been given to the servants, and distributed among the poor. Two of Fisher's guests died, as did the beggars who ate the pottage. Miraculously, a scandalised Chapuys reported, Fisher, 'who God no doubt considers very useful and necessary in this world' seemed to eat too little of the pottage to feel the full effects. It took little time to find the culprit – the cook, Richard Roose, was questioned by Fisher's brother, and confessed at once that he had actually put into the broth some powders, which he had been given to understand would only make his fellow servants very sick without endangering their lives or doing them any harm.[10]

We might ask who put Roose up to it? Chapuys does not attribute blame to Thomas, but does question who would have a motive and who would have gone to such lengths. With great prescience he actually reports to Charles that, although Thomas may have been innocent, it would be difficult to avert suspicion from falling on either him or the King.

> I have not yet been able to ascertain who it was who gave the cook such advice, nor for what purpose. The King has certainly shewn some displeasure at this, but whatever demonstrations of sorrow he makes he

will not be able to avert *suspicion* from falling, if not on himself, for he is too noble-minded to have resource to such means – at least on the Lady and her father.[11]

Fisher's first biographer, Edward Hall, also records the incident, but his account varies slightly. He states that the meal was especially served to Fisher but he had no appetite. He does not point to anyone other than the cook as being behind the deed.[12] Our third source is Nicholas Sander, whose hatred of the Boleyns and Anne in particular is evident in his highly embellished attacks on the family. Sander blamed Anne:

> To gratify her vengeance, she bribed his cook to poison him. As Fisher partook of the same food as his servants, the cook conveyed the poison into the common family pot; but Fisher, through the interposition of providence, did not dine at home that day, but the servants, who dined on the dangerous food, were immediately seized with violent pains, and nearly all of them died. The cook was apprehended and acknowledged the fact, and was executed, which redoubled the hatred of Anne against Fisher.[13]

While there is no doubt that this episode actually occurred, there is no evidence that any of the Boleyns were involved in the incident. Nor is there enough evidence to say with any certainty that Fisher himself was the target, or that political expediency was a motive. The Act of Parliament that sentenced the cook to death expressly stated that the powder was put in a vessel of yeast or barne, to make pottage for the family and poor people, and there is no evidence that Fisher intended to eat it.[14]

The punishment that Henry conjured for the cook showed a certain element of cruelty, and may well have been devised to deter anyone else from such an act. Henry decided that Roose should be condemned by attainder without a trial. This was an unusual measure, since an attainder was used for criminals who were at large and Roose had already been arrested. He then pushed through Parliament an act known as the Act for Poysoning, which made such an action treason. Roose was not executed in a quick manner. Parliament (urged by Henry) decreed that Roose should be boiled to death. The execution took place on 5 April, and Thomas and his son may have been present at Smithfield, where countless traitors to the Crown met their deaths. If they were present, they would have heard Roose's roars of pain as he was dipped slowly into a huge iron cauldron of either boiling water or oil, which he was suspended above. It was reported that the crowd could not muster the usual enthusiasm for the execution, and would have preferred to see the axeman at his work.

According to some narratives, Fisher's troubles were not over yet. The Bishop had only just recovered, when he suffered a different sort of attack.

A cannonball was shot thorough his house, close by his study window where he was used to spend much time in prayer and holy meditations. According to Edward Hall, it 'made such a horrible noyse and clutter, as it went through, that all the house were suddenly amazed'.[15] Hall adds that it was soon made clear that the cannon had been shot from across the river, specifically from Thomas' house on the Strand. When Fisher was informed of this fact, he called all his servants before him, declaring: 'Let us trusse up our baggage and be gone, this is no place for us to abide in any longer.'[16]

We have only Hall's account of this incident, but it is highly suspect that an event of such magnitude, a brazen attempt on the Bishop's life a second time, would not have been reported by Chapuys or any other ambassador, nor noted in court records. Thomas may have been powerful and influential, but attempted murder was not a trivial charge. It would have been far too diplomatically and politically dangerous, and apart from the ethical issue, Durham Place, Thomas' residence, lay 2.5 miles across the river. Modern weaponry would be necessary for the level of accuracy required for this shot.

It is also unlikely that an informal investigation would have been conducted so quickly, deducing the exact trajectory as having come from Thomas' residence, with no further investigation required or any charges laid. Such unreliable accounts have contributed greatly to negative historical opinion of the Boleyns, but we may assume that Hall fabricated the second incident to persuade historians that Thomas would stop at nothing to make Anne queen, and that the Boleyns were not hindered by scruples of conscience.

The court was rather crowded as Henry, his current queen, queen in waiting, and their large entourages remained under one roof, and despite his bravado in front of his clergy, Henry still seemed reluctant to act – instead Henry turned his attention back to Katherine to resolve their miserable situation. He sent a large delegation to visit her, including Thomas, the Marquis of Dorset, the Earl of Talbot, the Earl of Northumberland, and several other noblemen, as well as the bishops of Lincoln and London, and doctors Lee, Sampson and Stephen Gardiner.[17] This was not a polite morning meeting – Henry had instructed them to visit Katherine at 9pm, as she was preparing for bed. Norfolk and Suffolk were there to persuade her to allow the question of the annulment to be heard in England, rather than Rome, as if Katherine were still in control of the situation.[18] Norfolk took the lead, and explained that they were there in the name of the King, and listed the ways in which Katherine's actions had hurt and displeased Henry.[19] The Duke begged her to consider how many dangers they and the whole of England would risk by her refusing to comply with the King's wishes.[20] Katherine insisted that she had already appealed to the Pope to have the case heard in Rome with Henry's consent, to which Thomas politely answered that the licence for the appeal did not go so far as to have Henry summoned to appear before the Pope in Rome.[21] These were the more polite arguments – other members of the delegation spoke to the Queen in abominable terms, which made the whole evening, as Giles Tremlett described, a 'shameful episode' perpetrated by the bishops of Lincoln and Norfolk who were the main antagonists.[22] Thomas maintained civility by focusing on the legality of the issue, and who had the right to hear the matter. Once again he exercised his diplomatic skills and, as the father of Henry's future wife, have deemed it prudent to remain in the background. Out of respect for the Queen, he refrained from outbursts or rudeness towards the woman who had been his queen for over two decades.

By July, the membership of the Boleyn sphere began to change as tensions increased among the inner circle, hardly surprising considering the turmoil that had engulfed the country for five years. Anne had already fallen out with the Duke of Suffolk as he had foolishly repeated the rumour that Anne had been romantically linked to the court poet, Thomas Wyatt.[23] That Wyatt had written poems about Anne suggested some degree of courtly love, but there was no evidence it had gone further. Anne was sensitive to any possible stain on her reputation, which was under constant scrutiny, and demanded that Suffolk be banished from court. When Suffolk returned, he did not make the same mistake, but Anne's resentment had not abated and she accused Suffolk of 'having criminal intercourse with his own daughter'.[24] The irony of Anne's accusation is not lost on history. That summer, Henry Guildford, Comptroller of the Household and an old colleague of Thomas, openly criticised Anne, who immediately retaliated, threatening that, once she became queen, he would be on his way out. Guildford hotly retorted that he would save her the trouble and quit his post, making Henry aware that he had been threatened. Clearly tensions were running high, and something would have to change.

When Anne and Henry left Windsor and quietly rode out towards Woodstock on 11 July, Henry felt he was finally ready to leave his wife, and after 22 years of his marriage to Katherine, it was the first major step in years in a firm direction. Katherine would never see him again.

Some of the tension had been released at last. Anne and Henry spent the summer out in the fresh air, hunting, hawking, gambling, and tentatively enjoying their freedom with Katherine out of the picture. In July, Henry honoured several men within his inner circle. Nicholas Carew, Henry's Master of the Horse and also a Boleyn cousin, received various manors and parks with an annual rent of 40 pounds, and licence to hunt for small game. Henry also honoured his future father-in-law and brother-in-law in a lucrative joint grant of the offices of Steward of the Honour of Railegh, Keeper of Railegh Park, Master of the Hunt of Deer in Railegh Park and Thundersley Park, and Bailiff of the Hundred of Rochford, Essex. Thomas Cromwell, who had only recently been made Keeper of the Crown Jewels, was made Clerk of the Hanaper Chancery, supporting positions for the Keeper of the Privy Seal, and Lord Privy Seal.[25] For George, always with his sister and the King, it was an immense honour, but Thomas, in his role as Lord Privy Seal, continued an endless schedule of administration, sometimes related to Henry's annulment, as well as matters beyond.

In August, a herald arrived unannounced from Charles, Duke of Savoy, to visit the Earl. Charles' claim to Savoy had long been disputed by Francis, through his mother, Louise. The French were eager to annex the duchy, but at stake was not just Savoy, but the kingdom of Cyprus, a trade stronghold, which had been under Savoy rule but was sold to the Venetians decades earlier. When Thomas had passed through Chambery on his way back from his disastrous mission to Bologna, he had met with the Duke, and had promised to discuss the Duke's claims to the contested island. A promise the Duke had not forgotten. The herald was also at court to renew and confirm old alliances which had once existed between England and the House of Savoy. Thomas appeared to be defensive at first, lightly remarking that he heard a rumour that the herald had first visited Katherine.[26] When he heard that this was false, he dropped his defences, and told the herald frankly that now was not the time for any negotiations. He admitted that matters were rather confused and unsettled, and when things 'were no longer ambiguous and obscure, then would be the right time to treat about business of the kind'.[27] It was an honest response and, while the Earl was in favour of more alliances, matters were indeed uncertain and motives too cloaked and it was not the time to antagonise either Francis or Charles, especially when rumour reached court that these two monarchs, who were previously at war, were now preparing to meet.

Christmas of 1531 was held at Greenwich, but it was the first year without Katherine's gentle presence, or that of her ladies. Anne was flanked by a close-knit circle of women, including her sister Mary, her mother, and George's wife, Jane. Anne and Henry projected confidence and mirth, as she established her own style but, in abandoning the Queen, there was a sense that a line had been crossed. On New Year's Day, Henry and his court exchanged gifts – Henry gave Thomas and George a set of gilt goblets, bowls, cruses and cups, and for Jane, Mary, and Elizabeth Boleyn, gilt cruses, cups, salts, a lee pot, casting bottles and goblets. For his queen to be, Henry lavishly gifted a matching set of hangings for her room and bed, in cloth of gold, cloth of silver and richly embroidered crimson satin. The Boleyns would have had to spend a considerable amount for their own gifts to the King: from Anne he received a stunning set of richly decorated Pyrenean boar spears, Thomas gave him a box of black velvet, with a steel glass set in gold, and from Elizabeth Boleyn he received a coffer of needlework, containing six shirt collars, three in gold and three in silver.[28] George presented the King with gilt knives with velvet hilts, and from Jane he received four velvet and satin caps trimmed with gold buttons.

The same accounts which record Christmas gifts also offer some insight into various day-to-day activities, making an interesting diversion from the perpetual divorce issues. George and Thomas were particularly active in court entertainment – gambling, playing shuffleboard and tennis in Henry's palaces and, in good weather, hunting, hawking, holding archery contests, and racing greyhounds. Henry hated to lose, and although he was a competent jouster, it was often more politically expedient to ensure that he won.[29] This implies that he preferred his courtiers to be sycophants, yet both Thomas and his son often beat the King at various sports and games, as regular payments to both clearly show. George won four games of tennis, shooting, bowls and archery, and his father also demonstrated skill at bowls and shuffleboard, winning five angelots. Perhaps they were confident enough in their position to dispense with such dissimulation.

Besides leisure activities, the Earl had to deal with personal matters, in particular a matter brought by his one-time rival for the Earldom of Ormond, Piers Butler, who had written to Cromwell complaining that his rival in Ireland, the Earl of Kildare, was trying to supplant him by persuading Thomas to let him farm several garrisons. Piers sent a protest to Cromwell and Thomas, describing Kildare as a dangerous, untrustworthy man and suggested that if the Earl would not rent Carrick to him he 'should put some servant or an indifferent person on the land.'[30] But Thomas knew that Piers was jealous of Kildare, and proposed removing Piers from the situation by appointing him as deputy to Henry's illegitimate son, Henry Fitzroy. Thomas' response to matters suggests a certain ambivalence towards his Irish earldom – his mother had been born in Ireland, but he had never visited, nor was he heavily invested in the upkeep of the earldom, which yielded very little financial gain. It was the principle, as the earldom had belonged to his ancestors, and his affection for it had always stemmed from his mother. It is interesting, however, that Piers attempted to reach the Earl through Cromwell, now very much a valuable member of the Boleyn sphere, who would continue to prove himself dedicated to their cause, and whose religious affiliations would soon find traction with the younger Boleyns.

Cromwell had quietly become a central figure at court, steering Henry, as George Bernard noted, into more evangelical, reforming or protestant waters.[31] Under Cromwell's guidance, Henry continued to bully the English clergy and Parliament into confirming their allegiance to him rather than the Pope. In March 1532, a Supplication of the Commons against the Ordinaries, drafted by Cromwell, was delivered to Henry listing various grievances against the Church. Henry presented it to the clergy and Parliament, alleging that the English clergy's oaths to the Pope in violation of their oaths to the Crown. He insisted that all clerical legislation would henceforth require royal assent, existing legislation must be submitted for his approval and all laws must emanate from the Crown alone. Interestingly it was Gardiner, who had at first been a firm member of the Boleyn sphere, who objected to the clauses, writing a personal defence to the King. Parliament and clergy reluctantly agreed rather than face charges of treason. Thomas More immediately resigned as Lord Chancellor, unable to endorse where Henry was leading the church. As Henry's partner, Anne encouraged him and ensured he remained committed. On matters of policy, especially where the clergy was concerned, the Boleyns were united but were they like-minded because of political considerations or was it a meeting of religious minds?. The Imperial ambassador viewed them all as heretics especially when Thomas had interceded for a reformed priest in 1531, but matters were not as clear cut as Chapuys assumed or presented. The report came from Norfolk, who, despite benefitting from his niece's position, was never entirely 'with the programme', always keen to recommend himself to Charles. He was quite unlike the Boleyns, prepared to stand on their convictions even if it caused friction. The Papal Nuncio at court had complained to the slippery Duke that a preacher had called the Pope a heretic. The Duke responded that he was not in the least surprised, and if Thomas and his daughter had not interceded for the priest, he, Norfolk, would have burnt him and another doctor without mercy. *But please*, Norfolk begged wolfishly, do not write to the Pope about such little follies. *He, Norfolk*, would try and prevent them in the future.[32]

A month later, Chapuys reported that a young priest had been found guilty of filing the shavings from angelots, French coins. The ambassador reported that he did this out of simplicity rather than malice, but Henry had him imprisoned, due either to his violent dislike of priests or desire to please Anne. It was Thomas who interceded for the priest, asking Henry to spare him but to no avail. Anne, who had up to this point always shown deference to her father, publicly berated him, telling him that he should not speak for priests as there were already too many in England. Despite Thomas' pleas, the priest was executed for the minor crime.[33]

How might we explain Thomas' seemingly contradictory nature? Fiercely anti-clerical on one hand, and yet, as we have seen in previous chapters, religiously conservative and old-fashioned. This was a fraught century, with families like the Boleyns navigating the rough waters of religious change. Europe was assailed by complex religious discussions, with sacred thinking infusing political and economic realities, and strong convictions mingled with spiritual ambiguities and unresolved contradictions. Drawing clear lines around individuals is important if we are to understand the immense variety, and subtle differences that often were to be found in their religious positions.

By 1532, there were tendrils of spirituality evident in the lives of Thomas and his children. Christian humanists and evangelists of France had begun to influence Anne and George's religious affinity.[34] Their spirituality blossomed as they became exposed to reformist developments, but we should not assume that whatever religious beliefs Anne favoured, so too did every member of her family.

The tender green shoots of the early Reformation were already becoming the political and diplomatic sharp thorns of conflict between 'Protestant' and 'Catholic', and there are a few examples prior to 1530 of Thomas' personal pursuits at the height of his family's power.[35] One relationship in particular offers us an incredible personal insight into his spirituality – his correspondence with Desiderius Erasmus, one of the most famous humanist philosophers of the age. To correspond with the great Erasmus marked you as a person of high intellect and education. Men like Thomas More played on their friendship with Erasmus and the kudos it brought. Thomas' enduring friendship with the highly revered intellectual is therefore surprising, not in the connection itself, but in that it is rarely mentioned in most works on the Tudor period.

We have no records which prove that the two ever met, but it is entirely plausible that when the famous scholar visited England between 1509 and 1514, the two became acquainted. There seems to have been no letters of introduction between them, so we may reason that the first point of contact was in person.[36]

We do know that on 4 November 1529, Gerard of Friesland (referred to as Phrygius) wrote to Erasmus on behalf of his master, Thomas, with a request for a commentary on Psalm 23, 'The lord is my shepherd, therefore can I lack nothing.'[37] The letter remains:

You have in England, my beloved Erasmus, your Zoiluses and your Maecenases. The former are killing themselves with their own swords, the latter are doing all they can to share with others the fine producer of that divine mind. My master Viscount Rochford, by far the most accomplished expert in affairs, appeals to you by the great love he has for your kindly self that you employ all your skill and cleverness to open up for us in all its aspects the famous psalm 'The Lord ruleth me and I shall want nothing.' Apart from doing a service to others as well as to him, I know how much more closely you will bind the man to you as well as to him, I know many of his majesty's other councillors will be won over to become your friends.[38]

Thomas added a brief postscript in his own elegant hand: 'I pray yow gyff credit to thys, and pardon me thow I wryt nat at thys tyme to yow my self, yowr own assuredly, T Rochford.'[39] The letter ended with: 'Farewell again, do not be too hard on a pupil of Listrius!' This last sentence is intriguing; Listrius was a well-known scholar and theologian, who, in his later years, was influenced by Luther's teachings.[40]

The letter provides a fascinating insight into how Thomas fashioned himself for so great a scholar, and how intently he wished to be viewed as an individual worthy of Erasmus' respect.

That Thomas chose not to write his postscript in Latin has been seized upon as confirmation that the request was purely for show, without sincere purpose. Yet the letter to Erasmus is a clear introduction on Thomas' behalf, a respectful approach to someone of Erasmus' reputation, and it may have served a double purpose, as a valuable exercise in public relations and as the result of a genuine intellectual and religious interest in the work of the famous humanist. Nevertheless, historians have dismissed the letter, with many arguing that Thomas had no genuine reason to approach the scholar.[41] Although his dedication in *Ennaratio triplrex in Psalmum XXII* speaks of Thomas as a man of devotion to letters and divinity, it is assumed that Thomas would not have found the lengthy Latin text easy reading. As one scholar put it, 'he [Thomas] evidently had so little linguistic expertise that the composition of one simple Latin sentence was beyond him: would such a man really have enjoyed reading the text he later received?'[42]

This evaluation helps explain why Thomas and Erasmus have hardly been discussed together. George may have lamented his poor Latin, but Thomas spoke and wrote it fluently enough. His negotiations at Margaret of Austria's court involved writing and speaking in Latin, Henry praised his Latin to Chapuys, and his accounts book during his time as Comptroller of the Household were all written in Latin.[43] But for many, Anne was the reason for her father's contact with Erasmus: the pro-divorce party wished for their own Erasmian work to add lustre to their cause.[44] Such as the case may be, it should be kept in mind that the psalm had nothing to do with the divorce – it mattered little to the cause, as much as it could represent a genuine commission for a religious work from the most important writer of the day.

The English postscript also gives historians pause. It is generally assumed that Erasmus was little conversant with German, or English, and refused to speak French, finding the latter to be 'a barbarous tongue, with the shrillest discords, and words hardly human'.[45] Latin, Dutch and Greek were apparently the only languages he used; he risked his life in Italy by refusing to learn Italian and, while he did spend time in England, he similarly refused to learn the language, even sacrificing his benefice as a result.[46]

But it is possible that the address in English was simply to show that the commission was indeed from Thomas. In any case, Erasmus' response to Thomas, written in Latin, shows not just Erasmus' enthusiasm for the project, but his profound, and we can safely say sincere, respect for the Earl, for Erasmus was not prone to flattery.[47]

> To the right honourable Thomas, Viscount Rochford, from Desiderious Erasmus of Rotterdam, Greeting.
>
> Honoured sir, you have long given us since ample evidence of the excellence of your mind when you seemed not content with all the adornments that came to your lineage, from the busts of your ancestors, from gold rings and gold chains, adornments that you had gained the right to wear from the nobility of your ancient line and a character that did honour to your ancestry, but you wanted also to adorn your mind with a more precious chain, whose links are formed by the noble lessons of philosophy. But now I have even greater reason to congratulate you on your happy fortune, for I see you, a man of influence, a layman, taking to your heart the sacred word and craving to possess that noble pearl. So it was with increased pleasure that I proceeded to your most pious request. I have written a three-fold commentary on the psalm you chose. How well I succeeded is for you to judge. In any case, I myself have derived no small profit from this little effort, and for the work brought to my mind considerable pleasure and consolation. If it brings the same pleasure to your mind too, I shall be delighted to have obeyed your request. But if there are things in it that displease you, please do not hesitate to point them out. Let me thank you for the opportunity you have given me to expand my knowledge. St Jerome wrote on this psalm, but briefly, as his way. Arnobius is even briefer. St Augustine did not write a commentary; he added only the briefest of notes, the sort of thing I believe, which preachers did as an aide-memoir in the preparing to speak to the people. I wonder if by some chance a commentary has disappeared. Cassiodorus was not available to me, but he does not usually have much that is important to say. So for the most part, I was left, as the saying goes, to fend for myself. If however anything here has turned out well, the credit belongs wholly to Christ and him alone.[48]

Thomas was obviously stimulated by the religious and intellectual discussions of the age, and the Boleyn household has been described as a breeding ground or for the 'New Religion'. Certainly religion was an integral part of life for Thomas, his king and his countrymen, but he supported reform within the Church and accepted that Rome would have to change, or the world would change Rome. The political reformation was upon them; Henry was forging a protestant future in England, a cause which Thomas would dutifully champion. But Protestant reformers would take up some of the ideals espoused by Erasmus, but in far more thorough and trenchant ways than Erasmus, and even Thomas could have imagined. George and Anne's own spirituality became more apparent from 1530 onwards, but their father would continue to exhibit intellectual and spiritual interests that were a mix of old and new, just as Thomas was a product of both the old world and new one that was forming under Henry and his queen to be.

# CHAPTER TWELVE

# Nowe Thus

*The bravest are surely those who have the clearest vision of what is before them, glory or danger alike, and yet notwithstanding, go out to meet it.*

— Thucydides

Dawn had not yet broken on what promised to be a stiflingly hot August day, when Thomas was awoken by two men banging on the gates of his manor of Penshurst – John Comport and his servant, John Bensen. Bensen had been accused of murdering a man named Robert Grame and, as the evidence against Bensen was considerable, the Justice of the Peace for Surrey, Sir John Gaynsford, had locked Bensen up for questioning.[1] The two men escaped during the night, and foolishly made their way to Penshurst. Thomas was one of the most influential men in his county, and was frequently called up as a Commissioner of the Peace, and had been appointed as Sherriff of Kent.[2] Comport thought he could bribe Thomas to intercede for the pair. Thomas would never be persuaded to pervert the course of justice, and despite Comport offering to pay bail for his servant, the Earl brought both men straight back to Gaynsford for further examination.[3]

While Thomas spent time dealing with issues in his county, the political agenda intensified in 1532, as Charles staunchly continued to oppose Henry's attempts to dispose of his wife, leaving Henry once again seeking French support. Since the previous autumn, Henry's ambassadors in France, had been secretly canvassing the interest for another Anglo-French meeting. It had been 12 years since the two kings had come face to face on the glorious Field of Cloth of Gold – but by 1531 neither could afford such grand gestures. In many respects, this meeting signified far more, yet with Wolsey long gone, and Thomas not involved, arrangements were chaotic and convoluted. Instead, Thomas was busy concluding a minor negotiation with the French, represented by Giles de la Pomeraye, from the comfort of court. They were able to confirm former treaties, and agreed to supplying mutual aid when required against the Emperor.

Thomas' colleagues who were tasked with negotiating the French meeting were not so successful – they had reached an impasse because Francis' wife, Eleanor, was the sister of Charles V, and familial loyalty made a meeting between the two women awkward. Chapuys reported that Francis suggested that he (too) bring his mistress, Madame de Vendôme, rather than his queen, which was a diplomatic rebuke to Henry and would have humiliated both Eleanor and Anne, and was immediately refused.[4] It was decided that Anne should remain in Calais, while Henry and his male courtiers would ride on to meet Francis at Boulogne. Henry was exceptionally busy. Ships were being fitted out for the approximately 4,000 members of the party, and almost all the English nobles who were fit and could be spared from duties at home were to be part of the retinue.[5] To spare his nobles from excessive costs, a limit was placed on the extravagance of their attire, especially the wearing of cloth of gold or silver, but the limit did not apply to either Henry or Anne of course, with Henry's own expenditure exceeding £6,000. Anne longed to be attired as befitting a queen, and she would feel far closer to the throne if she were wearing the Queen's jewels. Henry indulged her, ordering much of the royal jewellery to be reset, setting aside the choicest stones for Anne: four bracelets, which yielded her no fewer than 18 tabled rubies.[6] But many of the Queen's jewels belonged to the Queen, and they were still in Katherine's possession. Henry sent his wolf, Norfolk, to fetch them, several pieces of which were actually gifts from Katherine's mother. According to Chapuys Katherine would not give up her jewels to 'ornament a person who is the scandal of Christendom'.[7] Katherine declared that if this was an express command, she would relinquish them. The command came swiftly.[8]

Anne was still only the daughter of an Earl, and required titled elevation in order to be presented in France as Henry's future queen. Her parents and siblings witnessed her elevatioh in a grand ceremony at Windsor, to the Marchioness of Pembroke, which made her a peer in her own right in September of 1532. Anne was breathtaking at the ceremony, her dark hair loose around her shoulders, wearing a robe of crimson velvet trimmed with ermine and encrusted with jewels.[9] Her uncle, Norfolk, and the Duke of Suffolk escorted her, her father and brother following in the entourage of nobles. Thomas proudly watched his daughter raised to heights beyond his own. A few nights later, the court celebrated as Anne hosted a banquet for the French ambassadors – Chapuys was not invited.

But at last, it must have felt as though events were moving apace towards their desired conclusion.

The English arrived in Calais on Friday 11 October and, four days later, Norfolk, Thomas, George, the Earl of Derby and a group of gentlemen met with 'the great mayster of Fraunce' Anne, duc de Montmorency, and his men at the English Pale, six miles outside of Calais.[10] John Hannaert, Viscount of Lombeke, Charles' Imperial ambassador to the French court, reported that: 'On three days a secret council and conference was held at which three persons assisted on each side besides the two kings, namely, on the side of the Most Christian King, the Legate, the Grand Master and the Great Admiral of France; on that of the English, the duke of Suffolk, his brother-in-law, the duke of Norfolk, and a bishop who is his chancellor.'[11] Henry left Anne at Calais on 21 October to meet the French king at Sandingfield; while Francis, brought an equally grand retinue, including the King of Navarre, the Cardinal of Lorraine and the Duke of Vendme. Here the kings embraced each other five or six times on horseback, and the lords on opposite sides followed their example. They rode hand in hand for a mile towards Boulogne, where they were joined by the Dauphin, the Duke of Orleans, the Count of Angoulme, and four cardinals, with a body of 1,000 men on horseback. The streets of Boulogne were lined with the Swiss, Scotch and French guards as they passed. On the following Friday, Francis, in return, visited the King at Calais, and was given a magnificent reception, where 3,000 guns were fired in his honour. The Boleyns were out in force – Thomas, his brothers, James and Edward, and of course George were all present.[12] Although we have no direct mention of his involvement, it is highly likely that both men accompanied Henry and his entourage to meet Francis, primarily because of their positions as future father-in-law and brother-in-law to the King, but also because of their command of French and courtly sophistication; they were immensely useful in Anglo-French relations. But it was the Duke of Norfolk who overshadowed the members of the retinue, as the premier noble in the realm. Despite his well-known dislike of the French, he enjoyed his esteemed position.

As Francis had no female companions, Anne was not supposed to be present for any events, even in Calais when Francis visited, but she found an ingenious way around the issue. The chronicler Edward Hall described the scene following a lavish supper in Boulogne, attended by all the men of court. The room for the banquet, and the stage itself, was decorated with gold bejewelled wreaths and draped with cloth of silver. Twenty different silver gilded candelabras, one of which could hold a hundred candles, provided the light for the performance.[13] The English and French contingency fell into hushed silence as eight ladies slipped into the hall, moving swiftly between the tables. These women were probably Anne and Mary Boleyn, the Countess of Derby, Lady Fitzwater, Jane Boleyn, Lady Lisle and Lady Wallop. Their gowns were of a 'straunge fashion, made of clothe of gold, compassed with Crimosyn Tinsell Satin, owned with Clothe of Siluer, liyng lose [loose] and knit with laces of Gold'. The leader, Anne, offered her petite hand to Francis, and before the court the ladies danced with their French counterparts. Henry, pleased to see Francis so charmed by the scene, stepped forward and removed Anne's mask, followed by the other ladies, and they were revealed. There could be no doubt that Anne was the centrepiece of the choreography, as she was of the highest rank among the ladies present and invited the man of highest rank, the king of France, to join the dance. It was a graceful and diplomatic sidestep of the issue of Anne not having a female French counterpart, but she was determined to see Francis. With her perfect command of French, which she spoke with a slight lilt, her clear favour and affection for the country, which her father had cultivated, and her intelligence and charm, it was Anne who would persuade Francis to their cause.

The next day, the two courts came together again in Boulogne for a final full day of celebrations. Thomas, among his fellow Knights of the Garter, dressed in their robes of crimson and fur, witnessed the ordination of two new members: Anne, duc de Montmorency, who Thomas knew well, and Philippe de Chabot, Admiral of France.[14]

The entertainment that day included bear baiting and a wrestling match, which saw the English Cornish wrestlers provided by Sir William Godolphin beat the French side. George and his fellow courtiers enjoyed the festivities, while Thomas probably spent time with his French counterparts, perhaps continuing to cultivate support for his daughter. On the final day, Francis escorted Henry and his retinue outside Calais, where they had a more subdued last meeting. In the middle of a green valley, a long table had been set with wine, hippocras, fruit and spiced wafers. Henry and Francis spoke quietly, the nature of their conversation not recorded. After a time, they mounted their horses, and with 'Princely countenaunce, loving behaviour, and hearty words, each embarrassed the other and so there departed.'[15] It had been a success, with Francis promising not only to support the match, but also to speak to the Pope in defence of his brother: his Cardinals 'shall do what they can in the matter of the king of England, as if it was the King's own affair'.[16]

The English had planned to sail from Calais to Dover, but the winds had whipped up the waters of the channel, and the ships turned back. They were stranded for eight days, as the harbour was besieged by storms and mist. There, it is believed, Anne and Henry finally consummated their relationship. Within weeks of returning to England, they felt emboldened and secure enough to wed and did so secretly, either in late 1532 or early 1533, despite the fact that Henry's marriage to Katherine was still considered valid.[17] We do not have the details of the wedding, who attended, or even when it took place, but her parents and her brother would have been present.

Rumours swirled around the court in early 1533 that Henry had married an already pregnant Anne in England on 25 January.[18] Something had shifted between the King and his mistress – they were calmer, more assured. Anne seemed lighter, and Chapuys reported that she had declared one evening during supper that she was as sure of her own death that she should be very soon married to the King. Her father was equally vocal, and in conversation with the Earl of Rutland, he confided that the King was determined no longer to be so considerate as he had been. In fact, Thomas added, once the marriage had taken place 'by the authority and sanction of Parliament it would be much easier to conciliate the opponents than at present'.[19] Rutland seemed hesitant to agree, especially when Thomas asked him outright which way he would vote, when the motion of marriage was brought forward in Parliament. Rutland vaguely answered that the matter was wholly of a spiritual nature and could not be decided by Parliament. Chapuys reported that Thomas 'got into a passion as though Rutland had uttered a blasphemy, and began to taunt him in very gross language, so much so that he at last promised to vote whatever the King wanted, and sent me a message to say how matters stood, and that I was not to expect that any member of Parliament would dare offer any opposition'.[20]

We have no way of knowing what language Thomas used, but it would be highly out of character for him to be vulgar. He may well have been forceful in his opinion, but then he probably knew what the rest of the court could not. Anne and Henry were married, and his daughter could even now be with child – which, as it happened, she was.

Chapuys further wrote that Thomas had not declared himself up to this moment. 'On the contrary, he has hitherto, as the duke of Norfolk has frequently told me, tried to dissuade the King rather than otherwise from the marriage.'[21] Thomas had always been a cautious man, especially considering the precedent of Henry's grandfather, the Yorkist Edward IV, whose marriage to Elizabeth Woodville had torn his family apart; nor did Edward have a queen who needed to be deposed first. But there is more evidence that Thomas supported his daughter, as so much of the last six years had been in the pursuit of the marriage – Norfolk or Chapuys may have been disingenuous.

By 1533 George was a key figure at court, his influence expanding when he was formally invited to Parliament on 5 February, taking his place beside his father and uncles. Both George and his father worked closely with two other influential and indispensable members of their sphere: Thomas Cromwell and Thomas Cranmer. While Cromwell maintained a professional relationship, Cranmer had developed a deep friendship with the Boleyn men, and was considered a confidant and trusted friend of the family.

In late February, Chapuys' spy informed him that the Papal Nuncio in England, Andrea del Borgho, was immersed in talks with Norfolk and Henry, and he immediately took a boat from his lodgings near the Tower to Greenwich, to interrogate the nuncio. Borgho strenuously denied that any meeting had taken place, despite the eyewitness accounts, which raised alarm bells with the ambassador. When further pressed about his stance on Henry's divorce, Borgho admitted that he supported the view that the matter not be heard in Rome, which would definitely please Henry.[22] Furthermore, William Warham's death the previous year had left a vacancy for the Archbishopric of Canterbury, the most powerful diocese in England. Henry had quietly and politely nominated 'a nobody', in Rome's eyes – Thomas Cranmer.[23] Clement, eager to please Henry on one issue at least, had to give his consent for Cranmer to be consecrated as archbishop, and the papal bulls were already drawn up. Chapuys hastily wrote to Clement, advising him to delay the bulls until after the case had been brought to a decision, so that Cranmer's involvement could be neutralised and the matter not brought to England.

Clement ignored Chapuys' warnings. In late March the bulls for the archbishopric of Canterbury arrived. Chapuys wrote that Henry was on his feet instantly, not wishing to waste another moment of being married to Katherine, and called Convocation at once, demanding the matter be decided immediately.[24] In the first week of April, Parliament passed the bill Cromwell had masterminded, the Act in Restraint of Appeals, meaning that any verdict concerning the King's marriage could not be challenged in Rome.

Henry's luck had unexpectedly turned, and Chapuys reported that on 15 February Anne had boasted quite openly to her uncle that if she was not pregnant by Easter she would undertake a pilgrimage to pray to the Virgin Mary.[25] A week later she said to one of her favourites, probably Wyatt, and again in the hearing of many courtiers, that she had developed a craving for apples, which the King said was a sign that she was pregnant before bursting into laughter.[26] Plans were put in motion immediately to have Anne crowned as Queen, even before the matter had been settled.

Thomas' Privy Seal duties kept him occupied for the first few months of 1533. He was part of the Parliament debate in January to decide whether to prorogue the Parliament on account of the unhealthy air, and was present for the 'Trial of the Pyx', the annual testing and evaluation of newly minted coins.[27] After almost three years, George was finally appointed for his second embassy, again to France in March. He was not appointed as a resident ambassador, but special envoy and, this time, he was more mature as a 29-year-old man, with some experience behind him. He would lead the embassy, and was instructed, according to Chapuys, to persuade Francis to 'take in hand the affairs of Scotland, with which they are already marvellously troubled; for there is no lord or other who would willingly go in the said enterprise'.[28]

George's lengthy instructions included presenting Francis with letters written in the King's own hand, and to inform Francis that 'from his anxiety to have male issue for the establishment of his kingdom, he has proceeded effectually to the accomplishment of his marriage'.[29]

George was to press Francis and remind him that in Calais he had promised to assist and maintain the King in the event of any excommunication from the Pope. He would also need to remind Francis that he would surely, as a true friend and brother, 'devise whatever he can for the establishment of the said marriage, preventing any impediment to it, or of the succession, which please God will follow, and which, to all appearance, is in a state of advancement already, as the King himself would do for Francis in like case'.[30] Most importantly, George was to convey the good news – his sister was pregnant. George arrived at the French court, confident in his position, and assumed Francis would be receptive to the news, but Francis seemed hesitant. Despite his grand gestures in Calais, he was less than willing to act on them. Charles and Clement had agreed to meet with Francis for a rapprochement, and George, obviously advised by his father, remained firm in the face of a monarch about to fall back on his word. Francis was finally induced to proceed with negotiating with Charles and the Pope on Henry's behalf.[31] George was also an integral part of negotiations between England and France over the growing tension with Scotland, which had in the past been a natural ally of France, and thereby a natural enemy of England. It was also possible, Chapuys surmised, that George would invite Francis to visit England, as he had promised at Boulogne. It made sense to the ambassador, who had noticed that Henry had ordered all his game parks to be put in order, and all licences for hunting revoked, which was a sign that he planned on entertaining special guests. Chapuys envisioned George Boleyn charming his way through the French court, but actually George's ambassadorial style seemed to irritate his French hosts. His determination that Francis write to the Pope supporting Henry's marriage to his sister made him somewhat belligerent, with du Bellay noting that at first he was very unreasonable, before he relaxed into the embassy. Du Bellay compared George to his father, declaring that the latter would not have behaved in such a way, and would have broken off the interview when he saw matters were not progressing. There was a faint suggestion that Francis preferred a man of more senior status, with du Bellay noting that Norfolk should have been present, and that he doubted whether Norfolk even approved of George being sent.[32]

Even if negotiations had not gone as smoothly as he hoped, his introduction to Francis' sister, Marguerite of Navarre, was considerable compensation. Highly literate, sensitive and famously beautiful, Marguerite spent her childhood in a large, aristocratic, cosmopolitan, educated, progressive and tolerant household. While her brother languished in Madrid as Charles' prisoner, Marguerite rode horseback with an armed escort, keeping within safe-conduct deadlines by riding 12 hours a day for several days, spending her nights writing her reports and diplomatic letters. As a Venetian ambassador commented, she knew the secrets and skills of the diplomatic arts and should be treated circumspectly and with deference.

Marguerite showed some sympathy for Henry's marital issues, and the religious direction Henry and Anne's marriage had taken them was, to Marguerite, an exciting development. Had George been dealing solely with her, he would have fared better and, although he convinced a hesitant Francis to write to the Pope, the tone of the letter was not what Henry had requested. For the time being, it would have to suffice.[33]

It was a short embassy. George returned in early April, having been awarded 2,000 crowns to celebrate his sister's marriage, but it had not been a resounding triumph.[34] Instead he resumed his domestic duties as Privy Councillor, and remained active in Parliament.[35]

In early May, a highly agitated Chapuys sat down and composed a lengthy report to the Emperor. He had attended a meeting of the King's Privy Council which included both Boleyn men, Cromwell and others.[36] Astoundingly, Charles had instructed Chapuys to write to Henry informing him of the Emperor's intention to appeal Cranmer's appointment with the Pope, and Chapuys had then taken it upon himself to add his own opinions, pointing out the errors in Henry's pursuit for an annulment.[37] Chapuys was surprised that, when he attended the meeting, he was confronted by an irate Thomas, who took the letter from his pouch and waved it around, asking the ambassador to explain its contents.

Thomas warned Chapuys that he had overstepped the mark and gone beyond what his duties dictated, but Chapuys was defiant, retorting that he had the power to act in Charles' name, though he was careful not to offend the Earl or the King: 'However, to show the King that I did not wish to be over-scrupulous, but on the contrary, was desirous of doing his pleasure in every respect, I would at once exhibit the powers, which I threw down on the table. This being done, I summarily declared the contents of my letter, and explained to them the nature and purport of the Papal briefs excommunicating the King and them all.'[38] Thomas was raring for an altercation with the Chapuys – his anger simmering for weeks as the ambassador had been avoiding him. When the two had met by chance at court earlier, Thomas had politely told him that Norfolk, who he had come to visit, was not at court, and the Earl was standing in for him. Chapuys flatly refused to do business with him or deal with him in any way. Thomas was offended, but again tried to mend fences by inviting Chapuys to dine, which Chapuys also ignored. It had been two snubs, and this latest evidence of his behaviour had tipped the Earl over the edge. Standing up, 'as a man who is at once vexed and surprised', Thomas declared that the letter was a most strange one, and of such a nature that had it been written by a man of this kingdom, however great and distinguished, he would certainly have had his property confiscated and himself cast in prison for setting at defiance the statutes, laws and ordinances lately passed in Parliament.[39]

If Chapuys continued to put on two faces, and exceed his functions of ambassador, that would be another matter. 'For that reason, he [Thomas] said, it was for me to consider whether I ought to mix myself up with the affairs alluded to in my letter.'[40]

Thomas continued to berate Chapuys, shaking the Statute in Restraint of Appeals which he held in his hand. Finally the argumentative ambassador agreed to stop meddling in Henry's divorce plans for a few days in return for an explanation in writing from Henry.

This behaviour at the Privy Council meeting would seem a departure from Thomas' usual diplomatic demeanour, and one of the few occasions in which he appears as the most vocal of the group, which Chapuys said was because neither Norfolk nor Suffolk were present. The dukes usually provided the muscular strikes while the Earl remained the more measured and reasonable councillor, in the background. With both men absent, Thomas took on their role which was to challenge the Imperial ambassador. Thomas was aware of the threat Charles posed and, with Anne pregnant and recently wed, and Katherine still living in exile, they were all dancing to a dangerous tune indeed.

But on 23 May, Cranmer, who had successfully been appointed Archbishop of Canterbury, pronounced Henry to be divorced from his queen of 24 years. Chapuys reported that the hearing was not held at Blackfriars but at Dunstable Priory in Bedfordshire. Chapuys remarked that Henry was anxious to avoid public involvement: 'A solitary place has been chosen for secrecy, as they fear that if the affair was managed [in London], the people would not refrain from speaking and perhaps rioting.'[41] It was remarkably quick, and Katherine had no chance to fight it – the court moved on.

Anne's coronation was set for 1 June, turning London into a construction site as the necessary preparations for the grand procession were put in place. Henry was personally involved in all the renovations made to the Tower of London, where Anne would spend the night before the coronation, but many of his trusted councillors were engaged elsewhere. Cromwell was busy drafting legislation to protect the King's new powers from opponents at home and abroad, and George had been appointed to yet another embassy to France, only weeks after arriving home. This time he was to accompany his uncle, Norfolk, who was usually sent north for diplomatic missions to Scotland, where they were more tolerant of his brusque manner. George may well have been sent to temper his uncle's lack of tact and charm, but their timing was most unfortunate, for George would miss his sister's moment of absolute triumph. The embassy to Paris left less than a week before, and we may speculate that George and his sister spoke privately of the impending event with excitement and apprehension. George must have had mixed feelings to be sent on another important mission which would help cement his role as a skilled and influential ambassador. Anne would have missed her brother, for there was tension between her and her father; just prior to Anne's coronation, she and her father had a loud argument.

Anne seemed to be feeling self-conscious and uncertain, and was letting out her gowns to cover and hide her growing belly. Her father, perhaps trying to be encouraging, told her to leave the gowns as they were, that 'she should be thankful to God for the state she was in, and to take away the piece she had put on her dress to denote her impending motherhood' (Anne was almost six months' pregnant at her coronation). Anne snapped at her father that she was in a better plight than he would have wished her to be.[42] Did Anne feel that she had not always had her father's support? In a conversation with Chapuys over the new marriage, Norfolk said that he had not originated or promoted the divorce. He said that the marriage would have occurred secretly a year earlier had not he and Thomas opposed it to the point of Anne's father feigning madness. It is impossible to verify Norfolk's statement but, with the strain of a coronation, and the expectation that the baby she carried would be the heir Henry craved, tempers were naturally fraying.

Thomas showed concern – if we may for a moment consider such things – and love for his daughter, and Anne was still a fiercely proud Boleyn. She had chosen for her royal crest a crowned white falcon, perched atop a tree stump, surrounded by white and red roses. The white falcon was the Butler falcon, her paternal grandmother's family crest. Even before her queenship when she was simply Mademoiselle Anne, she had always used the motto that had once adorned her great-great-grandfather's tomb in Salle, which had been favoured by her father, too – 'Nowe Thus.'

Anne's coronation had been planned on a spectacular scale, to rival Katherine's over 20 years earlier. Her brother may have been absent, but the pregnant Anne had her father by her side, as he was her personal escort for the four days of festivities. On Thursday, 29 May, Anne and her father were met at Greenwich by a delegation of the crafts from London headed by the Lord Mayor and most of the nobility, conveyed in 50 barges. It must have felt quite surreal that only three generations ago, a Boleyn as Mayor of London was the highest status the family had achieved.

The next day, Anne and her father progressed down the Thames from Greenwich Palace to the Tower of London, where she was greeted by her husband to the roaring fire of 1,000 guns. The following day a feast was held where 18 newly created Knights of the Bath attended upon her, one of which was her brother in law, Henry Parker. On Saturday, 31 May, Anne was conveyed by parade to Westminster over freshly gravelled London streets with hanging tapestries of cloth of gold, and past conduits which ran with free-flowing wine. She was carried in a litter followed by 12 ladies on hackneys and a chariot that contained the old Duchess of Norfolk and Anne's mother.[43] There, at Westminster, she spent her last night before being anointed Queen.

The next morning, Anne was brought from Westminster Hall to St Peter's Abbey in procession, with all the monks of Westminster going in rich copes of gold, with 13 mitred abbots; and after them all the King's chapel in rich copes with four bishops and two mitred archbishops. The lords, Thomas included, wore their parliament robes, and the Duke of Suffolk carried the crown in front of her as she made her way down the aisle, under a rich canopy of cloth of gold, dressed in a kirtle of crimson velvet decorated with ermine, and a robe of purple velvet also decorated with ermine.[44] Anne was crowned, transforming her from a mortal woman to Queen Consort. Chapuys describes the coronation as 'altogether a cold, poor, and most unpleasing sight to the great regret, annoyance, and disappointment not only of the common people but likewise of all the rest'. However, he was probably playing down the spectacle for Charles' sake, and for Katherine's, as he was lavishly entertained at a banquet held on the German ambassador's barge.[45] After the ceremony, Anne walked back through the hall, still under the canopy, but crowned, with two sceptres in her hands. Her father and Lord Talbot, whose daughter, Elizabeth was married to Henry Percy, escorted her.[46] We might well wonder whether either Talbot or Anne appreciated the irony. That night, a royal feast was held at Westminster, with Anne accompanied by her ladies, and Henry, swelling with pride at his new, pregnant queen, watched from a private gallery above for he did not want to overshadow her. This night belonged to the Boleyns.

# CHAPTER THIRTEEN

# Turning Tides

*Do not desire to constrain your face to feigned joy:*
*your sorrow is as lovely as your smile.*
*Thus is the dawn still beautiful when girded with clouds,*
*the melancholy moon is lovely in its pallor.*

*– Anna Bolena*, Donizetti

When George and his embassy arrived in France, they remained in Calais until they received instructions to travel to the French court, where George and his colleagues would meet Francis' sister, Marguerite.

While in Paris, he received news of his sister's triumph, and in the absence of extant communication between the family (we can assume Anne or her father wrote to George) we have a report of the event from Anne's new Chamberlain, William Baynton. He assured the ambassador that the coronation was honorably passed 'as ever was, if all old and ancient men say true'.[1] In the letter Baynton made reference to a private business arrangement between George and William Brereton, a fellow courtier, which George had relied on Baynton to complete. Baynton also wrote in jest of how merry Anne's court was, adding that 'If any of you that be now departed have any ladies that they thought favored you, and somewhat would mourn at parting of their servants, I can no whit perceive the same by their dancing and pastime they do use here.'[2] It sketches a portrait of Anne's new court, containing all the chivalric elements and intrigues, Anne herself surrounded by young courtiers and ladies, dedicated to 'pastimes', such as singing, playing music, dancing, gambling, and flirting – all wrapped in the revelry of a new beginning. But the observation that the men might be missed by particular ladies back at court is interesting, considering that George was married. Baynton also referred to a hawk called a Merlyon (Merlin) which

George, who was developing a passion for falconry, may have mentioned an interest in purchasing, but the hawk was young and not yet ready to 'fly at the larks in this country'. George would continue his search for the right bird of prey.

Marguerite hosted the embassy for several days, renewing her acquaintance with George. The nature of their conversations is not recorded; Marguerite may have spoken of her love of illustrated manuscripts, most of which were religious and devotional texts, including books of hours and antiphonals, traditional elements of medieval Catholicism. That she had a profound influence on the young ambassador was highly likely.[3] Perhaps as a present for the new queen, Marguerite gave George a copy of her work, *Miroir de l'âme pécheresse*, which would later be translated by George's niece, Elizabeth I. Tendrils of a literary and reformist connection between Marguerite, George and Anne and the future Queen Elizabeth are evident.

Norfolk's reports to Henry conveyed his deep admiration for Marguerite, declaring that he found her to be 'one of the most wisest frank women,' and was pleased that she supported Anne's cause. When she bid them farewell she promised that she would encourage her brother to support Henry. They continued to Riom, where Francis was staying, days before Francis' meeting with the Pope but, when they arrived, Francis explained that the meeting had been postponed due to the oppressive heat, and instead he took them on the scenic route, entertaining and treating them as 'though they were the Dauphin' as they accompanied him through various countryside towns.[4]

The congenial mood quickly dissipated – within days, Norfolk was taken ill, and travelled with some of the embassy to Lyon to recover, where his nephew would later reconvene with him. George was determined to push on; he did not need his uncle to assist him in negotiations.

Sir Anthony Browne, who accompanied the Duke, reported various dramatic events, including a thunderstorm which covered the field in which Norfolk had been dining, with lightning striking the very tree he had been sitting under: 'Within an hour after arose a great thunder, and burnt the same tree. One of the King's archers was also burnt, standing within three men of him.[5] George and his colleagues arrived a few days later, though we have no evidence of what they thought of Norfolk's streak of luck.

What the embassy did not know was that while they waited for a French-Papal summit, on 11 July, the Pope declared Cranmer's proceedings null and void, and excommunicated Henry. Clement graciously gave Henry a six-week window to leave Anne and return to Katherine.

When the pronouncement of the sentence of excommunication reached the English party in Lyon on 25 July, George was sent hurtling back to England with the news – Norfolk may have thought that the news coming from her brother would soften the blow to the very pregnant Anne.

George arrived at Windsor Castle within three days, bringing potentially disastrous news to a merry court. Henry convened a private meeting with his councillors, following which he issued new instructions which George would carry to his uncle. While he was privy to discussions we might wonder whether George continued to feel he was being under-utilised. Thomas' second embassy had lasted several months, and Thomas had been entrusted with enormous responsibilities. In George's case, Henry continued to treat him as a messenger, rather than an ambassador. George was a talented young man, and he was dedicated and reliable – he deserved more of an opportunity. George returned to France with the new instructions: they were still to prevent a meeting between Francis and the Pope until such time as the Pope acceded to Henry's wishes but, if possible, George was to 'tarry with him [Francis], and consult by what ways and means we can best annoy the Pope'. If the meeting could not be prevented, George was to inform Francis that Henry had commissioned his ambassadors Francis Bryan and John Wallop to accompany him to the interview, provided they would not present themselves to the Pope.[6]

By now, the King of France was almost entirely alienated by Henry's insistence on his support. Francis refused the English delegation's requests that he abandon the proposed Papal meeting completely, arguing that arrangements were too far gone to call it off and that it was in Henry's interests for it to go ahead. George's second embassy was proving even more disastrous and frustrating than his first.

Anne's first summer progress as Queen was shortened significantly as her due date neared, and she focused her efforts on preparing for the birth of a prince, and demanded that Katherine return the beautifully embroidered gown which she had brought from Spain which of course Katherine refused. While Anne focused on christening gowns, Henry was elsewhere – not able to lie with Anne, he had taken a mistress. Anne's fury at the betrayal resulted in an hysterical scene in which she belittled the King, who roared that 'she must shut her eyes, and endure as well as more worthy persons, and that she ought to know that it was in his power to humble her again in a moment more than he had exalted her'. The couple's fight blew out as quickly as it began, but it was unsettling for all concerned.

Despite his elevated status, Thomas remained one of the most approachable men of court – men of his own county of Kent continued to petition him for assistance, and he also assisted colleagues at court. In July, Cromwell received a self-pitying letter of introduction from his first cousin, Nicholas Glossop, who by his own admission was lame, impotent, suffering from gout and blind in one eye.[7] Nicholas had been in the service of the previous archbishop of Canterbury, William Warham, and was also a member of the Guild of Taylors but, following his guild master's death, the annuity that had been paid to him was stopped, and he now sought legal assistance to help him retain the benefit. Although the correspondence between Cromwell and Thomas cannot be located, Cromwell wrote a letter to the guild requesting that the annuity be paid and increased, and sent Glossop to the Earl, who seems to have taken good care of the Cromwell relative, with Glossop singling Thomas out as the man to whom he owed a great deal.[8] Cromwell could be equally generous to Thomas' relations and friends.

Thomas also introduced his godson to Cromwell, who would take him under his wing, and began sending the young man on missions throughout Europe, effectively forging his career. Even without extant correspondence between Cromwell and Thomas, we know that they worked well together much like Thomas and Wolsey had years earlier. Their arrangements were not always business related either – if they could assist each other even in personal matters, they would.

Thomas's personal relationship with Erasmus continued to flourish. In late 1532, Thomas had requested a second work from Erasmus and, in early 1533, *Explanatio Symboli apostolorum sive catechismus* was published, with another respectful dedication to the Earl. Erasmus wrote 'I do knowe also wel enough that you do not require of me to take this lytle laboure for your owne cause: whiche do not nede any instruction or infomacyon of me. But you do desire it foe other more ignoraunte and unlearned persones.'[9] Thomas enjoyed the work so much, he commissioned another.

Erasmus' admiration of Thomas had increased, with the scholar referring to Thomas as 'egregius eruditis', in other words, an extraordinary man of knowledge.[10] As with the first work, Erasmus claimed his second work to be so popular that it sold out within three hours at the Frankfurt Book Fair.[11] Written as a dialogue, it included Thomas's request of eight homilies by Chrysostom – Archbishop of Constantinople, an important Early Church Father – which had never been translated before.[12] The catechism request is worth noting – the commandment to honour one's parents 'doth not onely appertayneth to fathers and mothers: but also … to byshopes, teachers, and offycers and rulers'.[13] While

Cranmer had it translated and published by a Lutheran lawyer, William Marshall, the doctrine of *Explanatio* was essentially traditionalist, though it appealed to a broad range of English Christians.[14] Erasmus' phrases and commentary attempted to reconcile traditionalists to the concept of the supremacy; he wrote that his soul had longed to be enrolled in the society of the Catholic Church, the house of God, 'outside of which there is no hope of eternal salvation'.[15]

But this commission has been seen as more evidence of Thomas' Lutheran interests.[16] It has been argued that to possess and transmit such vernacular expressions of the Decalogue (Ten Commandments) was evidence of reformist belief, and certainly the Decalogue later played a role in reformist theology.[17] But Erasmian ideals were at times critical perspectives of traditional piety, and a yearning for a simpler, more direct and authentic relationship with God.[18] The reactions of some – perhaps many – Catholic reformers to Protestant doctrine may have been primarily about the problems of spirituality and salvation that Luther tackled; men like Thomas were not necessarily vexed by those problems. The work itself also suggests that Thomas believed that the Church was paramount but the king of England should rule on all matters in England. Neither Erasmus nor Luther wanted their works associated with the other – when Erasmus was accused of laying the egg that Luther hatched, he responded that he laid a hen's egg, and Luther had hatched a chick of a very different feather.[19]

Whatever spirituality Thomas exhibited, the scandal of Anne's marriage had tainted Thomas' reputation, with the general gossip suggesting he was a greedy and egotistical man for helping install his daughter as Queen, but Erasmus himself wrote a passionate defence of his patron to a fellow scholar, Damien de Goes, in July 1533, insisting that Thomas was not motivated by self-interest or ambition.[20] Thomas had earned the loyalty of the most upstanding men of the age. But the birth of a son and heir would put an end to the gossip.

Unusually, Anne was only in confinement for two weeks. On 7 September 1533, after seven years of waiting to be married and countless personal, religious and political sacrifices, her first pregnancy had resulted in the birth of a girl, and not the son she had promised. Regardless of the brave face the couple put on, a daughter did little to secure Anne as queen. Nevertheless, Henry and Anne, though disappointed, rallied quickly, and the child, named Elizabeth, was given a magnificent christening. Elizabeth was carried by her great-aunt, the old Duchess of Norfolk, her long train of purple velvet was carried by her grandfather, Thomas, and her uncle, George, carried the canopy over her head. This would be the first of many children, Anne and Henry must have assured themselves – for surely God smiled upon their marriage.

Norfolk seemed to take the news of the baby's gender quite personally and, within days, he and Anne had a heated argument; Anne accused him of being too free with his speech (as we have seen, Norfolk was hardly the most tactful man at court) and too familiar with her. Chapuys also reported that since his return from France, the Duke, who had always made a point of seeking Chapuys out in the past, was avoiding him. The ambassador's requests for a meeting had been ignored and, when he visited Norfolk in private, he found the Duke's rooms full of clerks and officials. When, by chance, they sat next to each other at dinner, Chapuys wrote with exasperated amusement that Norfolk had spoken earnestly and rather loudly about the French ladies at Francis' court and how strong the ties were now between England and France, impetuously declaring that there would never be peace in the world as long as Charles ruled so many kingdoms.

But Norfolk appeared to be playing both sides, writing to Montmorency in January of 1534 regarding Pope Clement, declaring that if the latter persisted in favouring the Emperor more than the two kings, he would 'give occasion to his loyal subjects to take every opportunity to impugn the authority which he unjustly usurps, and to allow the public discussion of questions which have been proposed by many famous clerks, prelates and doctors here, and which are very prejudicial to the Pope.'[21]

Norfolk dared to berate Montmorency: why had Francis recalled the theologian, Noel Beda, who had argued against Henry's cause, for had Francis not promised both George and Thomas that he would be banished from the kingdom? It was all rather suspicious to the Duke, but *his* behaviour was suspicious to the Boleyns.

Beyond the endless court intrigues, we continue to see fleeting glimpses of the aesthetic tastes of both Boleyn men. In 1534, George sent his servant, William Atkyns, to Flanders to purchase 'certain hawks' for his master. In October, Chapuys reported that a Venetian ambassador had been at court and, apart from relaying news of the Ottoman threat, he also presented Norfolk, Thomas, George, Cromwell and Fitzwilliam 'with certain gorgeous brigandines made of tortoise-shell and mother-of-pearl, having secret drawers inside, which the signory of Venice sends them at the request of the said Capello, their ambassador here, who, as I am told, must have received a hint from one of the parties to that effect'.[22] We do know that, like Wolsey, Thomas had developed a taste for 'Turkeye' carpets, many of which adorned Hever, where he spent a great deal of time. George was only beginning to amass his fortune, but he was slowly developing his own style, with a love of finery, both Anne and George were considered to be two of the most stylish and sophisticated individuals of court.

Christmas arrived with pomp and ceremony and, in the list of gifts, a new Boleyn had appeared on the scene – the wife of Thomas Boleyn's brother, Jasper, was now at court, and the position was probably sought through the Earl. Thomas' daughter, Mary, was also at court, and even had enough court influence to join with Sir William Kingston in requesting that Lord Lisle give 'a poor but deserving man a job'. It is possible that the Boleyns had begun to repair their relationship with the unpredictable member of the family.[23]

In April, Henry confirmed Cromwell as his principal secretary and chief minister, a position which he had held for some time in all but name. This suited the Boleyns who continued to work well with the opportunistic councillor. But Henrician diplomacy had undergone dramatic shifts since the death of Wolsey, with Cromwell at the helm. The structure and careful planning which Wolsey had put into each embassy had been cast aside. George's embassies throughout 1534 were short, hurriedly planned, but with the same, futile directions. George was neither resident ambassador, nor special envoy. He continued as a messenger, and his talents were wasted on such errands.

In April, George departed for France, this time alongside Sir William Fitzwilliam. Their instructions, much like they had been the last time, were to urge Francis to abandon his alliance with the Pope and declare himself against the latter; to suggest that Francis should invade Milan, but without taking subsidies from the Pope; to urge Francis to adopt similar legislation as had been passed in England against the Pope's supremacy; to arrange a meeting between the two kings, and Marguerite and Anne in the near future; and to further urge Francis to refuse to give the hand of his daughter to the King of Scotland. The men were due to land at Calais, and had been invited by Viscount Lisle, Constable of Calais, to dine with him and his wife. Lisle was probably aware that in a few months he would be working with George, and introductions were necessary and Lisle would have desired an opportunity to appraise his future colleague. Contrary winds had prevented the men from landing at Calais, and they landed at Boulogne-sur-Mer, but they would, George assured the Viscount, visit on their way back to court.[24] George and Fitzwilliam met Francis and his sister on 21 April at Coucy-le-Château, and were warmly received, but George sensed that Francis was humouring them. George must have felt the weight of his last embassy on his shoulders, and seemed determined to gain some ground, but they were only successful in obtaining Francis' agreement to a further meeting with Henry, not Francis' promise to intercede with the Pope. Three days later, the French king presented the embassy with a memorandum setting out the various demands and his answers to them. As to abandoning his alliance with the Pope, he had no such alliance and so could not break it. Francis also made it clear that he saw no reason why he should follow Henry's anti-papal direction blindly, which would doubtless cause trouble in his own kingdom – look where it got *Henry*, was the unspoken implication. Obviously, Francis declared, he supported Henry's choices, and he would comply with Henry's demand that he not marry his daughter to King James V of Scotland. It was not a complete failure, but Francis had rather neatly circumvented the main demand of the English embassy.

George and Fitzwilliam returned to England two days after receiving Francis' response, and as they had promised, they visited Lord Lisle and his wife on their way back to London. Lady Lisle presented him with 'dotterals' (plovers) as a gift to his sister, and George carried the birds all the way back from Calais to court, and presented his sister with the gift. He would rather have been able to present more from his French embassy.

George's return coincided with the news that on 23 March 1534, in Rome, Pope Clement pronounced Henry's marriage to Katherine valid.[25] In London that same day, the Act of Succession, which declared Thomas' granddaughter, Elizabeth, legitimate and Mary illegitimate, had its final reading in the House of Lords. In case Charles V decided to act against England in his aunt's defence, Cromwell, Audley and Thomas co-ordinated and increased the defence forces in the southern part of the country.

Thomas, now 57, had begun to step away from court life, spending more time at his estates in Kent, but Henry made a special request that he bring Mary, Henry's first daughter, 'into line'.[26] Thomas accompanied by Sir William Paulet, Comptroller of the Household, and visited her with the instructions to persuade her to accept her new status, that of Lady Mary.[27] She refused, but Henry persisted, sending Thomas again in July with the same request, but he made no progress with the young Mary.[28] Thomas admitted defeat, and slipped away from court, down to the peace of Hever. George and Anne were now the premier Boleyns at court, determined to usher in a new political and spiritual age.

Heretical literature had been flowing into the country for several years, with Anne and George's full support – Thomas probably approved of many too, though his focus was anti-clerical more than anything else. But since George's missions to France the spiritual connection had been forged, especially with French humanists. At court, surrounded by like-minded individuals such as Cranmner, Fox and Cromwell, religious reform and politics seem to have gone hand in hand for the younger Boleyns, and George, who now knew Marguerite well, continued as one of the primary links between her evangelical religious circle and that in England.[29] But networks of reforming piety amongst upper class people across Europe were still politically precarious, and discretion with letters was necessary. While Thomas had corresponded with Erasmus, Anne had requested that her brother translate two manuscripts, both based on works by Jacques Lefèvre d'Étaples, a Catholic humanist, titled *Les Epistles et Evangiles des cinquante et deux sepmaines de l'an* (*The Epistles and Gospels for the Fifty-two Weeks of the Year*) and *Book of Ecclesiastes*.[30] He had spent a great deal of time and money translating the works – they were beautifully made, with detailed gold borders framing the illustrations, and Anne's coat of arms were prominently displayed. The production speaks volumes of the tastes of a man often thought to be frivolous with his wealth, as a man capable of deep spirituality. His dedication to his sister in *Les Epistles* is also one of the few examples of their close bond:

> To the right honourable lady, the Lady Marchioness of Pembroke, her most loving and friendly brother sendeth greetings.

> Our friendly dealings, with so divers and sundry benefits, besides the perpetual bond of blood, have so often bound me, Madam, inwardly to love you, that in every of them I must perforce become your debtor for want of power, but nothing of my good will. And were it not that by experience your gentleness is daily proved, your meek fashion often times put into use, I might well despair in myself, studying to acquit your deserts towards me, or embolden myself with so poor a thing to present to you. But, knowing these perfectly to reign in you with more, I have been so bold to send unto you, not jewels or gold, whereof you have plenty, not pearl or rich stones, whereof you have enough, but a rude translation of a well-willer, a goodly matter meanly handled, most humbly desiring you with favour to weigh the weakness of my dull wit, and patiently to pardon where any fault is, always considering that by your commandment I have adventured to do this, without the which it had not been in me to have performed it.[31]

George's reputation as a poet also won him admirers at court and, while none of the surviving poetry carries his name, one in particular, often attributed to him, is named 'The Lover complaineth the unkindness of his love'. Like his translations, there is no evidence that his love of poetry was an affectation, and it is lamentable that we cannot identify his work.[32]

Thomas was less involved in the young, colourful circle of courtiers who surrounded Anne and George, but we do see elements of his own connection to France through his godson, who wrote to the Earl that he had made contact with those involved in the so-called Affair of the Placards – when anti-Catholic posters appeared in Paris, Orléans, Blois, Rouen and Tours late in 1534. He also sent his godfather an article published by Clement Marot, one of the most influential French poets of the age, whose work blended traditional medieval influences and Renaissance themes.[33] The work Thomas commissioned from Erasmus in June 1533, when the Boleyn family had reached the very pinnacle of success, was delivered to the Earl. The work called *Praeparatio ad mortem* (*Preparation for Death*), was dedicated to Thomas:

> To the ryght noble lorde Thomas, Erle of wylteshyre, and of Drmanie [Ormond?], sendeth gretynge.

> To the very perfyte conclusyon of Christes lore, your lordeshyp calleth me, mooste noble Erle, and yet more noble in the study of godlynes, than in the ornamentes of fortune, in that ye provuoke me to adde to my former bokes some lytle thynge, teachinge howe a man ought to prepare hym to deth. For this is of mans lyfe the last part (as it were) of the playe, wherof hangeth eyther euerlastynge blysse of man, or euerlastynge damnation. This is the laste fyghte with the enemye, wher| or |by the souldiour of Christe loketh for eter|or |nall triumphe, yf he ouercome: and euerlastynge shame, if he be ouercome.[34]

Its themes of death have a particular poignancy for us, considering that his two children had at this time less than two years to live. Thomas may have chosen the theme because he felt it·was 'necessary to contemplate death and the transience of this world'.[35] Erasmus gave powerful impetus to a shift in literature on the art of dying, moving away from a focus on the moment of death, towards a focus on how to live one's entire life to be *prepared* for the moment of death.[36] It fits with the literature of the *ars moriendi* tradition, which originated in the early fifteenth century, and reached a climax in the next hundred years in Catholic and some Protestant ideologies.[37] Erasmus began with the quote 'Death is the most terrible of all things, for it is the end', and this theme of *ars moriendi* was also present in Italian humanistic literature, and represents a different devotional tradition.[38]

Why, we might ask, would Thomas, at the very pinnacle of power, contemplate his own mortality? It is possible that 'modernity', the very idea of change, of the unknown, all greatly weighed on his mind. As for Erasmus, he concluded his work for Thomas with the following words: 'We may passe into eternall reste, through the ayde and grace of oure lorde Iesus Christe, to whom with the father and holy gooste be prayse and glorie without ende. Amen.' An early reformist biographer of Cranmer, John Strype, observed in the nineteenth century: 'The world is beholden to this noble peer [Thomas] for some of the labours that proceeded from the pen of that most learned man [Erasmus].'[39] We are left to wonder whether Thomas share these works with his children, but he was likely proud of their spirituality, even if it diverged somewhat from his own.

By the time Henry chose George, for the fourth time, as a special envoy to France, the latter may well have become weary of the task, not because he disliked diplomacy, but because he probably sensed the futility of these missions. By now, he had a clear view of Francis and what he would, and would not, agree to. But beyond this, it seemed that Henry never had any intention of utilising George as a resident ambassador, to serve as a special envoy in foreign courts. These brief missions to France must have been tedious; nevertheless, instructions were issued on 7 July, and George, described by Henry as one whom his grace 'specially loveth and trustith', departed England three days later. Henry and Francis were to meet in person for the third time in their reigns, but George was instructed to meet with Marguerite first, again entreating her to encourage her brother's support for Henry. He was also to attempt to postpone the royal meeting which had been scheduled to take place within weeks until the next year. He was to say that, although Anne was anxious to meet Marguerite, and indeed wished for nothing more, the meeting had to be deferred – Anne was pregnant once more.[40]

George arrived back in England on 27 July bringing with him confirmation that Francis had agreed to postpone the meeting until the following year. But sometime in the late summer of 1534, Anne suffered a tragic miscarriage. It was a devastating blow to the Queen, and Henry, who was not a man to whom one made promises one could not keep.

It was fortunate that George was back at court, for Anne's insecurities were getting the better of her, and she began to make wild threats against Katherine's daughter, Mary, who was still considered by much of Europe as Henry's legitimate heir. With Thomas occupied with his governmental position or away from court, it was left to George to carry the responsibility of protecting his sister, attempting to calm her, and encourage her to be guarded in her comments. Life was not idle or relaxing as brother to the Queen.

In early 1534, an opportunity arose for George when the Captain of Guisnes Castle, Lord Sandys, was taken grievously ill, and it seemed likely that he would die. Guisnes was an important fortress just outside of Calais and, while Sandys was incapacitated, Henry appointed George as Captain, with a salary and allowance which would total £1,000 a year. It was a highly prestigious and sought-after position, and some grumbled that George had jumped the queue. But this, like Thomas' position as Lord Privy Seal, was not a ceremonial position awarded to denote status. Sandys recovered, however, and George was transferred to another department, being appointed as Lord Warden of the Cinque Ports, which also included the Constableship of Dover Castle, awarded on 16 June. These positions on the south coast were both highly demanding, and kept George from court. Perhaps his interest in diplomacy had faded and he now preferred a government appointment. If this was the case, it was Henry's poor management of his embassies that had thwarted the enthusiasm and ambitions of a young courtier.

George immediately departed for Dover, determined to play an active role, but he was not steady on his feet to begin with. He had been thrown into the deep end, surrounded by far more experienced men who knew how the position worked, and his judgements were a little heavy handed. As brother of the Queen, every opportunity put his way was regarded simply as another gift from Henry. Many around him would happily take the opportunity to criticise him and label him as incompetent, of which he was only too well aware. But he did have his father's support, and Thomas stepped in for his son, taking over his administrative affairs when George was sent on another diplomatic mission to France.[41]

Throughout September and October, scandals threatened to engulf the Boleyn family – Mary Boleyn had secretly married a soldier and Gentleman Usher from Calais named William Stafford. Thomas learned of his daughter's actions when she suddenly appeared at court, clearly pregnant, and announced to her sister that she had married. While the romantic nature of her actions had captured imagination, it could have had very real ramifications. Mary was naive to have believed that, as sister of the Queen of England, she could marry well beneath her station, then expect her family's support. Thomas had great hope for Mary's first marriage to William Carey, introduced him to court circles, and welcomed him into the Boleyn family. But following Carey's death, Thomas would have wanted a similar match for Mary the second time – a man of court with station and financial security, as all parents desire for their children. A poor soldier had no prospects and subjected the family to ridicule. There is no evidence that Thomas and his wife did not love their other daughter, but she so often acted independently of her family, and almost brought them into disrepute.

Mary seemed shocked that her family, even George, showed no pleasure in her love match, which merely emphasised to Boleyn critics that the family was not worthy of the crown. The cast-off Mary fervently desired to reconcile with her family, and writing to Cromwell, she complained that both her sister and brother, and her parents, were all against her marriage and were cruel to her and her new husband.[42] No record of Cromwell's answer exists, but he did speak to Thomas, the implications of which would be felt years later after the Earl's death, as we shall see.

Apart from Mary, the other woman causing trouble in George's life was his wife, Jane. Jane's movements throughout these years are impossible to track, but we assume she remained at court as her husband moved between England and France, and she had always tried to fit in with Anne's social sphere. Jane saw her opportunity when, sometime late in 1534 Henry's eye had begun to wander, and Chapuys made note of a mysterious and unnamed woman whom Henry seemed particularly attached to. The young woman reportedly refused to pay deference to Anne, who then demanded her immediate dismissal, which Henry refused. Jane had sided with Anne, and made this mistress' life difficult, for which Henry banished her. Neither Anne nor George said a word in Jane's defence, at least none that survives, instilling a deep resentment.

In September, Thomas again left court and spent time in Hever, taking care of his mother who was living out her final years. From his estate, he received word that his friend Sir John Hackett, the King's representative in Flanders, had died. Thomas and Hackett had known each other for decades, and they had clearly been close, for Hackett left Thomas a fine gold chain with a whistle. Thomas mourned his old friend, but another death weeks later had less of an impact. Word reached court that Pope Clement, the most indecisive Pope his subjects could have imagined, died. Gregory Casale, Henry's ambassador in Rome, wrote not to Thomas, who was no longer diplomatically active, but to George. Rome, he reported, rejoiced at the death of Clement – his tomb had been broken open, and the inscription altered from 'Clementi [kind] VII. Pontifici Maximo, cujus invicta virtus sola clementia superata est' to 'Inclementi [unkind] VII. Pontifici Minimo, cujus victa virtus sola avaritia superata est' 'so that it had to be carved in marble and a guard set over it'.

But Casale also relayed news further afield, on a subject that we do not necessarily link with the Boleyns but which had occupied the court for some months. The Ottoman threat loomed over Europe, and Hyreddin Barbarossa, Suleiman the Magnificent's feared Admiral, had taken Tunis, a city as large as Rome, which threatened both Spain and Italy. The Emperor, Casale wrote, must either be strong enough to fight him or be continually on the defensive. Unfortunately for England, Charles united with the Persian Safavid Shah Tahmasp, who had been at war with the Ottomans for centuries. United, the Holy Roman Empire and the Persians enjoyed a resounding victory against the Ottomans. This would have meant little, had France not been Suleiman's ally at the time, their 'unholy alliance' having been forged between Louise of Savoy and Suleiman when Francis was Charles' prisoner. Charles took the opportunity to force France into another alliance and, when news reached

England, Cromwell, we are told, was scarcely able to breathe. French foreign policy now shifted.

The visit of Philippe de Chabot, Admiral of France, in December 1534, bordered on disastrous. George, as Constable of Dover, had the honour of first receiving the Admiral, and reported to Henry and Cromwell that the French retinue were certainly taking their time, although the fact that they had to move 350 horses from the ships to land may have been a factor. George waited patiently until he could escort the Admiral to Sittingbourne where he would stay the night, and then to Rochester on Tuesday, on Wednesday to Dartford, and on Thursday to Blackheath, where Norfolk would take over.

Henry put on a show for Chabot; Chapuys reported that he invited a group of pretty young ladies to amuse the Admiral, and a public declaration ordered that no one was to insult or attack him and his entourage on pain of death, nor were any men below the station of earl allowed near him. While Henry and Anne believed this meeting would be beneficial for both nations, Chabot made it very clear that he, in Chapuys words, 'cared not a straw for them' (the English).[43] Anne and Henry were desirous of a match between Elizabeth and the Dauphin, and assumed that this was what Francis too envisioned, but they soon discovered that in Francis' (recent) opinion, Anne's marriage was still not wholly accepted as lawful – there would forever be a line drawn under Elizabeth's legitimacy. Francis *was* willing to consider a marriage between Mary and his son, as there was no question of her legitimacy or royal lineage.

Chabot's reaction to his hosts was alarmingly cool and disinterested. He did not attend any of the tennis matches which were held for him, and in which Henry himself played: an unmistakable snub. He only visited Anne and her ladies twice, and Chapuys noted that he did so when prodded by Henry. In short, his mission was to tread on as many toes as he could, giving a clear message to Henry that a friendship with France was no longer reliant on Anne – quite the opposite. Chabot's attitude had convinced Henry that another visit to Francis was required and, again, George and his uncle were given orders to sail for France.

Absent from court and removed from the drama Chabot had caused, Thomas spent New Year at Hever, perhaps with his wife, and in January he received a letter from his godson. Tebald reported from Orleans that he had heard a rumour that the Bailey of Roan had gone on an embassy to England, being accompanied as far as Rouen by the Duke of Longfielde. It was Charles, Tebald reported, who had convinced Francis to send Roan, 'to admonish Henry to see correction upon heretics, or else the Emperor and he to make war on him'. But Tebald was sceptical of Francis declaring war on Henry. Francis' stance had hardened towards heretical notions in his realm: 'The receiver of Brytanne, about whom he wrote before Christmas, is condemned to be burned at Paris with his wife, one of the most beautiful ladies in France. His father will be publicly punished, lose his goods and be banished.' Francis' earnest persecution was probably to win the favour of the new Pope, for, as Tebald remarked, he had no such zeal in himself. Henry however, was fully committed to his course of action, and his determination to enforce the Act of Succession took a dangerous and bloody turn in 1535. The Act did not include a death penalty, but Henry had also introduced the Act of Treason which declared that any who spoke or wrote against his marriage to Anne, or against his title of Supreme Head of the Church, as well as any who called Henry a heretic, would be hanged, drawn and quartered. The first victims of these new acts were chosen carefully, and with an eye to driving home the point to Katherine and Charles: Bishop Fisher and Thomas More. Henry then decided to punish the Carthusians, one of the holiest orders in England and, to Henry, the most disobedient. For having maintained that the Pope was the true Head of the Church, three Carthusian monks (the Carthusian martyrs) and a Bridgettine monk were sentenced to death.[44] Chapuys reported Henry's increasing appetite for violence, which was not shared with those around him. He now insisted that his nobles witness executions, with Thomas, George, Norfolk and Henry's illegitimate son, Henry Fitzroy, present, and he even berated Thomas and Norfolk for not defending him against the sermon preached by Prior Houghton, one of the Carthusian monks, before his execution.[45]

The manner in which the nobles attended the executions was macabre. Among other members of the court, the men sat astride their horses, secretly armed, their faces hidden underneath the vizors of their helmets – a dramatic spectacle.[46]

What the men thought or felt we have no evidence, but within weeks, George departed for another mission to France, meeting with Chabot and the King. Just prior to leaving, George heard of Chabot's behaviour through Fitzwilliam, who had travelled to Dover before sailing for Calais. They spoke at length of the recent French visit and, as Fitzwilliam wrote to Cromwell, neither could believe that Chabot had 'arrived at Calais on Saturday, and was ready to leave upon Monday, making so light of the matter'. George was likely furious – Chabot would have been acting on Francis' orders. When Frenchmen are aloft, Fitzwilliam declared, 'they are the highest men in the world, and the soonest forget their benefactors: when they are a little under foot they are the humblest'.[47]

George had asked Fitzwilliam to wait at Dover for his return, though why is unclear, but Fitzwilliam reported that the weather was fair, and he loved to take to sea at the tail of a storm, and would therefore carry on. There was significant tension between the men, and even the French felt the difference in attitude from the young Lord – but the Admiral's treatment of his sister may have influenced his behaviour. George's mission was to convince the French to agree to a marriage alliance for Elizabeth, and force Francis to agree that neither the Henry nor Francis 'shall practise any marriage or league with the Emperor without mutual consent'.[48]

The Italian Bishop of Faenza at the French court sneeringly wrote that George 'came here for eight days, but, as far as could be seen, did nothing. It is only from his relation to the Queen that he is employed, for the King has very few to trust in.'[49] Despite George's best efforts and dedication to these thankless diplomatic tasks, his skills were always going to be overshadowed by his connection to the Queen.

George arrived back in England several weeks later, having left his uncle to conclude matters, and headed straight for his sister's rooms before seeing the King; this, Chapuys assumed, meant the news was anything but what Anne had hoped for. What Anne and George spoke of even Chapuys could not discover, but he did notice a marked antipathy towards the French ambassador and Francis at court following George's return. Eventually George had to present his news to Henry, and the Privy Council remained sitting for two days. Francis had once more refused a marriage contract between his son and Elizabeth. Henry had clearly hoped Chabot had persuaded his master that Mary should be ruled out, but the Admiral had done nothing of the sort. Henry took his rage out on Francis' representative, Jean Dinteville, as he so often did with the foreign ambassadors at his court, but this time Henry and Anne were deeply wounded. France had proven a fair-weather friend indeed to the Boleyns, and this may have been the first inkling that Cromwell, up until now a Boleyn supporter, was considering switching horses, for Cromwell also revealed that he had conspired to keep George from attending the meeting in Calais until matters reached a suitable conclusion. He was adamant that he be kept from any further missions to France for the pursuit of an alliance. But this order probably came from Henry himself, who publicly told Chapuys within days of his evening with Cromwell that he expected a reconciliation with Charles.

George resumed his duties as Constable of Dover, but it seemed to be above his level of competency. In an attempt to put his own seal of authority on the position, he made several heavy-handed moves which caused considerable consternation among his colleagues, demanding that every servant in each port, regardless of the family they served, wear either *his* Livery or that of the King's. He also clashed with Cromwell, who felt the need to keep an eye on the younger man. Cromwell intervened in one of George's determinations and, in late 1524, George wrote an indignant letter to Henry's Chief Minister.

> On Sunday last the mayor of Rye and others were with me at the Court, and I have taken such order and direction with them as I trust is right and just. I have commanded the mayor to return to Rye, and see the matter ordered according to the order I have taken in it before. He now advertises me that you have commanded him to attend you, and not obey the order. If you have been truly informed, or will command the mayor to declare to you the order I have taken, I trust you will find no fault in it.[50]

It was as far as George dared to take the matter, and the young man did not appreciated being undermined, but it was not a move Thomas would have approved of. Castiglione's ideals, still in currency among the older generations, were ignored by the younger men. It was no longer considered necessary to dissimulate, to fashion oneself and construct a persona. George, sister of the Queen, probably felt that he was untouchable, could speak to those around him as he pleased, and even felt that his own opinions carried more weight than those of his experienced colleagues.

He was also called on to determine a matter between two men – Robert Justyce and his son James – who refused to pay various fines and penalties. Hauled before George and several of his colleagues, the men again refused to pay what they owed and, without conferring with the others, George promptly sent both men to prison, a harsher judgement than necessary, evidenced by Richard Derring's letter to Lord Lisle complaining that he was being judged for George's actions. Eventually, the two men paid the sums they were ordered to pay, but George had not eased into his new career.[51]

George's personal life also seemed to be imploding. That same month, his wife Jane, humiliated by her banishment, threatened to embarrass the family. Numerous women partook in public demonstrations at Greenwich to show their support for Mary, who happened to be leaving Greenwich for Eltham. Some ladies of the royal household not on duty cheered for her, calling out that she was still their princess in spite of any laws to the contrary. Jane was one of these women, and she was reprimanded by being placed in the Tower for a short time, although the matter was kept quiet.[52] A rift had formed between the couple.

Henry's frustration continued to manifest itself in far more deadly ways, with his old adversaries, More and Fisher, firmly in sight. Until now, Henry had accepted that they could not in good conscience take the Oath of Succession and accept Henry has Supreme head of the church, and there had been an unspoken agreement that he would not ask, and they would stay silent. Now, Henry had changed his mind, and their refusal resulted in their arrests.

The trial was both significant at the time, and has retained its historical importance into the modern era: More's trial in particular is a turning point in English constitutional history, and his reputation as a pious, academic, humanist scholar and martyr has been enhanced over the centuries. He and Fisher were crowned with the highest honour that can be bestowed by the Catholic Church on martyrs to the faith; they were canonised in 1935 under Pope Pius XI.[53] At the trial itself, there were 12 jurors and 15 judges, including the newly appointed Lord Chancellor Audley, Royal Secretary Cromwell, the Duke of Norfolk, and Thomas and George Boleyn.

The focus for these events must lie with Henry, who wanted an end to the intransigence of his now former Lord Chancellor and Bishop of Rochester. Their executions are considered by most historians to be a stain on Henry's reign, one that also spread to the Boleyns, who have been labelled as the instigators of their executions.[54] After all, Thomas, George and Norfolk were, among others, judges at the trial and its outcome affirmed Anne's status – all of which reinforced the idea of the 'Boleyn faction' as the force behind the persecution of 'good men'. This view of events begins with those closest to More. More's son-in-law, William Roper, wrote a biography during the reign of Queen Mary called *The Mirrour of Vertue in Wordly Greatness, or the life of Syr Thomas More*. It is reputedly the earliest personal biography in the English language, and is favourable towards More, effectively influencing much of the subsequent writing on the former Lord Chancellor.

During More's examination, Roper wrote, Thomas had previously accused More of taking a bribe in the form of a gilt cup, from the wife of a man who wanted More to decide a legal case in his favour.[55] When More was asked about the suggestion of bribery, he admitted to accepting the cup. According to Roper, Thomas jumped up from his seat, triumphantly declaring: 'Lo, did I not tell you, my Lords, that you should find this matter true.'[56] Roper added that Thomas More went on to say that he filled the cup with wine, drank it, and then returned it to the family for a New Year's gift, greatly humiliating Thomas. This is repeated by historians who take the account at face value, without questioning his motives for More triumphing over a Boleyn in court.[57]

No other contemporary source cites Thomas as having said anything at More's interrogation, but only note in passing that he was a part of it. Chapuys further reported that Norfolk baited More at his trial.[58] But the most persuasive piece of evidence that puts the matter to rest is More's accounts of his own interrogation, in detailed letters to his daughter, Margaret. In his letter dated 3 June 1535, More listed Thomas, Cranmer, Audley, Cromwell and Suffolk in attendance, but only Audley and Cromwell addressed More directly.[59]

When Rome was made aware of the plight of one of its bishops, Pope Paul III appointed Fisher as Cardinal, mistakenly believing that if he sent the red Cardinal hat to England, with great ceremony and solemnity, Henry would not dare move against Fisher. Fisher was executed on the 22 June, and more on 6 July. Within days of their executions, there was another outbreak of the plague; Henry, Anne and Cromwell had already left London, George left for Dover, and Thomas returned to Kent.

For Thomas, this marked the beginning of his withdrawal from court life; he was no longer a stalwart of the court, and letters to and from him are all marked from Penshurst.[60] The deadly summer faded into a quiet autumn and winter for the Earl, and it is not until January of 1536 that he returned to London as events were fast overtaking the court.

# CHAPTER FOURTEEN

# Trying a Queen

*These violent delights have violent ends*
*And in their triumph die, like fire and powder*

*– Shakespeare, Romeo and Juliet*

Katherine of Aragon, who had been in exile for over five years, died on 7 January 1536 at Kimbolton, where she had been for some time. The ever-loyal Chapuys had visited her days before she died, and was devastated to hear the news on his return to London. At court, he found Henry and Anne's triumphant joy distasteful.[1] Of course we would be well served to know first hand Thomas' and George's reaction to these events, but we only have those from a third party. Firstly, we have the original report of Chapuys and the abridged version in the *Letters and Papers*. In the original report, Chapuys wrote: 'No words can describe the joy and delight which this King and the promoters of his concubine have felt at the demise of the good Queen, especially the earl of Vulcher [Wiltshire], and his son, *who must have said to themselves*, what a pity it was that the princess had not kept her mother company.'[2] In the *Letters and Papers* we have the following: 'You could not conceive the joy that the King and those who favour this concubinage have shown at the death of the good Queen, especially the earl of Wiltshire and his son, *who said it was* a pity the princess did not keep company with her.[3] Historians who have used the abridged version have either missed or chosen to ignore the fact that this is a deeply bitter comment by Chapuys; he is not reporting a remark, but rather expressing a sentiment.[4]

Jousts and tournaments were planned, to celebrate not only Katherine's death, but also Anne's latest pregnancy, which the royal couple were confident she would carry to term. On 25 January, George appeared in the jousts, performing well, and Henry, emboldened by Anne's condition, also chose to partake. The celebrations came to an abrupt halt when the King was thrown from his horse,which fell on top of him.[5] With Henry trapped and unconscious for two hours, the court was thrown into chaos, and Norfolk beat Thomas and George in bringing the pregnant Anne the news with his usual lack of sensitivity that Henry was near death.[6] Henry recovered, but several days later Anne miscarried, the same day Katherine's body was interred. It was a heartbreaking blow to the already vulnerable Queen.

Henry's fall may not have been the catalyst. He had embarked on a blossoming romance with a lady-in-waiting, Jane Seymour, once more seducing a lady under his wife's nose, in which he had considerable experience. Chapuys reported a distinct coldness between Henry and Anne; he hardly spent time with her and, when she miscarried, he darkly declared, 'I see that God will not give me male children.'[7] Chapuys reported that Henry had left Anne at Greenwich, telling her 'with ill grace' that he would speak to her when she recovered.

Apart from a marital rift, nothing else seemed amiss in the first months of 1536. Thomas split his time between Kent and London, and while at Hever received another detailed and deferential letter from his godson, that demonstrates the very close nature of their relationship:

> Please it your Lordship to understand I have received your most loving letters ... praying God to give me that power ... may once with my service and diligent endeavour reco[mpense] your great goodness, to the which my heart shall never ... [de]syrying your Lordship to continue this your good w[ill tow]erd me so long as you shall perceive me most willing [and] diligent to accomplish your pleasure, and to do that thy[ng] which I shall judge to be acceptable to you.[8]

Although Thomas' letters no longer exist, his financial generosity towards his godson is evident:

> This money came to me happily for two causes, because I fear war and because I have spent much in riding to Norenberg, Wy[ten]berg, Augusta, and Ulmes, from all which places I have written to you. I have had letters of commendation to the learned men there. It is costly at Tubynge, for you desired me to haunt the acquaintance of the best, and I am familiarly acquainted with the bishop of the town, the bishop and reformator of the whole country, the governor of the town, and most of the professors, being better esteemed than perhaps I am worthy, and of more credit than it becomes me to rehearse.[9]

Most significantly, Tebald's letter suggests that Thomas was a mentor, advising and guiding his godson. He was evidently highly desirous that Tebald continue his education, establish a network, hone his linguistic skills in French and Latin, and seek out learned men:

I have also bought books and raiment, and made journeys to Wyttemberge, Ausborge, and Noremberg, which cost me about seven weeks, and there are also my commons at Tubyng. I reckon the money well bestowed, for I have seen most of the chiefest cities in Almayne, and spoken with many of the best learned men. I could now travel to all these parts without a guide, and, if you were disposed, could cause works both in divinity and other subjects to be dedicated to you. You commanded me to tell you how I have profited in the Almain tongue and the Latin tongue, and al[though] I have tarried but little in one place since my coming ... but my being in France and learning French has made me less prompt, but a little use will make me prompter ... I will diligently labour at these two tongues. As for uttering my mind in speaking, I do not fear to whom I speak, not for excellency, but for true Latin, without studying or stumbling.[10]

It is frustrating for any scholar seeking out such personal insights into Thomas' relationship with his children that this correspondence with Tebald is all that remains. If this was how he treated his godson, how generous and involved must he have been with his children. George was again away from court, involved in royal plans to visit Calais, writing to Lord Lisle that Henry intended to depart for Calais in two weeks.

George spent most of his time away from court and his sister, his duties keeping him occupied, and with Thomas often absent, Anne must have felt isolated. She had lashed out already at her uncle, with whom she was no longer on speaking terms, but she made the mistake of arguing with Cromwell, who had always supported her cause. Henry's suppression of the monasteries had begun late in 1535, with Cromwell at the helm. Anne wanted a say in how the profit should be used, and was furious when she was sidelined. Later, Cromwell told Chapuys that she had declared that she would like to see his head off his shoulders.[11]

With Katherine out of the way, Charles appeared to soften his stance towards Henry's marriage, and an Anglo-Imperial alliance seemed possible. Charles had given his assent for his ambassador to proceed, and had written to Cromwell directly. It had been decided that Charles would agree to mediate between Henry and Pope Paul and, in return, Henry would assist in the war against the Turks and the French, and finally restore Mary to the succession.[12] It is possible that while Cromwell may have kept some details to himself, he shared the general gist of affairs with the Boleyns, none of whom had forgiven France for their rejection of Anne and her daughter.

On Easter Monday, Cromwell awaited an audience with Henry, arriving at court before the King was even awake, so eager was he to report his meeting with Chapuys and the letters from Charles. Henry was receptive and pleased by Charles' words and looked forward to healing the rift between the two. Before the King went out to Mass, Cromwell asked the ambassador who had also arrived at court early, if he would visit and pay his respects to Anne. In all the years Chapuys had been at court, while he had seen Anne, and she had seen him, there had not been any acknowledgement on either side. She had not requested an audience, which she could have done at any time, and the ambassador had been content to deal with her father and brother. Chapuys declined, and 'begged Cromwell to excuse it, and dissuade the said visit in order not to spoil matters'.[13]

Thomas and his son were at court at Easter. Both Boleyn men then warmly greeted the ambassador, and George was determined to grab Chapuys' attention; perhaps the Boleyns were apprehensive that things were beginning to slip away. George drew Chapuys away from the rest of court prior to Mass he seemed eager to not only strike up a conversation, but to be seen in cordial conversation with the Imperial ambassador.[14] George effusively greeted the ambassador, who tried to keep the conversation light and impersonal. Chapuys had never had an issue with George, but he did note that he was wary that George might launch yet again into an earnest conversation about religion, which he seemed to have enjoyed doing on numerous occasions with the ambassador, who disliked dining with him.

Chapuys walked with George, and asked what he thought of the Imperial proposal.

> Lord Rochefort, among the rest, signalised himself most particularly by his hearty congratulations. I could not help hinting to him that I had no doubt he was as much pleased as any other of the King's courtiers at the favorable prospect of affairs, and believed he would co-operate as well as the rest to ensure the success of one which could not fail to be beneficial to the community at large, and especially to himself and family. Rochefort seemed particularly pleased at this hint of mine.[15]

There is no reason to think George was insincere. If Charles was willing to work towards peace, and could accept Anne, then they could do business. George may have even assumed he would at some point be assigned to the Imperial court – a court he had never had the opportunity of visiting, but which his father knew well. But firstly, Anne and the ambassador would have to publicly acknowledge each other, if matters were to truly forge ahead. Who would break the seven-year stalemate?

What occurred is considered to be one of the most dramatic and significant events of Anne's last months, and the event might be construed as Anne's final triumph over Charles, making Chapuys look foolish. This would certainly make for a good story, knowing what would soon befall the Boleyns, but what Chapuys *actually* recounts to Charles differs significantly from the more popular version, namely that Chapuys was manipulated and 'tricked' into acknowledging Anne.[16]

In his original report, Chapuys makes it quite clear that George stood beside him and that he, Chapuys, did not object to being moved to where the royal couple would pass. Henry and Anne descended from the royal chapel and made their way to the altar. Chapuys wrote: 'I must say that she was affable enough on the occasion for on my being placed behind the door by which she entered the chapel, she turned round to *return the reverence which I made her* when she passed.'[17]

Popular history tells us that Anne stopped in front of Chapuys, who was then forced to bow, to the delight of both Henry and Anne. But we must bear in mind that Chapuys says he was already bowing as the royal couple passed; it was Anne who turned and acknowledged Chapuys' show of respect, which of course signified Charles' respect. These were formal recognitions, but significant for both sides.

That evening, George and Thomas dined with the ambassador and other councillors, and it seemed as though an Imperial alliance was a real possibility. But while Henry was pleased with events earlier that day (when he had just woken up), he had changed entirely by the evening. Cromwell, who had worked hard for Imperial peace, was accused of making his own policy, in cahoots with Chapuys. Henry railed at both men so violently that they both made quick exits. Both Cromwell and Chapuys seemed to think that Anne was at fault for changing Henry's mind, but this would negate what happened at Mass earlier that day. Clearly the Boleyns saw the logic in an Imperial alliance – why would Anne have wanted to disrupt it?

Cromwell disappeared from court for several days – ill or feigning illness, but Chapuys had reason to believe he was preparing himself.

Despite the drama at Easter, it was business as usual for the family. Thomas and his son were reconfirmed in their grants of several manors, for a period of 30 years. On 23 April, Thomas received all the sequestered property of the bishopric of Norwich, and two abbeys scheduled for suppression.[18] That same day, he attended a chapter meeting for the Order of the Garter. This is often seen as a crucial meeting amongst the significant events that would signal the fall of the Boleyns; it is believed that George was expected to be appointed to the Order. He missed out and the honour went to Nicholas Carew, who was a champion of Jane Seymour, widely known as Henry's new mistress.[19] However, on this occasion even voted for Carew, as there is credible evidence that Carew's appointment was a foregone conclusion because Henry had promised Francis in 1533 that Carew would be appointed.[20]

There is no evidence that this was a snub to George or the Boleyns, or a sign that the family had fallen from favour, and it was not the first time George's name had been put forward. He had been nominated in 1535 and had received a reasonable and promising amount of support, but James V of Scotland won by just two votes.[21] The next day, two separate commissions of Oyer and Terminer were quietly drawn up to investigate criminal activity and 'unspecified treasons'. These commissions were for offences committed in the counties of Middlesex and Kent, and covered various crimes including treason, rebellion, felonies, murder, rioting and conspiracy, among others. Norfolk was assigned to both, and Thomas, who had been a Commissioner of the Peace on countless occasions over the years, was appointed only to Middlesex. This commission would later be used to investigate four men – William Brereton, Henry Norris, Mark Smeaton and Francis Weston, but no one knew the specific offences or even who they would be used against. The Commission for Kent, which Thomas was not a part of, would be used for an unspeakably false crime.

Everything about these commissions is peculiar and suspicious. An Oyer and Terminer were usually provided after the arrest of an individual but, in Anne and George's case, they were issued six days before the arrests. Cromwell would have had an Oyer and Terminer drawn up before there was anyone to arrest, and this suggests that it was a matter of expedience. Delays between issuing an Oyer and Terminer could be as much as 11 days, but with a commission in place, the process could start at once, before any delays or doubts could occur.[22] Thomas must have felt deeply uneasy and, although we have no evidence, he most likely warned his daughter, for several days later, we have a credible report by Alexander Alesius, a Scottish theologian who happened to be at court, of an anxious Anne at Greenwich, carrying her daughter Elizabeth in her arms as she pleaded with Henry. Alesius reported later that it was most obvious to everyone that some deep and difficult question was being discussed.

Unbeknownst to the rest of the court, Cromwell quietly struck, beginning with the bottom of the pile – Mark Smeaton, a Flemish musician in Anne's household. He had apparently affected a rather theatrical display of despondency in Anne's rooms. Noticing the behaviour, Anne asked him what the matter was, to which he replied that it was no matter, before sighing again. Anne had no patience for such games, and slapped him down for his impertinence, reminding him that he should not expect her to speak to him as an equal. Cheekily Mark had replied that a look sufficed, and he left her chambers. Smeaton was a fool to act in such a manner, but someone had taken notice.

Two days later on 30 April, Smeaton was brought to Cromwell's house in Stepney where, under questioning, he admitted to carnal relations with Anne.[23] Anne's behaviour provided more ammunition. On 30 April, an already anxious Anne managed to have an altercation with Henry Norris, Henry's Chief Gentleman of the Privy Chamber and a member of her inner circle. Norris frequently visited Anne's rooms, ostensibly to court Madge Shelton, a cousin of Anne's, but he was taking his time proposing to her.[24] Again, Anne lost patience, asking him why he had not yet proposed to Madge, to which he replied that he wished to tarry a time. Anne's reaction was considerably disproportionate: she accused Norris of looking for dead men's shoes – if the King were to die, Norris wanted her for himself. Appalled, Norris rejected the claim, declaring that if he entertained such a thought 'he would his head were off'. Anne's retort suggested that she was only too happy to oblige.

May Day, 1 May, was a pagan celebration of love and renewal. Henry and Anne presided over the jousts; for the first time in several months, George had the leisure to joust, and was the principal challenger, with Norris the principal defender. At some point in the afternoon, Cromwell sent word to Henry: he had the confession from Smeaton. Henry abruptly left the joust with a small group of men, including Norris, without so much as a farewell to his queen. George, like the rest of the court, must have been confused and apprehensive about Henry's behaviour.

On the journey Henry questioned Norris, offering him a pardon if he would only confess adultery with Anne. Norris, indignant, refused, and he was committed to the Tower early the next morning. The details of these events are well documented in countless scholarly works, and there is no need to contribute to an already crowded field, beyond where we can locate either of the Boleyn men.

George, who weeks prior had been in preliminary discussions about another royal visit to France, was arrested in the early afternoon of 2 May and taken to the Tower. Finally, Norfolk, with several other members of the King's council, came to arrest Anne. They brought the terrified Queen to the Tower and, on her arrival, she dropped to her knees on the stone floor, 'beseeching God to help her as she was not guilty of her accusement, and also desired the said lords to beseech the king's grace to be good unto her'.

None of her ladies were allowed to attend her and she was surrounded by hostile women, including her aunt, the wife of Thomas' brother, Edward, who had loyally served Katherine. Meanwhile Cromwell and Thomas Audley, who had assisted in drawing up the Commissions against Anne, added more names to the list – William Brereton and Francis Weston.

Consensual adultery was not covered by the treason law of 1352, so the charges as they were would not necessarily result in execution. But Anne herself had provided the most damning evidence when she had taunted Norris.

The inclusion of George was the most surprising, and many assumed he would be charged with being an accessory to whatever crime Anne had committed.

As far as the evidence shows, neither Thomas nor his wife visited or officially communicated with their children in the Tower. This detail, that he lacked the compassion to even visit his own children in prison, has further conspired to shape the common view of Thomas and has become entrenched and overused in historical accounts, which have fed the frenzy of historical fiction. Might there have been unknown reasons for his and his wife's absence? They may have stayed away out of fear for themselves and for their family. It would not be surprising if they had little faith in Henry and the legal system to protect them. But it is much more likely that they were forbidden to visit their children. Norfolk, however, had abandoned his niece and nephew without a qualm. To preside over a trial which would result in the deaths of his sister's children took a certain type of man – in that sense, he was priceless to a king like Henry.

In the Tower, Anne's main concern was for her family. William Kingston, Constable of the Tower, was tasked with reporting Anne's every word, and one report shows her concern: 'And then she [Anne] asked me, when saw you the King? And I said I saw him not since I saw [him in] the Tiltyard. And then, Mr. K., I pray you to tell me where my Lord my father is? And I told her I saw him afore dinner in the Court. O where is my sweet brother? I said I left him at York Place; and so I did … O, my mother, thou wilt die with sorrow.'[25] Anne's words do not suggest a rift in the family. George's focus was elsewhere, for he makes no mention of his parents, and his concern was for those he had promised to assist at court, in particular a promotion for a 'white monk'.[26] George spent much of his time petitioning Cromwell from the Tower to assist in this matter, which it was reported 'touched his conscience'.

The Boleyns were surrounded by hostile families, many of whom were delighted by the turn of events. The Seymours – Sir John and his two ambitious sons Edward and Thomas – were networking and cultivating alliances. Courtiers were already eyeing Boleyn property and wealth, ready to pick their fortunes apart – Lord Lisle for example, who had worked with George for several years and so warmly invited him to dine, wrote to Cromwell, disowning any friendship with George, describing the charges as 'the most mischievous, heinous, and most abominable treason … I wholly trust that his Grace, being good lord unto me, will vouchsafe to employ some part of those same upon me; which I do well know may so much the rather be obtained by your good fortune.'[27] When the Crown was ready to divvy out the spoils, hungry courtiers would be waiting.

Even while the accused sat in the Tower, the specifics of the charges were still unknown.[28] The day before the trials were to begin, William Paulet wrote to Cromwell that:

> My lord of Norfolk showed me that he had no knowledge that the indictment was found, and asked me whether the parties should proceed to their trial or not. I told him I knew not. As to Commissioners he said he knew not how many were required, nor whether they ought to be barons or not. Therefore, he could not tell whom to name; and if he knew, yet he would name none till he learned the King's pleasure. So, he willed me to advertise you.[29]

The charges were still being determined, and the whole dramatic tale would be told before an eager court.

The four men were to be tried separately from Anne and George, but very few had any illusions about the trumped-up charges. Mark Smeaton admitted to having had liaisons with the Queen on three different occasions, but Chapuys made it clear that all the others were sentenced on mere presumption or on very slight grounds, without legal proof or valid confession.

Anne and George were tried separately on 15 May, before the Court of the High Steward in the Tower. Their uncle presided over both trials, under the cloth of state; Thomas Audley sat on his right, Charles Brandon, Duke of Suffolk, on his left, and Norfolk's son (the accused's cousin) was directly before him, as Lord Marshall.[30] It is also worth noting that, besides Norfolk, George's father-in-law Henry Parker, Baron Morley, was also on the jury.[31] There is no evidence he offered assistance to his son-in-law.[32] It was originally reported that among the 26 peers chosen for the trials of the Boleyn siblings, Thomas himself was present, but this is incorrect.[33] Chapuys, who was present for the trials, reported that: 'I am told that the earl of Wiltshire wished also to be present at the trial [of his daughter and son], as he had been at that of the other four [accused].'[34] Chapuys does not explain how he came across such information, but as there is no written record of Boleyn's reaction, we are left only with Chapuys' report.

The court might have expected Anne's emotions to flare, as had so often been witnessed, but she was calm and measured in her own defence, and declared that while she had not always treated the King with the respect he deserved, as God was her witness, she had not sinned against him with her body. Not that it made any difference, as the outcome of the 'trial' had been decided in advance. Anne was found guilty of treason, and sentenced to be beheaded, or burned, as the King pleased. When the sentence was read to her, she received it quite calmly, and said that she was prepared to die, but was extremely sorry to hear that others, who were innocent and the King's loyal subjects, should share her fate and die through her.[35] She ended by begging that some time should be allowed for her to prepare her soul for death. Her original sentence, to be beheaded or burned at the King's pleasure, was commuted to beheading by the sword.

Soon after, George entered the hall, not knowing his sister's fate. He seemed far more defiant than Anne, and those who witnessed his defence seemed sure he would be acquitted of so fanciful a charge as incest. As Chapuys noted, 'no proof of his guilt was produced except that of his having once passed many hours in her [Anne's] company, and other little follies'.[36]

There was some indication that George's wife had chosen to testify against her husband, and that her testimony helped convict George of incest and treason, but there is further evidence which puts this in doubt.[37] Cavendish, who, it seems, had an opinion on every member of the Boleyn family, hinted that she had made dishonest accusations, which sources further embellished. John Hussee had written to Lady Lisle of the trial, noting that three ladies had probably been coerced into giving evidence, the Countess of Worcester, Nan Cobham and another maid. Lady Jane Rochford was no maid.

The evidence suggests that Jane, at least outwardly, remained loyal to George's memory after his death.[38] She also appeared publicly as a dutiful wife during George's imprisonment, with the Lieutenant of the Tower recording that Sir Nicholas Carew and Sir Francis Bryan came with a message to George from Jane to 'see how he did' and also to declare that she would 'humbly suit unto the king's highness' on George's behalf.[39] Unfortunately, the letter in which this message was noted was later damaged in a fire and the nature of Jane's petition is lost, although it was 'for her husband' and such as that George 'gave her thanks', which implied that she offered to petition the King for his release. There had been much friction in the marriage and unhappiness, but this is not enough to stoop to a falsehood which would result in the death of one's husband. We may never know if, and to what extent, Jane was involved in the accusations.

There was another charge, put to George in writing, and he was forbidden to read it out and was told instead to quietly read it and plead accordingly. But George ignored the directive, and read it aloud much to the raucous amusement of the court. It was a joke regarding Henry's impotency – 'nestoit habile en cas de soy copuler avec femme, et quil navoit ne vertu ne puissance' –

saying that Henry was unable to copulate with any woman, and that he lacked vigour and staying power.

Shrugging, George slyly suggested that he could not possibly speculate, for fear of prejudicing Henry's future marriages. He knew this was about removing his sister so that Henry could remarry – why else make such a pointed comment? This caused a bawdy reaction from the witnesses at the trial but, when asked if he had ever expressed a doubt as to Anne's daughter being Henry's, he stayed unusually silent.[40] Despite his defence and the clear fact that the charges were fabricated, it came as a surprise to all who filled the courtroom that he too was found guilty. George was unsurprised at the sentence – he was well aware Henry had no intention of releasing the Boleyn siblings or they would not have been brought to trial in the first place. He quietly stated that he deserved death, apologised to those to whom he owed debts, and pleaded that they be paid by his estates after his death.

So much of the paperwork surrounding the arrests and trial have been lost, and only part of the indictment against Anne and the men survives.[41] But there is overwhelming evidence that Anne and her co-accused were innocent; a defence is neither necessary nor relevant.

Chapuys also wrote at length about the general mood of the populace as Henry's true passions became embarrassingly clear. 'Already it sounds badly in the ears of the public that the King, after such ignominy and discredit as the concubine has brought on his head, should manifest more joy and pleasure now, since her arrest and trial, than he has ever done on other occasions, for he has daily gone out to dine here and there with ladies, and sometimes has remained with them till after midnight.'[42]

Neither Thomas nor his wife were disgraced along with their children but they, and others among their generation in the Boleyn sphere, clearly were not the targets of Henry's purge; only the younger generation was targeted.

On 17 and 19 May 1536, two of the most infamous episodes of Henry's reign moved towards their inevitable conclusions. Anne's alleged lovers were all executed in the Tower of London. Chapuys was not present, but reported that George,

> before dying declared himself to be innocent of all the charges brought against him, though he owned that he deserved death for having been contaminated with the new heresies, and having caused many others to be infected with them. He had no doubt, said he on the scaffold, that God had punished him for that, and, therefore, he recommended all to forsake heretical doctrines and practices, and return to true faith and religion. Which words on the mouth of such a man as lord

Rochefort will be the cause of innumerable people here making amends for their sins, and being converted.[43]

Anne's death at the hands of the French swordsman two days later is so familiar to us that it is hard to imagine how shocking it must have been: the queen of England executed on charges of adultery, incest and conspiring to bring about the King's death. Centuries later, we are still pointing fingers. Was it Henry alone who wanted to be rid of his wife and gave the order, or was it Cromwell, conspiring to eliminate his rivals? Had a move been planned for some time, or was this a very recent development?

Weeks after the executions, Cromwell would confide in Chapuys that he dreamt it all up. But he would also say that Henry had first authorised and commissioned him to prosecute Anne in 1536, and 'quickly have her taken care of', which he added he had taken considerable trouble to do. We have no real reason to doubt him.

No one mentioned Anne's name, but George received a posthumous epitaph from Thomas Wyatt, who had been imprisoned briefly with the men on the same suspicion, but released on Cromwell's orders: 'Some say, "Rochford, haddest thou not been so proud, For thou great wit each man would thee bemoan, Since it is so, many cry aloud, it is a great loss that though art dead and gone".'[44] George had indeed been known as a man of wit and intelligence, but while the accusation of pride is a popular one, it was by no means a dominant character trait.

George and Anne lost their lives, while Thomas lost his reputation, not at the hands of his contemporaries, but generations of historians. For example, in his nineteenth-century work, Paul Friedmann wrote that 'Anne's friends were closely watched, but it was not thought necessary to interfere with the liberty of Lord Wiltshire. He was a mean egotist and coward, and from motives of prudence had always disapproved of his daughter's bold and violent courses. There was, therefore, no reason to fear that he would try to defend her.'[45] Decades later, even Eric Ives wrote that Thomas bought safety for himself by his willingness to condemn his daughter's alleged lovers.[46]

In a similar vein, if toned-down style, David Loades observed: 'In spite of his acquiescence in all that had happened, Boleyn now found himself excluded from the inner circle … he did not give up, but rather set out to recover his position.'[47] This is blatantly false – Thomas and his wife left court immediately, and remained at Hever for some time. Because their grief and distress were not officially recorded, or witnessed, does not mean he and his wife did not suffer over the loss of their children. Thomas' actions remain inconclusive; sources do not provide irrefutable evidence that he abandoned his children, and merely citing a lack of evidence is not enough. The depiction of Thomas as a nefarious character has served as a literary device in fictional portrayals of the period: he has been seen as a heartless father, absent during the trials of his children, even allowing their subsequent executions, despite the fact that he was powerless to intervene once the King had decided their fate.

This negative reputation probably would not have been so pronounced had he suffered the same fate as his children, but to ask how Thomas could stand by and watch the tragic events unfold for his children is the wrong question, and we are demanding answers from the wrong person. If Henry, the most powerful man in England, divinely appointed, had made clear his desire to be rid of Thomas' children, who logically would he have complained to and what would he have been able to achieve? While martyrdom for some would seem an honourable (but pointless) alternative to survival, Thomas had to consider the welfare of his remaining family. We know that Elizabeth had been ill just prior to these events as on 14 April 1536 Thomas Warley, Lord Lisle's servant, wrote to Lady Lisle, a friend of Elizabeth's, commenting that she was suffering from a bad cough:

> Also, this day my lady the Countess of Wiltshire [Elizabeth] asked me when I heard from your ladyship, and how you fared, and heartily thanks your ladyship for the hosen; and said you could not have devised to send her a thing that might be to her a greater pleasure than they were considering how she was then diseased; and further desired me that I would not depart over to Calais until I should speak with her, which, God willing, I will not fail. And I ensure your ladyship she is sore diseased with the cough, which grieves her sore.[48]

It may have been that Elizabeth was suffering from tuberculosis, a very common disease of the period. The sources fall silent on the Boleyns for a short time, as Henry and his court, Norfolk included, revelled around the new Queen, Jane.

The court had lost two of its brightest, most vivacious individuals. Anne had been queen for less than three years, and George, despite his best efforts, had been ill served by Henry. Had he lived in Wolsey's reign of power, he might have indeed become a highly respected ambassador, but Henry kept him on a tight leash, his brief embassies forever linked to Anne and Henry's issues. It is little wonder that he was not always taken seriously, and even as he attempted to cultivate a career in diplomacy and administration, yet no grant, award or position was linked to merit. But it should have been. For all his love of finery – books, art, hawks, elaborate clothing – there is a simpler image which has lasted the centuries. In Beauchamp Tower, where the men awaited their fate, was a crudely constructed (the carver was no Holbein) falcon. It was Anne's Boleyn falcon – the Butler falcon. Of all the men in the Tower, only one would have had the motive to do such a thing. The crest, which had been a part of the family for generations, could only mean the world to one man – George. He would have carved it in those last days, his thoughts fixed on his parents and sisters, the family that the King and his court were cheerfully tearing apart. The falcon had no crown or sceptre, it was plain, but it seems complete. It remains one of the most powerful lingering images of the family, who themselves were already entering into legend.

# CHAPTER FIFTEEN

# Aftermath

*Gentle visitor pause awhile, where you stand death cut away the light of many days. Here jeweled names were broken from the vivid thread of life, may they rest in peace while we walk the generations of their strife and courage under these restless skies.*
— Brian Catling, Tower of London Memorial to those executed

It is generally assumed that Thomas either spent the rest of his days a broken man in exile, or that he carried on despite the execution of his children, as evidenced by his communications with Cromwell, and reactions at court to his death in 1539. He undoubtedly was broken by the deaths of his children, but as a peer of the realm, a respected noble in his county of Kent, and Knight of the Garter he could not allow personal matters to interfere with his duties at court for long, nor could he dare display any grievance or disaffection towards his monarch.

Yet there is considerable evidence that Thomas did not have an easy or particularly cordial relationship with others involved in the downfall of children. We hear nothing of the Boleyns throughout May and June of 1536, most likely because they were in mourning at Hever. He quietly resigned his position of Lord Privy Seal, which was soon bestowed upon Cromwell. On 2 July, Thomas received two letters at Hever, one from the King, and one from Cromwell, each requesting an augmentation of the allowance for Jane, George's widow. Thomas' written response to Cromwell, with whom he had not been in communication with since the death of his children, made it clear that he did 'thys alonly for the Kyngs plesur . . . I thank yow for your goodnes to me when I am far off, and cannot always be present to answer for myself'.[1]

His letter was business-like, to the point, and could even be interpreted as terse.[2] Thomas agreed to allocate Jane the sizable annual pension of £100, precisely what Thomas had given his daughter Mary.[3] Jane would also have to rely on her own father, who, having sat on the jury for the trial of her husband, must have felt somewhat obliged.

The pace of religious change in the early years of the Reformation was too fast for many in various regions across the country as not everyone was ready to embrace the break with the Roman Catholic Church. Civic unrest was growing into civic insurrection. The autumn of 1536 brought violent religious riots against the King's dissolution of the monasteries, known as the Pilgrimage of Grace. Thomas' many years as Commissioner of the Peace made him the ideal individual to muster troops in Kent, and Cromwell quickly wrote to the Earl. But Thomas was furious that he received the notice over a week after Cromwell had written it, leaving him only a few days to gather 300 men and march to Northampton. Had Cromwell allowed the letter to be delayed? We have no way of knowing, but Thomas wrote to Cromwell: 'It is very hard for me to be there by that day, as the letter was so long in coming to me, as Cromwell's clerk, Jeffrey, the bearer, can show. Has come here today and appointed the said number or very near to be with him here tomorrow night or Sowlmas day in the morning. As it is rumoured that the rebels have fled or yielded, asks for further orders.'[4]

The fact that Thomas managed to attain the men and march to London in two days is impressive, and suggests he was highly respected in his county. There is no further correspondence, so it appears that Thomas must have returned home.

In May of 1537, Thomas served on a special commission of 17 peers to arraign the northern rebels of the Pilgirmage of Grace. Meeting on 15 May, they charged 11 people including Lords Hussey and Darcy, Sir Francis Bigod and Robert Aske, historically considered the ring leader of the rebellions.[5] Thomas then sat on the court of the Lord High Steward that found the rebel peers guilty. It was the first case Thomas had been a part of since the dreaded Oyer and Terminer a year before. Hostility between Thomas and his brother-in-law, the Duke of Norfolk, who presided over the trials of the Boleyn children, had overtaken a relatively productive working relationship. In July that year, Norfolk wrote to Cromwell, complaining that Thomas' minstrel had sung derogatory songs about the Duke. Several people had heard the ballad, and the sensitive Duke accused Thomas of having approved of it:

> As to the song of my lord of Wiltshire's minstrel, begs Cromwell to write to him in a letter apart that such and such men heard him say that he had sung it before the Duke, and that the Duke was privy thereto. Will then, after convicting him by his own confession, as he has already denied it, order him so that he shall be afraid hereafter to sing songs of any gentlemen without their knowledge, and if his

master heard the same and did not advertise me thereof, as he did not, *Judas non dormit*, though I have not deserved it to him, as ye know.[6]

That Norfolk chose to make the matter public, rather than deal with Thomas himself, is evidence of a breach in their relationship, and we never learn if the matter was resolved. Cromwell hounded Thomas when he could, and was particularly harsh on him when it came to payment of legal subsidies and rents, insisting that all of Thomas' payments be paid strictly on time. Although other nobles, including Norfolk, were also in arrears, they were never pressured for payment.[7] In September of 1537 Thomas wrote to Cromwell regarding his stewardship of St Albans. Thomas had relinquished the wealth of the stewardship to Thomas Audley, Keeper of the Privy Seal, but it was still in his name. Cromwell had questioned this situation, and Audley's response was that he:

> Was much troubled by Cromwell's late letters, that it was reported to the King he had attempted to take the stewardship of St. Albans. Reminds Cromwell he spoke about it to him before he did anything, showing that the earl of Wiltshire had offered him his patent, and Cromwell encouraged him to believe the King would be content. Obtained the patent from the earl under the convent seal: the fee is 20*l*. If he may not take a free gift from his friend, he is worse than a friar Observant.[8]

There is a hint of sarcasm in Thomas' response to Cromwell which suggests he did not voluntarily give up the Stewardship, and was less than impressed that Cromwell was choosing to take an interest now:

> Has received today a letter from him touching the stewardship of St. Alban's. Last term delivered his patent of the office and released his right in it to the Lord Chancellor. If it had been in his hands, trusts Cromwell would rather have helped him to have kept it for his weal, than helped him from it to his loss.[9]

The relationship between Cromwell and Thomas remained tense, yet has been misinterpreted as evidence that Thomas, in Ives' words: 'Set himself with enthusiasm once more to climb up the greasy pole ... he buttered up and co-operated with ministers, even lending Cromwell his chain and best garter badge.'[10] Cromwell was admitted to the prestigious order on 5 August 1537 and, as a member – Thomas should have been present, but he was conspicuously absent.[11] This may well explain Cromwell's personal letter to Thomas, prior to the installation set for 26 August. Thomas did not, as Ives wrote, happily offer his Garter collar to Cromwell to win favour. We do not have Cromwell's letter, but Thomas' response is quite clear: 'According to your letter I send you my collar with my best George [the Garter's symbol] and request that it may be delivered when done with to Mr. Thornham, my chaplain, at Darby Place.'[12] It seems that Thomas did not voluntarily give his collar to Cromwell, and he would not leave Hever to witness Cromwell wearing what was once his.

One final duty of note was Thomas' required attendance at the christening of Prince Edward, the son of Henry and his third queen, Jane Seymour, on 15 October. Thomas had been present at the christenings of all of Henry's legitimate children, but it was cruel of Henry to demand him to participate in the baptism of Jane's son.[13] He was given the role of bearing a taper of virgin wax in a towel hung around his neck; what he felt, and what those around him felt about him being there, is not known.[14]

On 1 November, in another twist of fate, Thomas was present for the funeral of Jane Seymour, who died just 12 days after giving birth, and Thomas was tasked with assisting about Jane's corpse, which lay in state.[15] It seems likely that he felt little at her death.

Thomas then returned to Hever, but in January of 1538, the Boleyns were back at court, and John Hussey, a servant of Lord Lisle's, reported that Thomas was 'Again now in the court and very well entertained.'[16] It is unclear in what manner Thomas was 'entertained,' or perhaps Hussey was merely noting that the Boleyns were not in disgrace or ignored at court. None of Thomas' roles following the deaths of his children are indicative of being back in favour. Especially considering his rival, Piers Butler, received the Earldom of Ormond on 22 January. But Thomas no longer seemed to feel so strongly about the title- he had no son to bequeath it to. He remained as he had always been, a servant of the Crown.

Just two months later, on 7 April, Elizabeth Boleyn died in a house near Baynard's Castle in London. We have no record of Thomas' reaction, but can assume it was one of grief. Within a few days of her death, her body was taken by barge to Lambeth, accompanied by her brother, Lord Edmund Howard, and half-sister, Lady Daubney, as chief mourners.[17] Elizabeth was not buried at Hever, but at Lambeth, which was close to her brother's London residence.

This has always been seen as a sign that the Boleyn marriage was strained, further evidence that the events of 1536 had caused a rift between the couple, but Lambeth was commonly used as a burial place for members of the Howard family who died in the capital. Choosing Lambeth might simply demonstrate Elizabeth's pride in her lineage and may be the reason she did not select Hever as her burial place, where her husband later chose to be buried.

Within months of his wife's death, a frankly ridiculous rumour spread round the court that Thomas planned to marry, of all women, the King's niece:

'I heard say that my lord of Wolshyre [Boleyn] will marry lady Margaret Dowglas.'[18] It is highly unlikely that Henry would consent to such a match. There is no further evidence to suggest Thomas was interested in remarrying; instead, it appears that he had returned to his intellectual pursuits, aided by his godson, Thomas Tebald.[19] Tebald wrote to his godfather, keeping him up to date with the latest scholarly publications and ideas. It must have been one of the few comforts Thomas now had, who could no longer converse on such subjects with his brilliant children. It was kind of Tebald to be so concerned for his godfather in what would be the last few months of his life.

On 13 March 1539, Cromwell, now Lord Privy Seal and the most powerful man bar the King, received a note. It was short and to the point, in the hand of Thomas' steward, Robert Cranewell: 'My good lord and master is dead. He departed this transitory world I trust to the everlasting Lorde, for he made the end of a good Christian man, ever remembering the goodness of Christ.'[20] Thomas was about 62. To have been closely involved with Henry VIII and yet lived so long was testament to his survival skills; many who had lived so near the sun had been fatally burnt. So many others had fallen by the wayside of Henry's whims.

Henry's response appears to be a testament to the enormous respect he held for his former father-in-law. Henry spent £16 (over £5,000 in today's currency) on 'Certain orasions, suffrages, and masses to be said for the soul's health of the Erle of Wiltshire, late deceased'.[21] Parliament then collected an order for £200 (almost £60,000 in today's currency) for more masses for Boleyn's soul.[22]

Following his death, his devoted friend, Cranmer, along with other trusted servants, hastened to Hever, and showed their respect for Thomas by carefully going through his property and personal belongings to remove anything he might have wished be kept private. It was timed well, for within two weeks Cromwell sent Sir Thomas Willoughby to assist with disposing of all his goods. He was not allowed to move Thomas' mother, for Thomas stipulated that she was to remain at Hever, and he left a generous sum for her upkeep.[23] With no heir, Thomas' properties reverted to the Crown, including his earldoms. Prior to his death, it seemed that Thomas had begun to reconcile with his only living daughter, Mary. Within weeks, Thomas' daughter Mary Stafford and her husband, who had petitioned Cromwell years earlier, received much of Boleyn's property portfolio, including Hever and Rochford Hall. The indenture between the King and Mary and William has remained hidden in an archive over the years, but the eight pages, written in Henry's hand, suggests that Thomas negotiated with Cromwell and the King before his death and left his brother James and his lawyer to ensure it was carried out – whatever their issues had been, Boleyn had shown signs of softening towards his only remaining child. He would not have wanted her to go through the rest of her life destitute. But the indenture written by Henry is far harsher than Thomas had intended, Henry included a number of penalty clauses and steep fines if any property was undervalued. The King seemed less than pleased with the deal. Mary would live only a few years beyond her parents, and it seemed that Thomas' siblings would outlive everyone – they continued their careers, but none of them had ever displayed the wherewithal to excel at court, and their lives ended as quietly as they began. The Boleyn name was not spoken at court any longer, as Henry helped himself to one wife and then another. The rest of Henry's story is well known.

* * *

The Boleyn story traced its way from the late Middle Ages to the early modern period, animated by events in individual lives with consequences that went far beyond the people involved: they shaped and were in turn shaped by the backdrop of the times in which they lived. Epochal changes in this period – of which the Boleyns were a part – included the advancement of those recognised as 'new men', from humble origins on the land and small business, to positions of power, influence and wealth centred on the English court. They valued education and culture, acquiring the skills to become professional administrators of government and to participate in the affairs of state under the first Tudors. Henry VII and Henry VIII would reward these men with promotion, titles and land to become the new Tudor aristocracy, whilst remaining distinct in many ways from the older aristocracy; at the same time they introduced an influential strand into the English social fabric.[24] Thomas' career in Wolsey's stable of ambassadors was impressive, rising to become one of his most skilled and respected diplomats. He was viewed as a loyal and trusted servant of Cardinal Wolsey for many years, and it is important that this 'lost thread' of a relationship between the two is restored. Despite how the story ended, the evidence is overwhelming that Thomas cared for his children, did all he could to nurture their educations, and was fiercely proud of their meteoric rise at court.

Both George and Thomas served Henry VIII well, possessing attributes that the King required, and were well rewarded with promotions and titles for themselves and their family, ambitions of any courtier. While it would be unreasonable to argue that Anne had nothing to do with the royal preferences bestowed on her father and brother, the political culture of the day was extremely personal, so that Boleyn's familial connection with Anne *of course* brought favour, but this was not unusual or morally suspect as much as reflecting the importance of blood ties among the many elements that connected individuals at court, and influenced their fortunes. They have been judged throughout the centuries, not because they attained such heights as father and brother of the Queen, or even that they fell from them, but that they set out to secure them in the first place.

Years after their deaths, another Boleyn would surpass even their expectations.

Against all the odds, and she did indeed have the odds stacked against her, Anne's daughter outlived the heir *and* the spare, Edward, Jane Seymour's son, and Mary, Katherine of Aragon's daughter. Elizabeth was crowned exactly 20 years after the death of her grandfather, Thomas, and her coronation mirrored that of her mother in 1533.

In 1578 Queen Elizabeth visited Norwich as part of her East Anglia Progress. She stayed in Norwich for five days, and the feasts that she held, in the cloisters of Norwich Cathedral, almost bankrupted the town. She had never spoken of her mother, or her Boleyn lineage, and she was always sensitive to attacks on her pedigree, and thus identified closely with her Tudor lineage.

And yet, she had never come to the part of England from where her mother's family hailed. She probably did not visit Blickling, where her mother, uncle and aunt, and her grandfather, were born, or the church where her ancestors lay. But she did visit the Cathedral of Norwich, for the upkeep of which the Boleyns had donated considerable funds decades before. It must have shimmered with Boleyn ghosts. The Queen explored the cathedral, as she was escorted through the various archways and knaves. Her jewel-encrusted heavy dress may have brushed the tombs of her great-grandfather, William Boleyn, or his mother, Anne, who lay next to each other under the cold stone floor. She made no remark, nor gave any indication that she knew whose tombs she crossed. But, as she prepared to hear Mass, she quietly insisted that her throne be placed on the north side of the high altar, in front of the reliquary arch. When she sat down, she sat facing the Boleyn chapel. Above, the square arches showed panels with shields of arms, all of which were the Boleyn bull heads and the Ormond crest, supposedly a memorial of Sir William Boleyn. She sat facing her family crest, and that of her ancestors. What she must have felt, gazing up at the proud bull heads, the azure and gold shields, was the weight of generations of Boleyns, who had endured triumph, sacrifice and loss but none of whom could have ever imagined that a Boleyn would one day hold the sceptre and wear the crown of England.

APPENDIX I

# Grants, Positions, and Titles given to Thomas Boleyn

1509 – Knight of the Bath.
 – Keeper of the Exchange, Calais; Keeper of the Foreign Exchange, England.
1511 – Keepership of the Park of Beskwode, Nottinghamshire, Borham and Powers, Essex; Busshy, Hertfordshire; Henden, Kent; Purbright, Surrey.
1512 – Manor of Walkerfare and Wykmere, Norfolk.
 – Keeper and Constable of the Norwich Castle and Gaol.
1513 – Partial Wardship and custody of the lands and of Elizabeth Grey, daughter and heir of Viscount Lisle.
1514 – Life grant of the Norfolk manors of Saham Tony, Nekton, Panworth Hall, Cressingham Parva, and the hundreds of Waylond and Grymmeshowe.
1520 – Comptroller of the Household.
1521 – Treasurer of the Household.
 Manor of Fritwell, Oxfordshire.
1522 – Manor of Fobbing, Essex; survivorship (alongside his son, George) the manor, honour, and town of Tunbridge; the manors of Brasted, Penshurst Place and Park, Northeligh, and Northlands, Kent.
1523 – Knight of the Order of the Garter.
 – Joint office keeper of Bekeswood Park, Nottinghamshire, with herbage and pannage of 4 pence a day.
1524 – Parker of Thundersley, Essex, with herbage and pannage;
 Issues of the manor of Railegh, Essex 3 pence a day.
1525 – Made Viscount Rochford.

Steward of the Lordship of Swaffenhan, and the crown lands, parcel, and the honour of Richmond, Norfolk.

1529 – First presentation to the recotyr of All Hallows *ad Fenum, alias* 'the More'.

– Elevated to Earldom of Wiltshire and the Irish Earldom of Ormonde Custody of lands and tenements in Lathingdon and Hadley, Essex. Also wardship of William, son and heir of John and Mary Strongman.

1530 – Appointed Lord Keeper of the Privy Seal.

Wardship of Robert, kinsman and heir of Edward Knyvett.

1531 – Fee of the manor and park of Henden *alias* Hethenden, Kent.

Joint grant with George Boleyn, the offices of steward of the honour of Railegh, keeper of Railegh park, master of the hunt of deer in Railegh park and Thundersley park, and bailiff of the hundred of Rachford *alias* Rochford, Essex.

1533 – Grant of the parks called 'le Posterne' and 'le Cage', Kent.

– Grant of a fair at the town of Blickling, Norforflk on St. John Baptist's Day (24 June) and 25 June.

1534 – Feodary of the honor of Clare in Norfolk and other counties.

1536 – Temporal goods of the bishopric of Norwich, 'worth 3,000 of rent', 'Two of the abbeys that are to be suppressed.'

# Grants, Positions, and Titles given to George Boleyn

**1522** – Granted alongside his father the manor, honour, and town of Tunbridge; the manors of Brasted, Penshurst Place and Park, Northeligh, and Northlands, Kent.

**1524** – Grant of the manor of Grymston, Norfolk.

**1525** – Appointed as a gentleman of the King's Privy Chamber.

**1526** – Appointed Royal Cupbearer.

**1528** – Made Squire of the Body.

– Appointed Master of the King's Buckhounds.

– Made Keeper of the Palace of Beaulieu, alias the manor and mansion of Newhall, Essex; gardener or keeper of the garden and orchard of Newhall; warrener or keeper of the warren in the said manor or lordship; keeper of the wardrobe in the said palace or manor in Newhall, Dorhame, Walkefare Hall and Powers, Essex; with certain daily fees in each office, and the power of leasing the said manor, lands for his lifetime.

**1529** – Appointed as chief steward of the honor of Beaulieu, Essex, and of all possessions which are annexed by authority of Parliament or otherwise, and keeper of the New Park there, in the manor of Newehall; with 10l. a year for the former, and 3d. a day for the latter.

– Made Governor of the hospital of St. Mary of Bethlem, near Bishopesgate, London.

– Elevated as his father's heir, to Lord Rochford.

**1532** – Wardship of Edmund, son and heir of Sir Robert Sheffield.

**1533** – Granted the Manor of Southe, Kent.

**1534** – Appointed as Constable of Dover Castle and warden of the Cinque Ports.

# Notes

## INTRODUCTION

1. There are several versions of George's scaffold speech, but I have chosen to use *The Chronicle of Calais in the Reigns of Henry VII and Henry VIII to the Year 1540*, edited by John Gough Nichols (London: J. B. Nichols & Son, 1846), 46.
2. Hall, Edward. *Henry VIII*. Vol II. (London: T. C. & E. C. Jack, 1904), 268–269
3. The main argument regarding George's sexuality stems from Retha Warnicke's *The Rise and Fall of Anne Boleyn: Family Politics at the Court of Henry VIII*, 214–16.
4. J. S. Brewer *Letters and Papers, Foreign and Domestic, of the Reign of Henry VIII, 1509–1547* (London: 1888), IV, Introduction (hereafter cited as L&P).
5. P. W. Sergeant, *The Life of Anne Boleyn* (London: Hutchinson & Co, 1923), 75; Eric Ives, *The Life and Death of Anne Boleyn: 'The Most Happy'* (Oxford: Blackwell Publishing, 2004), 6.
6. Paul Friedmann, *Anne Boleyn: A Chapter of English History, 1527–1536* (London: Macmillan, 1884), 155.
7. David Loades, *The Boleyns: The Rise and Fall of a Tudor Family* (Stroud: Amberley, 2011), 8.
8. William H. Dean, 'Sir Thomas Boleyn: The Courtier Diplomat, 1477–1539' (PhD thesis, West Virginia, 1987), 3.

## CHAPTER ONE   MEN OF MARK

1. As noted by Elizabeth Norton, in *The Lives of Tudor Women* (London: Head of Zeus, 2017), 86.
2. Walter Langley Edward Parsons, 'Some Notes on the Boleyn Family,' *Norfolk Archaeology* 25 (1935): 386–407; Francis Blomefield and Charles Parkin, *An Essay Towards a Topographical History of the Country of Norfolk, Containing a description of the Towns, Villages, and Hamlets, with the foundations of monasteries, churches, chapels, chantries, and other religious buildings ... likewise, an historical account of the castles, seats, and manors, their present and ancient owners*, Vol. VI (London: William Miller, 1805).
3. Blomefield and Parkin, *An Essay Towards a Topographical History of the Country of Norfolk*, 386.
4. For example, another John may have succeeded John Boulen, from whom it is believed our Thomas is descended, but some records identify a Nicholas Boleyn.

Blomefield and Parkin, in their work on Norfolk families, contributed to the confusion, adding two more Thomases and Johns as successors. As William Dean noted in his thesis, these men could be siblings rather than children, and the discrepancies as to the number of generations (and who inherited from whom) continued until 1370. See Blomefield and Parkin, *An Essay Towards a Topographical History of the Country of Norfolk*, 386; William H. Dean, 'Sir Thomas Boleyn: The Courtier Diplomat, 1477–1539' (PhD thesis, University of West Virginia, 1987), 1–2.

5. Ibid.

6. Sylvanus Urban, 'The Family of Boleyn,' *The Gentleman's Magazine* 32, N.S. (August 1849): 155.

7. For general discussion of Eustasius, or Eustace, see *The Study of the Bayeux Tapestry*, ed. Richard Gameson (London: Boydell and Brewer, 1997), 2–8.

8. Ibid.

9. John S. Ott, 'Reviewed Work: Heather J. Tanner, Families, Friends and Allies: Boulogne and Politics in Northern France and England, c. 879–1160,' *Speculum* Vol. 81, No. 2 (Apr., 2006): 613–15.

10. Peter Cross, *The Origins of English Gentry* (Cambridge: Cambridge University Press, 2005), 12.

11. Ibid.

12. John S. Ott, 'Reviewed Work: Families, Friends and Allies,' 613–15.

13. Blomefield and Parkin, *An Essay Towards a Topographical History of the Country of Norfolk*, 386.

14. Parsons, 'Some Notes on the Boleyn Family,' 387.

15. Ibid., 389–90.

16. Ibid.

17. Blomefield and Parkin, *An Essay Towards a Topographical History of the Country of Norfolk*, 388.

18. Parsons, 'Some Notes on the Boleyn Family,' 390–1.

19. Theresa Coletti, *Mary Magdalene and the Drama of Saints: Theater, Gender, and Religion in Late Medieval England* (Philadelphia: University of Pennsylvania Press, 2013), 31.

20. Eamon Duffy, *Saints, Sacrilege and Sedition: Religion and Conflict in the Tudor Reformations* (London: Bloomsbury Publishing, 2012), 84.

21. Norfolk and Norwich Archaeological Society and Contributors, *Norfolk Archaeology* (1935): 391. See also Walter Langley Edward Parsons, *Salle: The Story of a Norfolk Parish: Its Church, Manors & People* (London: Jarrold & Sons, 1937), 117–78.

22. Ibid.

23. A. B. Emden, ed. *Biographical Register of the University of Cambridge to 1500* (hereafter cited as *BRUC*) (Cambridge: Cambridge University Press, 1963), 70–5.

24. Michiel Decaluwe, Thomas M. Izbicki and Gerald Christianson, *A Companion to the Council of Basel* (Brill, 2016), 93.

25. *BRUC*, 70, 74–5. In 1439, Thomas obtained a Papal dispensation to hold an additional benefice which had been deemed incompatible, and this success emboldened him to apply three more times for similar benefices, all which were awarded.

26. *Calendar of Close Rolls*, Edward IV, II, 409.

27. Other companies included Grocers, Fishmongers, Brewers, Ironmongers, Cutlers and Bakers, to name a few. See Robert Seymour, 'Twelve Principal Companies of the City of London,' *Survey of the Cities of London and Westminster*, Vol. II (London: J. Read, 1735).

28. *The Medieval Account Books of the Mercers of London*, ed. Lisa Jefferson, Vols. I and II, item 1435 (London: Routledge, 2016).

29. *Calendar of Letter-Books preserved among the Archives of the Corporation of the City of London at the Guildhall. Letter-Book K: Temp. Henry VI*, ed. Reginald Robinson Sharpe (London: John Edward Francis, 1911), Fol. 158b.

30. See Geoffrey's will, which is printed in Daniel Gurney, Esquire, *Supplement to the Record of the House of Gournay* (London: Thew & Son, 1858), 831–40.

31. C. H. Cooper, *Memorials of Cambridge*, Vol. I (Cambridge, 1860), 298.

32. Anthony Richard Wagner, *English Genealogy* (Oxford: Clarendon Press, 1972), 157.

33. Blomefield and Parkin, *An Essay Towards a Topographical History of the Country of Norfolk*, 77.

34. *Calendar of the Fine Rolls*, 130. Parsons, 'Some Notes on the Boleyn Family,' 395.

35. Reginald Robinson Sharpe, ed. *Calendar of Letter-Books preserved among the Archives of the Corporation of the City of London at the Guildhall. Letter-Book K: Temp. Henry VI.* (London: John Edward Francis, 1911), 392.

36. Dale Hoak, *Tudor Political Culture* (Cambridge: Cambridge University Press, 2002), 35. Also, F. J. Furnivall, 'Early English Meals and Manners,' *Early English Text Society* 32 (1868): 70–2.

37. *Calendar of the Patent Rolls Preserved in the Public Record Office: Henry VI. AD 1452–1461 (November, 1457)*, Vol. 6 (London: HMSO, 1910), 444.

38. *C.C.R.*, VI, 410.

39. Gordon Home, *Medieval London* (New York: George H. Doran, 1927), 216.

40. *Acts of the Mercer's Company* 1461 (London: Lyell and Watney, 1936), 54.

41. HMC, *Report on The Manuscripts of the Marquess of Lothian: preserved at Blickling Hall Norfolk* (London: HMSO, 1905), 29–30.

42. Ibid.

43. Ibid.

44. Cross, *The Origins of English Gentry*, 2.

45. Nicholas Harris Nicolas, *Testamenta Vetusta*, Vol. I, 299–300.

46. John Stow, *A survey of London*, ed. 1603, reprinted (London: J.M. Dent & Sons Ltd, 1940) 246–7.

47. Nicolas, *Testamenta Vetusta*, Vol. I, 299–300.

48. Ibid.

49. Ibid., 299–300.

50. Ibid., 322. William is described in his father's will as 'within age' in 1463, which would have been 15 years old. Additionally, a bequest from his father of money and jewels, exactly like that left to his brother Thomas and under the same terms, was to be his upon marriage or attaining the age of 25, which William acknowledged in 1473, suggesting he was that age.

51. Blomefield and Parkin, *An Essay Towards a Topographical History of the Country of Norfolk*, 34.

52. See George E. Cokayne, *The Complete Peerage*. London: St. Catherine Press, 1940. X, 126–7, Joseph Foster, *Collectanea Genealogica* (Oxford: Oxford University Press), 43.

53. See Elizabeth Griffin, 'The Boleyns and Blickling, 1450–1560,' *Norfolk Archeology*, XLV (2009): 453–68.

54. *L&P*, XIII, i, 937. 'Directly he knew of their offence, sent them to Islee, saying they should never enter his house again except at Islee's intercession.'

55. *The Posthumous Works of Sir Henry Spelman, Kt. Relating to the Laws and Antiquities of England. Published from the Original Manuscript*. 'Bolannorum aliquando sedes, e quibus orti funt Thomas Bolen, comes Wiltsheriae, et Anna Bolen uxor Regis Henrici VIII., optimae principis Divae Elizabethae mater, natalitium hic sortita.' (London: D. Brown, W. Mears, F. Clay, and Fletcher Gyles), 151.

56. William Campbell, ed., *Materials for a History of the Reign of Henry VII*, Vol. II (London: John Cambell: 1873), 135.

57. Blomefield and Parkin, *An Essay Towards a Topographical History of the Country of Norfolk*, 34.

## CHAPTER TWO    FORTUNE RULETH OUR HELME

1. Blomefield and Parkin, *An Essay Towards a Topographical History of the Country of Norfolk*, 34.

2. Letters of the Kings of England, now first collected from Royal archives, and other authentic sources, private as well as public, ed. James Orchard Halliwell, Vol. I. (London: Henry Colburn, 1848), 171.

3. S. B. Chrimes, *Henry VII* (Yale: Yale University Press, 1999), 75–8.

4. Ibid.

5. *Letters of the Kings of England*, 71.

6. As discussed in Dean, 'Sir Thomas Boleyn: The Courtier', 18–19; Campbell, *Materials for a History of the Reign of Henry VII*, Vol. II, 135.

7. James Gairdner, ed. *Paston Letters*, A.D. 1422–1509 (London: Chatto & Windus, 2015), I, 312.

8. *Calendar of Patent Rolls preserved in the Public Records Office, Henry VII*, I (London: HMSO, 1907), 357.5.

9. Polydore Vergil, *The Anglica Historia of Polydore Vergil, 1485–1537*, ed. Denys Hay (London: Royal Historical Society, 1950), 52.

10. Ibid.

11. Ibid.

12. James Gairdner, *Letters & Papers, Illustrative of the Reigns of Richard III and Henry VII* (London: HMSO, 1861), I:410. 402–3.

13. Edward Hall, *Hall's Chronicle: Containing the History of England, During the Reign of Henry the Fourth, and the Succeeding Monarchs, to the End of the Reign of Henry the Eighth, in Which are Particularly Described the Manners and Customs of Those Periods* (London: J. Johnson, 1809), 476.

14. Ibid., 478.

15. Vergil, *Anglica Historica*, 94.

16. Ibid.

17. *L&P*, IV, Section 5.

18. *Calendar of the Charter Rolls Preserved in the Public Record Office, 1427–1516* (London: HMSO, 1927), VI: 74–5.

19. David Mathew, *The Courtiers of Henry VIII* (London: Eyre & Spottiswoode, 1970), 32.

20. *L&P*, XI, 17.
21. Samuel Bentley, 'The Privy Purse Expenses of Henry VII,' in *Excerpta Historica* (London, 1889), 158. *C.C.R Henry VII*, II, 54, 63.
22. *Calendar of Fine Rolls*, XXII, 324.
23. Ibid.
24. Lawrence Stone, 'Ages of Admission to Education Institutions in Tudor and Stuart England: A Comment,' *History of Education* 6 (1977): 9.
25. Carey wrote to Lord Burghley: 'My late father, on the authority of heralds and lawyers, ever assured me that a title to the earldom of Ormond was to desend to me, which, if he had lived until this Parliament, he meant to challenge, unless Her Majesty had bestowed some greater honour upon him. His claim to the title was, that Sir Thomas Boleyn was created Viscount Rocheford and Earl of Ormond, to him and his heirs general, and Earl of Wiltshire, to him and his heirs male; by his death without issue male the earldom of Wiltshire was extinguished; but the earldom of Ormond he, surviving his other children before that time attainted, left to his eldest daughter Mary, who had issue, Henry, and Henry had issue, myself.' *Calendar of State Papers Domestic: Elizabeth, 1595–97*, ed. Mary Anne Everett Green (London, 1869), 135.
26. See W. H. Dixon, 'Anne Boleyn,' *Gentleman's Magazine*, New series, XVI (1876): 296.
27. Henry Clifford, *Life of Jane Dormer* (London, 1887), 80.
28. Retha Warnicke, *The Rise and Fall of Anne Boleyn: Family Politics at the Court of Henry VIII* (Cambridge: Cambridge University Press, 1989), 7.
29. Hugh Paget, 'The Youth of Anne Boleyn,' *Bulletin of the Institute of Historical Research* LIV (1981): 162–70.
30. Paget, 'The Youth of Anne Boleyn', 164–5.
31. Ibid.
32. See Steven Gunn, *Henry VII's New Men and the Making of Tudor England* (Oxford: Oxford University Press, 2016). In Gunn's words, these men brought with them a galaxy of talents.
33. Ibid.
34. John Leland, *Antiquarii de rebvs britannicis collectanea*, Vol. 5 (London: Impensis Gvl. & J. Richardson, 1770), 356–67.
35. Ibid., 358.
36. Ibid., 360–1.
37. Steven Gunn and Linda Monckton, *Arthur Tudor, Prince of Wales: Life, Death & Commemoration* (London: Boydell Press, 2009), 64–70.
38. Ibid.
39. Ibid.
40. See Giles Tremlett, *Catherine of Aragon: Henry's Spanish Queen* (London: Faber and Faber, 2010), 101–12.
41. *Hall's Chronicle*, 355.
42. HMC, *The Manuscripts of His Grace the Duke of Rutland preserved at Belvoir Castle*, IV, 12 (London, 1888), 17.
43. Ibid., 18.
44. John Leland, *Antiquarii de rebvs britannicis collectanea*, IV, 265–71.
45. Ibid.

46. Nicholas Harris Nicolas, *Testamenta Vetusta*, Vol. II, 465. It was reported that, from 1519 onwards, Margaret was unable to take care of herself or her affairs, and so Thomas moved his mother down to Hever, where he could care for her for the rest of her life.

47. *Calendar of Patent Rolls, Henry VI*, Vol. II (London: HMSO, 1907), 445.

48. Richard E. Brock provides a valuable summary in his doctoral thesis, 'The Courtier in Early Tudor Society, Illustrated from Select Examples' (PhD thesis, University of London, 1963), 31.

49. David Starkey, 'Representation through Intimacy: A Study in the Symbolism of Monarchy and Court Office in Early Modern England,' in *Symbols and Sentiments: Cross Cultural Studies in Symbolism*, ed. Ioan Lewis (London, New York and San Fransisco: Academic Press, 1977), 202–7.

50. *Calendar of Patent Rolls*, Henry VII, II, 445.

51. See Samuel Pegge, *Curialia: Or An Historical Account of Some Branches of the Royal Household* (London: B. White, 1791), 22.

52. There were three categories of Yeoman, all with different duties: Yeoman of the Guard, Crown and Chamber. For a general discussion of their duties, see Anita Rosamund Hewerdine, 'The Yeomen of the King's Guard 1485–1547' (PhD Thesis, University of London, 1998), 19–24, and her book, *The Yeomen of the Guard and the Early Tudors: The Formation of a Royal Bodyguard* (London: I.B.Tauris, 2012). See also Rosemary Horrox, *Richard III: A Study of Service* (Cambridge: Cambridge University Press, 1991), 245.

53. *L&P*, I, 81.

## CHAPTER THREE  A COURTIER TO HIS FINGERTIPS

1. David Starkey, 'The Court: Castiglione's Ideal and Tudor Reality; Being a Discussion of Sir Thomas Wyatt's Satire Addressed to Sir Francis Bryan,' *Journal of the Warburg and Courtauld Institutes* 45 (1982): 235; Susan Brigden, '"The Shadow That You Know": Sir Thomas Wyatt and Sir Francis Bryan at Court and in Embassy,' *HJ* 39 (1996): 1–31.

2. As Sarah Cockram notes, Castiglione was himself a courtier who had an impressive career trajectory, and his book can be viewed in a multitude of different genres, as a courtesy book, an elegant dialogue, a philosophical treatise, and so on. Sarah Cockram, 'The Author–Actor in Castiglione's "Il Cortegiano": "lo esser travestito porta secouna certa liberta e licenzia"' in *The Tradition of the Actor–author in Italian Theatre*, ed. Donatella Fischer (New York: Legenda, 2013), 11–13. Most Renaissance advice books followed the 'mirror-for-princes' genre established in the Middle Ages. For discussion, see Quentin Skinner, *The Foundation of Modern Political Thought*, Vol. 1, 'The Renaissance' (Cambridge: Cambridge University Press, 1978), 123–7.

3. This book cannot confirm with any certainty that Thomas owned a copy or read the work, especially as it was not translated into French or English until 1537 and 1561 respectively, but we do know that Thomas Cromwell owned a copy of the book, and there was certainly interest, evidenced by Bishop Bonner's letter to Cromwell in 1530, asking to loan 'the book called Cortegiano in Ytalian'. See Henry Ellis, *Original Letters, Illustrative of English History*, Vol. II (London: Richard Bentley, 1848), 177–8. Peter Burke, *The Fortunes of a Courtier: The European Reception of Castiglione's Cortegiano* (Malden, MA: Polity, 1995), 61–6.

4. Jon Robinson, *Court Politics, Culture and Literature in Scotland and England, 1500–1540* (Aldershot: Ashgate, 2013), 84–6.

5. Baldesar Castiglione, *The Book of the Courtier*, trans. George Bull (London: Penguin Books, 1967), I:67. See Frank Lovett, 'The Path of the Courtier: Castiglione, Machiavelli, and the Loss of Republican Liberty,' *The Review of Politics* 74 (2012): 593.

6. Cockram, 'The Author–Actor in Castiglione's 'Il Cortegiano,' 10–11.

7. Stephen Greenblatt, *Renaissance Self-Fashioning from More to Shakespeare* (Chicago: University of Chicago Press, 2005), xi.

8. Woodhouse, J. R., 'Honourable dissimulation: Some Italian Advice for the Renaissance Diplomat,' *Proceedings of the British Academy* 84 (1994): 28.

9. *L&P*, I, 81.

10. Ibid.

11. Ibid.

12. George John Younghusband, *The Tower of London* (London: George H. Doran, 1925), 213.

13. *The Household of Edward IV: The Black Book and the Ordinance of 1478*, ed. Alec Reginald Myers (Manchester: Manchester University Press, 1959), 133.

14. Ibid.

15. F. G. Tomlins, ed. *A History of England: combining the various histories by Rapin, Henry, Hume, Smollett, and Belsham: corrected by reference to Turner, Lingard, Mackintosh, Hallam, Brodie, Godwin, and other sources*, Vol. 1 (London: Kendrick, 1841), 716.

16. Francis Lancelott, *The queens of England and their times: From Matilda, queen of William the Conqueror, to Adelaide, queen of William the Fourth*, Volume I (New York: D. Appleton and Co., 1859), 334.

17. Edward Hall, *The Lives of the Kings, The Triumph of King Henry VIII, with an introduction by Charles Whibley*, Vol. 1 (London: T.C & E.C. Jack, 1904), 4.

18. John Skelton, ed. Reverene Alexandr Dyce, 'A Lawde and prayse made for our souereigne Lord the Kyng,' in *The Poetical Works of John Skelton: with notes, and some account of the author and his writings* (London: Thomas Ross, 1843), IX.

19. George Cavendish, *The Life and Death of Cardinal Wolsey* (New Haven: Yale University Press, 1962), 11.

20. Thomas More, 'On the coronation day of Henry VIII,' in *The Complete Works of Thomas More*, Vol. III, ed. C. H. Miller *et al.* (New Haven: 1984), 104–5.

21. As Martin Allen notes, Henry VIII's reign marked an almost immediate change in policy towards the exchanges, which were to be leased at a lower fixed farm of 30 pounds, six shillings, and eight pence. Martin Allen, *Mints and Money in Medieval England* (Cambridge: Cambridge University Press, 2012), 234.

22. Lorne Cameron George Greig, 'Court Politics and Government in England, 1509–1515' (PhD thesis, University of Glasgow, 1996), 27–9.

23. Ibid.

24. See Clayton J. Drees, *Bishop Richard Fox of Winchester: Architect of the Tudor Age* (Jefferson, NC: McFarland, 2014).

25. Greig, 'Court Politics and Government in England,' 3. As Greig noted, 'William Compton rose from humble beginnings to become one of the king's closest confidants, recognised by many as the man to befriend.'

26. *C.P.R,. Henry VII*, 122; *Letters of the Kings of England, now first collected from Royal archives, and other authentic sources, private as well as public*, Vol. I, James Orchard Halliwell, ed. (London: Henry Colburn, 1848), 171.

27. *L&P* II, 1490.

28. Ibid.

29. For the list of opponents, see *L&P*, I, Appendix 9.

30. 'Whereas it has ever been the custom in this realm for gentlemen to pass the summer season in 'disportes,' as in hunting and hawking and other pastimes; and because all such sports be not ready in May and June, to eschew idleness, the ground of all vice, and give honorable and healthy exercise, 'two gentlemen, associating to them two other gentlemen to be their aids' beseech the King's licence to furnish certain feats of arms, as follows: – A green tree shall be set up in the 'lawnd' of Greenwich park on 22 May, bearing a white shield on which those who accept this challenge may subscribe their names. On Thursday, the 23 May, and every Thursday and Monday until 20 June, the said two gentlemen and their aids will on foot meet all comers 'at the feat called the barriers' with casting spear (headed with 'the morne') and target and with bastard sword (point and edge rebated) from 6 a.m. till 6 p.m.' *L&P*, I, 467.

31. Edward Hall, *Hall's Chronicle: Containing the History of England, During the Reign of Henry the Fourth, and the Succeeding Monarchs, to the End of the Reign of Henry the Eighth, in Which are Particularly Described the Manners and Customs of Those Periods* (London: J. Johnson, 1809), 519.

32. Ellis, *Original Letters, Illustrative of English History*, Vol. II (London: Richard Bentley, 1848), Vol. I, 2nd series, 185.

33. See Garrett Mattingly's vivid description in *Catherine of Aragon* (Boston: Little Brown and Co., 1941), 142.

34. *L&P*, I, 707.

35. *L&P*, I, 546, 604; Polydore Vergil, *The Anglica Historia of Polydore Vergil, 1485–1537*, ed. Denys Hay (London: Royal Historical Society, 1950), 3–4.

36. *L&P*, I, 734. We learn of Compton's political approbation from the French ambassador who in 1511 reports that he enjoyed more 'credit' with the King than anyone else: 'Wrote in his last [letter] about one Conton's credit with the King of England. Is advised that a pension of 400cr. or 500cr. would be well bestowed upon Conton. Is sure Robert would pay it himself if he knew how much the man can do for the maintenance of the amity. It should be done as soon as possible and the letters sent to the writer, as was done in the case of the Great Treasurer and the Great Master [Thomas Howard, Lord Treasurer and Charles Somerset]. Some who have the King's pension here are very old and the pensions will cease when they die.'

37. *L&P*, I, 1960. Fox wrote to Wolsey: 'Brother master Almoner [Wolsey], Yesternight, in my bed and in sleep after ten of the clock, I received your letters, with the letter to the King of Scots, a minute for a warrant for the deliverance of Steward out of the Tower, and the instructions for Thomas Spynell, the which, with a letter directed to Mr. Compton to get them signed of the King's grace.'

38. Greig, 'Court Politics and Government in England,' 2.

39. *L&P*, IV, 4442. In Compton's will, he states: 'Bequeaths to the King his little chest of ivory with gilt lock, and a chest bourde under the same, and a pair of tables upon it,'

with all the jewels and treasure enclosed, now in his wife's custody; also 'certain specialties to the sum of 1,000 marks, which I have of Sir Thos. Bullen, knight, for money lent to him.' Original found in PROB: *Will Registers*, National Archives, 11/23, fol. 219 r.

40. Ibid.
41. On 18 October 1518, Compton bought a moiety of the nearby manor of Long Compton from Thomas for £400, which raised Thomas from a man simply in debt to Compton, to an equal, a principal, someone with whom Compton conducted business.
42. *L&P*, I, 604.
43. See Peter Gwyn, *The King's Cardinal: The Rise and Fall of Thomas Wolsey* (New York: Random House, 2011), 2.
44. Vergil, *Anglica Historia*, 196.
45. See George Cavendish, *The Life and Death of Cardinal Wolsey* (New Haven: Yale University Press, 1962), 11–13; *L&P*, I, 568.
46. David M. Head, *The Ebbs and Flows of Fortune: The Life of Thomas Howard, Third Duke of Norfolk* (Athens, GA: University of Georgia Press, 1995), 28–9.
47. Ibid.
48. Ibid.
49. Vergil, *Anglica Historia*, 162–5.
50. The commission states that the men are 'To treat with the Pope, Maximilian (both as Emperor elect and tutor of the Prince of Spain), the Duchess of Savoy and the King of Aragon (in his own name and that of the Queen of Castile), a league for defence of Holy Church, recovery of its Patrimony and defence of the Pope.' *L&P*, I, 1524.
51. In conversation with Barry Collett, whose monograph study, *The Fox and the Tudor Lions*, is forthcoming. Also noted in Eric Ives, 'Henry VIII: The Political Perspective.' In *The Reign of Henry VIII: Politics, Policy, and Piety*, ed. Diarmaid MacCulloch (New York: St. Martin's Press, 1995), 24. Further discussion can be found in Nadine Lewycky, 'Serving God and King: Cardinal Thomas Wolsey's Patronage Networks and Early Tudor Government, 1514–1529, With Special Reference to the Archdiocese of York' (PhD thesis, University of York, 2008).

CHAPTER FOUR  FORTUNE, INFORTUNE

1. *L&P*, I, 156.
2. See Geoffrey Elton, *England Under the Tudors* (London: Routledge, 1991), 71–8; Garrett Mattingly, *Renaissance Diplomacy* (New York: Cosimo Classics, 2008), 161; J. J. Scarisbrick, *Henry VIII* (Berkeley and Los Angeles: University of California Press, 1968), 26; Polydore Vergil, *The Anglica Historia of Polydore Vergil, 1485–1537*, ed. Denys Hay (London: Royal Historical Society, 1950), 161.
3. Elton, *England Under the Tudors*, 76–8.
4. Betty Behrens, 'The Office of the English Resident Ambassador: Its Evolution as Illustrated by the Career of Sir Thomas Spinelly, 1509–22,' *Transactions of the Royal Historical Society* 16 (1933): 167.
5. Martin Allen, *Mints and Money in Medieval England* (Cambridge: Cambridge University Press, 2012), 234.
6. *L&P*, I, 1213.
7. Ibid.

8. Ibid.

9. *BL* Cotton MS, Galba B III, 27.

10. Ibid.

11. Ibid.

12. Cotton MS, Galba B III, fol. 33. *L&P*, I, 1279.

13. Maximilian, *et al. Correspondance de l'empereur Maximilien Ier et de Marguerite d'Autriche de 1507 à 1519, publiée après les manuscrits originaux par Le Glay* (Paris: Renouard, 1839. Reprinted by New York: Johnson, 1966), 14.

14. *L&P*, I, 1258.

15. Ibid.

16. Cotton MS, Galba, fol. 33. *L&P*, I, 1279. 'Thereupon we desired Thomas Spynell [Spinelly] to learn whether we might speak with my Lady [Margaret] that night; and meanwhile I, Sir Thomas Boleyn, copied the obligation.'

17. Maximillian, Parm Le Glay, *Correspondance de l'empereur Maximilien*, 19.

18. *L&P*, I, 1338.

19. *L&P*, I, 1322.

20. *L&P*, I, 1338.

21. Ibid.

22. Ibid.

23. Cotton MS, Galba B III, fol 44.

24. Ibid.

25. Ibid.

26. Ibid.

27. Ibid.

28. Maximilian, Parm Le Glay, *Correspondance de l'empereur Maximilien*, 'Laquelle desirons que recevez benignement dudit seigneur d'Aremberch, et que après, vous faictes refaire ledit coffin qui est couvert de cuyre pardessus, ou lieu dudit cuyre, d'argent dore, et puis le tour faire presenter a nosyre frère, Le roy d'Angleterre,' 410.

29. *L&P*, I, 1436.

30. Ibid.

31. Cotton MS, Galba B III, fol. 49. *L&P*, I, 1430.

32. Ibid.

33. Ibid.

34. Cotton MS, Galba B III, fol. 53. *L&P*, I, 3500.

35. Additionally, Thomas was irritated by Spinelly's decision to send two brothers from the town of Serizee (Cerezay) to England, but Spinelly reasoned that Thomas was with Margaret in Antwerp at the time. Regardless, Thomas valued communication, and he also had a sense that the embassy may have lost some of its cohesion and effective identity, which had always been one of Fox's main foci when it came to foreign embassies.

36. Cotton MS, Galba B III, fol. 96.

37. Thomas Rymer, *Foedera, Conventiones, Literae, Et Cujuscunque Generis Acta Publica, Inter Reges Angliae, Et Alios quosvis Imperatores, Reges, Pontifices, Principes, vel Communitates, Ab Ineunte Saeculo Duodecimo, viz. ab Anno 1101, ad nostra usque Tempora, Habita aut Tractata; Ex Autographis, infra Secretiores Archivorum Regiorum Thesaurarias, per multa Saecula reconditis, fideliter Exscripta*, XIII, 'Appunctuamenta cum Leone Papa, pro Defensione Ecclesiae' (London: A. & J. Churchill, 1727), 354–8.

38. Ibid., 432.
39. Peter G. Bietenholz and Thomas Brian Deutscher, *Contemporaries of Erasmus: A Biographical Register of the Renaissance and Reformation* (Toronto: Toronto University Press, 2003), 388.
40. Hugh Paget, 'The Youth of Anne Boleyn,' *Bulletin of the Institute of Historical Research* LIV (1981):162–70.
41. *L&P*, I, 2053.
42. See David M. Loades, *The Boleyns: The Rise and Fall of a Tudor Family* (Stroud: Amberley, 2011), 26.
43. *The Chronicle of Calais in the Reigns of Henry VII and Henry VIII to the Year 1540*, ed., John Gough Nicols (London: J. B. Nichols & Son, 1846), 12. 'The last day of June kynge Henry landyd at Caleys; with hym landed the bysshope of Wynchestar lord prevye seale.'
44. Louis had no intention of relinquishing his claims to Italy, but a war with England equally undesirable. For general discussion, see Scarisbrick, *Henry VIII*, 37–40; C. S. L. Davies, "Tournai and the English Crown, 1513–1519," *HJ* 41, no. 1 (1998): 1–26. 44.
45. *L&P*, I, 3146.
46. Paget, 'The Youth of Anne Boleyn,' 167.
47. See Cotton MS, Vitelli, C, XI, fol. 155.; *L&P*, I, 3357.
48. Ibid.
49. *L&P*, II, Revel Accounts, 1501.
50. Edward Hall, *Hall's Chronicle: Containing the History of England, During the Reign of Henry the Fourth, and the Succeeding Monarchs, to the End of the Reign of Henry the Eighth, in Which are Particularly Described the Manners and Customs of Those Periods* (London: J. Johnson, 1809), 580. Also see Neil Samman, 'The Henrician Court During Cardinal Wolsey's Ascendancy c. 1514–1529' (PhD thesis, University of Wales, 1988), 168.
51. See *L&P*, II, Revel Accounts, 1501. Also cited in Samman, 'The Henrician Court During Cardinal Wolsey's Ascendancy,' 147.
52. *L&P*, II, Revel Accounts, 1501.
53. *L&P*, X, 450.

CHAPTER FIVE   THE PICKLOCK OF PRINCES

1. *L&P*, I, 1221.
2. *L&P*, II, 207. Between 1509 and 1532, Thomas would be appointed Commissioner over a hundred times for various counties.
3. It was, according to Butler 'mine ancestors at first time they were called to honour, and hath since continually remained in the same blood; for which cause my lord and father commanded me upon his blessing, that I should do my devoir to cause it to continue still in my blood.' *Will of Thomas, Earl of Ormond*, The National Archives, Kew, PROB 11/18/184.
4. *Archaeologica: or Miscellaneous Tracts Relating to Antiquity*, III (London, 1775), 20–21.
5. *Will of Thomas, Earl of Ormond*, The National Archives, Kew, PROB 11/18/184.
6. *L&P*, I, 5784.
7. Ibid.
8. *L&P*, II, 1277. Also found in *Calendar of State Papers relating to Ireland of the reigns of Henry VIII, Edward VI, Mary, and Elizabeth, 1509–1573*, I (London, 1860), 2.

9. *A Descriptive Catalogue of Ancient Deeds in the Public Record Office*. London: HMSO,1890 VI, 4700.

10. *Calendar of Ormond Deeds* IV, ed. Edmund Curtis (Dublin: Stationery Office, 1937), 111, 116.

11. Ibid.

12. King's Book of Payments, 1516, *L&P*, II, p. 1470.

13. *L&P*, II, 3756.

14. *L&P*, II, 1573.

15. *L&P*, II, King's Book of Payments, 1473.

16. George Goodwin, *Fatal Rivalry, Flodden 1513: Henry VIII, James IV and the Battle for Renaissance Britain* (London: Hatchette, 2013).

17. Cited in G. W. Bernard, 'The Rise of Sir William Compton, Early Tudor Courtier,' *The English Historical Review* 96, no. 381 (1981), 762. He had held a moiety of this manor between about 1514 and 3 May 1516. Also see Northamptonshire County Record Office, *Typescript Catalogue of the Muniments of the Compton Family preserved at Castle Ashby*, ed. I. H. Jeayes, 461–2, 464–6.

18. *L&P*, II, 4409.

19. Ibid.

20. Ibid.

21. See J. J. Scarisbrick, *Henry VIII* (Berkley and Los Angeles: University of California Press, 1968), 71–4; *Cal. Ven.*, II, 1085, 1088.

22. *Cal. Ven.*, II, 1088.

23. *The Cambridge Companion to Thomas More*, ed. George M. Logan (Cambridge: Cambridge University Press, 2011), 75.

24. David Starkey, *The Reign of Henry VIII: Personalities and Politics* (London: Vintage, 2002), 76.

25. *L&P*, II, 4469.

26. Cotton MS, Caligula. D, VII, fol. 85.

27. *L&P*, II, 4674.

28. Ibid.

29. John Stevens Cabot Abbott, *The Empire of Austria: Its Rise and Present Power* (New York: Mason, 1859), 103.

30. Martyn Rady, *The Emperor Charles V* (New York: Routledge, 2014), 14; Scarisbrick, *Henry VIII*, 97–105.

31. Kenneth M. Setton, *The Papacy and the Levant, 1204–1571, Volume III, The Sixteenth Century to the Reign of Julius III to Pius V* (Philadelphia: The American Philosophical Society, 1984), 192.

32. *The Richest Man Who Ever Lived: The Life and Times of Jacob Fugger* (New York: Simon & Schuster, 2015), 157.

33. A. F. Pollard argued that 'The Papal Tiara hovered in Wolsey's eyes over his own uplifted brow,' but D. S. Chambers makes a convincing case that Wolsey's ambitions were lukewarm at best. See A. F. Pollard, *Wolsey* (London: Longmans, Green, 1929), 25; D. S. Chambers, 'Cardinal Wolsey and the Papal Tiara,' *Bulletin of the Institute of Historical Research* 28 (1965): 20–30. Also discussed in Luke MacMahon, 'The Ambassadors of Henry VIII: The Personnel of English Diplomacy, c.1500–c.1550.' (PhD thesis, University of Kent, 1999), 5.

34. For example, Cotton Caligula, D, VII, Fol. 105, 108, 112; *L&P*, III, 223.

35. Cotton Caligula, D, VII, Fol. 88, *L&P*, III, 70.
36. Thomas also informed Wolsey that his reports were being carried by his servant to Calais which cost nine or ten crowns – an exorbitant amount – Wolsey immediately arranged for Boleyn's reports to be sent through trusted couriers via Calais.
37. Cotton MS, Caligula, D, VII, 106.
38. Ibid.
39. Ibid.
40. *L&P*, III, 92.
41. Cotton MS, Caligula, D, VII, 96.
42. *L&P*, III, 222.
43. *L&P*, III, 111.
44. Cotton Caligula, D, VII, 96–8; *L&P*, III, 122. 'Yesterday in the morning I resceived owt of England…a pacquett of letters wherin was a letter from the king's highnesse to the king here with a copy of the same, a letter from your grace to the king here, a qwere of instrucions signed with the king's hand concemyng in the begynnyng the deliverance of the king's letter with recommendacions … And a letter from your grace to me concemyng most the thorder to be takyn for the marchants spoyled in the sea in September and October last year.'
45. Cotton MS, Caligula D VII, Fol. 102.
46. *L&P*, III, 111.
47. Cotton MS, Caligula, D, VII, 121.
48. Ibid.
49. Ibid.
50. It clearly alarmed Thomas, who did not want to breach protocol or cause offence, and his letter to Wolsey shows that he was concerned enough at this surprise request for money to enquire if what he had given had been honourable.
51. *L&P*, III, 223. Thomas wrote: "Four years ago, when I first sued to the King in this matter, said that he wished to serve the King in the court all his life, if on Lovell's leaving the office of treasurer he [the king] would appoint him to that place or to the controllership, and that if he would grant me that he would never sue for any higher place. The King then faithfully promised that when Lovell should quit his office Ponynges should be treasurer and Boleyn controller; and at Boleyn's last departing from him, he bade him undoubtedly trust thereto." It nevertheless remains unclear from this letter which position Henry promised, and when.
52. Ibid.
53. Ibid.
54. *L&P*, III, 447.
55. Cotton MS, Caligula, D, VII, fol. 140.
56. *L&P*, III, 514 "I told my Lady that I have here afore time known when the King's Grace hath worn his long beard, that the Queen hath daily made him great instance, and desired him to put it off for her sake."
57. Cotton MS, Caligula, D, VII, 95.
58. Ibid., D, VII. 182. 'The time of the meeting shal be the hottest season of all the year,.. Whan folks drynk most, and thinketh that amongs such a multitude of pepull some drunken personne might cause invovicneces.' This letter is incorrectly labelled as

Wingfield to Henry in Henry Ellis *Original Letters*, but in the Caligula MS the writing is clearly Thomas', as is the signature, 'beseching the Holy Trinite long to Preserve your Highnesse'. Wingfield usually ended with 'Beseching the Holy Goset to have your Grace in hys most blessed kepyng'.

59. *L&P*, III, 666.
60. L&P, III, Introduction.
61. *Cal. Ven.*, II, 1235.
62. *L&P*, III, 629.
63. So styled by Elizabeth Benger, author of *Memoirs of the Life of Anne Boleyn, Queen of Henry VIII* (Philadelphia: Parry and Macmillan, 1854), 50.

## CHAPTER SIX  BETWIXT TWO PRINCES

1. *L&P*, III, introduction. Chapter 6.
2. Edward Hall, *Hall's Chronicle: Containing the History of England, During the Reign of Henry the Fourth, and the Succeeding Monarchs, to the End of the Reign of Henry the Eighth, in Which are Particularly Described the Manners and Customs of Those Periods* (London: J. Johnson, 1809), 604.
3. *L&P*, III, 728.
4. Ibid.
5. The prevailing practice of the day (at least as far as the Imperial Empire was concerned) was that a sovereign should meet the Holy Roman Emperor in the latter's realm, as an inferior prince to a superior one.
6. J. G. Russell, *The Field of Cloth of Gold: Men and Manners in 1520* (London: Routledge & Kegan Paul, 1969), 48–9.
7. Ibid., 48–9.
8. *Rymer*, XIII, 711.
9. *The Chronicle of Calais, in the Reigns of Henry VII. and Henry VIII. To the Year 1540. Ed. from Mss. in the British Museum.* Edited by John Gough Nichols (London: J. B. Nichols and Son, 1846), 22.
10. *L&P*, III, 869. 'La description et ordre du camp, festins et joustes'.
11. *L&P*, III, 702; *Rymer*, XIII, 710.
12. Hall, *Hall's Chronicle*, 606–8.
13. Ibid.
14. *Cal. Ven.*, III, 60.
15. Ibid.
16. Ibid., *L&P*, III, 869.
17. *L&P*, III, 1011.
18. Cotton MS Caligula D, VIII, 149. 'On my return I will talk with you how to bring about the marriage between his son and Sir Thomas Boleyn's daughter, which will be a good pretext for delaying to send his son over.'
19. 'It is generally believed that the violent manner in which the Cardinal governs England will produce great inconvenience in that country.' Charles himself was reported to have remarked: 'A butcher's dog has killed the finest Buck in England.' Thomas Boleyn's younger brother, Edward, was among seven men who later questioned two supporters of the Duke before sending them to trial. Cal.Span, II, 336.

20. Such a move caused considerable tension, and when Charles was asked about the state of his relationship with Francis, he quipped "My cousin Francis and I are in perfect accord: he wants Milan and so do I."

21. J. D. Mackie, *The Earlier Tudors* (Oxford: Clarendon Press, 1952), 310.

22. *L&P*, III, preface section 2.

23. *L&P*, III, 1458.

24. William Robertson, *The History of the Reign of the Emperor Charles V with a View of the Progress of Society: From the Subversion of the Roman Empire, to the Beginning of the Sixteenth Century* (New York: Harper Brothers, 1838), 151.

25. *L&P*, III, 1508.

26. Ibid.

27. Ibid., 1555.

28. For general discussion, see J. G. Russell, "The Search for Universal Peace: The Conferences at Calais and Bruges in 1521," *Bulletin of the Institute of Historical Research* XLIV (1971): 93. Boleyn and Docwra were entertained as special envoys, lodged separately from the normal English ambassador, and their pay was better.

29. *L&P*, III, 1694.

30. Ibid., 1705, 1706, 1715.

31. Ibid., 1724.

32. *L&P.*, III, ii, 2446.

33. Ibid. See the deposition of Perpoynte Devauntter in *L&P*, III, 2446.

34. As noted by J. J. Scarisbrick in *Henry VIII* (Berkeley and Los Angeles: University of California Press, 1968), 95.

35. *Cal. Span.*, II, 430. Also see Scarisbrick, *Henry VIII*, 95.

36. State Papers, Henry VIII, VI. 108.

37. Cotton MS, Vespasian C. II. 28.

38. Ibid., III, 2591.

39. Cotton MS, Vespasian C. II. 28.

40. Ibid., 36.

41. Ibid.

42. Ibid.

43. Western Manuscripts, BL, f. 217–34. 'The negotiations of Cardinal Wolsey: transcripts of correspondence, etc., mostly between Cardinal Wolsey and various ambassadors, with short introductory comments; 1522–1525.' Copy. Seventeenth century.

44. Harleian MS. 295. f. 133. Also see discussion in Garrett Mattingly, *Renaissance Diplomacy* (New York: Cosimo Classics, 2008), 150; Dean, 'Sir Thomas Boleyn: The Courtier Diplomat, 93.

45. *L&P*, III, 2878. 'Quod si mihi evenisset paulo benevolentior collega, multo facilius transegissem; cujus tamen mores ita fero constanter ut simultati locus alicui non pateat. Neque tam illibenter sentiret me affore ita rerum omnium inopem, ut nihil non egerem ope sua: neque res alia mihi obtingeret ingrate.'

46. *L&P*, IV, 960.

47. *Haus Hoff und Staat Archiv*, England, Berichte, Karton 3, f 2.

48. *L&P*, III, 3386.

49. State Papers, VI, 167.

50. *L&P*, IV, 1939.

51. See Josephine Wilkinson, *Mary Boleyn: The True Story of Henry VIII's Favourite Mistress* (Stroud: Amberley, 2009).

52. *L&P*, IV, 83. Note that it is first spelled as Boloyne, and then Boleyn, which is not significant as spellings of the name constantly varied.

53. L&P, III, 3256. 'The King will perceive by the letters of Fitzwilliam that from the contrarious weather he has not been able to keep his enterprise against Boulogne, and, as the victuals expire on the 28th, he wishes to know whether he shall lay up his ships at Portsmouth or not. Wolsey thinks the Vice-admiral has done as much as he could, and according to the King's pleasure, signified to him by Sir Edward Guyldford, has sent him word to despatch one ship of 400 tons, and another of 200, to join Sir Anthony Poynes westward, to intercept Albany.'

54. *L&P*, IV, 83.

55. *L&P*, IV, 5013.

56. *L&P*, IV. 'List of prizes taken by Captain Coo since leaving the Thames on 22 Jan to the present date of his discharge from the King's wages. A ship of 50 tons, laden with salt, taken in the Tradde, sold for 70l. 2 ships, laden with Danske rye, taken from the gallies of Dieppe and Homflete, 140l. The Mary of Homflete, 90 tons, with ordnance, delivered to Thos. Clere for the King's service. The Galley of Dieppe, 50 tons, 40 men, taken in the Narrow Seas. The Yennett Purwyn, taken in the North Parts, with 16 pieces of ordnance, delivered by the Admiral's commandment to the mayor of Hull. The Michael of Depe, the Mary of Boloyn, the Griffin of Depe, a ship of Rouen, laden with Newfoundland fish, fisher boats, crays, &c. Total 1213l. 16s. 8d.83.'

57. *L&P*, IV, 136.


CHAPTER SEVEN   THE BALANCE OF POWER

1. Thomas Martin, *The history of the town of Thetford, in the counties of Norfolk and Suffolk, from the earliest accounts to the present time* (London: J. Nichols & Son, 1779), Appendix VIII, 38–41.

2. Ibid.

3. Marie Axton, James P. Carley, David Starkey, *et al.*, *Triumphs of English: Henry Parker, Lord Morley, Translator to the Tudor Court* (London: British Library, 2000), 165.

4. Retha Warnicke provides an interesting insight into the Parkers' relationship with Katherine of Aragon. See Retha Warnicke ' The Fall of Anne Boleyn: A Reassessment' *Historical Journal*, 70, (1985): 1–15.

5. *L&P*, VI, 1213.

6. See Steven Gunn, *The English People at War in the Age of Henry VIII* (Oxford: Oxford University Press, 2018), 6.

7. Kenneth Pickthorn, *Early Tudor Government* (Cambridge: Cambridge University Press, 2015), 67.

8. *L&P*, IV, 1234. 'I have received your gracious token by the hands of Sir Thos. Boleyn, treasurer of your household, who tells me that you will come here if it be to the advancement of your affairs. Nothing would be better for the speedy execution of your causes than your presence, where I could from time to time consult you. Wherefore, if it shall please your Grace to take the pain to come to this my poor house, the same shall not only be to the setting forth of your said causes, but also to

my singular rejoicing, consolation, and comfort. And as welcome shall your Grace be as heart can think.'

9. *L&P*, IV, 1319. As noted in Dean, Sir Thomas Boleyn: The Courtier Diplomat, 98.

10. Ibid., IV, 1243, 1260, 1266, 1318.

11. Edward Hall, *Hall's Chronicle: Containing the History of England, During the Reign of Henry the Fourth, and the Succeeding Monarchs, to the End of the Reign of Henry the Eighth, in Which are Particularly Described the Manners and Customs of Those Periods* (London: J. Johnson, 1809), 699.

12. Ibid., 699. The Duke of Norfolk, who was in charge of collections in his own county, reported that that the citizens there offered undervalued plate. As well as an intrinsic value, plate often had a cultural significance for the middle and upper classes – often used as gifts, personalized, or engraved in some way as a remembrance or for some other purpose. He suggested that the plate could be melted down to make substandard coin to be fobbed-off in France.

13. See *L&P, IV*, Appendix 9. The account is from 1525, and offer details of his household expenses for November and December of that year. It would appear that a certain "Sir Harry" was in charge keeping abreast of expenses, but he also wrote several entries himself.

14. *L&P*, IV, 1550.

15. Ibid.

16. *L&P*, IV, 1431.

17. Ibid.

18. Ibid.

19. *Cal. Span.*, III, i, 111.

20. Ibid.

21. Ibid.

22. Ibid.

23. Ibid.

24. *L&P*, IV, 1628.

25. Ibid.

26. *L&P*, IV, 1633.

27. Ibid.

28. The original from Vienna can be found on plate 16.

29. See Peter Gwyn, *The King's Cardinal: The Rise and Fall of Thomas Wolsey* (New York: Random House, 2011), 365–7.

30. Ibid.

31. Ibid.

32. David Starkey, *Six Wives: The Queens of Henry VIII* (London: Random House, 2004), 319.

33. Gwyn, *The King's Cardinal*, 368–70.

34. *L&P*, IV, 1939.

35. Ibid.

36. Ibid., IV, 3105.

37. Ibid.

38. Ibid.

39. Ibid., IV, 3124.

40. In fact the only reference we have to Lisle is in a commission to France in October: 'to Arthur Plantaginet, viscount Lysle, John Taylour, LL.D., archdeacon of Buckingham, vice-chancellor, Sir Nic. Carewe, master of the stable, Sir Ant. Browne, and Sir Thos. Wriothesley, Garter king-at-arms, to signify to Francis I. his election into the Order of the Garter, to place the collar on his neck, to present him with the mantle, garter, and statutes, and to take his oath according to the said statutes. If he does not wish to take the oath, his simple word will be sufficient.' *L&P*, IV, 3508.

41. *L&P*, IV, 3185, 3194.

42. Ibid., IV 3171.

43. Cotton MS, Caligula, D. X. 47. 'We suppy[d] … and passed three or four hours in dancing [until] midnight and past, at which time the da[ncing was] finished. My lord of Rocheford took his leave [of the] King and of my Lady, and so we departed f[or that] night to our lodging.'

44. Ibid.

45. Ibid.

CHAPTER EIGHT   DECLARE, I DARE NOT

1. Edward Hall, *Hall's Chronicle: Containing the History of England, During the Reign of Henry the Fourth, and the Succeeding Monarchs, to the End of the Reign of Henry the Eighth, in Which are Particularly Described the Manners and Customs of Those Periods* (London: J. Johnson, 1809), 630–1.

2. Ibid.

3. Ibid., 707–8.

4. *Cal. Ven.*, IV, 366.

5. David M. Loades, *The Boleyns: The Rise and Fall of a Tudor Family* (Stroud: Amberley, 2011), 267.

6. *L&P*, IV, Introduction.

7. Loades, *The Boleyns: The Rise and Fall of a Tudor Family*, 87.

8. See James Tracy, *Emperor Charles V, Impresario of War: Campaign Strategy, International Finance, and Domestic Politics* (Cambridge: Cambridge University Press, 2002), 48; Luigi Guicciardini, *The Sack of Rome*, trans. and ed. James H. McGregor (New York: Italica Press, 1993), 10–14.

9. *Cal. Span.*, III, ii. 113.

10. State Papers, I, 278.

11. George Cavendish, *The Life and Death of Cardinal Wolsey* (New Haven: Yale University Press, 1962), 29–34. Cavendish claimed that Henry already had a personal interest in Anne at this point, forcing Wolsey to part the couple, but this is highly debatable.

12. Cavendish, *The Life and Death of Cardinal Wolsey*, 34.

13. As noted in Ives, *The Life and Death of Anne Boleyn*, 65.

14. For example, see Samman, 'The Henrician Court During Cardinal Wolsey's Ascendancy, 180; Steve Gunn, 'Wolsey's foreign policy and the domestic crisis of 1527–1528,' eds. Steve Gunn and P. Lindley, *Cardinal Wolsey: Church, State and Art* (Cambridge: Cambridge University Press, 1991), 149–77; Eric Ives, 'The Fall of Wolsey,' in Gunn and Lindley, eds., *Cardinal Wolsey*, 286–315.

15. HHStA, *England Berichte*, Karton 4, fol 224, No. 18. Also in *Cal. Span.*, III, ii, 69.

16. Ibid.

17. See Dean, 'Sir Thomas Boleyn: The Courtier Diplomat, 111. Eric Ives, *Faction in Tudor England* (London: Historical Association, 1979); Robert Shephard, 'Review: Court Factions in Early Modern England,' *Journal of Modern History* 64 (1992): 721–45; David Starkey, 'Intimacy and Innovation: The Rise of the Privy Chamber, 1485–1547.' In *The English Court from the Wars of the Roses to the Civil War* (London: Longman, 1987), 108.

18. *L&P*, IV, 3360.

19. *Cal. Span.*, III, ii, 224.

20. *L&P*, IV, 4106.

21. Ibid., 3937.

22. Ibid. Curiously, Thomas' mother, Margaret, did not sign her full name, only marking M.B. It is said that Margaret later suffered from dementia, and certainly Thomas' care for her down in Hever suggests that she required care. As she was certainly literate, judging from her earlier letters to her son, this use of initials may well point to a mental decline.

23. *L&P*, IV, 3950.

24. J. A. Froude, *History of England from the Fall of Wolsey to the Death of Elizabeth*, Vol. 3 (London: Longman, Green, and Co, 1866), 521, 525.

25. Exactly when Cromwell joined Wolsey's services is the subject of much dispute. See M. Everett, 'Qualities of a Royal Minister: Studies in the Rise of Thomas Cromwell, c. 1520–1534' (PhD thesis, University of Southampton, 2012), 43.

26. Cromwell wrote to Thomas that he was to 'be of co unsayll' to his sister in a dispute with Elizabeth Fyneux, wife of the deceased Sir John Fyneux, a former chief justice of King's Bench. Cromwell gave his opinion of the matter, advising that Thomas' sister was 'vtterlye without Remedye by course of the common lawe.' Interestingly, he advised Thomas to speak to Wolsey and convince him to 'to graunt a wryt of Injunctyon,' directed to Elizabeth Fyneux, the respondant, commanding her to prevent the execution of her writs, and to ensure that no 'wryttes of liberata goo out of the sayd courte vntyll Chauncerye [vntyll] suche time [as] the hole matyer tochyng the premysses may dulye and accordyng to conscyence be harde and examyned.' *L&P* IV, 3741.

27. Ibid., IV, 4188.

28. Ibid., 4189, 4190.

29. Ibid., 4167.

30. Ibid.

31. Wolsey owned numerous fisheries at Norham, hence the extravagant seafood orders.

32. David Knowles, 'The Matter of Wilton,' *Bulletin of the Institute of Historical Research* 31 (1958): 92–6.

33. *L&P*, IV, 448.

34. As Dr Bell, Wolsey's commissioner, wrote to Anne: 'I would not for all the world clog your conscience nor mine to make her ruler of a house which is of so ungodly demeanour; nor, I trust, you would not that, neither for brother (Carey) nor sister, I should so distain mine honour or conscience. And, as touching the prioress (Isabella Jordan), or dame Elinor's eldest sister, though there is not any evident case proved against them, and that the Prioress is so old, that of many years she could not

be as she was named; yet, notwithstanding, to do you pleasure, I have done that neither of them shall have it; but ... some other good and well disposed woman.' *L&P*, IV, Section 8.

35. See Samman, 'The Henrician Court,' 271; Starkey *Six Wives: The Queens of Henry VIII*, 334–5; *L&P*, IV, Introduction, ccclxxxvi.

36. Starkey, *Six Wives*, 334–5; Friedmann, *Anne Boleyn*.

37. Samman, 'The Henrician Court,' 270.

38. Cotton MS Vespasian f. 13.

39. As Brewer notes: 'Never before had Wolsey stood so high in the favour of his master. He had triumphed over every obstacle. He had propitiated the Pope, and won over his consent to the divorce.' *L&P*, IV, Introduction.

40. Thomas Osborne, ed. *The Harleian Miscellany, Or, A Collection of Scarce, Curious, and Entertaining Pamphlets and Tracts, as Well in Manuscript as in Print, Found in the Late Earl of Oxford's Library: Interspersed with Historical, Political, and Critical Notes: With a Table of the Contents, and an Alphabetical Index*, Vol. III letter XI, 56.

41. Brewer notes that although translations often use the word 'deceive' the original says 'dyslave'. *L&P*, IV, 4410.

42. *L&P*, IV, 4993. The post came into effect in February 1529, see *L&P*, IV, 5248.

43. *Cal. Span.* III, ii, 621.

44. *L&P*, IV, 5774. Wolsey wrote frequently to Rome on Henry's behalf, and many of his letters can be found in the Biblioteca Apostolica Vaticana.

45. *Ambassador du Bellay*, 118, *L&P*, IV, 5210.

46. Giles Tremlett, *Catherine of Aragon: Henry's Spanish Queen* (London: Faber and Faber, 2010), 309.

47. *L&P*, IV, 5774.

48. Cavendish, *The Life and Death of Cardinal Wolsey*, 118.

50. Ibid.

51. State Papers, I. 55, 25–6. Gardiner wrote to Wolsey after visiting Boleyn, 'I have spoken with my Lord of Rocheforde and shewed unto him howe your Grace offerith to wryte your letters to such as wer your offcers in Durham, to cause them to make payment here, with al diligence, of the haulf yeres rent due at Our Ladyes Day last past; for the which he most hertely thankith your Grace and sayth he shal requite it with like kindness.'

## CHAPTER NINE   TREASONOUS WATERS

1. Robert Knecht, *The Valois: Kings of France 1328–1589* (London: Bloomsbury, 2007), 142–3.

2. Cotton MS, Caligula, D. XI. 15.

3. *L&P*, IV, 5877.

4. See Edward Hall, *Hall's Chronicle: Containing the History of England, During the Reign of Henry the Fourth, and the Succeeding Monarchs, to the End of the Reign of Henry the Eighth, in Which are Particularly Described the Manners and Customs of Those Periods* (London: J. Johnson, 1809), 758–9.

5. Ibid.

6. Ibid.

7. State Papers, I. 342.

8. Ibid.

9. Ives, *The Life and Death of Anne Boleyn*, 122.

10. Ibid.

11. *L&P*, IV, 5918.

12. John Foxe, *The Acts and Monuments of John Foxe*, ed. George Townsend (London: R.B. Seeley and W. Burnside, 1841), 541.

13. I understand, though I do not know for certain, that they are consulting the theologians of the University of Paris about the case. *L&P*, IV, 5636.

14. *L&P*, IV, 5862.

15. John Strype (ed.), *Memorials of Thomas Cranmer. 2 Vols.* (Oxford: Clarendon Press, 1840), 4.

16. Du Bellay reported that 'On the return of Suffolk, Wolsey complained to the King that the Duke had put him out of favor with Francis by some of his conversations. On which the King asked Suffolk if it was true. The Duke said he had not spoken of it. Wolsey further said it was I that had informed him. So that, whenever the Duke could meet me, after long protests, and after confessing that he had had some conversation with Francis about Wolsey, but he had made sure that if Francis had sent word of it I would not have repeated it, he pressed me so hard for an answer that I knew not what to say, except that I had never spoken of it, – which, in truth, I never did.' *L&P*, IV, 5862.

17. George Cavendish, *The Life and Death of Cardinal Wolsey* (New Haven: Yale University Press, 1962), 238.

18. Du Bellay, *Correspondance*, 105.

19. Cal. Span., IV, i, 6073.

20. Chapuys does make mention of being introduced to a gentleman named Poller, or something to that effect, which some historians have assumed was George Boleyn, but Chapuys had already written about George, calling him Boulan, and when they first met, in early 1530, Chapuys refers to him Rochford, Boleyn's son, it is unlikely this was George.

21. *L&P*, IV, 6147. 'The unlearned Spaniard, Dr. Petre Garray, who has circulated a bill, drawn up by Beda, notwithstanding the admonition of the Great Master, against our opinion, and circumvented some of the Doctors. They have, however, recanted, and we are sure of the congregation of the faculty ... We would rather have their help now than when they have their desires, for by this means our enemies have undermined many, but if my Lord speed our desires we shall be able to bring them round, and even if the King (Francis) deny our requests, we trust to prevent further signatures against our opinions.'

22. Ibid., 6253. Henry VIII to Boleyn: '[Unclear]...has shown us your letters to himself, in which you appear particularly desirous that we should write to the dean and heads of the faculty of theology at Paris. We send you accordingly our letter to them, with a copy, so that if you and our kinsman think it will promote our cause, you may deliver them; but you must take the greatest care to be sure of the good will of the majority beforehand, lest you give an advantage to our enemies.'

23. H. F. M. Prescott, *Mary Tudor* (London: Hatchette, 2012), ii.

24. Cal. Span., IV, 132.

25. Cal. Span., IV, 160.

26. Ibid.
27. Peter Gwyn, *The King's Cardinal: The Rise and Fall of Thomas Wolsey* (New York: Random House, 2011), 594.
28. *HHStA England Berichte*, Karton 4, c. 226, 23.
29. Ibid.
30. *L&P*, IV, 6114. 'Yf the desspleasure of my lady Anne be [some]what asswagyd, as I pray God the same may be, then yt shuld [be devised t]hat by sume convenyent meane she be further laboryd, [for th]ys ys the only helpe and remedy. All possyble means [must be used for] atteynyng of hyr favor.'
31. Stanford E. Lehmberg, *The Reformation Parliament: 1529–1536* (Cambridge: University Press, 1970), 3. Relatively little is known about parliamentary procedure during the early Tudor period because there were so few records kept: there was no journal of proceedings, and only a handful of letters directly concerning the Parliament survive, making it is difficult to draw any conclusions of the Boleyn's actions or involvement in Parliamentary discussions or debates.
32. Ibid., 75.
33. Hall, *Hall's Chronicle*, clxxxiii.
34. Lord Herbert of Cherbury, *The Life and Reigne of Henry the Eighth* (London: E.G, 1649), 266–71. 7. *L&P*, IV, 6075.
35. Hall, *Hall's Chronicle*, 767–8.
36. G. W. Bernard, 'The Fall of Wolsey Reconsidered.' *The Journal of British Studies* 35, no. 3 (1996): 277–310, 96.
37. Du Bellay, *Correspondance*, 112. 'Le duc de Norfoch est faict chief de ce Conseil et en son absence celluy de Suffoch, et par dessuz tout mademoiselle Anne.'
38. Cavendish, *Life and Death of Cardinal Wolsey*, 288.
39. *Cal. Span.*, IV, I, 232.
40. See *L&P*, IV, 6324.
41. Ibid., 5983. Du Bellay writes: '[Boleyn] allowed everything to be said, and then came and suggested the complete opposite, defending his position without budging, as though he wanted to show to me that he was not pleased that anyone should have failed to pay court to the Lady [Anne], and also to make me accept that what it pleased the lady to allow them, and that is gospel truth. And because of this he wanted with words and deeds to beat down their opinions before my eyes.' Remy Scheurer, *Correspondance du cardinal Jean du Bellay* Volume 1; Volumes 1529–1535 I, 41.
42. Remy Scheurer, *Correspondance du cardinal Jean du Bellay* Volume 1; Volumes 1529–1535 I, 41.
43. *L&P*, IV, 6085.
44. *HHStA, England Bericht*, Karton 4, Fasc. 227, 50.
45. His maternal grandfather was the seventh earl of Ormond and his great uncle had been Earl of Wiltshire prior to achieving the Ormond peerage.
46. For general discussion of its medieval function, see Thomas Frederick Tout, *Chapters in the Administrative History of Mediaeval England*, 1 (Manchester: Manchester University Press, 1937), 282–313.
47. While the origins and functions of the Privy Council and of the royal seals have received scholarly attention, research remains to be undertaken of the office of Lord Privy Seal. The office is one of the traditional sinecure offices of state, and the calibre

of those appointed suggest that it was a role of distinction. It would be most enlightening for a study comparing the effectiveness of incumbents from Henry VII's reign through to Elizabeth I (that is from Fox's position in 1487–1516, through to Boleyn 1530–36, Cromwell 1536–40, William Fitzwilliam 1540–42, John Russell 1542–55, William Paget 1555–58, Nicholas Bacon 1558–71 and finally William Cecil 1571–72) to name the most significant of the early modern period, which would indicate how the position evolved, the extent of its power, and whether the incumbent limited or increased its importance. Many of the incumbents were functioning bishops: Cuthbert Tunstall, Bishop of London, held the position from 1523 to 1530, one of the longer tenures under Henry, about which historians are silent for its lack of innovation. When Wolsey was stripped of his government offices and property in 1529, Tunstall succeeded him as Bishop of Durham, vacating the position of Lord Privy Seal, when Thomas Boleyn was appointed in 1530.

48. The Star Chamber comprised seven privy councillors, the Chancellor, the Treasurer, the Keeper of the King's Privy Seal, a bishop, a temporal lord and two common law judges. It used the Council's powers, but remained a distinct Court and could separately receive petitions involving property rights, public corruption, trade and government administration, disputes arising from land enclosures, and cases of public disorder. See A. F. Pollard, 'Council, Star Chamber, and Privy Council under the Tudors: 1. The Council' and 'Council, Star Chamber, and Privy Council under the Tudors: 2. The Star Chamber,' in *English Historical Review* 17 (1922): 337–60, 516–39, respectively.

49. Many historians consider Thomas' tenure as Lord Privy Seal unremarkable, conservative and predictable, noting only his dates of service, before they move on to discuss Thomas Cromwell's high distinction in the position immediately following Thomas' resignation. However, during his term, the role extended to the oversight of a wide range of matters – from legal disputes, summonses to appear before the council, orders to the chancellor to issue letters under the great seal, and directions to the exchequer to make money payments. He was there to preserve the status quo, and made no attempt to change the nature of the position – unlike his successor, Cromwell, who dismantled it. It could have been an opportunity to wield power – in 1536 when he became Lord Privy Seal, Cromwell had an unprecedented overarching view of the entire governmental system from which he could use the confluence of these roles to run the entire bureaucracy of the country, along with which came concentration of power in the hands of a single minister of the king, rather than several.

50. Geoffrey Elton, 'Presidential Address: Tudor Government: The Points of Contact. III. The Court,' *Transactions of the Royal Historical Society* 26 (1976): 211–28.
   During Boleyn's six-year term, the role extended to the oversight of a wide range of matters – from legal disputes, summonses to appear before the council, orders to the chancellor to issue letters under the great seal, and directions to the exchequer to make money payments.

51. *Cal. Span.*, IV, 224.

52. Ibid., 241.

53. Ibid., 257.

54. Ibid.

55. Ibid.

CHAPTER TEN   THE BOLEYN ENTERPRISE

1. Starkey, *Six Wives*, 400. Charles was crowned on 24 February in the church of San Petronio.

2. William Robertson, *The History of the Reign of the Emperor Charles V with a View of the Progress of Society: From the Subversion of the Roman Empire, to the Beginning of the Sixteenth Century* (New York: Harper Brothers, 1838), 117.

3. *L&P*, IV, 1939.

4. The mission might have been futile but it was well funded – Henry provided the group with £1,743, almost £800,000 by today's currency as well as 80 horses and 20 mules.

5. *L&P*, IV, 6253. Henry VIII to Boleyn: '[Unclear]…has shown us your letters to himself, in which you appear particularly desirous that we should write to the dean and heads of the faculty of theology at Paris. We send you accordingly our letter to them, with a copy, so that if you and our kinsman think it will promote our cause, you may deliver them; but you must take the greatest care to be sure of the good will of the majority beforehand, lest you give an advantage to our enemies.'

6. *HHStA, England Bericht*, Karton 4, fol. 126; *Span. Cal*, IV, i. 250.

7. Ibid.

8. *HHStA, England Bericht* Karton 4, England, c. 226, 6. 'Besides which, it is rumoured in certain quarters – and the rumour has been adroitly circulated – that this embassy is not so much sent for the purpose of this marriage as for the conclusion of perpetual peace with Your Majesty.'

9. Ibid., c. 226, 3.

10. *HHStA, England Bericht*, Karton 4, England, c. 226, 6.

11. Ibid. The meeting had no effect on Chapuys' policy, but his letter to Charles, urging him to assemble as many learned men as possible to combat Boleyn's arguments, as Henry was sending some of the ablest men to argue Henry's case, gives some indication of how Chapuys saw Boleyn.

12. *L&P*, 6254.

13. Ibid.

14. 'Then the Duke went on to say that he was now going to speak to me rather as a friend and brother than as a foreigner and ambassador. "You are aware (he said), that my brother-in-law, the Sr. de Vulchier (Wiltshire) is not of a warlike disposition; on the contrary, he is very timid, and if, on his arrival in Italy, he should find any danger abroad, or even suspicion of it, I believe him capable of not venturing to proceed on his journey." The Duke, therefore, begged me to write to Your Majesty, that some precautions should be taken for his security.' *Cal. Span.*, IV, I, 255.

15. *Cal. Span.*, IV, I, 255.

16. Ibid.

17. J. J. Scarisbrick, *Henry VIII* (Berkeley and Los Angeles: University of California Press, 1968), 255.

18. *Cal. Span.*, IV, i, 252, 432. As evidenced by du Bellay's letter to Francis: 'The king of England is very anxious that your Majesty would get the faculty of Paris to give its opinion in writing in favor of his Majesty's cause. You could not do him a greater pleasure, or bind him to you more effectually. We hear he is sending the said opinions, along with others, to the earl of Wiltshire (Boleyn) to show to the Pope, so

as to incline him to the King's will in good time; if, at least, your Majesty, conceiving the cause to be a just one, will take such expedients as shall seem good to you and your Council. For this reason he wishes justifications and final proofs sent by the Pope and Emperor. Moreover, the present earl of Wiltshire, as a person greatly in the King's confidence, interested though he be, and, some say, in order to obtain from the Pope what is desired, had a commission to make great expense, and promise assistance...with a good sum of money. But this I hear from others, not from "S. P.," who thanks your Majesty much for your reception of the said Earl. I can learn no other cause for the Earl's mission, unless there be some promise for the restitution of the Queen's dower to the Emperor, with security for the Queen's good treatment.'

19. *Cal. Span.*, IV, 265.
20. *L&P*, IV, 6539.
21. Ibid.
22. *Cal. Milan*, I, 813.
23. Ibid.
24. *L&P*, IV, 6324.
25. Ibid., IV, 6290, 6293.
26. Ibid.
27. Ibid.
28. Ibid., 6285.
29. John Foxe, *The Acts and Monuments of John Foxe*, ed. George Townsend (London: R.B. Seeley and W. Burnside, 1841), 9.
30. Ibid.
31. *Cal. Span.*, III, 434.
32. *L&P*, 6293.
33. Ibid., 6293.
34. Ibid.
35. *Cal. Milan.*, I, 815, 816.
36. Ibid., 838.
37. *L&P*, IV, 6355.
38. *L&P*, IV, 6307.
39. Starkey, *Six Wives*, 405.
40. Ibid.
41. *L&P*, IV, 6393.
42. Ibid.
43. *L&P*, IV, 6304.
44. Ibid., 6397.
45. Ibid., 6563.
46. *Cal. Span.*, IV, I, 790.
47. Ibid. 'Just as I was leaving the room the earl of Wiltshire arrived, at which the Duke said he was glad, as I had not seen the Earl since his return from Italy. The Earl having enquired after Your Majesty's health and most courteously offered his services, began slandering the Pope and cardinals so violently that full of horror at what was being said I took leave and left the room immediately.'
48. Ibid.
49. Ibid., 799.
50. *Cal. Span*, IV, II, 915.

51. *HHStA, England Bericht*, Karton 5, 17.
52. George Cavendish, *The Life and Death of Cardinal Wolsey* (New Haven: Yale University Press, 1962), 20–1.
53. Ibid.
54. *Cal. Span*, IV, i, 270.
55. *L&P*, IV, 6579.
56. George Godfrey Cunningham, *Lives of Eminent and Illustrations Englishmen from Alfred the Great to the Latest Times*, Vol. 2 (Glasgow: A. Fullarton & Co, 1837), 8.
57. *Cal. Span.*, IV, ii, 615.
58. Ibid.
59. Seymour Baker House, 'Literature, Drama, and Politics', in *The Reign of Henry VIII: Politics, Policy, and Piety*, ed. Diarmaid MacCulloch (New York: St. Martin's Press, 1995), 183.
60. Greg Walker, *Plays of Persuasion: Drama and Politics at the Court of Henry VIII* (Cambridge: Cambridge University Press, 1991), 20.
61. Edward Hall, *Hall's Chronicle: Containing the History of England, During the Reign of Henry the Fourth, and the Succeeding Monarchs, to the End of the Reign of Henry the Eighth, in Which are Particularly Described the Manners and Customs of Those Periods* (London: J. Johnson, 1809), 764.
62. *Cal. Ven*, IV, 693.
63. *Cal. Span*, IV, 584: 'In two former letters I mentioned the impossibility of doing anything in the matter enjoined me by your Excellency's Lord Lieutenant, by reason of the absence from this Court of the Earl of Wiltshire [Thomas]; the King's Almoner [Edward Lee] being of opinion that this business should not be attempted through any other channel than that of the Earl.'
64. *Sforza Archives*, Milan, 642.
65. Greg Walker, 'Persuasive Fictions: Faction, Faith and Political Culture in the Reign of Henry VIII,' *Sixteenth Century Journal* 29 (1998): 20.

CHAPTER ELEVEN   AINSI SERA, GROIGNE QUI GROIGNE

1. *L&P*, V, 27.
2. See Lehmberg, Appendix B, which lists Thomas as being in attendance for 42 out of 45 days. George Boleyn was in attendance for 41, and Norfolk for 38. The attendance list is found in the House of Lords Record Office, Lord's Journal.
3. Stanford E. Lehmberg, *The Reformation Parliament: 1529–1536* (Cambridge: University Press, 1970).
4. Gerald Lewis Bray (ed.), *Documents of the English Reformation 1526–1701* (Cambridge: James Clarke & Co, 1994), 115.
5. Original is in the National Archives: Records assembled by the State Paper Office, including papers of the Secretaries of State up to 1782, SP 6, Theological Tracts Henry VIII, Folio 94 'Rochford MS,' *A treatise delivered to the Convocation of the Clergy on 10 February 1531, by George Boleyn, Lord Rochford. Previously described as 'treatise upon whether certain texts pertain especially to spiritual prelates or to temporal princes, viz John, XX, 'Sicut misit me pater, ita et ego mitto vos'; and Acts, XX, 'Attendite vobis et cuncto gregi in quo vos Spiritus Sanctus posuit episcopas etc.' In defence of the royal supremacy.'*

6. The Boleyns formed a powerful political circle in Parliament – including Thomas Cranmer, Thomas Cromwell, Thomas Boleyn, his nephew James and his son George Boleyn, whose attendance, Stamford Lehmberg believes, helped to 'popularize the Boleyn cause with younger generations,' Lehmberg, *Reformation Parliament*, 30.

7. Richard Hall, *The Life and Death of the Renowned John Fisher, Bishop of Rochester: Who was Beheaded on Tower-Hill, the 22d of June, 1535*, ed. Thomas Bayly (Princeton: Princeton University Press, 1739), 79.

8. See John Guy, *Henry VIII: The Quest for Fame* (London: Allen Lane, 2014), 498–99.

9. *Cal. Span*, IV, ii, 641. 'The bishop of Rochester [Fisher] is quite ill in consequence. He has made, and is still making, as much opposition as he can to the measure; but as he and his followers have been threatened with death, by being cast into the Thames.' It is not clear who, if anyone, actually threatened to throw Fisher into the Thames.

10. *Cal. Span*, IV, ii, 646.

11. Ibid.

12. Hall, *The Life and Death of the Renowned John Fisher*, 109.

13. Nicholas Sanders, trans J. Christie, *The Rise and Progress of the English Reformation* (Dublin: J Christie, 1827), 83. 'This yere was a coke boylyd in a cauderne in Smythfeld for he wolde a powsyned the bishop of Rochester Fycher with dyvers of hys servanttes, and he was lockyd in a chayne and pullyd up and downe with a gybbyt at dyvers tymes tyll he was dede.'

14. K. J. Kesselring, 'A Draft of the 1531 "Acte for Poysoning"', *The English Historical Review* Vol. 116, No. 468 (September 2001), 894–9.

15. Hall, *The Life and Death of the Renowned John Fisher*, 109–11.

16. Ibid.

17. *HHStA*, England, Karton 5, c227, 5.

18. Ibid.

19. *HHStA*, England, Berichte Karton 5, 227.

20. Ibid.

21. Ibid.

22. Giles Tremlett, *Catherine of Aragon: Henry's Spanish Queen* (London: Faber & Faber, 2010), 348–9.

23. *Cal. Span.*, IV, ii, 765.

24. Ibid.

25. *L&P*, V, 1207.

26. *L&P*, V, 375.

27. Ibid.

28. *L&P*, V, 686. Shirts and material for shirts and collars seemed to be one of the most popular gifts from the wives of court –perhaps there was a concerted effort to ensure Henry would not have to go back to his wife to have any more shirts made.

29. Samman, 'The Henrician Court, 321–2.

30. *L&P*, V, 688. Piers wrote to Boleyn: 'Your grandfather, by his deed gave me and my heirs the manors of Tullagh and Arcloo; whereupon I recovered them out of the possession of Irishmen. Yet Kildare boasts he has obtained of you a lease of the said manors, with the Karig; whereof I marvel. He covets them for no love of your Lordship, but only to confound me. The late insurrection was made by his kinsmen, and all the Pale would have been destroyed if I had not come to the rescue in the

dead winter at my own cost, and incurring debt, of which I shall not be free this seven years . . . I give you yearly 10l. sterling to have your good will and to further my causes. I pray you suffer me to have the benefit of the said deed; and, if you cannnot be content that I shall have the Carryk for a reasonable rent, that you would set thereon one of your servants or some indifferent person. I pray you to assign no default in me for not paying your rent for Michaelmas term last. "It chanced me then to be in Dublin at the Parliament, where I continued seven weeks, spending much more than my ordinary revenues and rents would maintain; natheless, at my returning home, I prepared your payment, and there was no passage with whom I might have conveyed your money to you, unto now that this bearer departed, by whom I have sent your payment.'

31. Bernard, *The King's Reformation*, 512.
32. *Cal. Span.*, V, 1013.
33. *Cal. Span.*, V, 1165.
34. See Ives' discussion of Anne's collection of French manuscripts, including her French bible, translated by Jacques Lefevre d'Etaples, 270. His arguments regarding Anne's collection of French reformist works as a definitive sign of her intellectual and religious preferences are applicable here in terms of Thomas' Erasmian interests. Ives, *The Life and Death of Anne Boleyn*.
35. See Barry Collett, *A long and troubled pilgrimage: the correspondence of Marguerite d'Angoulême and Vittoria Colonna, 1540–1545* (Princeton: Princeton Theological Seminary, 2000) 11; J. K. McConica, *English Humanists and Reformation Politics under Henry VIII and Edward VI* (Oxford: Clarendon Press, 1952).
36. For further discussion, see Alois Gerlo (trans.), *La Correspondance D'Erasme, VIII* (Brussels: University Press, 1979), L. 2266.
37. Desiderius Erasmus, Epistle 2322, trans. Alexander Dalzell, cited in *The Correspondence of Erasmus: Letters 2204–2356 (August 1529–July 1530)* (Toronto: University of Toronto Press, 2015), 86.
38. Ibid.
39. Ed Bailey, *The Colloquies of Erasmus* (London: Reeves and Turner, 1878).
40. Cited in J. Austin Gavin and Thomas M. Walsh, 'The Praise of Folly in Context: The Commentary of Girardus Listrius', *Renaissance Quarterly* 24 (1971): 198. Before we presume that this Lutheran influence is what Friesland is alluding to, we must go further back. Listrius had met Erasmus years before, and is most famous for his defence of Erasmus' *The Praise of Folly*, a work for which Erasmus was widely criticised; Listrius' commentary is almost as an apologist. The most provocative passages of the *Folly* revolved around matters of liturgy – the public worship and the morals of the clergy, and thus viewed by some as almost heretical; Erasmus was highly critical of indulgences, ridiculing those 'fools who seek to buy salvation by indulgences. But this one thing I know, that what Christ promised in the gospel concerning the remission of sins is more certain than what men promise, especially since this whole affair is recent and but lately discovered. Lastly, many men, trusting in these pardons, take false comfort and give no thought to reforming their lives.'
41. In Peter G. Bietenholz's *Contemporaries of Erasmus: a biographical register, of the Renaissance* and Maria Dowling's work on the English Reformation, both scholars are sceptical about Boleyn's actions and argue that Erasmus could not explain why Boleyn had approached him. Maria Dowling, *Humanism in the Age of Henry VIII*

(London: Croom Helm, 1986), 221–4. G. Peter Bietenholz and Thomas Brian Deutscher, *Contemporaries of Erasmus: A Biographical Register of the Renaissance and Reformation* (Toronto: University of Toronto Press, 2003), 87–90.

42. Emily Kearns, *A Threefold Exposition of Psalm 22, In psalmum 22 enarratio triplex, in Exposition of Psalms* (Toronto: University of Toronto Press, 2005), 120.

43. See Plate 10.

44. Kearns, *Expositions of the Psalms*, 120.

45. H. H. Milman, 'Life of Erasmus' in *The Quarterly Review* 106 (London: John Murray, 1859), 42.

46. Ibid.

47. Desiderius Erasmus, *The Correspondence of Erasmus: Letters 2204–2356 (August 1529– July 1530)* trans. Alexander Dalzell (Toronto: University of Toronto Press, 2015), 2266. Erasmus gave three systematic interpretations of the psalm for Thomas, beyond what he would usually write, as nowhere else does he do this.

48. The work was titled *Ennaratio triplrex in Psalmum XXII*, has the dedication: 'Clariffimo Angliae Baroni, D. Thomae Rochefordo', *Opus Epistolarum Des. Erasmi Roterodami, denuo recognitum et auctum*. Vol. IX, eds. Percy Stafford Allen, Helen Mary Allen and William Garrod Heathcote (Oxford: Clarendon Press, 1906), 350. See also Letters (Epistles) 2512, 2576 and 2266. Erasmus also claimed satisfaction at having admirers in both Katherine of Aragon's and the Boleyns' camp.

## CHAPTER TWELVE   NOWE THUS

1. *L&P*, V, 1592.

2. *L&P*, I, 3774.

3. Ibid. Boleyn was elected Sherriff in 1517, though in some modern accounts, he is erroneously listed as Mayor. *L&P*, IV, 3783. For a full list of Boleyn's appointments as Commissioner of the Peace, see Appendix.

4. *Cal. Span.*, IV, ii, 1003.

5. Ibid., IV, ii, 802.

6. Ibid.

7. Ibid.

8. Ibid.

9. *L&P*, V, 1274.

10. See Ives for a detailed account of the meeting. Ives, *The Life and Death of Anne Boleyn*, 158–60.

11. *Cal. Span.*, IV, ii, 1023.

12. *The Chronicle of Calais, in the Reigns of Henry VII. and Henry VIII. To the Year 1540. Ed. from Mss. in the British Museum.* Edited by John Gough Nichols (London: J. B. Nichols and Son, 1846), 41–2.

13. Hall's Chronicle, 793–4.

14. *L&P*, V, 1474.

15. *L&P*, IV, ii, 1541.

16. Ibid.

17. Nicholas Harpsfield, *Treatise on the Pretended Divorce between Henry VIII and Catharine of Aragon*, ed. Nicholas Pocock (London: Camden Society 1878), 234–5.

18. *HHSTA* England Berichte, *c.* 228, No. 13. *Cal. Span.*, IV, ii, 1048.
19. Ibid.
20. Ibid.
21. Ibid.
22. *Cal. Span.*, IV, ii, 1047.
23. *Cal. Span.*, IV, ii, 1051.
24. *Cal. Span.*, IV, ii, 1047.
25. Ibid.
26. Ibid.
27. *L&P*, VI, 1481.
28. *Cal. Span.*, IV, ii, 1056.
29. *L&P*, VI, 230.
30. Ibid.
31. A letter from Francis makes clear his position: The King will therefore be glad if Francis will despatch an agent to the Pope to intimate to him the following points: 1. That if he refuses to admit the King's excusator, and proceeds against the King, Francis will not allow it, but both will resist it to his great disadvantage; but if he will maintain the King's privileges, and not intermeddle in the cause, he will find us his true friends; otherwise, we will never enter into any alliance with him.

    2. And then he will be obliged to Francis if he will order his Ambassadors at Rome to join with the King's in persuading the Pope and the Cardinals to be satisfied with what is done, and not attempt to contravene it; or, in case the Pope should attempt it, will be glad if Francis will gain over as many Cardinals as he can for the King's support. The Ambassador is to tell the Grand Master and the Admiral that the King has great confidence in them, and appoints them protectors of his cause in the Court of France, and he is to deliver them the letters herewith sent. Also, they shall make what interest they can for him there. They shall assure Francis that there is no prince or personage on whose support and comfort he relies so much, and that his kind words and promises are a great consolation to Henry, especially as he vows never to abandon the King in this cause, but aid and maintain him in his succession, declaring that he will hold all that trouble him or condemn his proceedings, whether it be Pope or Emperor, as his adversary.
32. *L&P*, V, 882. The letter is listed under 1532, but the contents of the letter suggests such a date is illogical.
33. *L&P*, VI, 255.
34. *L&P*, VI, 351. When he returned, he was granted the wardship and marriage of Edmund Sheffeld, son and heir of Sir Robert Sheffeld during his minority. *L&P*, VI, 419.
35. Stanford Lehmberg, *Reformation Parliament 1529–1536* (Cambridge: Cambridge University Press 1960), 30.
36. *Cal. Span.*, IV, ii, 1072.
37. Ibid.
38. Ibid.
39. Ibid.
40. Ibid.
41. *L&P*, VI, 391.
42. *Cal. Span.*, IV, ii, 1077.

43. *L&P*, VI, 601. Also mentioned in Charles Wriothesley, ed. William Douglas Hamilton, *A Chronicle of England During the Reign of the Tudors* (London: Camden Society 1875), 21–2.

44. Ibid.

45. HHStA, England Berichte Karton 5, 228, 46.

46. *L&P*, VI, 601. Also mentioned in Wriothesley, *A Chronicle of England During the Reign of the Tudors*, 21–2.

CHAPTER THIRTEEN   TURNING TIDES

1. *L&P*, VI, 613.

2. Ibid.

3. I am grateful to Professsor Barry Collett for his view of Marguerite as an ardently devout young Catholic woman 'who became restless with her religion', a frustration she shared with George and Anne.

4. *L&P*, VI, 831. 'Within all the way the King went the t[own was] hanged over with fair linen cloths upon bowe ... walls hanged with arras, children to the num[ber of] 40 in garments of silk, spears in their hands [crying] *viva le Roy*. In the midst of the town three o[r four] young women upon a stage in like gorgeous a[pparel]. In the third place, likewise the fyft, with tr[umpets] and other minstrelsy.'

5. *L&P*, VI, 891, 892.

6. *L&P*, VI, 954.

7. Glossop's letter still exists in which he sends '12 Banbury cheeses, half hard and half soft, and wish they were worth 20,000*l*. I am almost four-score years old, impotent, lame of the gout and cramp, and one of my eyes is gone. I hope you will help me [to] 4 nobles more of my masters the Taylors, for I have 4 paid me every year; or else 2 nobles more, to make even 40*s*., with a chamber, and 4 qrs. of coal amongst their beadmen. I have a feather-bed with a bolster for Master Will. Wellyfed's son, who is at Cambray at your finding. My mistress your mother was my aunt. Thos. Allkoke's wife, of Werkworth-in-the-Peak, was my godmother and my aunt. "Loke upon my byll at the instance of Owre Blessed Lady of Sumshon," sending to Master Hubbulthorne, who will serve you with the master of the Taylors' fellowship. "Thus blessed St. John Baptist have you in keeping night and day". *L&P*, VI, 696.

8. Clearly Boleyn went above and beyond his duty, as Glossop later wrote: 'I dwell with my good lord of Lincoln. My lords of Norfolk, Wiltshire, and Windsor put me to him. I am bound to thank them, especially my lord of Wiltshire.' *L&P*, VI, 697.

9. Erasmus, *A playne and godly Exposytion or Declaration of the Commune Crede (which in the Latin tonge is called Symbolum Apostolorum) and of the x. Commaundementes of goddes law, newly made and put forth by the famouse clarke Mayster Erasmus of Roterdame. At the requeste of the moste honorable lorde, Thomas Erle of Wyltshyre: father to the moste gratious and vertuous Quene Anne wyf to our most gracyous soueraygne lorde kynge Henry the VIII*, trans. William Marshall (London: Robert Redman, 1733), 1–4.

10. J. K. McConica, *English Humanists and Reformation Politics under Henry VIII and Edward VI* (Oxford: Clarendon Press, 1952), 61.

11. *Opus Epistolarum Des. Erasmi Roterodami, denuo recognitum et auctum.* Vol. IX, eds., Percy Stafford Allen, Helen Mary Allen, and William Garrod Heathcote (Oxford: Clarendon Press, 1906), Letter 2845.

12. Alois Gerlo (trans.), *La Correspondance D'Erasme, VIII* (Brussels: University Press, 1979), 224.

13. See Aysha Pollnitz, *Princely Education in Early Modern Britain* (Cambridge: Cambridge University Press, 2015), 125.

14. Ibid.

15. *Spiritualia and Pastoralia: Disputatiuncula de Taedio, Pavore, Tristicia Iesu/Concio de Immensa Dei Misericordia/Modus Orandi Deum/Explanati,* Vol. 70, eds., John W. O'Malley, Beatrice Corrigan and John Schoeck (Toronto: University of Toronto Press, 1998), 236.

16. Jonathan Willis, *The Reformation of the Decalogue: Religious Identity and the Ten Commandments in England, c.1485–1625* (Cambridge: Cambridge University Press, 2017), 284.

17. Ibid.

18. Peter Marshall, *Heretics and Believers: A History of the English Reformation* (New Haven and London: Yale University Press, 2017), 140.

19. Erasmus, *Correspondance of Erasmus, Letters 1356–1534,* X, 464.

20. Ibid. Boleyn did show signs of being deeply involved in an Erasmian blend of humanism and piety.

21. *L&P,* VII, 111.

22. *Cal. Span,* V, i, 22.

23. I desire you and my good lady to be good unto Thomas Hunt, a poor man at Calais, for the room of soldier with 6d. a day in the King's retinue, when any such is vacant.' *L&P,* VII, 177.

24. Muriel St Clare, *The Lisle Letters* (University of Chicago Press, 1981), 167.

25. Henry Gee and William John Hardy, *Documents Illustrative of English Church History, Compiled from Original Sources* (London: Macmillan, 1896), 232–7.

26. Ibid.

27. Paulet to Cromwell, 'This day my lord of Wiltshire and I go to my lady Mary; thence to court to; make report; and so to my house for 12 days.' *L&P,* VII, 529.

28. *Cal. Span.,* V, i, 71.

29. See Maria Dowling, 'William Latymer's Cronickille of Anne Bulleyne,' Camden Forth Series, vol. 39, (1990): 56–60; Thomas Freeman, 'Research, Rumour and Propaganda: Anne Boleyn in Foxe's Book of Martyrs,' *Historical Journal* 38 (1995): 806.

30. James P. Carley, '"Her moost lovyng and fryndely brother sendeth gretyng": Anne Boleyn's Manuscripts and their Sources,' in *Illuminating the Book: Makers and Interpreters, Essays in Honour of Janet Backhouse,* eds, Michelle P. Brown and Scot McKendrick (Toronto: University of Toronto Press, 1998), 261–80.

31. 'Her moost lovyng and fryndely brother sendeth gretyng – Anne Boleyn's Manuscripts and Their Sources' by James P. Carley in *Illuminating the Book* edited by Michelle P. Brown and Scot McKendrick (London: the British Library and University of Toronto Press, 1998).

32. George Ellis, *Specimens of the Early English Poets, to which is Prefixed an Historical Sketch of the Rise and Progress of the English Poetry and Language* (London: Bulmer and Co, 1803), 94.

33. Ibid.

34. Helen Allen, *Opus epistolarum Des. Erasmi Roterdami,* 2824.

35. Michael Welker, Michael Weinrich, and Ulrich Möller, *Calvin Today: Reformed Theology and the Future of the Church* (London: Bloomsbury, T & T Clark, 2011), 186.

36. *Collected Works of Erasmus: Spiritualia and Pastoralia: Disputatiuncula de Taedio, Pavore, Tristicia Iesu/Concio de Immensa Dei Misericordia/Modus Orandi Deum/Explanati*. Vol. 70. Edited by Beatrice Corrigan, John O'Malley and Richard Schoeck (Toronto: University of Toronto Press, 1998), xxviii.

37. See Bettie Anne Doebler, *Rooted in Sorrow: Dying in Early Modern England* (New Jersey: Fairleigh Dickinson University Press, 1994).

38. See Alberto Tenenti, *Il senso della morte e l'amore della vita nel* Rinascimento (Francia e Italia) (Turin: G. Einaudi, 1977).

39. *L&P*, III, ii, 3232.

40. 'The Queen his mistress much rejoices in the deeply-rooted amity of the two kings, but wishes her to get the interview deferred... Her reasons are, that being so far gone with child, she could not cross the sea with the King' *State Papers*, vii, 565.

41. *L&P*, VIII, 776.

42. *L&P*, VII,1655.

43. *Cal. Span.*, V, i,

44. Boleyn was part of the special commission of Oyer and Terminer, called to hear the cases of the monks, and decided that the case should go to a grand jury. *L&P*, VIII, 609.

45. *Cal. Span.*, VIII, 666.

46. Ibid.

47. *L&P*, VIII, 760.

48. Ibid., 793.

49. Ibid., 909.

50. Ibid., 1478.

51. As evidence in a letter from the Mayor and Jurats of Rye to Cromwell: 'We have informed the Council, and sent letters to my lord of Rochford, the warden of the Cinque Ports, but he is one of the King's ambassadors beyond sea. In his absence my lord of Wiltshire has opened the letters, and shown them to Mr. Chr. Hales, the King's Attorney, who advises us to send the parties to you.' *L&P*, VIII, 776.

52. *L&P*, IX, 566. In the margin, the names are given as 'Millor de Rochesfort et millord de Guillaume.'

53. J. Duncan M. Derrett, 'The Trial of Sir Thomas More,' *EHR* 79 (1964): 451.

54. For example, see David Loades, *The Tudor Queens of England* (London: Bloomsbury, 2010), 123.

55. William Roper, *The Mirrour of Vertue in Worldly Greatnes, or, the Life of Syr Thomas More, Knight, Sometime Lo. Chancellour of England*. (Paris: English College Press, 1626).

56. Ibid.

57. Dean, 'Sir Thomas Boleyn: The Courtier Diplomat', 173.

58. *Cal. Span.*, V, i, 180.

59. Thomas More, *The Last Letters of Thomas More*, ed. Alvaro De Silva (Michigan: W. B. Eerdmans, 2001), 112.

60. Evidently Thomas moved between his Kentish estates, but his presence at Penshurst is interesting as we tend to link him primarily to Hever.

CHAPTER FOURTEEN　TRYING A QUEEN

1. *Cal. Span.*, V, ii, 3, 9.
2. *Cal. Span.*, V, ii, 9. The original is in cipher, but we owe a great deal to Garrett Mattingly who translated this report in his PhD thesis on the Imperial ambassador, and his translation corresponds with Gayangos' translation.
3. *L&P*, X, 141. The original is found in *HHStA, England Bericht*, Karton 7, fasc 236, 3.
4. For example, Robert Hutchinson, *House of Treason: The Rise and Fall of a Tudor Dynasty* (London: Hachette, 2009), 207; Elizabeth Norton, *The Boleyn Women: The Tudor Femmes Fetales who changed English History* (Stroud: Amberley, 2013), 237.
5. *Cal. Span.*, V, ii, p. 39.
6. Ibid.
7. *Cal. Span.*, V, ii, 29.
8. *L&P*, X, 458.
9. Ibid.
10. *L&P*, X, 458
11. *Cal. Span.*, V, ii, 43.
12. *HHStA, England Berichte*, Karton 7, 270–1.
13. *Cal. Span.*, V, ii, 699.
14. Ibid.
15. Ibid.
16. Ibid.
17. Ibid.
18. *Cal. Span.*, V, ii, 43.
19. For example, Tracy Borman, *Thomas Cromwell: The Untold Story of Henry VIII's Most Faithful Servant* (Hodder and Stoughton, 2015), 212; Ives, *The Life and Death of Anne Boleyn*, 295; David Starkey, *Six Wives*, 588.
20. Aldrich, *The Register of the Most Noble Order of the Garter*, 496. *Dictionary of National Biography*, ed. Leslie Stephen (London: Macmillan, 1887), 9:58.
21. Robert Aldrich, *The Register of the Most Noble Order of the Garter, from its cover in black velvet, usually called The Black Book* (London: J. Barber, 1724), 394–5.
22. Ives, *Anne Boleyn*, 323.
23. *HHStA, England Bericht*, Karton 4, Fasc. 230, 29.
24. *Cal. Span.*, V, ii, 48.
25. *L&P*, X, 793.
26. *L&P*, X, 902.
27. Muriel St Claire, *Lisle Letters*, 161.
28. Ives, *Anne Boleyn*, 323.
29. *L&P*, X, 843.
30. *Cal. Span.*, V, ii, 55.
31. *L&P*, X, 876.
32. Further to the point, when Jane Boleyn, George's widow, herself was executed in 1542 for treason, again her father seems to have given no opposition. For further discussion, see Marie Axton, James P. Carley, David Starkey, *et al.*, *Triumphs of English: Henry Parker, Lord Morley, Translator to the Tudor Court* (London: British Library, 2000), 165.
33. T. B. Howell, comp., *A Complete Collection of State Trials and Proceedings for High Treason and Other Crimes and Misdemeanors from the Earliest Period to the Year 1820*,

Vol. 33 (London: Longman, 1826), 417. He notes that Boleyn was not part of the trial at all.

34. *Cal. Span.*, V, ii, 55. 'Neither the concubine nor her brother were taken to Westminster as the other criminals had been; they were tried within the Tower, and yet the trial was far from being kept secret, for upwards of 2,000 people were present.'

35. *Cal. Span.*, V, ii, 55.

36. Ibid.

37. Gilbert Burnet, *Bishop Burnet's History of the Reformation of the Church of England* (R. Priestley, 1820), I: 306. Burnet believed that Jane played a major role in providing evidence against her husband and sister-in-law due to the fact that she was jealous of her husband's close relationship with his sister and was 'a woman of no sort of virtue'.

38. See Elizabeth Norton, *The Boleyn Women*, 25. George Cavendish, who knew her, described her as 'a widow in black'. The evidence of Jane's possessions also suggests that she habitually wore black, something that, given that her widowhood lasted for nearly six years, was far above what was required by convention.

39. MS Cotton, Otho C, X, fol. 225;

40. *Cal. Span.*, V, ii, 55.

41. *L&P*, X, 876.

42. *Cal. Span.*, V, ii, 55.

43. *Cal. Span.*, V, ii, 55.

44. Thomas Wyatt, ed. Kenneth Muir, Patricia Thomson, *Collected works of Sir Thomas Wyatt* (Liverpool: Liverpool University Press 1969), 157.

45. Paul Friedmann, *Anne Boleyn: A Chapter of English History, 1527–1536* (London: Macmillan, 1884), 51.

46. Ives, *Anne Boleyn*, 329.

47. David M. Loades, *The Boleyns: The Rise and Fall of a Tudor Family* (Stroud: Amberley, 2011), 86.

48. Thomas Warley to Lady Lisle, 14 April 1536, *Lisle Letters*, III, 673.

## CHAPTER FIFTEEN  AFTERMATH

1. Ellis, *Original Letters, Illustrative of English History,* Vol. II (London: Richard Bentley, 1848), Vol. III, 22–3.

2. Dean, 'Sir Thomas Boleyn: The Courtier Diplomat', 180.

3. *BL* Cotton Vespasian, F XIII, fol. 109. The original letter is as follows: 'Mayster Secretory, as a power desolate widow wythoute comfort, as to my specyall trust under God and my Pryns, I have me most humbly recommendyd unto youe: prayng youe … my father payed great soms of money for my Joynter to the Errell of Wyltchere to the some off too thowsand Marks, and I not assuryd of no more duryng the says Errells natural lyff then one hundredth Marks; whyche ys veary hard for me.'

4. *L&P*, XII, ii, 926.

5. Ibid., 1199.

6. Ibid., 291.

7. *L&P*, XII, 1310, 782. Ives sees his prompt payments as evidence of Boleyn 'buttering up' Cromwell. Ives, *The Life and Death of Anne Boleyn*, 353.

8. Ibid., XII, 738.

9. Ibid., 722.
10. Ives, *The Life and Death of Anne Boleyn*, 353.
11. *L&P*, XII, 445.
12. *L&P*, XII, 580.
13. Dean, 'Sir Thomas Boleyn: The Courtier Diplomat,' 184.
14. *L&P*, XII, 610.
15. He was also one of the banner bearers in the cortege along with Suffolk, the Marquis of Dorset, and the Earls of Surrey and Sussex. *L&P*, XII, ii, 1060.
16. *Lisle Letters*, V, 1086.
17. It would not have been customary for Boleyn to be chief mourner, as the position was always held by the closest relative, in this case, Elizabeth's brother.
18. *L&P*, XIII, I, 1419.
19. *L&P*, X, 458.
20. P. H. Ditchfield and George Clinch, *Memorials of Old Kent* (London: Bemrose and Sons, 1907), 237; *L&P*, XIV, I, 511.
21. Ibid., II, 781.
22. Ibid., I, 950.
23. Ibid., 608, 609.
24. Brock, 'The Courtier in Early Tudor Society,' 11.

# Select Bibliography

ARCHIVAL SOURCES

Exchequer Series: Exchequer, King's Remembrancer: *Accounts Various Account book of Thomas Boleyn, Controller of the Household.* 22 April 1520–21 April 1522. E 101/419/5.

Haus-, Hof- und Staatsarchiv: Österreichisches Staatsarchiv, Vienna.
Diplomatie und Außenpolitik vor 1848, Großbritannien (England) (1495–1867) Varia, *Korrespondenz, Instruktionen und Berichte*, Karton 1–9, 10.

PROB 11: Prerogative Court of Canterbury and related Probate Jurisdictions, Will Registers SP 6/2/94; 11/18/184.

Records assembled by the State Paper Office, including papers of the Secretaries of State up to 1782, SP 6, Theological Tracts Henry VIII, Fol. 94. *'Rochford MS.'*

Records created, acquired and inherited by Chancery, and also of the Wardrobe, Royal Household, Exchequer and various commissions. Original files of writs and returns, Henry VIII, C131/108/30–31; C131/269/2; C131/269/4; C1/488/45; C1/490/33.

State Papers, Henry VIII, National Archives, Kew.

*Typescript Catalogue of the Muniments of the Compton Family preserved at Castle Ashby.* Edited by I. H. Jeayes. 5 Vols. Northhamptonshire County Record Office: 1921.

Manuscripts:

Over the decades, some of the folios have been renumbered, but not on the online catalogue, causing endless confusion. For example, in the Cotton MS Caligula, which contains correspondence between Thomas Boleyn and Cardinal Wolsey during his embassies, one folio numbered 105, named: *Sir Tho. Boleyn, to Card. Wolsey; various intelligence about the election to the empire,* &c is actually 108r–108v, and the original folio 108 is now 111–12. For the sake of clarity and ease of comparison, any references to the Cotton Manuscripts will correspond with the library catalogue.

British Library
Caligula
Cleopatra

Cotton Manuscripts
Galba
Harleian
Othos
Titus
Vitellius
Vespasian

## PRINTED PRIMARY SOURCES

### Calendars

*Calendar of State Papers and Manuscripts relating to English affairs, existing in the Archives and collections of Venice, and in other libraries of Northern Italy.* Edited by Rowdon Lubbock Brown. London: Longman, HMSO, 1864.

*Calendar of State Papers and Manuscripts Existing in the Archives and Collections of Milan.* London: HMSO, 1912.

*Calendar of State Papers Relating to Ireland of the Reigns of Henry VIII, Edward VI, Mary, and Elizabeth, 1509–1573.* Vol. I. London: HMSO, 1860.

*Calendar of State Papers Domestic: Elizabeth, 1595–97.* Edited by Mary Anne Everett Green. London: Her Majesty's Stationery Office, 1869.

*Calendar of the Charter Rolls preserved in the Public Record Office. AD 1427–1516, with an appendix, AD 1215–1288.* London: HMSO, 1927.

*Calendar of the Close Rolls preserved in the Public Record Office: Henry VII. 2 vols. 1500–1509.* London: HMSO, 1963.

*Calendar of the Fine Rolls preserved in the Public Record Office: Vol. XVIII. Henry VI. AD 1445–1452.* London: HMSO, 1939.

*Calendar of the Patent Rolls preserved in the Public Record Office: Henry VI. Vol. II.* London: HMSO, 1907.

*Calendar of the Patent Rolls Preserved in the Public Record Office: Henry VI. AD 1452–1461 (November, 1457). Vol. VI.* London: HMSO, 1910.

*Calendar of Patent Rolls Preserved in the Public Records Office, Henry VII. Vol. I.* London: HMSO, 1907.

*Calendar of the Patent Rolls Preserved in the Public Record Office: Henry VII, AD 1485–1509.* Vol. II. London: HMSO, 1907.

*Calendar of Letter-Books preserved among the Archives of the Corporation of the City of London at the Guildhall. Letter-Book K: Temp. Henry VI.* Edited by Reginald Robinson Sharpe. London, 1911.

*Calendar of Letters, Despatches, and State Papers, Relating to the Negotiations between England and Spain: Preserved in the Archives at Simancas, and Elsewhere.* Gustav Adolph Bergenroth, *et al.* London, Longman, Green, Longman, and Roberts, 1940.

*Letters and Papers, Foreign and Domestic, of the Reign of Henry VIII, preserved in the Public Record Office, the British Museum, and Elsewhere.* Edited by J.S. Brewer, J. Gairdner, and R.H. Brodie. 22 vols. London: HMSO, 1862–1932.

*Letters and Papers Illustrative of the Reigns of Richard III and Henry VII.* Edited by James Gairdner. London: Longman, Green, Longman, and Roberts, 1861.

PRIMARY SOURCES

*Acts of Court of the Mercers Company: 1453–1527*. Edited by Laetitia Lyell and Frank Dormay Watney. Cambridge: Cambridge University Press, 1936.

Aldrich, Robert, et al. *The Register of the Most Noble Order of the Garter, from its Cover in Black Velvet, usually called the Black Book*. London: J. Barber, 1724.

*Archaeologia, or, Miscellaneous Tracts relating to Antiquity*. Vol. 3. London: Society of Antiquaries of London, 1775.

Ashmole, Elias. *The History of the Most Noble Order of the Garter: And the Several Orders of Knighthood Extant in Europe. Containing I. The Antiquity of the Town, Castle, Chapel, and College of Windsor; II. The Habits, Ensigns, and Officers of the Order*. London: A. Bell, E. Curll, J. Pemberton, and A. Collins, 1715.

*Autographs of Royal, Noble, Learned, and Remarkable Personages Conspicuous in English History, from the Reign of Richard the Second to That of Charles the Second: With Some Illustrious Foreigners: Containing Many Passages from Important Letters; Accompanied by Concise Biographical Memoirs, and Interesting Extracts from the Original Documents*. Edited by Nichols, John Gough. London: John Gough Nichols, 1829.

Bellay, Jean Du, et al. *Ambassades en Angleterre de Jean du Bellay: la première ambassade (Septembre 1527–Février 1529)*. Paris: S.n., 1905.

—— and R. Scheurer. *Correspondance du cardinal Jean du Bellay*. Paris: Klincksieck, 1969.

Boom, Ghislaine de. *Marguerite d'Autriche*. Bruxelles: La Renaissance du livre, 1946.

Castiglione, Baldassarre, and George Bull. *The Book of the Courtier*. Harmondsworth: Penguin, 1976.

Cavendish, George. 'The Life and Death of Cardinal Wolsey,' in *Two Early Tudor Lives*, Edited by R.S. Sylvester and D.P. Harding. New Haven: Yale University Press, 1962.

—— and A.S.G. Edwards. *Metrical Visions*. Columbia, SC: University of South Carolina Press, 1980.

*The Chronicle of Calais, in the Reigns of Henry VII. and Henry VIII. To the Year 1540. Ed. from Mss. in the British Museum*. Edited by John Gough Nichols. London: J.B. Nichols and Son, 1846.

*Collectanea Genealogica*. Edited by Joseph Foster. Oxford: Oxford University Press, 1881–85.

Curtis, Edmund, ed. *Calendar of Ormond Deeds*. Vol. IV. Dublin: Stationery Office, 1937.

Ellis, Henry. *Original Letters, illustrative of English history: including numerous royal letters, from autographs in the British Museum, and one or two other collections*. 2 and 3 series, 11 vols. London: Richard Bentley, 1824–46.

Erasmus, Desiderius. *D. Erasmi Roterodami Purgatio adversus epistolam non sobriam Martini Luteri*. Coloniae, Ex aedibus Eucharij Ceruicorni. Basel, 1534.

—— *A playne and godly exposition or declaration of the commune crede (Which in the Latyn tonge is called Symbolum Apostolorum): and of the. X commaundementes of goddes law, newly made and put forth by the famouse clerke, Mayster Erasmus of Roterdame, at the requeste of the moste honorable lorde, Thomas Erle of wyltshyre: father to the moste gratious and vertuous Quene Anne wyfe to our moste gracious soueraygne lorde kyng Henry the VIII. Cum priuilegio*. Translated by William Marshall. London: Robert Redman, 1534.

—— *Preparation to Deathe, a boke as devout as eloquent*. London: Thomas Berthelet, 1543.

——*The Colloquies of Erasmus*. II Vols. Translated by N. Bailey. Edited by Reverend E. Johnson. London: Reeves & Turner, 1878.

—— *Opus Epistolarum Des. Erasmi Roterodami, denuo recognitum et auctum*. 9 volumes. Edited and Translated by Percy Stafford Allen and Mary Helen Allen, Heathcote William, Garrod. Oxford: Clarendon Press, 1906.

—— *et al. La correspondance d'Erasme*. Translated by Aloïs Gerlo. Vol. 8. Brussels: Presses Académiques Européennes, 1979.

—— *Collected Works of Erasmus: Spiritualia and Pastoralia: Disputatiuncula de Taedio, Pavore, Tristicia Iesu/Concio de Immensa Dei Misericordia/Modus Orandi Deum/Explanati*. Vol. 70. Edited by Beatrice Corrigan, John O'Malley and Richard Schoeck. Toronto: University of Toronto Press, 1998.

—— *Disputatiuncula de taedio, pavore, tristicia Iesu; Concio de immensa Dei misericordia; Modus orandi Deum; Explanatio symboli apostolorum sive catechismus; De praeparatione ad mortem*. Edited by O'Malley, John W. Toronto: University of Toronto Press, 1998.

—— *Collected Works of Erasmus: Expositions of the Psalms*. Vol. 64. Edited by Baker Smith, Dominic. Translated by Emily Kearns. Toronto: University of Toronto Press, 2005.

—— *The Correspondence of Erasmus: Letters 2204–2356* (August 1529–July 1530). Translated by Dalzell, Alexander. Toronto: University of Toronto Press, 2015.

—— *The Correspondence of Erasmus: Letters 1356–1534, 1523–1524. Translated by Dalzell, Alexander*. Toronto: University of Toronto Press, 2015.

*Exchequer, treasury of the receipt: Ancient deeds*. Vol. VI. List and Index Society, 1978.

Foxe, John. *The Acts and Monuments of John Foxe*. Edited by George Townsend. London: R.B. Seeley and W. Burnside, 1841.

Gairdner, James. *The Paston Letters: A.D. 1422–1509*. London: Chatto & Windus, 1904.

*The Great Chronicle of London*. Edited by Robert Fabyan, *et al*. Gloucester: Alan Sutton, 1983.

Hall, Edward. *Halls chronicle; containing the history of England, during the reign of Henry the Fourth, and the succeeding monarchs, to the end of the reign of Henry the Eighth, in which are particularly described the manners and customs of those periods. Carefully collated with the editions of 1548–1550*. London: J. Johnson, 1809.

Hall, Richard. *The Life and Death of the Renowned John Fisher, Bishop of Rochester: Who was Beheaded on Tower-Hill, the 22d of June, 1535*. Edited by Thomas Bayly. Princeton: Princeton University Press, 1739.

*Historical Manuscripts Commission, Report on the Manuscripts of the Marquess of Lothian, Preserved at Blickling Hall, Norfolk*. London: HMSO, 1905.

*The Household of Edward IV: The Black Book and the Ordinance of 1478*. Edited by Alec Reginald Myers. Manchester: Manchester University Press, 1959.

*Letters of the Kings of England, now first collected from Royal archives, and other authentic sources, private as well as public*. Edited by James Orchard Halliwell, ed., Vol. I. London: Henry Colburn, 1848.

*Manuscripts of His Grace the Duke of Rutland, G.C.B., Preserved at Belvoir Castle*. London: HMSO, 1888.

*Materials for a history of the reign of Henry VII: From Original Documents Preserved in the Public Record Office*. II Vols. Edited by William Campbell. London, 1873.

Maximilian, *et al. Correspondance de l'empereur Maximilien Ier et de Marguerite d'Autriche de 1507 à 1519, publiée après les manuscrits originaux par Le Glay*. Paris: Renouard, 1839. Reprinted by New York: Johnson, 1966.

Nicolas, N.H. *Testamenta Vetusta: Being Illustrations from Wills, of Manners, Customs, &c. as Well as of the Descents and Possessions of Many Distinguished Families. From the Reign of*

*Henry the Second to the Accession of Queen Elizabeth.* Vols. 1 and 2. London: Nichols & Son, 1826.

—— *Proceedings and Ordinances of the Privy Council of England.* Edited by Nicolas Harris. London: The Commissioners on the public records of the kingdom, 1837.

Roper, William. *The Mirrour of Vertue in Worldly Greatnes, or, the Life of Syr Thomas More, Knight, Sometime Lo. Chancellour of England.* Paris: English College Press, 1626.

Rymer, Thomas. *Foedera, conventiones, literae, et cujuscunque generis acta publica, inter reges Angliae, et alios quosvis imperatores, reges, pontifices, principes, vel communitates, ab ineunte saeculo duodecimo, viz. ab anno 1101, ad nostra usque temopora, habita aut tractate.* London: A. & J. Churchill, 1727–1735.

Vergil, Polydore. *The Anglica historia of Polydore Vergil, AD 1485–1537.* Edited and translated by Denys Hay. London: Offices of the Royal Historical Society, 1950.

Wyatt, Thomas. *The works of Henry Howard and Thomas Wyatt the Elder.* Edited by F. Nott. London: T. Bensley, 1816.


PhD Theses

Brock, Richard Egbert. 'The Courtier in Early Tudor Society, Illustrated from Select Examples.' PhD thesis. University of London, 1963.

Campbell, D.S. 'English Foreign Policy: 1509–21.' PhD thesis. Cambridge University, 1980.

Dean, William H. 'Sir Thomas Boleyn: The Courtier Diplomat, 1477–1539.' PhD thesis. University of West Virginia, 1987.

Everett, M. 'Qualities of a Royal Minister: Studies in the Rise of Thomas Cromwell, c. 1520–1534.' PhD thesis. University of Southampton, 2012.

Greig, Lorne Cameron George. 'Court Politics and Government in England, 1509–1515.' PhD thesis. University of Glasgow, 1996.

MacMahon, Luke. 'The Ambassadors of Henry VIII: The Personnel of English Diplomacy, c.1500–c.1550.' PhD thesis. University of Kent, 1999.

Samman, Neil. 'The Henrician Court during Cardinal Wolsey's Ascendancy c.1514–1529.' PhD thesis. University of Wales, 1988.

Starkey, David. 'King's Privy Chamber 1485–1547.' PhD thesis. University of Cambridge, 1974.


SECONDARY SOURCES

Axton, Marie, James P. Carley, David Starkey, *et al. Triumphs of English: Henry Parker, Lord Morley, Translator to the Tudor Court.* London: British Library, 2000.

Bacon, Francis. *History of the Reign of King Henry VII and Selected Works.* Edited by Brian Vickers. Cambridge: Cambridge University Press, 1998.

Baldwin, David. *The Kingmaker's Sisters: Six Powerful Women in the Wars of the Roses.* Stroud: History Press, 2009.

Behrens, B. 'The Office of the English Resident Ambassador: Its Evolution as Illustrated by the Career of Sir Thomas Spinelly, 1509–22.' *Transactions of the Royal Historical Society* 16 (1933): 161.

Benger, E. *Memoirs of the Life of Anne Boleyn, Queen of Henry VIII.* Philadelphia: Parry & McMillan, 1854.

Bentley, Samuel. 'The Privy Purse Expenses of Henry VII.' In Samuel Bentley. *Excerpta Historica.* London, 1889.

Bernard, G.W. 'The Rise of Sir William Compton, Early Tudor Courtier.' *The English Historical Review* 96, no. 381 (1981): 754–77.

────── 'The Fall of Anne Boleyn: A rejoinder,' *EHR* 107 (1992): 665–74.

────── 'Anne Boleyn's Religion.' *The Historical Journal* 36, no. 1 (1993): 1–20.

────── 'The Fall of Wolsey Reconsidered.' *The Journal of British Studies* 35, no. 3 (1996): 277–310.

────── *Power and Politics in Tudor England: Essays*. Aldershot: Ashgate, 2000.

────── *The King's Reformation: Henry VIII and the Remaking of the English Church*. New Haven: Yale University Press, 2005.

────── *Anne Boleyn: Fatal Attractions*. New Haven: Yale University Press, 2010.

Betteridge, Thomas, and Lipscomb, Suzannah, eds. *Henry VIII and the Tudor Court: Art, Politics and Performance*. Farnham, Surrey: Ashgate, 2013.

Bietenholz, Peter G., and Deutscher, Thomas Brian. *Contemporaries of Erasmus: A Biographical Register of the Renaissance and Reformation, volumes 1–3, A–Z*. Toronto: University of Toronto Press, 2003.

Block, Joseph S. *Factional Politics and the English Reformation, 1520–1540*. London: Boydell Press, 1993.

Blomefield, Francis and Parkin, Charles. *An Essay towards a Topographical History of the Country of Norfolk, containing a Description of the Towns, Villages and Hamlets, with the Foundation of Monasteries Churches, Chapels, Chantries and other religious buildings*. London: Miller, 1805.

Bray, Gerald, ed. *Documents of the English Reformation*. Cambridge: James Clarke, 1994.

Burke, Peter. *The Fortunes of the Courtier: The European Reception of Castigliones Cortegiano*. Cambridge: Polity Press, 1995.

Byrne, Muriel St. Clare. *The Lisle Letters*. Vol 3. Chicago: University of Chicago Press, 1981.

Campbell, John. *Lives of the Lord Chancellors and Keepers of the Great Seal of England: From the Earliest Times till the Reign of King George IV*. London: John Murray, 1869.

Campbell, William, ed. *Materials for a History of the Reign of Henry VII. From original documents preserved in the Public record office*. London: Longman & Co., 1873.

Carley, James P. '"Her Moost Lovyng and Fryndely Brother Sendeth Gretyng": Anne Boleyn's Manuscripts and Their Sources.' In *Illuminating the Book: Makers and Interpreters: Essays in Honour of Janet Backhouse*. Edited by Michelle P. Brown and Scot McKendrick. Toronto: University of Toronto University Press, 1998.

Chambers, D.S. 'Cardinal Wolsey and the Papal Tiara.' *Bulletin of the Institute of Historical Research 28* (1965): 20–30.

Cockram, Sarah. 'The Author–Actor in Castiglione's "Il Cortegiano": "lo esser travestito porta secouna certa liberta e licenzia"' In *The Tradition of the Actor–author in Italian Theatre*. Edited by Donatella Fischer. New York: Legenda, 2013, 11–19.

Cooper, William. 'The Families of Braose of Chesworth, and Hoo.' In *Sussex Archaeological Collections Relating to the History and Antiquities of the County*. Vol. 8. London: John Russell Smith, 1856.

Davies, C.S.L. 'Tournai and the English Crown, 1513–1519.' *The Historical Journal* 41, no. 1 (1998): 1.

Derrett, J. D. M. 'The Trial of Sir Thomas More.' *The English Historical Review* 79 (1964): 449–77

Doebler, Bettie Anne. *'Rooted Sorrow': Dying in Early Modern England*. Rutherford, NJ: Fairleigh Dickinson University Press, 1994.

Doran, Susan. *England and Europe in the Sixteenth Century.* New York: St Martin's Press: 1999.

Dowling, Maria. 'Anne Boleyn and Reform.' *The Journal of Ecclesiastical History* 35, no. 1 (1984): 30–46.

—— *Humanism in the Age of Henry VIII.* London: Croom Helm, 1986.

—— William Latymer's Cronickille of Anne Bulleyne. Camden Forth Series, vol. 39, (1990): 23–65.

Drees, Clayton J. *Bishop Richard Fox of Winchester: Architect of the Tudor Age.* Jefferson, NC: McFarland, 2014.

Duffy, Eamon. *Saints, Sacrilege and Sedition: Religion and Conflict in the Tudor Reformations.* London: Bloomsbury, 2012.

Ellis, George, *Specimens of the Early English Poets, to which is Prefixed an Historical Sketch of the Rise and Progress of the English Poetry and Language* (London: Bulmer and Co., 1803.

Elton, Geoffrey, 'Thomas Cromwell.' *History Today* 6 (1956): 528–36.

—— *Henry VIII: An Essay in Revision.* London: The Historical Association, 1962.

——'Presidential Address: Tudor Government: The Points of Contact: I. Parliament.' *Transactions of the Royal Historical Society* 24 (1974): 183–200.

—— 'Presidential Address: Tudor Government: The Points of Contact. II. The Council.' *Transactions of the Royal Historical Society* 25 (1975): 195–211.

—— 'Presidential Address: Tudor Government: The Points of Contact. III. The Court.' *Transactions of the Royal Historical Society* 26 (1976): 211–28.

—— *Studies in Tudor and Stuart Politics and Government.* Vol. 4. Cambridge: Cambridge University Press, 1983.

—— *England under the Tudors.* London: Routledge, 1991.

Emden, A.B. *A Biographical Register of the University of Cambridge to 1500.* Cambridge: Cambridge University Press, 1963.

Erickson, Carolly. *Mistress Anne.* New York: St. Martin's Press, 1984.

Everett, Michael. *The Rise of Thomas Cromwell: Power and Politics in the Reign of Henry VIII, 1485–1534.* New Haven: Yale University Press, 2015.

Fletcher, Catherine. *Our Man in Rome: Henry VIII and his Italian Ambassador.* London: Bodley Head, 2012.

Freeman, Thomas S. 'Research, Rumour and Propaganda: Anne Boleyn in Foxe's "Book of Martyrs".' *The Historical Journal* 38 (1995): 806.

Friedmann, Paul. *Anne Boleyn.* Edited by Josephine Wilkinson. Stroud: Amberley, 2010.

—— *Anne Boleyn: A Chapter of English History, 1527–1536.* London: Macmillan, 1884.

Froude, James Anthony. *History of England from the Fall of Wolsey to the Death of Elizabeth.* Vol. 3. 12 vols. London: Longman, Green, and Co., 1866.

Gavin, J. Austin and Walsh, Thomas M. 'The Praise of Folly in Context: The Commentary of Girardus Listrius', *Renaissance Quarterly* 24 (1971).

Greenblatt, Stephen. *Renaissance Self-Fashioning: From More to Shakespeare.* Chicago: University of Chicago Press, 2005.

Guicciardini, Luigi. *The Sack of Rome.* Translated and edited by James H. McGregor. New York: Italica, 1993.

Gunn, Steven J. *Charles Brandon, Duke of Suffolk, c.1484–1545.* Oxford: Basil Blackwell, 1988.

—— 'Tournaments and Early Tudor Chivalry.' *History Today* 41, no. 6 (1991): 15–21.

—— 'Wolsey's Foreign Policy and the Domestic Crisis of 1527–1528.' In *Cardinal Wolsey: Church, State and Art,* edited by P.G. Lindsey and Steven Gunn, 149–77. Cambridge: Cambridge University Press, 1991.

—— 'The Structures of Politics in Early Tudor England.' *Transactions of the Royal Historical Society* 5 (1995): 59–90.

—— *Henry VII's New Men and the Making of Tudor England*. Oxford: Oxford University Press, 2016.

—— *The English People at War in the Age of Henry VIII*. Oxford: Oxford University Press 2018.

Guy, John. *The Public Career of Sir Thomas More*. New Haven: Yale University Press, 1980.

—— 'Henry VIII and the Praemunire Manoeuvres of 1530–1531,' *EHR* 97 (1982): 481–503.

—— 'Thomas Wolsey, Thomas Cromwell and the Reform of Henrician Government.' In *The Reign of Henry VIII: Politics, Policy and Piety*, edited by Dairmaid MacCulloch, 35–59. New York: St. Martin's Press, 1995.

—— 'Thomas Cromwell and the Intellectual Origins of the Henrician Reformation.' In *The Tudor Monarchy*, edited by John Guy, 213–33. London: Arnold, 1997.

—— *Henry VIII: The Quest for Fame*. London: Allen Lane, 2014.

Gwyn, Peter. *The King's Cardinal: The Rise and Fall of Thomas Wolsey*. New York: Random House, 2011.

Haigh, Christopher. *English Reformations: Religion, Politics, and Society under the Tudors*. Oxford: Oxford University Press, 1993.

Hare, Christopher. *Maximilian the Dreamer, Holy Roman Emperor, 1459–1519*. New York: Charles Scribner's Sons, 1913.

Head, David M. *The Ebbs and Flows of Fortune: The Life of Thomas Howard, Third Duke of Norfolk*. Athens, GA: University of Georgia Press, 1995.

Hoak, Dale. *Tudor Political Culture*. Cambridge: Cambridge University Press, 2002.

House, Seymour Baker. 'Literature, Drama, and Politics.' In *The Reign of Henry VIII*, edited by Diarmaid MacCulloch, 181–203. New York: St. Martin's Press, 1995.

Howell, T.B., comp. *A Complete Collection of State Trials and Proceedings for High Treason and Other Crimes and Misdemeanors from the Earliest Period to the Year 1820, vol. 33*. London: Longman, 1826.

Hutchinson, Robert. *House of Treason: The Rise and Fall of a Tudor Dynasty*. London: Hatchette, 2009.

Ives, Eric. 'Faction at the Court of Henry VIII: The Fall of Anne Boleyn.' *History* 57, no. 190 (1972): 169–88.

—— *Faction in Tudor England*. London: Historical Association, 1979.

—— 'The Fall of Wolsey.' In *Cardinal Wolsey: Church, State and Art*, edited by Steven Gunn and Phillip Lindley, 286–315. Cambridge: Cambridge University Press, 1991.

—— 'The Fall of Anne Boleyn Reconsidered.' *The English Historical Review* 107 (1992): 651–64.

—— 'Anne Boleyn and the Early Reformation in England: The Contemporary Evidence.' *The Historical Journal* 37, no. 2 (1994): 389–400.

—— 'Henry VIII: The Political Perspective.' In *The reign of Henry VIII: Politics, Policy, and Piety*, edited by Diarmaid MacCulloch, 13–35. New York: St. Martin's Press, 1995.

—— *The Life and Death of Anne Boleyn: 'The Most Happy'*. Oxford: Blackwell Publishing, 2004.

—— *Henry VIII*. Oxford: Oxford University Press, 2007.

Jefferson, Lisa, ed. *The Medieval Account Books of the Mercers of London: An Edition and Translation, Item 1435*. 2 Vols. New York: Routledge, 2016.

Kearns, Emily, *A Threefold Exposition of Psalm 22, In psalmum 22 enarratio triplex, in Exposition of Psalms*. Toronto: University of Toronto Press, 2005.

Kesselring, K.J. 'A Draft of the 1531 "Acte for Poysoning",' *The English Historical Review* 116, No. 468 (September 2001): 894–99.

Knecht, Robert, *The Valois: Kings of France 1328–1589*. London: Bloomsbury, 2007.

Knowles, M.D. 'The Matter of Wilton.' *Historical Research* 31, no. 83 (1958): 92–6.

Lehmberg, Stanford E. *The Reformation Parliament: 1529–1536*. Cambridge: University Press, 1970.

Lewis, John. *The Life of Dr. John Fisher, Bishop of Rochester, in the Reign of King Henry VIII*. London: Joseph Lilly, 1855.

Loades, David M. *The Tudor Queens of England*. London: Bloomsbury, 2010.

―――― *Henry VIII*. Stroud: Amberley, 2011.

―――― *The Boleyns: The Rise and Fall of a Tudor Family*. Stroud: Amberley, 2011.

Logan, George M., ed. *The Cambridge Companion to Thomas More* (Cambridge: Cambridge University Press, 2011), 75.

Lovett, Frank. 'The Path of the Courtier: Castiglione, Machiavelli, and the Loss of Republican Liberty.' *The Review of Politics* 74, no. 4 (2012): 589–605.

MacCulloch, Diarmaid. *The Reign of Henry VIII: Politics, Policy, and Piety*. New York: St. Martin's Press, 1995.

―――― *Thomas Cranmer: A Life*. New Haven: Yale University Press, 1996.

―――― *All Things Made New: The Reformation and Its Legacy*. New York: Oxford University Press, 2016.

Mackie, J.D. *The Earlier Tudors, 1485–1558*. Oxford: Clarendon Press, 1952.

MacMahon, Luke. 'Courtesy and Conflict: The Experience of the English Diplomatic Personnel at the Court of Francis I.' In *The English Experience in France C. 1450–1558: War, Diplomacy and Cultural Exchange*, edited by David Grummitt, 182–99. Surrey: Ashgate, 2002.

Martin, Thomas, *The History of the Town of Thetford, in the Counties of Norfolk and Suffolk, from the Earliest Accounts to the Present Time London*. London: J. Nichols & Son, 1779.

Marshall, Peter. *Heretics and Believers: A History of the English Reformation*. New Haven and London: Yale University Press, 2017.

Mathew, David. *The Courtiers of Henry VIII*. London: Eyre & Spottiswoode, 1970.

Mattingly, Garrett. 'An Early Nonaggression Pact.' *The Journal of Modern History* 10, no. 1 (1938): 1–30.

―――― *Catherine of Aragon*. Boston: Little, Brown, 1941.

―――― *Renaissance Diplomacy*. New York: Cosimo, 2008.

McConica, James. *English Humanists and Reformation Politics under Henry VIII and Edward VI*. Oxford: Clarendon Press, 1952.

McGrath, Alister E. *The Intellectual Origins of the European Reformation*. Oxford: John Wiley & Sons, 2008.

Mears, Natalie. 'Courts, Courtiers, and Culture in Tudor England.' *The Historical Journal* 46, no. 3 (2003): 703–22.

Murphy, Virginia. 'The Literature and Propaganda of Henry VIII's First Divorce.' In *The Reign of Henry VIII: Politics, Policy, and Piety*, edited by Diarmaid MacCulloch. New York: St. Martin's Press, 1995.

Norton, Elizabeth. *The Boleyn Women: The Tudor Femmes Fatales Who Changed English History*. Stroud: Amberley, 2013.

Paget, Hugh. 'The Youth of Anne Boleyn.' *Historical Research* 54, no. 130 (1981): 162–70.

Parsons, Walter Langley Edward. 'Some Notes on the Boleyn family.' *Norfolk and Norwich Archaeological Society* 25 (1935): 386–407.

—— *Salle: The Story of a Norfolk Parish: Its Church, Manors & People.* London: Jarrold & Sons, 1937.

Pegge, Samuel, and Nichols, John. *Curialia, or An Historical Account of Some Branches of the Royal Household.* London: B. White, 1791.

Penn, Thomas. *Winter King: The Dawn of Tudor England.* New York: Simon & Schuster, 2011.

Pickthorn, Kenneth. *Early Tudor Government.* Cambridge: Cambridge University Press, 2015.

Pollard, A.F. 'Council, Star Chamber, and Privy Council under the Tudors: 1. The Council.' *The English Historical Review* 37 (1922): 337–60.

—— 'Council, Star Chamber, and Privy Council under the Tudors: 2. The Star Chamber.' *The English Historical Review* 37 (1922): 516–39.

—— *Wolsey.* London: Longmans, Green, 1929.

—— *Henry VIII.* London: Longmans, 1963.

Pollnitz, Aysha. *Princely Education in Early Modern Britain.* Cambridge: Cambridge University Press, 2015.

Potter, D.L. 'Foreign Policy.' In *The Reign of Henry VIII, Politics, Policy and Piety*, edited by D. MacCulloch, 101–35. New York: St. Martin's Press, 1995.

Queller, Donald E. *The Office of Ambassador in the Middle Ages.* Princeton: Princeton University Press, 2017.

Rady, Martyn C. *The Emperor Charles V.* New York: Routledge 2014.

Reid, Jonathan A. *King's Sister – Queen of Dissent: Marguerite of Navarre (1492–1549) and her Evangelical Network.* Leiden: Brill, 2009.

Richardson, Glenn, Susan Doran. 'Eternal Peace, Occasional War: Anglo-French Relations Under Henry VIII.' In *Tudor England and its Neighbours*, edited by Susan Doran and Glenn Richardson, 44–74. Basingstoke: Palgrave Macmillan, 2005.

—— *The Field of Cloth of Gold.* New Haven: Yale University Press, 2013.

Richardson, Walter. *Stephen Vaughan, Financial Agent of Henry VIII.* Baton Rouge: Louisiana State University Press, 1953.

Robertson, Mary L. 'Wingfield, Sir Richard', (b. in or before 1469, d. 1525). In *Oxford Dictionary of National Biography.* Oxford: Oxford University Press, 2004.

Robertson, William. *The History of the Reign of the Emperor Charles V. with a View of the Progress of Society; from the Subversion of the Roman Empire, to the Beginning of the Sixteenth Century.* New York: Harper Brothers, 1838.

Robinson, Jon. *Court Politics, Culture and Literature in Scotland and England, 1500–1540.* Aldershot: Ashgate, 2013.

Russell, Joycelyne Gledhill. *The Field of Cloth of Gold: Men and Manners in 1520.* London: Routledge & Kegan Paul, 1969.

—— 'The Search for Universal Peace: The Conferences at Calais and Bruges in 1521.' *Historical Research* 44, no. 110 (1971): 162–93.

—— *Peacemaking in the Renaissance.* London: Duckworth, 1986.

Ryan, Lawrence V. 'Book Four of Castigliones Courtier: Climax or Afterthought?' *Studies in the Renaissance* 19 (1972): 156–79.

Sanders, Nicholas, trans. *The Rise and Progress of the English Reformation.* Dublin: J Christie, 1827.

Scarisbrick, J.J. *Henry VIII*. Berkeley and Los Angeles: University of California Press, 1968.

Sergeant, Philip W. *The Life of Anne Boleyn*. London: Hutchinson, 1923.

Seton-Watson, R.W. *Maximilian I, Holy Roman Emperor: Stanhope Historical Essay 1901*. London: Constable & Co, 1901.

Setton, Kenneth Meyer. *The Papacy and the Levant: 1204–1571, Sixteenth Century to the Reign of Julius III*. Vol. 3. Philadelphia: American Philosophical Society, 1984.

Shulman, Nicola. *Graven with Diamonds: The Many Lives of Thomas Wyatt: Poet, Lover, Statesman, and Spy in the Court of Henry VIII*. Hanover: Steerforth Press, 2013.

Silva, Alvaro De, ed. *The Last Letters of Thomas More*. Michigan: W.B. Eerdmans, 2001.

Slavin, Arthur Joseph. *Politics and Profit: A Study of Sir Ralph Sadler, 1507–1547*. Cambridge: Cambridge University Press, 1966.

Smith, Thomas. *De Republica Anglorum: A Discourse on the Commonwealth of England*. Cambridge: Cambridge University Press, 2013.

Starkey, David. 'Representation through Intimacy: A Study in the Symbolism of Monarchy and Court Office in Early Modern England.' In *Symbols and Sentiments, Cross Cultural Studies in Symbolism*, edited by Lewis Ioan Myrddin, 187–224. London: Academic Press, 1977.

—— 'The Court: Castigliones Ideal and Tudor Reality; Being a Discussion of Sir Thomas Wyatts Satire Addressed to Sir Francis Bryan.' *Journal of the Warburg and Courtauld Institutes 45* (1982): 232–39.

—— 'Intimacy and Innovation: The Rise of the Privy Chamber, 1485–1547.' In *The English Court from the Wars of the Roses to the Civil War*. London: Longman, 1987.

—— 'Court, Council, and Nobility in Tudor England,' In *Princes, Patronage and the Nobility Princes, Patronage, and the Nobility: The Court at the Beginning of the Modern Age, C. 1450–1650*, edited by Ronald G. Asch and Adolf Matthias Birke, 175–203. Oxford: Oxford University Press, 1991.

—— *The Reign of Henry VIII: Personalities and Politics*. London: Vintage, 2002.

—— *Six Wives: The Queens of Henry VIII*. London: Random House, 2004.

Stephen, Leslie, ed. *Dictionary of National Biography*. London: Macmillan, 1887.

Strype, John, ed. *Memorials of Thomas Cranmer*. 2 Vols. Oxford: Clarendon Press, 1840.

Tenenti, Alberto, *Il senso della morte e l'amore della vita nel Rinascimento* (Francia e Italia) Turin: G. Einaudi, 1977.

Totten, Mark. 'Luther on "unio Cum Christo": Toward a Model for Integrating Faith and Ethics,' *Journal of Religious Ethics* 31, no. 3 (2003): 444–7.

Tout, T.F. *Chapters in the Administrative History of Mediaeval England: The Wardrobe, the Chamber and the Small Seals*. Vol. 1. Manchester: Manchester University Press, 1937.

Tracy, James D. *Emperor Charles V, Impresario of War: Campaign Strategy, International Finance, and Domestic Politics*. Cambridge: Cambridge University Press, 2002.

Tremlett, Giles. *Catherine of Aragon: Henry's Spanish Queen*. London: Faber and Faber, 2010.

Urban, Sylvanus. 'The Family of Boleyn.' *The Gentleman's Magazine* 32 (Aug. 1849): 155.

Vincent, Nicholas. *A Brief History of Britain 1066–1485*. London: Hatchette, 2011.

Wagner, Anthony Richard. *English Genealogy*. Oxford: Clarendon Press, 1972.

Walker, Greg. *Plays of Persuasion: Drama and Politics at the Court of Henry VIII*. Cambridge: Cambridge University Press, 1991.

—— *Persuasive Fictions: Factions, Faith and Political Culture in the Reign of Henry VIII*. London: Aldershot, 1996.

—— 'Persuasive Fictions: Faction, Faith and Political Culture in the Reign of Henry VIII.' *Sixteenth Century Journal* 29 (1998): 20.

—— 'Rethinking The Fall Of Anne Boleyn.' *The Historical Journal* 45 (2002): 1–29.

Warnicke, Retha. *The Rise and Fall of Anne Boleyn: Family Politics at the Court of Henry VIII.* Cambridge: Cambridge University Press, 1989.

—— "Debate: The Fall of Anne Boleyn Revisited." *The English Historical Review* 108 (1993): 653–65

—— The Rise and Fall of Anne Boleyn: Family Politics at the Court of Henry VIII. Cambridge: Cambridge University Press, 1989.

Wilkinson, Josephine, Mary Boleyn: The True Story of Henry VIII's Favourite Mistress (Stroud: Amberley, 2009).

Williams, Penry. *The Tudor Regime.* Oxford: Clarendon Press, 1979.

Willis, Jonathan. *The Reformation of the Decalogue: Religious Identity and the Ten Commandments in England, c.1485–1625.* Cambridge: Cambridge University Press, 2017.

Woodhouse, J.R. 'Honourable dissimulation: Some Italian Advice for the Renaissance Diplomat,' *Proceedings of the British Academy* 84 (1994): 25–50.

Wriothesley, Charles. *A Chronicle of England during the Reigns of the Tudors from 1485 to 1559.* Edited by William Douglas Hamilton. Westminster: The Camden Society, 1875.

Younghusband, G.J. *The Tower of London.* New York: George H. Doran, 1925.

Zagorin, Perez. 'Sir Thomas Wyatt and the court of Henry VIII: The Courtier's Ambivalence.' *Journal of Medieval and Renaissance Studies* 23 (1993): 113–41.

# Index

Anne of France, 50
Aparre, Thomas, 68
Arthur, Prince of Wales, 28–9,
    29–31, 40, 49, 117, 128
Aske, Robert, 220
Audley, Thomas, Keeper of the
    Privy Seal, 140, 193, 203–4,
    211, 213, 221
Austria, Margaret of, 26, 47, 49–50,
    60, 72, 76, 80–1, 84, 86, 89–90,
    132, 136, 160, 171, 174

Barbarossa, Hyreddin, 198
Barlow, William, 123
Beaufort, Edmund, 12
Beaufort, Eleanor, 82
Beaufort, Margaret, 29, 32, 82
Beckett, Agnes, 65
Beckett, Thomas, 65
Beda, Noel, 154, 191
Bedingfield, Edmund, 22
du Bellay, Jean, French ambassador
    128, 132, 134, 136, 138, 141, 142,
    144, 154, 181
Blickling, Norfolk, 15, 17–20, 25, 27,
    33, 225

Blount, Elizabeth, 62, 106
Blount, Gertrude, 114
Boleyn, Alice, 11
Boleyn, Anne, 60, 61, 69, 71, 76, 84,
    87, 91, 120–2, 136, 137, 139,
    142, 149, 144, 181, 190, 191, 193,
    194, 196, 198, 199
    birth, 26–7, 114
    birth of Elizabeth, 190
    in Calais, 175–8
    and Cardinal Wolsey, 62, 87, 118,
        120, 124–8, 135, 140, 141, 145
    coronation, 183
    at Court, 91, 113–15, 179
    downfall, 210–18, 224, 225
    education, 54, 57–8, 62, 68
    execution, 211–14, 216
    Henry VIII, 77, 98, 115–18, 121,
        125, 143, 178, 201, 203–11
    made Marchioness of Pembroke, 175
    relationship with her father, 71, 76,
        114, 116
Boleyn, Dionise, 13, 14
Boleyn, Dionysius, 13, 14
Boleyn, Edward, 18, 19, 62, 84,
    176, 211

Boleyn, Geoffrey, 11, 12, 13–17
Boleyn Geoffrey (elder), 10, 11
Boleyn, George, 2, 3, 4, 7, 27, 33, 36,
    60, 61, 62, 67, 71, 84, 86, 100,
    120, 142, 150, 152, 154, 161,
    167, 176, 191, 200, 201, 203,
    204, 205, 216
  and Arthur Plantagenet, Lord Lisle,
    192, 193, 202, 207, 212
  birth, 18, 19
  Constable of Dover, 196–8, 201
  created Lord Rochford, 149
  and Cromwell, 201–2
  education, 25
  Eltham Ordinances, 109–10
  execution, 209, 210, 211–15
  Field of Cloth of Gold, 79, 82–4,
    86, 174
  First Mission, 136–7, 156
  in France, 177, 180, 181, 183, 186,
    188, 192, 193, 199
  and Henry VIII, 116, 125–8, 130,
    148, 168, 171, 179, 196
  historical views of, 1–6, 35
  and Marguerite of Navarre, 187,
    192, 193, 196
  marriage, 103–4, 198
  personal interests, 187, 194,
    205, 211
  relationship with Anne, 170, 173,
    202, 207
  religious translations, 194
  trial, 212–15
Boleyn, James, 18, 19, 176, 223
Boleyn, Mary, 2, 3, 6, 25, 26, 27, 61,
    62, 63, 81, 84, 85, 98, 99, 106,
    113, 114, 116, 117, 118, 122,
    125, 126, 142, 167, 177, 192,
    197, 223, 224

Boleyn, Nicholas, 9, 10
Boleyn, Simon, 9
Boleyn, Thomas, Earl of Wiltshire,
    2, 7, 23, 24, 27, 28, 43, 60, 63, 64,
    65, 67, 86, 92, 93–6, 99, 104,
    105, 107, 114–18, 120, 123, 125,
    128, 160–3, 168, 183–5, 197,
    203, 206, 210, 211, 212, 216, 217,
    218, 220, 221, 222, 224, 225
  ambassador, 69, 70, 84, 88, 89, 90,
    91, 93, 96, 97, 108–12, 114, 117,
    126, 174–5, 176
  birth of, 17, 19
  Comptroller of the Household,
    3, 78, 84
  and Imperial ambassador Eustace
    Chapuys, 137, 138, 139, 141,
    142, 143, 147, 148, 149, 155–8,
    178, 181–3, 208, 209
  correspondence with Desiderius
    Erasmus, 170–2, 189, 190, 195
  correspondence with Thomas
    Tebald, 154, 199, 200, 206,
    207, 223
  courtier, 25, 27, 28, 29, 30–45,
    47–55, 56–60, 61, 62, 67, 68,
    99–100
  created Earl of Wiltshire and
    Ormond, 142, 143
  created Lord Rochford, 106
  death of, 26, 223, 224
  family ties, 9, 19, 25, 33, 40,
    65, 66, 67, 82, 87, 102,
    103, 198
  first diplomatic mission, 46–58
  and Imperial ambassador Eustace
    Chapuys, 137, 138, 139, 141,
    142, 143, 147, 148, 149, 155–8,
    178, 181–3, 208, 209

involvement in the Field of
  Cloth of Gold, 79, 80, 81, 84,
  85, 86
Lord Privy Seal, 143, 158,
  167, 196
mission to Bologna, 146–57, 167
negative perceptions of, 3, 4, 5, 35
Order of the Garter, 97, 98, 130
pilgrimage to Santiago de
  Compostella, 42
relationship with Wolsey, 75–81,
  87, 89, 91–4, 97, 105, 108, 109,
  120, 121, 122–3, 124, 125–32,
  133–5, 136, 157, 158, 159
religion, 168, 169, 170, 172, 173,
  190, 193, 195–6
retirement, 193, 204, 219
second diplomatic mission, 70–8
Treasurer of the Household, 92,
  97, 106
Boleyn, Thomas (elder), 11–13,
  15–17
Boleyn, William, 16–20, 21–5, 29,
  30, 32, 33, 128, 225
Boleyne, John, 9
Bouton, Claude, 26, 58
Brandenburg, Albrecht Von,
  Archbishop of Mainz, 72
Brandon, Charles, Duke of Suffolk,
  41, 42, 44, 98, 106, 113, 213
Brereton William, 1, 186, 210, 211
Browne, Sir Anthony, 112,
  187, 246
Bryan, Francis, 109, 188, 214, 234
Butler, James, 87, 115, 121, 122
Butler, Margaret, 25
Butler, Piers, 168, 222
Butler, Thomas, 21, 23, 40, 65,
  66, 67, 239

Calthorp, Philip, 24
Cambridge, Gonville Hall, 12
Cambridge Queen's College,
  12, 13
Campeggio, Lorenzo, 88, 126,
  127–30, 135, 136
Carew, Nicholas, 62, 109, 113, 166,
  209, 214
Carew, Richard, 59
Carey, Eleanor, 125
Carey, George, Baron Hundson,
  25, 233
Carey, Mary (*see* Mary Boleyn)
Carey, William, 67, 81, 86, 108, 125,
  126, 127, 197
Carthusian Monks, 200
Casale, Gregory, 150, 198
Castiglione, Baldasarre, 35, 36,
  44, 202
Cavendish, George, 38, 44, 120, 129,
  135, 139, 156, 214
Cecil, William, Lord Burghley,
  25, 251
Chapuys, Eustace, Imperial
  ambassador, 136–9, 141–5,
  147–51, 155–9, 161, 163, 165,
  171, 175, 178–84, 191, 198,
  199, 200–2, 204, 205, 206–12,
  214–16
Charles V, 50, 52, 55, 72, 75, 78, 79,
  83, 84, 86–93, 100, 104, 106–10,
  113, 118, 119, 127, 132–4, 137,
  145–9, 157, 158, 163, 167, 169,
  174–6, 180–2, 185, 191, 193,
  198–201, 207–9
  and Thomas, 94–6, 137–9, 141,
  151–6
Charles of Castille, 60
Charles of France, 23, 47

Claude, Queen of France, 26, 62, 71, 74, 76, 77, 81, 82, 117, 118

Clere, Robert, 24, 244

Clifford, Henry, 26, 106

Compton, William, 34, 42, 43, 45, 68, 109, 126

Cornish, William, 110

Cranewell, Robert, 223

Cranmer, Thomas, 134, 135, 149, 161, 162, 179, 181, 183, 187, 190, 195, 204, 223

Cromwell, Thomas, 2, 4, 18, 122, 123, 139, 140, 160–9, 179, 181, 183, 189, 191, 192, 193, 197, 199, 200–4, 207–13, 216, 219–24, 247

De Chabot, Phillip, Admiral of France, 177, 199, 200, 201

De Croy, Guilliam, Lord Chievres, 84

De Grammont, Gabriel, Bishop of Tarbes, 110, 151, 152

De La Marck, Robert, Duke of Bouillon, 89

de la Pole, John, Earl of Lincoln, 22

De la Sauch, Jean, French ambassador, 83

De Mendoza, Don Inigo Lopez, 119, 121, 128, 137

De Montmorency, Anne, Duke, 100, 111, 142, 176, 177, 191

De Salinas, Martin, 92, 93

Derring, Richard, 202

Devauntter, Perpoynte, 91

Dinteville, Jean, 201

Docwra, Thomas, Lord of St John, 89, 90, 91, 108

Dormer, Jane, 26

Douglas, Archibald, Earl of Angus, 68

Du Praet, Louis, Lord Chancellor, 90

Edward III, King of England, 12, 18, 28, 47, 96

Edward IV, King of England, 11, 15, 18, 21, 97, 103, 109, 178

Edward VI, 225

Eleanor of Austria, sister of Charles V, 50, 110, 132, 175

Elizabeth I, Queen of England, 225

Elizabeth of York, 21, 28, 31, 33, 34, 40

Erasmus, Desiderius, 12, 28, 35, 58, 170–3, 189, 190, 194, 195

Eustace II, Count of Boulogne, 8

Falstolf, Sir John, 15, 16

Ferdinand of Aragon, 31, 37, 47, 49, 59, 116

Fisher, John, Bishop of Rochester, 34, 40, 163, 164, 165, 200, 202, 203, 204

Fitzroy, Henry, 105, 106, 114, 168, 200

Fitzwilliam, William, 106, 110, 121, 142, 191, 192, 193, 200, 201

Fox, Edward, 132, 133, 134, 149, 162, 192

Fox, Richard, 39, 40, 43–9, 59, 92, 102, 117, 130

Foxe, John, 151, 152

Francis I, 62, 63, 50, 69, 71–8, 80–91, 99, 100, 101, 110, 111, 112, 118, 132, 133, 134, 136, 137, 138, 149, 151, 152–5, 158, 162, 175, 176, 177, 180, 181, 186, 187, 188, 191, 192, 193, 196, 198, 199, 200, 209

Frowik, Henry, 13

Fugger, Jacob, 72, 73

Gardiner, Stephen, 123, 124, 133, 134, 135, 141, 166
Garnish, Christopher, 61
George, Duke of Clarence, 21, 103
George, Duke of Saxony, 72
Ghinucci, Girolamo, 150, 152
Glossop, Nicholas, 189, 259
Gouffier, Artus, Lord of Boissy, 76, 80
Gresham, Richard, 86
Grey, Elizabeth, 65
Grey, Thomas, Marquess of Dorset, 42, 107, 141, 142, 165
Guildford, Henry, 42, 62, 97, 105, 108, 123, 142, 166

Hackett, Sir John, 198
Hall, Edward, 140, 164, 165, 176
Hastings, George, 65, 142
Henry II, 65, 103
Henry V, King of England, 15
Henry VI, King of England, 15
Henry VII, 19, 21–9, 31, 34, 36, 37, 40, 42, 43, 45, 49, 85, 97, 103, 224
Henry VIII, 2, 3, 4, 7, 12, 21–9, 33, 37, 45, 46, 48, 49, 82, 97, 105, 109, 113, 199, 223, 224
Heydon, Henry, 17, 22
Holyrood, Edinburgh, 32
Hoo, Anne, 14
Hoo, Lord Thomas, 14, 20, 98
Howard, Edward, 34, 41, 48, 57, 103
Howard, Elizabeth (nee Boleyn), 2, 24, 27, 56, 84, 116, 124, 167, 168, 217, 222
Howard, John, Duke of Norfolk, 20
Howard, Thomas, 2nd Duke of Norfolk, 24, 31, 32, 33, 38, 39, 40, 41, 44, 88, 102, 103

Howard, Thomas, 3rd Duke of Norfolk, 40, 57, 86, 87, 107, 109, 110, 121, 122, 128, 123, 131, 133, 138–42, 144, 145, 147, 148, 149, 155, 157–61, 165, 166, 169, 175–9, 181–4, 187, 188, 190, 191, 199, 200, 203, 206, 210, 211, 212, 213, 217, 220, 221
Hungerford, Edward, 59, 142

Isabella of Castile, 37, 47, 49, 50, 117

James IV, King of Scotland, 23, 31, 32, 33, 40, 68
Jerningham, Richard, 95, 96
Juan, Prince of Castile and Aragon, 49, 50

Katherine, Queen of England, 29, 30, 31, 37, 38, 40, 41, 42, 46, 49, 50, 61, 67, 68, 79, 81, 83, 84, 85, 92, 95, 108, 110, 115, 117, 118, 119, 125, 127–32, 143, 145, 151, 156, 161, 162, 163, 165, 166, 167, 175, 178, 179, 182, 183, 184, 185, 187, 188, 193, 196, 200, 205, 206, 207, 211, 225
Kildare, Earl of (Gerald FitzGerald), 22, 168
Kingston, William, 109, 113, 192, 212
Knight, William, 118, 121, 122
Knyvett, Anthony, 40, 48, 113

Lee, Edward, ambassador, 137, 147, 166
Lisle, Lady (Grenville, Honor), 177, 193, 214, 217

Lisle, Lord (Plantaganet, Arthur), 59, 65, 111, 142, 192, 193, 202, 207, 212, 217, 222

Louise of Savoy, 50, 71, 73, 74, 79, 80, 81, 101, 104, 106, 108, 110, 111, 132, 138, 142, 153, 154, 167, 198

Louis XII, King of France, 46, 47, 60

Lovell, Thomas, 39, 77

Manners, Henry, Earl of Rutland, 106

Manners, Thomas, 113

Margaret of Austria, 26, 27, 47, 49–59, 60, 72, 76, 80, 81, 84, 86, 89, 90, 132, 136, 160, 171

Margaret of Burgundy, 22, 23

Maximilian I, Holy Roman Emperor, 23, 47–56, 58, 59, 60, 70, 72, 73, 95, 237

More, Thomas, 1, 39, 89, 132, 140, 158, 161, 163, 169, 170, 200, 203

Neville, George Lord Abergavenny, 23

Neville, Richard, Earl of Warwick, 15

Norris, Henry, 1, 135, 139, 210, 211

Oldcastle, John, 15

Owen, Sir David, 68

Pace, Richard, 73, 76, 100

Parker, Henry, Baron Morley, 1–3, 184, 213

Parker, Jane, 103, 114, 150, 167, 168, 177, 198, 202, 214, 219

Parr, Thomas, 59

Percy, Henry, 120, 158, 185

Philibert of Savoy, 49

Pio, Ridolf, Bishop of Faenza, 63

Plantaganet, Edward, Earl of Warwick, 21, 22

Pole, Reginald, 149, 153, 221

Pope Clement VII, 100, 108, 114, 118, 119, 121, 122, 124, 126, 127, 129, 132, 136, 144, 146, 147, 148, 151, 152, 153, 155, 156, 157, 161, 162, 166, 169, 177, 179, 180, 187, 188, 191, 192, 193, 198

Pope Julius II, 47, 49, 52, 57, 117, 127

Pope Leo, 57, 60, 72, 73, 89, 91, 117, 119, 127

Pope Paul III, 200, 204, 207

Pope Pius XI, 203

Poullain, William, 61

Poynings, Sir Edward, 24, 39, 45, 77, 78, 84, 91

Rene of Savoy, 75

Renee, Princess of France, 117, 118

Richard III, King of England, 17, 20, 22, 103

Roper, William, 203

Russell, John, 144, 251

Ruthall, Thomas, Bishop of Durham, 39, 89

Salle, 7, 9, 10, 11, 17, 184

Sampson, Richard, 93–6, 108, 167

Seymour, Jane, 206, 209, 217, 222, 225

Seymour, John, 59, 212

Sforza, Francesco, Duke of Milan, 150, 153, 159

Simnel, Lambert, 21, 22, 24

Skelton, John, 38

Smeaton, Mark, 1, 210, 211, 213

Somerset, Charles, 39

Spinelly, Thomas, 49, 50–4, 56, 73, 93, 94

Stafford, Edward, Duke of Buckingham, 27, 88

Stafford, William, 197

Stokesley, John, ambassador, 136, 137, 146, 149, 151

Stuart, John, Duke of Albany, 68, 75, 100

Strype, John, 135, 195

Symonds, Richard, 21, 22

Talbot, George, 39, 97, 107, 167, 185

Tebald, Thomas, 154, 199, 200, 206, 207, 223

Tournai, 59, 69

Treaty of Bruges, 89, 90, 91, 92

Treaty of Windsor, 92

Tudor, Margaret, Queen of Scotland, 31, 32, 33, 40, 60, 68

Tudor, Mary, Princess, 93, 98, 106, 107, 110, 115, 117, 119, 193, 196, 199, 201, 202, 203, 207, 223, 225

Tudor, Mary, Queen of France, 27, 114

Tunstall, Cuthbert Bishop of London, 108, 132

Vaux, Nicholas, 59, 68

Walter, Theobald, 65

Warbeck, Perkin, 23, 31

Warham, William, Archbishop of Canterbury, 39, 65, 73, 99, 105, 117, 123, 140, 179, 189

Weston, Francis, 1, 210, 211

Weston, Richard, 70, 109

Wingfield, Richard, 45, 49, 50, 52, 53, 56, 57, 80, 81, 82, 90, 91, 108, 109

Wolfe, Reginald, 154

Wolsey, Thomas, Cardinal, 2, 34, 38, 39, 40, 43–9, 52, 58, 59, 60, 62, 69, 70, 72, 73, 74, 75, 76–81, 83–8, 100, 104–12, 113, 114, 117–21, 123–30, 131–42, 144, 145, 151, 153, 157, 158, 159, 174, 189, 191, 192, 217, 224

Wyatt, George, 117

Wyatt, Henry, 39, 64, 113, 38, 39

Wyatt, Thomas, 35, 166, 117

Young, John, 45, 48, 49, 50, 52, 53, 56, 57